String Music

Also by Chris Dortch

Blue Ribbon College Basketball Forecast (editor)
Blue Ribbon College Football Forecast (editor)
Gentleman Champion

String Music

Inside the Rise of SEC Basketball

Chris Dortch

Brassey's, Inc.
Washington, D.C.

For Patty, Chris, and Jennifer.
Thanks for your daily inspiration.

Published in the United States by Brassey's, Inc. All rights reserved. No part of this book may be reproduced in any manner whatsoever without written permission from the publisher, except in the case of brief quotations embodied in critical articles and reviews.

Library of Congress Cataloging-in-Publication Data
Dortch, Chris.
  String music : inside the rise of SEC basketball / Chris Dortch.
    p. cm.
Includes index.
  ISBN 1-57488-439-5 (hardcover : alk. paper)
  I. Title.
  GV885.415.S68 D67 2002
  796.323'62'0975--dc21

                          2002151497

Printed in the United States of America on acid-free paper that meets the American National Standards Institute Z39-48 Standard.

Brassey's, Inc.
22841 Quicksilver Drive
Dulles, Virginia 20166

First Edition

10 9 8 7 6 5 4 3 2 1

Contents

Photographs

Acknowledgments

A n author's name might appear on the front cover, but the process of nurturing a book from the first proposal to the final printing is far from a one-person job. Were it not for the collective efforts of several friends and colleagues, I'm not sure you'd be reading these words today. Without further adieu, I'd like to thank those people whose invaluable assistance made this book possible.

My first words of thanks go to Joe Dean, Jr., a good friend who shares my addiction to college basketball. I can say with absolute certainty that this is a better book because of Joe's immense contributions.

It's appropriate to mention a bit of Joe's background. He grew up in the heart of Southeastern Conference country in Baton Rouge, Louisiana, and thus developed at an early age an appreciation for basketball, SEC style. Joe went on to play at an SEC school, Mississippi State, and also coach there. He spent time as an assistant coach on Joe B. Hall's staff at Kentucky, where he was a part of the 1978 national championship team. Joe later ran his own programs at Birmingham Southern and Central Florida. After leaving the coaching profession, Joe followed in the footsteps of his father and became a color analyst for SEC games, on radio and television. He spent six years working for the Auburn radio network and still works several television games a year for Fox Sports Net and Jefferson Pilot Sports.

Few people, if any, know SEC basketball as well as Joe. I knew if I were to do a thorough job recounting what was perhaps the most significant ten-year period in the league's history, I would need Joe's guidance.

With nary a bit of arm-twisting on my part, Joe graciously agreed to read my manuscript. As I finished each chapter, I would send it via e-mail attachment to Joe's office at Birmingham Southern College, where he serves as athletic director. It was uncanny that if I had the slightest question or reservation about something I had written, Joe would pick up on it and red flag it. I looked forward to his e-mail critiques of my chapters. Sometimes, he liked what I'd written so much that he didn't offer any changes. Other times, he suggested wholesale alterations. Seldom did I disagree with any of his input. Joe didn't seek nor would he have accepted compensation for his work. He was thrilled to be part of a project he thought was a long time coming. Just seeing this book come to fruition was payment enough for Joe.

I'd be remiss if I closed my thoughts on Joe without mentioning a bond that exists between us. Both of us survived college basketball–related plane crashes, which, by eerie coincidence, happened on the same day (albeit six years apart) and involved the same airport.

On December 16, 1978, Joe and his wife Ellen were flying into the Tri-Cities Airport in Blountville, Tennessee. Joe had been sent by Hall to scout a player from Bristol, Tennesee, Derrick Hord. Disoriented by darkness, Joe's pilot clipped some trees on his descent, causing the plane to crash-land. The pilot was killed, but somehow, Ellen was able to free herself from the wreckage and run to a nearby home for help. Joe was banged up but also able to walk away.

Six years to the day after Joe's accident, on December 16, 1984, I was part of a traveling party that included East Tennessee State's basketball team. The trip originated from Tri-Cities Airport and would take the Buccaneers to Birmingham, where they would play UAB, and on to Oxford, Mississippi, for a game against Ole Miss.

The flight to Birmingham, ironically, was the best I'd ever been on, smooth and quick. It was hardly a harbinger of things to come. The morning after ETSU played UAB, the traveling party departed for Oxford. Ten minutes into the flight, the plane's right engine caught fire. Thus began a slow, terrifying descent. The hilly, tree-lined Alabama terrain loomed closer by the second.

Were it not for a small landing strip in Jasper, Alabama, that day might have taken its grim place in college basketball history, alongside the 1977 plane crash that claimed the lives of every member of the University of Evansville's team. Somehow, our pilot brought the plane in for a crash-landing. Miraculously, everybody on board survived, though the plane, which spun off the runway, was badly damaged and eventually gutted by fire.

The kind people of Jasper came to our rescue, and one woman who was nice enough to take us to shelter was a personal friend of Joe Dean's. She recounted his horrifying crash and told us how he'd coped. I remember thinking that I'd like to meet Joe one day and share our experiences.

Like his son, Joe Dean, Sr., helped make this a better book. Searching for a perfect title, my editors at Brassey's, Inc. wanted to find a catch phrase that was synonymous with SEC basketball. Allyson Bolin, Brassey's former marketing manager, played soccer at Kentucky and has the proper reverence for basketball. She suggested "string music." Immediately I knew that was perfect.

Anyone who has followed SEC basketball for any length of time knows what string music means. Let Joe Dean, Sr., the first person to serve as a color commentator for league games, tell the story about how two words came to define him, and SEC basketball.

"When I began doing TV in the early going—this is the late sixties—we had some terrible games," Joe recalled. "Arenas were just fair. Coaching was maybe a little

Acknowledgments

shaky. We've come so far. Anyway, the games were on Saturday afternoons. Eddie Einhorn, who now is part owner of the Chicago White Sox, owned Television Sports—TVS—out of New York. I remember him asking us to do something to make the telecasts more interesting—to juice them up a little.

"So somebody would hit one, and I'd holler, 'String music!' I started talking about 'Heartbreak Hotel' if a shot went in and out. Or 'stufferino' when somebody dunked one. I just came up with stuff to stimulate things a little bit. Some were maybe cornball. But for all of the little things I threw out there, the one that caught on was string music. And everywhere I go, to this day, people will see me and shout out 'string music.' It's amazing."

The famous phrase had been inside Joe's head since childhood. String music, it seems, was the forerunner of modern-day trash talking.

"I grew up in a little town in Indiana," Dean recalled. "On weekends, a group of us, maybe forty or fifty kids, would gather in a backyard where a man had stripped his whole yard and created a basketball court. There were baskets at each end. It's where I learned to play.

"The games back there were notorious. A lot of times we'd all put up a nickel into the pot. The winning team got the pot. There were a lot of sayings that came out of that backyard. It was just kids hollering and carrying on. They'd holler stuff like 'in the blue for two' or 'a tickling of the twine.' 'String music' was just one of the many things that was said. I don't really know where it came from. It could have been me or anyone."

Regardless of who might have coined the phrase, it was Joe Dean, Sr., who popularized it. And thanks to his generosity, "string music," a phrase with which SEC basketball so closely identifies, fittingly became part of this book's title.

Without question, *String Music* could not have been written without the cooperation of the twelve SEC coaches. Thanks go to Mark Gottfried (Alabama), Cliff Ellis (Auburn), Billy Donovan (Florida), Jim Harrick (Georgia), Tubby Smith (Kentucky), John Brady (LSU), Rick Stansbury (Mississippi State), Rod Barnes (Ole Miss), Dave Odom (South Carolina), Buzz Peterson (Tennessee), and Kevin Stallings (Vanderbilt). Former Arkansas coach Nolan Richardson also graciously granted an extended interview just weeks before he was bought out of his contract.

Anyone who covers college basketball knows that assistant coaches are often the best sources a writer can have. Toward that end, I can't thank several SEC assistants enough. I had a key contact on every team, but every assistant coach I talked to was gracious with his time and insight.

Thus, special thanks go to Philip Pearson and T. R. Dunn (Alabama); Mike

ix

Anderson (Arkansas); Shannon Weaver, Charlton Young, and Reggie Sharp (Auburn); John Pelphrey and Donnie Jones (Florida); James Holland (Georgia); Kermit Davis, Jr., and Butch Pierre (LSU); Phil Cunningham and Robert Kirby (Mississippi State); Marc Dukes and Wayne Brent (Ole Miss); Ernie Nestor and Rick Duckett (South Carolina); Chris Ferguson, Kerry Keating, Al Daniels, and Ed Conroy (Tennessee); and Tim Jankovich (Vanderbilt). Several of these coaches have since moved on to other jobs, and some are running their own programs.

Several former SEC coaches also were gracious enough to share their recollections with me. Thanks go to Sonny Smith, Wimp Sanderson, Eddie Fogler, Richard Williams, Ed Murphy, and Dale Brown.

I'm especially grateful to Smith for helping shape my career when he was coach at East Tennessee State and I wrote for the student newspaper there. Smith took me under his wing and allowed me to see how college basketball coaches really work. That inside knowledge helped cement my love for the game and convinced me I wanted to cover college basketball for a living. Had Smith been short with me or run me off the first time I tried to interview him, I might have chosen a far less interesting career track.

A project as extensive as this would not be possible were it not for the efforts of the most unsung heroes in college athletics, the sports information directors. The SEC is blessed with some excellent SIDs who focus their attention on basketball. Thanks go to Becky Hopf (Alabama), Robby Edwards (Arkansas), Chuck Gallina (Auburn), Steve McClain (Florida), Tim Hix (Georgia), Brooks Downing (Kentucky), Kent Lowe (LSU), David Rosinski (Mississippi State), Lamar Chance (Ole Miss), Brian Binette (South Carolina), Craig Pinkerton (Tennessee), and Brent Ross (Vanderbilt).

Charles Bloom and DeWayne Peevy in the Southeastern Conference office were also extremely helpful. It was Charles's encouragement that helped me make the decision to write this book.

My many friends in the media also lent invaluable support by supplying background information or insight. Thanks to Neal McCready of the *Mobile (Alabama) Register*; Wally Hall and Bob Holt of the *Arkansas Democrat-Gazette*; Mark Schlabach of the *Atlanta Journal-Constitution*; Trent Rosecrans of the *Athens (Georgia) Banner-Herald*; Jerry Tipton of the *Lexington (Kentucky) Herald-Leader*; Larry Vaught of the *Danville (Kentucky) Advocate-Messenger*; Rusty Hampton, Mark Alexander, and Todd Kelly of the *Jackson (Mississippi) Clarion-Ledger*; Chris Low and Mike Organ of *The Tennessean*; Mike Strange of the *Knoxville News-Sentinel*; and Ron Higgins of the *Memphis Commercial-Appeal*.

Thanks also to Dudley Dawson, who sent me a copy of his comprehensive book on

Acknowledgments

Arkansas basketball, *Razorbacks Handbook*, and Tom Wallace, who gave me a copy of the book he co-wrote with Jim Harrick, *Embracing the Legend: Jim Harrick Revives the UCLA Mystique.*

Few people have greater insight into a college basketball program than the men who broadcast games on radio. Several voices of SEC basketball teams provided invaluable assistance. Charlie McAlexander, who surely belongs in the *Guiness Book of World Records* after serving four schools (Ole Miss, Vanderbilt, Kentucky, and South Carolina) in the same league as a play-by-play man, graciously opened his library to me, sending me on my way with a box of invaluable books and video tapes. Mike Nail, who calls Arkansas games, generously gave of his time, sharing his thoughts about his long relationship with former Arkansas coach Nolan Richardson. Bob Kessling and Bert Bertlekamp, who call Tennessee games, were supportive throughout the project.

A special thanks goes to Mike Dodson of Host Communications, who sent me tapes of legendary Kentucky play-by-play announcer Cawood Ledford's final game. Ledford's call of Kentucky's heartbreaking loss to Duke in the 1992 NCAA Tournament East Regional finals was valuable for a lot of reasons.

Before I wrap this up, I have to thank my family. My wife Patty has put up with my sports addictions for longer than she probably thought she could. She's been a great source of encouragement in my various endeavors over the years. And my children, Chris II and Jennifer, have long supported their father's work, even though their respective talents don't have a thing to do with sports. More power to them.

Thanks also to my parents, Bill and Helen Dortch, for giving me my love of sports, reading, and writing. They were extremely supportive during this project.

Finally, thanks to my editor at Brassey's, Chris Kahrl, and to all the Brassey's team for helping make this book possible.

I hope you enjoy reading *String Music: Inside the Rise of SEC Basketball* as much as I enjoyed writing it.

Introduction

In *Southern Fried Football*, his thorough look at the proud history of Southern college football, Tony Barnhart, long-time sportswriter for the *Atlanta Journal-Constitution* and commentator for ESPN, offers a telling summary of the game's importance, as quoted from a sign he once saw hanging in the office of a coach.

"College football is not a matter of life and death," the sign read. "It's much more important than that."

So it is in the twelve towns and nine states that are home to Southeastern Conference schools. From Tuscaloosa, Alabama, to Gainesville, Florida, to Knoxville, Tennessee, and points in between, football is followed with a fervor unseen in the rest of the country.

Everyone has probably heard some variation of the old line about the typical SEC fan's three favorite sports: football, spring football, and football recruiting. For a long time that might have been true. But in the last decade, SEC basketball has forced its way in between recruiting and spring football and into the hearts of fans in such previously unlikely places as Florida and Mississippi.

Traditionally, only at Kentucky, where the success over the years of the mighty Wildcats helped transform basketball into a statewide religion, was the sport held in higher esteem than football.

In the new millennium, fans are packing the University of Florida's O'Connell Center, and the O-Dome is now one of the most feared places to play in the country. They're filling Tad Smith Coliseum at the University of Mississippi, where, years ago, the sports information department sent out a press release to announce that an assistant basketball coach had been "promoted" to freshman football coach. And at Tennessee, which had been mired in the league's longest NCAA Tournament dry spell throughout most of the 1990s, suddenly four straight trips to the Big Dance weren't good enough.

How did the transformation of SEC basketball take place? And when did it occur? *String Music: Inside the Rise of SEC Basketball* will focus on a ten-year period during which the SEC not only took its place alongside the Big Ten, the Atlantic Coast Conference, and the Big 12—established basketball powers all—but in the opinion of some surpassed them.

The rise of SEC basketball can be traced back to the 1991–92 season, when two significant events took place that would eventually elevate the level of play throughout the league. That season, Rick Pitino's excellent work in rebuilding a Kentucky

Buzz Peterson. *Elizabeth Olivier/UTSports.com*

program that had been shattered by a recruiting scandal came to fruition. The Wildcats, banned from the SEC Tournament the previous two seasons, won the event, thus ending a three-year run by Alabama. The Wildcats would go on to win twenty-nine games, losing out on a Final Four berth only after a miracle three-point shot by Duke's Christian Laettner gave the Blue Devils an East Regional championship in a game some consider the greatest of all time.

That same year, the SEC expanded to twelve teams, becoming the pioneering "super conference" by adding Arkansas and South Carolina. Arkansas, which had played in the Final Four in 1990, brought from the Southwest Conference a swagger, an attitude, and a style of play that wreaked havoc in the SEC. The Razorbacks won the league's first Western Division championship, played in a memorable SEC Tournament semifinal game against Alabama and transformed the event into an instant sellout by bringing along a small army of fans.

With the resurgence of Kentucky and the addition of Arkansas, the SEC could claim two superpowers equal to the best programs in the country. For the next six years, one of those teams would advance to the Final Four. Arkansas won the national championship in 1994 and was runner-up in 1995. Kentucky won two championships, in 1996 and 1998, and was runner-up in 1997. In that same six-year period, the SEC was also represented in the Final Four by Florida (1994) and Mississippi State (1996).

Following the lead of Kentucky, Arkansas, and upstarts Florida and Mississippi State, the rest of the SEC's schools saw that college basketball, with television contracts and an ever-increasing pool of money being disbursed to NCAA Tournament, had become big business. And they all wanted a piece of the action. All of a sudden, a major, leaguewide emphasis was placed on basketball. Facilities were upgraded. Salaries were increased. Successful, experienced coaches were hired. Marketing and promotional efforts were increased tenfold.

The unprecedented focus on basketball paid big dividends. By the 2001–2002 season, the SEC was generally considered the strongest league in the country from top to bottom, and there were several statistics to support that contention. The SEC led the nation's conferences in nonconference winning percentage and had the highest Ratings Percentage Index (RPI) of any league. And those numbers weren't put together through creative scheduling. The schedules of nine SEC teams were ranked among the top twenty-five toughest in the country by CollegeRPI.com.

Inside the conference, balance was the order of the day. In the first ten years of expansion, every SEC team won or shared a regular-season division or overall championship. And from the 1996–97 season to 2001–2002, every league team played in at least one NCAA Tournament.

The SEC's 5-6 records in the 2001 and 2002 NCAA Tournaments did nothing to enhance its growing reputation, but coaches around the league weren't worried. Their response was to go out and restock their rosters.

This book traces the evolution of SEC basketball from the 1991–92 season to 2001–2002, which was the tenth anniversary of the league's expansion. Consider *String Music* a document of that era, the most important in SEC history. A chapter has been devoted to each school, giving the reader a choice to read the book from start to finish or skip around to different chapters. A recap of each school's 2001–2002 season ends its respective chapter, and the final chapter chronicles the 2002 SEC Tournament. In the epilogue, 2002 postseason play, recruiting, and personnel moves are recounted as the SEC begins its second decade after expansion.

In some cases, it was necessary in the interest of historical perspective to discuss the successes or failures of a school that occurred before 1991–92. But for the most part, each chapter focuses on how a particular school was built for success in the first ten years of expansion. All twelve coaches will be profiled—fitting, in that their respective programs have tended to take on their personalities.

3

An SEC coach doesn't have an easy job, though all of them are compensated well enough to help them cope with the demands that come with the position. The pressure to win is constant. Recruiting has become a war, as so many schools in such close proximity are battling for the wealth of talent that exists in the South.

Often, the struggle to sign players pits one school squarely against another. Occasionally, hints of impropriety are tossed about among coaches, the media, and

fans. SEC schools have run afoul of NCAA rules just often enough in the last fifteen years to keep the specter of violations hovering above the recruiting process. Particularly when SEC football schools have their own brushes with the NCAA, as was the case in 2002, the league's image suffers.

The mission of this book was neither to prove nor disprove whether that image is justified. But some well-publicized recruiting stories will be retold, and the principle characters will be allowed to tell their side. Readers can draw their own conclusions.

Telling evidence of the pressure to win came in the last two years of the decade this book chronicles. Three coach-

Eddie Fogler. *USC Sports Information*

ing changes underscored the fact that the what-have-you-done-for-me-lately attitude that exists among fans is alive and well in the SEC, where past laurels cannot be rested upon. Not even a future hall-of-fame coach could escape scrutiny and criticism.

As losses mounted for Arkansas in 2001–2002, coach Nolan Richardson's relationship with the media and a small group of disgruntled fans had become increasingly tense. Amid rumblings that Richardson, then sixty, had grown too complacent and let some of the league's energetic young coaches outwork him in recruiting, the

4

coach couldn't resist taking little shots back at his critics.

When Richardson won his five hundredth game on December 10, 2001, he told reporters that it felt as though he'd won a thousand, given all the hardships he'd endured as a pioneering African-American coach. During his weekly television show in mid February, Richardson made comments that essentially suggested Fayetteville, Arkansas, where the university is located, was a hick town where black athletes would find nothing to do socially.

That potentially damning comment didn't cut Richardson's throat, but it was a harbinger of things to come. After a late-February loss to Kentucky that dropped the Razorbacks to 13-13 and 5-9 in the SEC, Richardson inserted a surprising and unprompted comment into his remarks to the media. If university officials felt compelled to exercise the buyout option of his six-year contract, which paid him $1.03 million annually, Richardson said, they should go ahead.

Two days later at his weekly press conference, Richardson stopped hinting at what was bothering him and let it all out, lambasting the media with an irrational diatribe that focused on the issue of race. One reporter called Richardson's rant a "meltdown" as Richardson claimed he was treated differently than Arkansas's other coaches because he was black and that he was the "the greatest thing going at the University of Arkansas." That comment would offend other coaches, athletes, administrators, and professors at the school.

Richardson wasn't finished. He also railed against the media, barring reporters from practice for the first time in his career and questioning why no one in the room was black. As Richardson was winding down, he invited the broadcast journalists at the press conference to "run that on every TV station in the country."

Of course, that's exactly what happened. Richardson's remarks were televised on ESPN and CNN and Fox Sports and seen by millions. Arkansas fans and influential media in the state and across the country were outraged. Several key Arkansas boosters called athletic director Frank Broyles and demanded Richardson's ouster. Richardson tried to exercise damage control later in the week by issuing an apology and proclaiming his renewed enthusiasm to continue coaching, but there was no taking back some of his more incendiary comments. Four days after the press conference, the coach who had won the 1994 national championship and whose program had helped lift Southeastern Conference basketball to the upper level of Division I leagues was unceremoniously dismissed.

Eleven months before Richardson's ouster, coaching changes at Tennessee and South Carolina helped underscore the emerging status of basketball at schools where football had always commanded the most attention.

On fall Saturdays, Tennessee's Neyland Stadium becomes the state's fourth-largest city as more than 105,000 people pile inside to watch their beloved Volunteers, who have become consistent national championship contenders under coach Phillip Fulmer. At South Carolina, a program recently revitalized by Lou Holtz, the grizzled coach who has seen and done it all marveled during his 0-11 first season in 1999 at how 80,000 Gamecock fans turned out, undaunted, every game. That interest only intensified after Holtz guided the Gamecocks to two consecutive bowl games.

As important as football is to both those schools, their respective athletic directors didn't have to be told about the growing importance of basketball in the SEC. Both Tennessee's Doug Dickey and South Carolina's Mike McGee agonized in the spring of 2001 over hiring the right coach to run their basketball programs. A mistake, in a league as strong in the SEC, could mean a setback of several seasons.

On April 3, more than five hundred orange-clad fans showed up for a press conference inside Tennessee's Thompson-Boling Arena. Several dignitaries were there, including then–university president J. Wade Gilley, athletic director Doug Dickey, Fulmer, and women's basketball coach Pat Summitt.

Anyone who didn't know beforehand what the fuss was all about might have thought they had wandered into a gathering to announce that some new benefactor had donated ten million dollars to the football program, or that Summitt—the John Wooden of women's basketball—was being honored yet again.

On this day, neither Fulmer nor Summitt was on center stage. That honor belonged to men's basketball coach Robert Peterson—better known to his friends as Buzz—who was just beginning his first day on the job in Knoxville.

Here was a perfect example to illustrate the evolution of basketball in the SEC. In a building where six national championship banners—won by the *women's* basketball team—hang, where the streets that run alongside are named for quarterbacks and football coaches, a men's basketball coach was being introduced amid adulation by the masses. The room where the Big Orange faithful gathered was decked out in balloons and banners. Southern delicacies, Peterson favorites such as Krystal hamburgers and Krispy Kreme donuts, were served. People seemed genuinely enthused. Basketball, it seemed, actually mattered at one of the SEC's staunchest football strongholds.

A long-suffering Tennessee basketball fan might have had to pinch himself to realize he wasn't dreaming or in the throes of some chemically induced stupor. But the day was very real. The occasion was the hiring of Peterson, one of the college game's hot young coaches, away from Tulsa University.

Volunteer fans who had grown weary of the tantalizing but disappointing four-year

6

career of former coach Jerry Green were ecstatic over Peterson's hiring. Here was a man who grew up just a few mountains over in Asheville, North Carolina, who as a child had been driven to Tennessee football games by his father. Peterson, a high school basketball hero who, in 1981, was chosen the North Carolina player of the year as a senior—over some guy named Michael Jordan—went on to notoriety at the storied University of North Carolina. His roommate there was none other than M. J., the man who would later become known as the greatest player of all time.

Peterson's association with Jordan had given him a certain claim to fame over the years. But his UNC connections had also served him well as he rose through the coaching ranks, as an assistant at East Tennessee State, North Carolina State, and Vanderbilt, then as a head coach at Appalachian State and—for all of one season—at Tulsa. How many people could list Dean Smith and Roy Williams on their resumes and expect to get glowing recommendations from both? Peterson could, and did.

In accepting the job as Tennessee's fourth basketball coach in an eight-year span, Peterson impressed his ready-made fans, not with any great oratorical style or sense of humor but through honesty and the sheer force of his personality. Peterson told the crowd that when he asked Smith, his former college coach and lifelong mentor, about the Tennessee job, the reply was that his decision to accept the position was a "no-brainer." Peterson was quick to give the proper reverence to King Football, and talked about how he negotiated some 50-yard line tickets in his contract talks with Dickey. He was careful to show Summitt the respect her considerable accomplishments deserve.

Most importantly, Peterson shared with the crowded room his philosophy of the game. Finally, Tennessee appeared to have gotten this hiring thing right. After enduring in the previous eight years one coach who took the program to the bottom of the league standings, another who micromanaged with an iron fist, and another whose hands-off approach with his players was widely criticized, Vols fans had what they thought was the perfect man for the job. In Peterson, Tennessee hired a coach who is stern but not too stern, who wants to play an exciting brand of basketball but not out of control, and who would do all the right things off the court. Peterson loves to entertain his players at home, and even encourages them to attend church with him. This was a far cry from the days of no study halls or curfews under Jerry Green's watch.

In the minds of Tennessee fans, their team had fired the first shot of the 2001–2002 Southeastern Conference basketball season. Not in a literal sense, but with a loud and clear declaration. Twenty-two wins a year, which Green had averaged during his four seasons, were not good enough if the Vols were going to vanish every March, when the real basketball programs identify themselves in the crucible of the NCAA

Tournament.

After a series of player defections, injuries, and uncanny last-second losses, the Vols finished 15-16 and missed the NCAA Tournament in Peterson's first year. But ironically, Tennessee fans had more respect for a team that fought adversity until the bitter end and ending up with a losing record than the previous four teams that played in the Big Dance and underachieved.

Green's ouster was hardly an isolated incident in a conference that, in the 1990s, began to shed its image of a football-only league and discovered the virtues of winning basketball.

At South Carolina, it had been widely rumored for a couple of years that former coach Eddie Fogler had grown weary either of the off-the-floor responsibilities of coaching or his athletic director, Mike McGee. And McGee was in no rush to give Fogler—one of the most successful and respected coaches in the game—a vote of confidence. That much was clear after the Gamecocks' mildly disappointing 2000–2001 season, when McGee refused to roll over Fogler's contract, which had three years remaining. "Coach Fogler's contract was not extended because there were certain standards and expectations such as finishing in the upper half of the SEC and advancing to the NCAA Tournament that were not met," McGee said.

After that decision, Fogler began to seriously think about leaving. South Carolina's then-president John Palms joined in the negotiations and Fogler was paid $735,000 to step away.

Long considered one of the game's best coaches and winner of the SEC's 1993 coach-of-the-year award while at Vanderbilt, Fogler managed to turn around a struggling program in his eight years at South Carolina. Despite all Fogler's efforts, though, some will choose to remember his tenure at South Carolina for two celebrated first-round NCAA Tournament flameouts. In 1997, after winning the SEC's regular-season championship and earning a No. 2 seed in the East Regional, the Gamecocks were stunned by fifteenth-seeded Coppin State. A year later, seeded No. 3 in the East, South Carolina was beaten by No. 14 seed Richmond.

The program fell on lean times after that. The Gamecocks finished 8-21 in 1998–99 and 15-17 in 1999–2000. In Fogler's final year, South Carolina was 15-15 after suffering through a rash of injuries, the most critical a season-ending knee blowout suffered by the team's most versatile player, small forward Chuck Eidson. That the Gamecocks wound up in the NIT after a two-year postseason drought mattered little. McGee had made up his mind not to extend Fogler's contract.

Publicly, SEC coaches expressed regret and dismay over the fates of Green and Fogler. But eventually most were to benefit from the departures of their former colleagues. The ensuing coach searches at both schools ultimately netted half the league's coaches a pay raise.

For a time, it had been rumored that Tennessee was going to try and pursue Ole Miss coach Rod Barnes, whose team had laid a pair of humiliating whippings—the latter in the second round of the SEC Tournament—on the Vols that season. But Gilley, who claimed to have played a part in hiring then–twenty-eight-year-old Billy Donovan at Marshall in 1994, had admired the job Billy the Kid had done at Florida, which had also beaten Tennessee twice in 2000–2001. Gilley wanted to find another young star like Donovan, and fairly quickly Tennessee's search centered on Peterson, Jeff Lebo of Tennessee Tech, and Gregg Marshall of Winthrop.

Though Tennessee's pursuit of a new coach was followed with great interest, it was South Carolina's search that sent shock waves around the league. McGee had encouraged Peterson to apply for the Gamecocks job, which forced a sense of urgency on Tennessee to hire Peterson or risk losing him to an SEC Eastern Division rival. The fourth time proved to be the charm for Dickey, who went after his man and got him with an offer Peterson couldn't refuse—a five-year contract worth $700,000 a year. Dickey also agreed to pay half of Peterson's $500,000 contract buyout at Tulsa.

With some big bucks of his own to throw around, McGee went fishing in deep waters. McGee spent a considerable amount of time in a futile effort to hire Kentucky's Tubby Smith. Though most people didn't expect Smith to leave what many believe is the best coaching job in the college game, the money McGee was reportedly offering was intriguing. And incredibly, Smith had been underappreciated at Kentucky, despite winning a national championship in 1998, his first season in Lexington.

Kentucky administrators took South Carolina's interest in Smith seriously, eventually offering their coach a four-year extension worth $1.5 million annually. Smith's contract also called for a $1 million bonus if he stayed for its duration.

Two other SEC coaches who reportedly had contact with McGee also ended up with sweet deals by staying put. Rod Barnes, who had signed a contract for a substantial pay increase—from $300,000 to $450,000—midway through the 2000–2001 season, received yet another new contract in early April after leading the Rebels to the Sweet 16. That arrangement included an extension and tacked a few more shekels onto his compensation package, including incentives for academic and athletic success. Barnes also extracted a promise from Ole Miss's then–athletic director John Shafer to upgrade the school's facilities and better compensate his staff and support personnel.

Alabama's Mark Gottfried probably wasn't seriously thinking about leaving his alma mater, but the mention of McGee's possible interest sent athletic director Mal Moore scurrying to put a new contract in front of his coach. Gottfried negotiated an even nicer deal than Barnes. In addition to getting his pay increased from about $387,000 annually to $650,000—$500,000 of which comes from a radio and TV package—Gottfried got a four-year extension, to seven years overall. And, like Barnes, he also elicited a promise from Alabama's administration to improve the Crimson Tide's arena and other facilities.

The cushy deals handed to Peterson, Smith, Barnes, and Gottfried might have created some contract envy around the league. Though no schools were apparently trying to hire away Vanderbilt's Kevin Stallings or Georgia's Jim Harrick, both men were given new contracts. Vanderbilt, which had already made a commitment to improve the Commodores' venerable Memorial Gym with a multimillion dollar facelift, tied up Stallings for six years with a deal that pays him between $700,000 and $800,000 annually. And Harrick, who led his team to an improbable NCAA Tournament appearance in 2001, got a raise and two-year extension. Like Stallings and Peterson, Harrick is in the $700,000-a-year neighborhood.

Still intent on hiring a coach with a solid record of achievement, McGee—who had offered the job to Connecticut's Jim Calhoun and approached Oklahoma's Kelvin Sampson, John Calipari of Memphis, Quin Snyder of Missouri, and Tommy Amaker of Seton Hall, among others—eventually turned his attention to Wake Forest's Dave Odom. Odom had done all he could battling against Duke, North Carolina, Maryland, and others in the rugged Atlantic Coast Conference. Odom had been underappreciated in Winston-Salem, and he was looking for a change.

After searching a month and a day for a new coach, McGee finally had his man. Odom, then fifty-eight, was given a five-year contract worth $750,000 annually. South Carolina's state-of-the-art arena, scheduled to open in time for the 2002–2003 season, was yet another enticement for Odom. Huge contracts. Arena upgrades. Coaches paid as well as the CEOs of major corporations. Perhaps the coaching searches at South Carolina and Tennessee produced a domino effect. But the kind of money being spent on basketball around the SEC is more than a short-term phenomenon sparked by a month-long hunt for coaches. The level of commitment seen in these ten years illustrates how important basketball has become in the SEC.

The league's coaches have argued for years that the SEC is the toughest basketball conference in the nation. You get the feeling they would say that even if they weren't all millionaires in the making.

Chapter One

Alabama

A labama's reemergence as a Southeastern Conference basketball power began in Big Ten country.

As long as he coaches at his alma mater, Mark Gottfried won't forget the night of March 23, 2001, when his young team finally fought off a road-game jinx and won a third-round National Invitation Tournament game at Purdue. Though the program had already begun a gradual return to the level of success it had enjoyed under the tenures of coaching legends C. M. Newton and Wimp Sanderson, Gottfried's freshman- and sophomore-dominated group needed something to help accelerate its progress. The Purdue game, won in two overtime periods, was the kick in the backside Alabama needed.

Ironically, this side trip to the NIT might have benefited the Tide more than playing in the NCAA Tournament, though Gottfried had hoped Alabama's 2000–2001 resume was good enough to impress the NCAA selection committee. A weak non-conference schedule, a poor road record, and consecutive losses to Auburn, Florida, Arkansas, and Ole Miss to end the regular season doomed the Tide's chances of playing in its first NCAA Tournament since 1995. Selection Sunday was a downer for Alabama, which accepted an NIT bid with a vow to atone for that late-season collapse and to make people aware that the program was back.

The NIT run started at home, with consecutive victories over Seton Hall and Toledo. Gottfried had hoped to stay in Tuscaloosa for yet another game, but all those two wins earned Alabama was the chance to go on the road to play at Purdue's Mackey Arena, where through the years the Boilermakers had compiled a 13-0 record in NIT games. Considering the Tide's road record in Gottfried's three seasons was 3-27, the chances of advancing to the NIT's Final Four in New York seemed remote. But Gottfried used Alabama's road woes to his advantage. Here was a chance, he told his team, to cast aside old demons and strike a blow, not just for the present, but for the future.

The Tide took Gottfried's words to heart. Alabama reached back and gave its best effort on the road in Gottfried's tenure, holding Purdue to 35 percent shooting and bashing the Boilermakers on the boards, 55-44. Kenny Walker, the junior center

11

Gottfried had to beg to shoot earlier in the season, put together a career game with 24 points and eight rebounds. Erwin Dudley contributed 20 points and 16 rebounds. "Walker and Dudley just kicked our behinds," Purdue coach Gene Keady told reporters after the game.

Despite its physical dominance, the Tide had to overcome an 11-point deficit to tie the game in the closing minutes. Alabama lost a five-point lead with forty-five seconds to play in the first overtime and had to survive the second overtime without Walker, who had fouled out. In Walker's absence Dudley took over, scoring two important baskets to give the Tide the lead for good. The road curse had been vanquished at last, and Alabama was on its way to New York, where it advanced to the NIT title game but lost to Tulsa.

The loss did nothing to dampen Alabama's spirits, or diminish the importance of the win at Purdue.

"That win really elevated our confidence," Gottfried recalled. "We had struggled on the road. We put a whole bunch of young guys out there, and it's hard to do that. Now you beat Purdue in a tough environment. That carried over."

"The Purdue win was huge," Dudley said. "People didn't think we could win on the road. We proved we could do it. Beating a Big Ten team like that on their home court really gave us a lot of confidence."

That boost of confidence had a lasting effect. A year later, Alabama, with a new attitude and a new point guard, would become the best team in the SEC.

———

In 1960, Wimp Sanderson, then coaching high school basketball at Carbon Hill, Alabama, loaded his wife, young son, and all their possessions into an old coal truck. Their destination was the University of Alabama, where Sanderson had hoped to serve Crimson Tide basketball coach Hayden Riley as a graduate assistant for one year, earn his master's degree, and find a better-paying high school job. Sanderson ended up staying in Tuscaloosa a little longer than he planned.

By the time Sanderson left thirty-two years later, he had served two head coaches as a trusted assistant and, as head coach, turned Alabama into a perennial NCAA Tournament team. Along the way, he became an icon in a football-crazy state through creative use of poor-mouthing, a bone-dry wit, and a brightly colored array of plaid jackets. Sanderson had more trademarks than any ten college basketball coaches. And to hear him tell it, he needed them all.

"Alabama was a football school, is a football school, and always will be a football school," Sanderson said. "Hell, it's a football state. I was coaching basketball. We needed something to make us stand out."

In his own droll fashion, Sanderson stood out. He mastered the art of downplaying his team's chances every year—"He was the king of the poor mouthers," said his old friend, former Auburn coach Sonny Smith—and was hilarious in media gatherings. In the late 1980s, the SEC's pre-season media tip-off resembled open mic night at a comedy club. Every year the press could count on being entertained by Smith's homespun humor, Georgia coach Hugh Durham's tongue-in-cheek rants, LSU coach Dale Brown's compassionate ramblings, and Sanderson's wry wit. Sanderson's pre-season assessment of his team was predictable. In an era when Alabama won SEC Tournaments and played in the Sweet 16 with regularity, Sanderson always made it seem as though the Tide didn't stand a chance to win.

Durham told a classic tale of Sanderson's glass-is-half-empty mentality in the foreword of Sanderson's biography, *Plaid and Parquet*.

"So comes to mind a round of golf," Durham wrote. "Wimp made an 8-iron shot from 140 yards for an eagle. Most golfers would have been ecstatic. But my loyal friend Wimp quickly said, 'I probably won't hit another good shot all day.' That's Wimp, a guy who poor-mouths all the way to the bank."

In the latter stages of Sanderson's Alabama career, the program had begun to take on some of his personality traits. Sanderson's players were tough and competitive. They had to be to survive their coach. "I was pretty tough on them," Sanderson recalled. "Latrell Sprewell never did choke me, but I was a damn good candidate."

Off the floor, Sanderson's penchant for wearing garish plaid jackets gave Alabama basketball its own identity and made it independent from King Football.

"I wore plaid, and the press wrote about it," Sanderson recalled. "And they wrote about it some more. I had no idea we'd have the band in plaid, the ushers in plaid, the midcourt [at Coleman Coliseum] in plaid. They called it the Plaid Palace. Once that got started, I said why not use it? It took on a life of its own."

Sanderson, and Alabama basketball, didn't need any gimmicks to attract attention. Winning would have sufficed, and under Sanderson's watch, the Crimson Tide won often. From 1980, when Sanderson replaced C. M. Newton as head coach, until he was forced to resign twelve years later, Alabama appeared in ten NCAA Tournaments and one NIT. The lone year the Crimson Tide missed a postseason tournament under Sanderson's watch, Derrick McKey, the team's star, bolted early for the NBA, leaving Alabama without an experienced big man.

McKey wasn't the only future NBA player turned out by Alabama in Sanderson's tenure. Eight other players recruited by Sanderson became first-round draft picks, including Robert Horry, Latrell Sprewell and Antonio McDyess.

Under Sanderson, Alabama dominated the SEC Tournament, reaching the finals nine times in twelve seasons and winning five championships.

"I think two significant things stand out in my time there," Sanderson said. "Being in the finals nine out of twelve years was a mark of consistency. We didn't win it but five times, but could have won it six times. And getting to the Sweet 16 six times was big. We never got past that, but for a so-called football school, that wasn't too bad."

Sanderson had guided Alabama basketball to the highest point in its long history in the early 1990s, a period that begins the focal point of this book. In 1991–92, Sanderson's last season, Alabama was 26-9 and 10-6 in the SEC. Arkansas won the division in its inaugural SEC season, but Alabama extracted revenge in one of the most memorable SEC Tournament games ever.

Both teams were loaded with future NBA players. Arkansas featured Todd Day, Oliver Miller, and Lee Mayberry, and Alabama, Robert Horry, Latrell Sprewell, and James "Hollywood" Robinson. The game was close throughout. With thirty-eight seconds left, Alabama trailed 89-85. Sprewell scored to cut the lead to a basket. Alabama fouled the Razorbacks' Roosevelt Wallace, who missed the front end of a one-and-one. Alabama rebounded and called time. Twenty-three seconds remained.

"We go out there [after the time out] and the ball ends up in James Robinson's hands," Sanderson recalled. "We'd take a two to tie or a three to win. Generally speaking, when James had the ball, he wouldn't throw it to his mother. It was going up."

This time, Robinson fooled everyone. Double-teamed and forced to give up the ball, Robinson spotted Eric Washington alone in the left corner. Washington, a guard Sanderson had signed the year before only after another player he wanted went elsewhere, had taken one shot in the previous thirty-nine minutes and change. Then Robinson fired a pass toward him as the final seconds were ticking down.

Washington, stunned to be so wide open, knew he had to shoot quickly. Time seemed suspended as the ball made its way to the rim.

"I really thought Latrell or Robert or James was going to take the shot," Washington told the media after the game. "When James drove the lane and he got double-teamed, he threw me the ball and told me to shoot it before I even got it."

"I went down to the baseline," Sanderson recalled. "I said, 'I believe that thing's going in.' It hit nothing but bottom."

Alabama won 90-89. It's amazing how many SEC fans today don't recall the game was only in the tournament semifinals. It had all the makings of a championship game.

The Tide lost to Kentucky in the championship game the next day, ending a streak of three straight tournament titles. The resurgence of Kentucky under Rick Pitino and the presence of Arkansas might have eventually slowed down Alabama's SEC Tournament run, but there was no question Sanderson had the Tide in a good place. Arkansas and Alabama had split their regular season games, the Tide winning by a basket in Tuscaloosa and the Hogs winning by three points in Fayetteville.

"No doubt in my mind that our three games with Arkansas this season were the greatest games I've ever been involved with," Sanderson told the media after the epic semifinal game. Sanderson couldn't have imagined at the time that he'd coached his last game against Arkansas. Two months later, Sanderson, voted the SEC's coach of the decade in the 1980s, was gone.

In the spring of 1992, Sanderson's long-time secretary filed a sexual harassment suit against him and the university. Amid the turmoil that followed, Sanderson was forced to leave the program he had devoted himself to most of his adult life.

Sanderson stayed out of basketball for a year, but in 1994, at age 57, he got the urge to coach again. He eventually resurfaced at Arkansas–Little Rock, where he coached for five seasons before retiring.

These days, Sanderson keeps his hand in basketball by doing color commentary on television and radio. And every day during the week, he drives to Birmingham, where he joins Sonny Smith for a talk show that basically reprises the stand-up routines they gave for the media during their SEC days.

"It's a crazy little old show, but we have a lot of fun with it," Sanderson said. "Half the time we don't know what we're talking about, but we act like we do."

———

Sanderson was replaced by David Hobbs, Sanderson's assistant the previous seven seasons. Hobbs was a likeable person and an excellent bench tactician who had been the architect of Alabama's trademark man-to-man defense, but he had one problem. He wasn't Wimp Sanderson.

"David is a good basketball coach," Sanderson said. "He did a nice job for me. But it was probably going to be hard to follow what we had done. That didn't help him any. And I don't want this to come out wrong, but he wasn't as much a people person. Even if you're pretty successful and win some games, if your attendance is down, your athletic director is going to get out of sorts."

Hobbs's record, especially early in his six-year tenure, was good enough for most programs. Alabama dropped to 16-13 in 1992-93, the year after Sanderson left, but played in the NIT. The Tide was 20-10 in 1993–94 and 23-10 the next season. Both years Alabama played in the NCAA Tournament and won its first-round game.

Alabama won nineteen games in Hobbs's fourth season and advanced to the NIT finals in New York. Again, that was an accomplishment that might have been acceptable at other schools. By that time, Hobbs had begun to catch heat from Alabama fans.

After a 17-14 season in 1996–97, the fans and media in Alabama had Hobbs all but out the door and replaced by former Alabama player Mark Gottfried, then the coach at Murray State. Hobbs survived, but the end was near. Twenty-one games into the 1997–98 season, Alabama athletic director Bob Bockrath announced he was firing Hobbs. Alabama was 9-12 at the time and had just been beaten, 94-40, by Auburn. That was the worst loss in school history, and for Alabama fans it underscored the difference between the two rival programs.

Bockrath said his decision was based on "a whole culmination of events over the course of the year."

At the time, most critics blamed Hobbs's troubles on recruiting. During his tenure, several good players left the state and excelled at other programs, including Anthony Williams, the all-time leading rebounder in Alabama high school history who was signed by Vanderbilt, and Greg Stolt, who became an All-SEC player at Florida and is the Gators' all-time three-point field goal leader. Chris Williams was the 1997–98 Alabama high school player of the year out of Birmingham Minor High School, and both his parents went to Alabama. Still he was never offered a scholarship. Williams went on to become a four-year starter and All-ACC player at Virginia.

"They passed on a guy or two they shouldn't have," said one SEC assistant. "How do you pass on a guy like Greg Stolt? How do you miss on a kid like Chris Williams?"

Hobbs had a lot of turnover on his staff, and the lack of continuity had to hurt recruiting. The program was dealt a setback in 1998 when assistant coach Tyrone Beaman committed two major NCAA rules violations. Beaman had asked for five thousand dollars from an Alabama booster in Montgomery to pay the coach of a Texas high school recruit, then subsequently lied about it to the NCAA.

Alabama, which had run afoul of the NCAA in football, quickly fired Beaman in an effort to avoid any sanctions. The strategy worked, but Beaman's follies were clearly a factor in Hobbs's dismissal.

Hobbs didn't stay away from basketball long. In 2000, Hobbs's old friend Tubby Smith brought him to Kentucky as an assistant. In 2001–2002, with fifteen seasons of experience in the SEC, Hobbs was the senior-most coach in the league.

16

———

Mark Gottfried's career at Alabama began on the roof of a taxi on a cold winter day in 1983. Alabama coach Wimp Sanderson, who had pursued Gottfried to Tulsa, Oklahoma, to get his signature on scholarship papers, didn't want to take any chances. He'd lost Gottfried the first time he recruited him, so Sanderson wanted the player's name on the dotted line as soon as he could get it. In lieu of a desk or other firm surface for Gottfried to sign on, the roof of a taxi would do just fine.

In 1982, Gottfried played his senior season at Mobile's UMS–Wright Prep, but resisted the overtures of Alabama and Auburn and several other upper-level Division I schools, including Duke and Ohio State, to sign with Oral Roberts. If that seems a curious choice in an age where Duke has become the dominant program in the country, Gottfried's decision was perfectly logical at the time.

Before taking over as assistant athletic director at South Alabama, Gottfried's father Joe coached basketball at Southern Illinois. While competing in the Missouri Valley Conference, he became friendly with New Mexico State coach Ken Hayes. When Hayes left for Oral Roberts, the Gottfrieds kept up with him.

"During Mark's junior year in high school, Ken let my [Southern Illinois] team work out at the Mabee Center at Oral Roberts," Joe Gottfried said. "Mark had made the trip with us, and he became infatuated with that facility. From that point, Ken made an aggressive effort to recruit him. Not only did he sign Mark, but he also came close to getting Mark Price to come to Oral Roberts."

Mark Gottfried eventually signed with Oral Roberts. But five games into Gottfried's freshman season Hayes was fired. Several players left after that, including Gottfried.

"I don't recall who called me [when Gottfried wanted to transfer]," Sanderson said. "But I had gotten to know the family a little bit when Mark was in high school. I felt like we had a chance to recruit him. So I flew out there and visited him. It was during the school day, and I was in a taxi. Mark said he'd sign, so I signed him on top of a taxi. The rest is history."

"Wimp had gotten a hotel room in Tulsa," Gottfried recalled. "He told me he wasn't going to leave until I signed. He took a taxi over to my dorm, and I went ahead and signed so he could go home."

Sanderson couldn't have known it at the time, but Gottfried became one of the key cogs in two successful eras of Alabama basketball. In 1987, Gottfried helped lead the Crimson Tide to the SEC's regular-season championship. It would be another fifteen years before Alabama won another SEC title—with Gottfried as its coach.

17

In many ways, Gottfried had prepared his whole life to become a coach. He had a unique, front-row view of the life, and what he saw interested him. Joe Gottfried coached high school basketball, entered the college ranks at Division III Ashland (Ohio) College and later moved to Division I at Southern Illinois. His son couldn't help but be drawn into the game.

"I remember when he was this five-foot-eight, 140-pound freshman with horn-rimmed glasses," Joe Gottfried said. "He'd just made the decision to play one sport. I can still see the note he put above his bed. It said he wanted to earn a Division I scholarship. From then on, I don't think he ever took a day off from doing something to try and improve. His skill level began to get better."

Even as the younger Gottfried was elevating his game and making his dream of becoming a Division I player come true, he must have known his limitations. Most young players fantasize about playing in the NBA. Gottfried dreamed of becoming a coach.

"I wanted to be a basketball coach from the time I was very young," Gottfried recalled. "I'd grown up around coaching. I made a decision I wanted to coach. Not necessarily for the wins and losses, but for the relationships you develop with players. I watched my dad make an impact with his players that extended well beyond the time those kids were done playing. That excited me more than anything."

"Mark was young and doesn't have any memories of when I was a high school coach," Joe Gottfried said. "And even when I was at Ashland, he couldn't wait until the games were over so he could play on the court with his buddies. Mark saw the rough times at Southern Illinois. When I went there, I tried to change the philosophy [of the previous coach], and that didn't go over too well. I ended up getting fired after three years. That had to impact Mark. But the thing that influenced him most was the relationship I had with the players. We had players at our house all the time. Mark felt like that was something he wanted to do."

Gottfried was drafted by the Detroit Pistons after his senior season at Alabama. He showed up at preseason training camp, but quickly discovered he didn't have the drive to try and beat the odds and make the Pistons' roster. Gottfried traveled with the Athletes in Action team for a season, but he knew his playing days were coming to an end. Coaching was in his future.

Knowing that Gottfried had hoped to coach, Wimp Sanderson offered him a graduate assistant's position at Alabama. But Gottfried thought he could benefit more by learning another coach's system. Gottfried didn't want to learn just any system, so he set his sights high, applying in 1988 for a graduate assistant's position at UCLA. Legendary coach John Wooden had long since retired by that time, but Gottfried knew Jim Harrick, then coaching the Bruins, was a Wooden disciple. Harrick picked Gottfried from among two hundred applicants.

"That was huge for me," Gottfried said. "I learned a great deal from Jim Harrick, and I got to spend a lot of time with coach Wooden. That was an unbelievable opportunity for a young coach. He helped me develop a philosophy that will never leave me. He laid a foundation for me."

Gottfried rose through the ranks on Harrick's staff. Joe Gottfried recalls the day his son called with the news that the third assistant's job had opened.

"I said, Jim's not going to promote you to the part-time [third assistant's] job," Joe Gottfried said. "Three days later, Jim gave him the job. He was in that spot for three years. Counting the graduate assistant's job, he spent four years learning how to coach without ever leaving campus [to recruit]. And he was around John Wooden all the time. Mark learned the UCLA system, not only from the master himself, but from Jim Harrick, who I think is one of the all-time underrated coaches."

Eventually, Gottfried became Harrick's top assistant on a staff that included two other coaches who would go on to run their own programs, Lorenzo Romar (Pepperdine, Saint Louis, Washington) and Steve Lavin (UCLA). In 1995, Gottfried's last season in Los Angeles, the Bruins won the national championship.

"That was a fantastic experience," Gottfried said. "To win the national championship was something that few people in this business get a chance to do. Coach Harrick deserved it. After working for him, I really do think he's one of the undervalued coaches in America. He's got a great feel for people. And he's at his best when the game starts. He can really coach the game. That's a term people throw out all the time, but don't really understand what it means. Jim really knows how to make adjustments while the game is going on."

By 1995, Gottfried was ready to take over his own program. Because of UCLA's success, he had opportunities. Better still, he could afford to be selective.

"A lot of people at UCLA said I should go right into a big-time job," Gottfried recalled. "People are so interested in how much money you can make, or if you're in the spotlight. But I didn't want the biggest job. I wanted a job where I'd have the ability to learn. I wanted to be able to make mistakes, because I knew I'd make some."

As it turned out, Gottfried found the perfect place to start his career as a head coach. For years Murray State, tucked away in a remote corner of southwestern Kentucky, had dominated the Ohio Valley Conference, seemingly regardless of who was coaching. The program's tradition sustained it. It was a can't-miss situation for Gottfried, who was reasonably sure he was going to win, and that his every move wouldn't be scrutinized. He was right on the former assumption, wrong on the latter.

19

Gottfried, who inherited a team of seniors from former coach Scott Edgar, guided the Racers to a 19-10 record, the regular-season OVC championship, and an NIT berth in 1995–96, his first season.

"Mark made a decision that first year," said former Alabama player Philip Pearson, whom Gottfried hired as an assistant at Murray State and would later take with him to Alabama. "We inherited a team of seniors, but they honestly weren't the kind of kids we would have recruited. But we worked with them and worked with them, and ended up winning the [OVC regular season] championship that first year.

"The next year, we went out and signed eleven players. Six of them were from Alabama. Some didn't make grades right away, but everybody was scratching their heads, wondering how we were going to work things out. But Mark made a lasting impression. He was going to get his guys, and do it his way."

In 1996–97, Murray State was 20-10, won the OVC again, and added the league's tournament title, thus earning a trip to the NCAA Tournament. That season, Gottfried realized he was wrong about being able to coach in obscurity at Murray State. Alabama fans and the media were already watching his every move. And athletic directors at several other schools were discreetly observing him as well. Gottfried's name was mentioned in connection with several jobs, including Tennessee.

The 1997–98 season would be Gottfried's last at Murray State. The Racers won twenty-nine games and the OVC's regular-season and tournament championships. Well before the season was over, Alabama sports writers had been dispatched to Kentucky to write magazine-length features on Gottfried, touted as the replacement for Alabama coach David Hobbs almost from the day he became a head coach. Gottfried told no one other than his family, but he had long dreamed of returning to his alma mater.

"When Mark was at UCLA, we talked about Alabama," said Gottfried's father Joe. "He hoped that one day, he would eventually put himself in position to go back there as the head coach."

When Hobbs was fired midway through the 1997–98 season, Gottfried hoped he'd get a chance to interview at his alma mater. He needn't have worried. If there were any other serious candidates for the job, their names didn't surface.

As obvious as his decision to leave Murray State for Alabama appeared to be, Gottfried nevertheless sought advice from his most trusted advisers. One thought from an impeccable source stood out in his mind.

"Coach Wooden and I talked about the job before I took it," Gottfried recalled. "He thought it was a great move. He did tell me that at your alma mater, expectations are a little higher. But he told me that's something you should never be afraid of."

Gottfried wasn't afraid of the challenge of coaching Alabama, but he was concerned about the players he inherited from Hobbs.

"We have a large number of players, and they all do something different well," Gottfried diplomatically told *Blue Ribbon College Basketball Yearbook* before the 1998–99 season. "But not many of them have made an impact on the SEC level."

And not many of them would make an impact in the SEC. The lone exceptions were Brian Williams, a senior guard, and junior center Jeremy Hays. Gottfried didn't have time to recruit once he arrived in Tuscaloosa, though he thought Chris Williams, the Alabama high school player of the year from Birmingham, was going to be available after a coaching change at Virginia. The rumor was that Williams was going to ask for his release, but new Virginia coach Pete Gillen talked him back into the fold.

Gottfried might have arrived too late to do anything about Williams, but he vowed to put a fence around the state of Alabama and keep in-state recruits at home. True to his word, the foundation of his program would be built on Alabama high school players.

———

With his goal of keeping the better in-state high school players at home in mind, Gottfried hired as his chief recruiter Robert "Rah-Rah" Scott, a Birmingham native who had starred at Alabama in the 1970s, coached high school basketball in his hometown, and later joined the staff at UAB.

The first Alabama high school star targeted by Gottfried and his staff was Marvin Stone, a six-foot-ten center from Huntsville. But Gottfried gave away too much ground to Kentucky, which had a substantial head start recruiting Stone, a *Parade* and McDonald's All-American. Gottfried was disappointed but not surprised when Stone announced for Kentucky.

Undaunted, the Alabama coaches turned to other players. The first was Rod Grizzard, a six-foot-seven forward from Birmingham. Grizzard played for a tiny Christian school and thus didn't face demanding competition. But if some experts thought Stone was the No. 1 player in Alabama, others thought that honor belonged to Grizzard.

"I had decided on Alabama all along," Grizzard recalls. "I'd followed Alabama basketball when it was good; they had guys like the Robert Horrys, the James Robinsons. I wanted to help put Alabama basketball back on the map."

With Grizzard in the fold, Gottfried and his staff had a strong ally who could help them recruit other in-state stars.

The next target was Erwin Dudley, a six-foot-eight forward who had played high school basketball in obscurity in Uniontown, Alabama.

"Rubble-strewn lots and abandoned hulls of buildings are blights on the bleak land-scape of this rural, poverty-riddled town in central Alabama," Thomas Murphy of the *Mobile Register* wrote of Uniontown. "Uniontown had the misfortune of lying on the U.S. Highway 80 corridor, down which drug traffic made its insidious trail through the Deep South, further deepening the town's plight."

Out of such grim surroundings Dudley emerged, determined that basketball would be his ticket to a better life. Gottfried was taken by Dudley's character and his remarkable consistency—Dudley reached double figures in points and rebounds in seventy-three of the eighty high school games he played.

Grizzard, who played AAU basketball with Dudley, put the hard sell on his friend during the summer of 1999.

"Rod had signed first," Dudley recalled. "I remember him coming to my house, trying to get me to come to Alabama, too. I didn't tell him at the time, but Alabama was where I wanted to go. I liked coach Scott and I thought coach Gottfried was going to do a great job. I wanted to be a part of what was going on."

So too did Terrance Meade, a sweet-shooting guard from Scottsboro, Alabama. Meade had played AAU basketball with Dudley and Grizzard and wanted to join them in Tuscaloosa. The Alabama coaches took particular delight in signing Meade, who was from the same hometown as Auburn assistant coach Eugene Harris.

The final player in what would become one of the most significant recruiting class-es in Alabama history was Kenny Walker, a six-foot-nine forward. He was the only player in the class not from Alabama; Gottfried and Scott went to Jacksonville, Florida, to get him.

———

Gottfried's first season at Alabama went about as well as could be expected. Gottfried had vowed to better utilize guard Brian Williams—miscast as a point guard much of his career—as a scorer, and Williams responded by averaging 17 points a game. Center Jeremy Hays averaged 12 points and eight rebounds. With that nucleus, Gottfried fash-ioned a team that won seventeen games and played in the NIT. Considering the state of the program before he arrived, the NIT was considered real progress.

In the summer before his second season, Gottfried surprised the rest of the SEC with what appeared to be a recruiting coup when two in-state stars committed to Alabama. Six-foot-seven forward Gerald Wallace, of tiny Childersburg, Alabama, would later be ranked by several recruiting analysts as the top high school player in the class of 1999–2000. And Mario Austin, a six-foot-nine center from York, Alabama, would be chosen a *Parade* and McDonald's All-American after his senior season.

Wallace and Austin, friends from their AAU basketball days, had talked about going to school together. But after the announcement that the two players were bound for Alabama, Austin said his decision to commit had been announced prematurely by his AAU coach, Kenny Harris, and in November signed with Mississippi State. Wallace stayed the course, resisted the lure of the NBA, and enrolled at Alabama.

Gottfried's second year in Tuscaloosa turned out to be difficult, professionally and personally. In September 1999, assistant coach Robert Scott was diagnosed with stomach cancer. Somehow, he found the courage to press on. He made a vow to attend every game, and nearly did, despite his ever weakening condition and the fact he had to make an hour drive to Birmingham for weekly chemotherapy treatments. No one who was in Coleman Coliseum the night of February 12, 2000, will forget Scott's dramatic entrance with just two minutes to play against Vanderbilt. Scott wound up missing only two regular-season games.

"I feel like if I can just come in, sit down and watch, it's better than not being here," Scott told the *Birmingham News*. "If I can get up and say one or two things, I want to try to do something. That just keeps me going."

Scott fought his illness through the regular season, but died in May. "That was a tough, tough thing," Gottfried said.

Nearly two years after Scott's death, in the 2001–2002 season, Alabama's players hadn't forgotten their coach. They honored him by their appearance in the Jimmy V Classic, an annual double-header named for Jim Valvano, the former North Carolina State coach who died of cancer. And Erwin Dudley pays his own tribute to Scott in every game he plays. Dudley prints the letters RAH on one side of his shoes and RIP on the other side.

"He stays with me," Dudley once told the *Anniston Star*. "He's in my heart all the time."

On the court, the 1999–2000 season seemed cursed, from the beginning to the bitter end. Because of an ankle injury, Hays missed the Tide's first two games in a tournament in St. Louis. Alabama lost them both, to lightly regarded Northern Iowa and Saint Louis. Tide fans expecting big things from their team were shocked.

Hays recovered and showed signs of putting together a year good enough to impress NBA scouts. But in a late-November game against LaSalle, Hays, who had made his first seven shots and scored 24 first-half points against the Explorers, tore the anterior cruciate ligament in his left knee. His season was done, and so, essen-

Erwin Dudley. *University of Alabama Media Relations Office*

tially, was Alabama's. The Tide finished 13-16 without its leading scorer and rebounder.

Hays wasn't the only player to battle injuries. Schea Cotton, a talented junior-college transfer, missed several games and considerable practice time with a variety of ailments. Cotton stayed just one season before declaring for the NBA draft. Sam Haginas, Kenny Walker, Alfred Moss, Travis Stinnett, and Terrance Meade all missed games with injuries.

"It was scary at times," Gottfried recalled. "We ended up playing basically freshmen on the road. We very rarely had more than seven or eight guys in practice."

Some good did come out of the season. Even before Hays's injury problems, Gottfried decided to play his freshmen as much as he could. The experience they gained was invaluable.

"We'd made the decision to recruit high school kids, and if that's what we were going to do, they had to be good enough to play," Gottfried said. "We decided to throw Rod and Erwin and Kenny and Terrance in there and see how they handled it. Those guys helped us lay a foundation."

Gottfried couldn't have asked for much more production than he got from Grizzard, Dudley, and Meade. All three averaged double figures in scoring, and Dudley finished sixth in the SEC in rebounding. Despite his injury problems, Walker showed he could handle himself at the SEC level.

The end of the season didn't mean the Tide's troubles had ended. Incredibly, assistant coach Tom Kelsey was also diagnosed with cancer; he underwent surgery to remove his left kidney. Guard Doc Martin broke his foot.

"We were wondering when it was all going to end," Gottfried said.

———

With Gerald Wallace joining Alabama's young nucleus, much was expected of Alabama in 2000–2001. But again, a major injury hampered the Tide's progress. Jeremy Hays, who had worked hard to rehabilitate his knee, was slowed by a stress fracture in his lower right leg. Hays tried to play, but later decided the pain was too much to bear and reluctantly gave up basketball.

With Hays gone for good, Gottfried needed Wallace to pick up some of the scoring load. And Wallace did nothing to diminish his reputation in the first month of the season, scoring 26 points in a win over Grambling and 27 as the Tide beat Akron. Alabama won its first nine games, lost by just three points to Cincinnati, then won three more in a row before a familiar problem resurfaced.

The previous two years, Alabama had been a horrible road team, losing fifteen-of-sixteen SEC away games. As league play began in 2000–2001, the Tide appeared ready to end its road woes. Alabama won at LSU in its SEC opener, but a few days later was soundly beaten at Tennessee. The Tide didn't win a league road game the rest of the season.

As Alabama struggled in SEC games, so did Wallace, a great athlete put a poor shooter. He scored in double figures just four times in league play. In late-season losses at Florida and Ole Miss, he contributed a grand total of one point.

Though the Tide won twenty regular-season games and another in the SEC Tournament, the NCAA Tournament berth that Gottfried had so coveted never came.

Some teams that get snubbed by the NCAA selection committee reluctantly accept NIT bids and get knocked out in the first round. But Alabama chose to make the most of its NIT trip. The positive mindset the Tide took on made for a successful NIT run, but paid even greater dividends the next season.

———

A year after his arrival in Tuscaloosa, Gottfried made a risky personnel decision. Gottfried knew Alabama was in dire need of a point guard, but rather than do what some coaches would have and find a quick fix via the junior-college route, Gottfried decided to wait. Instead of signing a player who would be around for only two years or another freshman that wasn't equal to the responsibilities he placed on the position, Gottfried would focus on one particular point guard and pursue him relentlessly.

That player was Maurice "Mo" Williams.

Williams—who had attended Alabama camps during his high school days—stood proud in a long line of great players to emerge from Murrah High School in talent-rich Jackson, Mississippi. And just as Othella Harrington, James Robinson, Ronnie Henderson, and others did before him, Williams had his choice of schools. Gottfried knew he would have plenty of competition, not the least of which would come from the SEC's two Mississippi schools. In the 1990s, Mississippi State's Rick Stansbury and Ole Miss' Rod Barnes had greatly reduced the talent exodus from Mississippi, so it was going to be difficult to extract Williams from his home state.

"We kind of left the cupboard bare on purpose for him," Gottfried recalled, "so it would be his position. Yeah, we were anxious about it. But in this case, we had to have a point guard. He was the one we wanted."

It wasn't hard to see why Gottfried had become infatuated with Williams, who possessed a rare blend of talent, basketball savvy, and competitive spirit, even at an early age. Gottfried wasn't the first coach to notice that.

Williams started playing basketball at nine years old. At that impressionable age, he was fortunate enough to come under the tutelage of AAU coach Fred Williams.

"He just had this little team," Williams recalled. "He took a group of kids, picked them up and spent time with them, teaching them basketball. I guess I kind of stood out. He must have seen something in me, because he took me in and helped me."

Fred Williams instilled in his young protégé a solid grasp of the fundamentals, but one lesson stood out above all others.

"He just told me to always play hard," Mo Williams said. "If you play hard, good things will happen."

Because he was always willing to expend his last bit of energy every time he played, Williams quickly developed a reputation. At Murrah, Williams played shooting guard for three seasons, but before his senior year, Murray coach Bob Frith asked him to move to the point. Williams was only too happy to do so, and he made the difficult switch with ease.

"Point guard is a tough position," Frith told the *Jackson Clarion-Ledger*. "Maurice just knows the game—how the flow is going, who's open and when they're open. If you get open, he's going to try to get the ball to you. His second option is to shoot, because he wants to pass the ball if he can. That's a good point guard's mentality."

In his final season at Murrah, Williams averaged 8.6 assists. He was more proud of that than his 25.7 scoring average, but statistics meant little to him.

"I don't really get caught up in points or assists," Williams said. "I just try to play the game. As long as I play hard, I'm happy."

For three years, Gottfried and his staff recruited Williams, eventually convincing him that he would run the show from his first day on campus.

26

"I eventually took that to heart," said Williams. "I had an opportunity to come in and play around a great group of guys. It's a great feeling to know they had that much confidence in me."

Though Williams narrowed his list of schools to Alabama, Ole Miss, Miami, and Georgetown, he seriously considered only one of them.

Williams couldn't wait to get to Tuscaloosa. He enrolled in school for the summer term so he could get to know his new teammates. Williams was an instant hit in pick-up games.

"We all knew he was the real deal," Rod Grizzard said.

"He fit in right away," Erwin Dudley recalled. "You like playing with a guy who gives up the ball and tries to spread the points around. He plays the same way in pick-up games as he does in SEC games."

And so Williams was the real deal. Not hesitant about leading a team dominated by juniors, the rookie took over the team. "They opened up to me and took me in real easy," Williams said. "And I just tried to lead the team in a positive way, on and off the court."

Williams didn't seem to need an adjustment period. Crimson Tide fans couldn't help but be exited by the opening minutes of Alabama's first game of the season, against Mississippi Valley State. First, he hit a three-pointer from the right wing. Next, he threw a perfect alley-oop pass to Rod Grizzard for a dunk. Then he knocked down a three-pointer from the left wing.

Williams finished with 15 points, eight assists, six rebounds, and three three-pointers. The opponent was hardly the strongest Alabama would play all year, but Tide fans knew after that performance that their team finally found a true point guard. And Gottfried, though he never doubted Williams's ability, got to see him perform in the spotlight and was satisfied his gamble had paid off.

"I didn't know for sure," Gottfried said. "But I expected Mo was going to have a chance to play. I knew he had the physical tools to be as good as anybody out there. With freshmen you can't lump guys into one category. Every one is a little bit different. You never know how they'll respond. We knew early on that Mo had adapted well, and we looked forward to see what he could do leading our team."

———

Gottfried took a lot of criticism during the 2000–2001 season because of Alabama's nonconference schedule, which, save for games against Cincinnati and Ohio State, was weak. But Gottfried didn't want to overly tax his team, then dominated by sophomores, until he thought it was time. By the 2001–2002 season, it was time. Gone were the Gramblings, the Troy States, and the Arkansas Pine Bluffs. In their place were Missouri, Memphis, Utah, UCLA, Temple, and Notre Dame. It was the kind of schedule that could show Gottfried exactly how far his team had progressed and how much of a factor Mo Williams would become.

Gottfried was counting on Williams to make an impact, and for his guards to play a bigger role in general, because the Tide had lost some firepower. In the spring of 2001, Gerald Wallace, though he didn't appear to be ready, declared for the NBA draft and was chosen in the first round by the Sacramento Kings. Two junior college players Gottfried had hoped to plug into his front line were academically ineligible, which meant Alabama had no low-post depth behind Erwin Dudley and Kenny Walker.

Early in the season, Gottfried had to get creative, sometimes putting four guards on the floor at the same time. And defense, always emphasized, would become even more of a focal point. Before the season, Gottfried filled a vacancy on his staff by hiring former Alabama star T. R. Dunn, one of the most popular players in school history, and letting him whip the defense into shape. Dunn, never a great shooter, had forged out a lengthy NBA existence on the strength of his defensive prowess.

The smaller lineup and emphasis on defense were big keys as Alabama showed considerable progress in wins over Memphis and Utah and a narrow defeat against Missouri, then ranked among the top five teams in the country. But some regression in early December caused Gottfried to take some drastic measures.

The first signs of slippage were subtle. Poised to blow out a seemingly out-manned Chattanooga team at home, Alabama instead allowed the Mocs to erase a double-figure deficit and hang around a lot longer than Gottfried would have preferred before escaping with a six-point win. Afterward, Gottfried said his players looked as though they were running in mud, but he didn't seem overly concerned. "We did what we needed to do to win the game," Gottfried said.

Things got muddier and Gottfried was overly concerned five days later in a much larger forum—the Wooden Classic in Anaheim. Given his reverence for former UCLA coach John Wooden and the fact he was a UCLA assistant for seven years, Gottfried wanted to put on a good show when his team traveled west to take on the mighty Bruins. Instead the Tide struggled.

The game was actually close throughout much of the first half. The Bruins led 30-25 with just under four minutes to play, but a late run increased the advantage to 40-25 by halftime.

The Tide battled back to trim UCLA's lead to 56-50 with 8:23 to play, but the Bruins pulled away again and won handily.

Afterward, Gottfried could only shake his head as he looked at the final box score. It didn't take the Wizard of Westwood to figure out why the game was so lopsided. Alabama made just 19-of-64 shots, including 7-of-33 from three-point range. The shooting woes even carried to the free throw line, where the Tide made just 12-of-20.

"We got open looks, but just couldn't seem to make a shot," Gottfried said. "It was a frustrating day."

Alabama felt Gottfried's frustration when it took the floor again six days later. The Tide was back home in Tuscaloosa, and the opponent was Jacksonville State. When the starting lineups were announced, Kenny Walker and Rod Grizzard stayed on the Alabama bench as little-used Reggie Rambo and Travis Stinnett took their places.

Grizzard knew why his string of fifty-five consecutive starts had ended.

"Basically, he said that I was not playing as hard as I should," Grizzard told reporters after the game. "It's not set in stone that it's going to be the same five every night."

Walker wound up having his best game to that point of the season, coming off the bench and scoring a career-high 20 points. Grizzard played just twenty-two minutes and scored eight points.

Gottfried's message had been sent.

"We've just got to have five guys on the floor playing extremely hard," Gottfried said in his post-game press conference. "If you're fortunate enough to be on the floor, you better play with all you have."

Alabama closed out its nonconference schedule with two more significant victories, over Temple and Notre Dame. In both games, the Tide had taken substantial leads, only to let its opponents come back. Alabama led Notre Dame by 18 points at halftime, but with 3:13 to play was ahead by just a point at 70-69. Rod Grizzard took control from that point, knocking down a three-pointer, a ten-foot jumper, and four free throws to secure Alabama's victory. The Tide finished 12-2 in nonconference games and was ranked No. 18 by the Associated Press heading into the SEC portion of its schedule.

Alabama started 2-0 in the league by winning at home, but followed that good start with a troubling loss at Auburn, which was in the middle of its worst season in coach Cliff Ellis's seven-year tenure. The Tide had won just two of twenty-four SEC road games in Gottfried's three previous seasons. Had an old nemesis returned?

Alabama had an answer for that question in its next game at Georgia, a matchup that would feature several interesting story lines. Gottfried would once again be matched against his former boss at UCLA, Jim Harrick. The Bulldogs, ranked twentieth at the time, were one of college basketball's surprise teams, having been picked by many to finish last in the SEC's Eastern Division. Two Georgia players, Tony Cole

29

and Steven Thomas, had been suspended after being accused of rape by a Georgia student. Finally, there was that little matter of Alabama's road jinx.

Few Alabama fans, had they been told Erwin Dudley and Terrance Meade would be in foul trouble most of the game, would have predicted the Tide could have gone to Georgia and won. But that's what happened as Gottfried turned to his bench.

Sophomore guard Antoine Pettway, a former walk-on, played a career-high thirty-six minutes and came up with 15 points, seven rebounds and five assists. Reggie Rambo contributed 10 rebounds and six assists in a career-high twenty-two minutes as Alabama stole away with a 77-72 win.

Considering Georgia's personnel problems, Alabama's win there didn't convince skeptics that the Tide had suddenly become road warriors. But a week later, after Alabama had won at Kentucky for the first time since 1989, any doubters were silenced.

Once again, walk-on Pettway came up big with a pair of three-pointers and 10 points. But Erwin Dudley, who led Alabama with 16 points and seven rebounds, was the key to the win. It was at this point of the season that SEC coaches, media, and fans began to realize that Dudley might be the best player in the league.

Dudley's career had been building to that point. He arrived in Tuscaloosa at 218 pounds, no featherweight but hardly large enough to endure the pounding he would receive in the paint.

"I came in here from day one knowing I had to work hard," Dudley said. "I just wanted to do anything I could to get better."

The first step was the weight room.

"Alabama has historically and traditionally taken guys like Erwin Dudley and have helped them improve their bodies," Gottfried said. "I played with Derrick McKey and Keith Askins, and physically, you'd think they had no chance to be NBA players. But both worked on their bodies and played in the league for over a decade. We knew our strength program could help Dudley if he committed to it."

Dudley did commit to weight training. By his second season, he had added twenty pounds of muscle and was starting to reap the benefits of his increased strength, leading the league in rebounding. By his junior season, Dudley had added twenty more pounds and become a hulking, physical presence inside without losing any mobility or quickness.

While he was working on his body, Dudley also worked on his game. Early in Dudley's career, Gottfried decided the young post man should concentrate on a few scoring moves and become proficient with them.

"A lot of time with post players we all become clinic instructors and try to teach

30

them twenty-five post moves," Gottfried said. "They end up not being any good at any of them. I call it being a jack of all trades and a master of none. With Erwin, we tried not to have him do too many things. He developed a nice jump hook and can really turn and face the basket. He can count on those shots."

The results of Dudley's hard work were obvious. Once SEC games began, he quickly became a favorite of the league's coaches, who watch tape after tape of an opponent's games in an effort to establish trends. Alabama had flashier players—the high-flying Rod Grizzard, the cat-quick point guard Mo Williams—but its most solid player, by far, was Erwin Dudley.

"To be honest with you, and I love Erwin Dudley, he's probably gotten better than we thought he could be," said Alabama assistant Philip Pearson. "He's become a special player, and that's a tribute to his work ethic."

Given a huge confidence boost by its win at Kentucky, Alabama won five of its next six games and improved its SEC record to 10-2 as it continued to ride the broad shoulders of Dudley. In four of those games, Dudley scored 20 or more points and was the Tide's leading scorer. In all six games, Dudley led Alabama in rebounding.

A loss at Arkansas on February 20 mattered little. Three days later, the Tide returned to Tuscaloosa for a key game with Florida. A win would give Alabama the overall regular-season SEC championship. Not since 1987, when Gottfried played, had Alabama won a regular-season league title.

Predictably, the Florida game was hotly contested. With just seconds to play and Alabama trailing 64-63, freshman Earnest Shelton found himself in the left corner stuck between two Florida defenders. Shelton had to make a quick decision.

"I was thinking shot," Shelton told the *Birmingham News*. "I was going to throw it at the basket."

Before he could toss up a last-second prayer that had little chance of going in, Shelton alertly kept his pivot foot. He moved back, then forward, and as he did spotted Antoine Pettway streaking toward the basket. Somehow, Shelton squeezed a pass between two defenders and Pettway caught it in perfect stride for an uncontested lay-up. The final horn sounded, and Alabama, by this time ranked No. 5 in the country, had come away a 65-64 winner, improving its overall record to 23-5 and its SEC mark to 11-3. The shot touched off bedlam at Coleman Coliseum as Pettway ran to the press table, right where CBS broadcasters were seated, and started jumping up and down in sheer joy.

On a team full of stars and players with interesting stories, Pettway's might have been the most compelling. It doesn't happen often in a league as powerful as the SEC, but every now and again, a player who isn't rated that highly by the recruiting services gets overlooked by upper-level Division I schools, or otherwise falls through the cracks, and winds up walking on and playing a key role. Such was the case with Pettway. His last-second shot against Florida, combined with his earlier heroics at Georgia and Kentucky, had more than earned the scholarship he'd been given before the season started.

That was the deal that Pettway and Gottfried had worked out before the player ever set foot on campus. Pettway had been an all-state player for three years in high school, the last at Wilcox Central in Camden, Alabama. But because he wasn't invited to any of the major camps, Pettway wasn't spotted by recruiting analysts.

Much to his disappointment, Pettway couldn't do much to boost his notoriety after his junior year at Camden, when a high ankle sprain kept him out of summer basketball. So despite the fact Pettway averaged 24.2 points, 5.2 rebounds and 6.7 assists in leading Wilcox Central to the 2000 Alabama 5A championship and was a 4.0 student, SEC schools didn't give him a look. At six feet tall and 160 pounds on his best day, Pettway was hardly an imposing physical specimen, another factor that might have caused SEC schools to look the other way.

Pettway did have his pick of smaller Division I schools. Tulane wanted him. So did Jacksonville State, Troy State, Alabama State, Alabama A&M, and Louisiana Tech. Pettway could have been given a full scholarship by any of them, but he wanted something more.

"I always felt I could play at the [SEC] level," Pettway recalled. "I was always confident in my ability."

Pettway's school of choice was Alabama, which his father Joseph, who coached him in high school, had attended.

"I wanted to go to Alabama," Pettway said. "My dad saw that I really wanted to go there, and he supported me."

Pettway's task was to get Gottfried to notice him.

"He saw me play in the state championship game my senior year," Pettway said. "I'd hoped I'd done enough to impress him."

He had, sort of. Gottfried offered Pettway a chance to come to Tuscaloosa as a walk-on. "He told me if I came and showed I belonged, he would give me a scholarship my sophomore year."

Pettway lived up to his part of the bargain in his freshman year, proving he belonged with an eight-point, six-assist game against Louisville and a seven-point, three-assist effort against Cincinnati. Pettway's final statistics were meager, but when Gottfried assessed his chances of playing the next year, he thought back to a regular-season ending blowout at Ole Miss, when Pettway fought his way to 19 points, three rebounds and four assists. The kid had guts, Gottfried reasoned, and had earned his opportunity.

Gottfried honored his commitment to Pettway before the 2001–2002 season, placing him on scholarship.

Pettway didn't disappoint. He averaged twenty minutes of playing time and was Gottfried's insurance policy. In a year where Alabama basketball took a major step forward, there was room in the mix for a former walk-on who always dreamed of playing for the Tide and had the fortitude to turn that dream into reality.

"Antoine's story is beautiful," Gottfried said. "He had an opportunity to go to several mid-major schools in our state, but he wanted to come here. So many times, young people are influenced by friends. But Antoine didn't let anybody influence him. He knew what he wanted, and that was to come to Alabama."

Alabama
All-SEC Expansion Era Team
F-Erwin Dudley
F-Robert Horry
C-Antonio McDyess
G-Latrell Sprewell
G-Maurice Williams
Top Reserves-Rod Grizzard, James Robinson

Alabama's regular season ended, just as it had the year before, with a lopsided loss at Ole Miss. But the defeat didn't diminish the Tide's accomplishments. Alabama finished 24-6 overall and 12-4 in conference games, claiming the SEC regular-season overall championship and the Western Division title. When the SEC's post-season awards were announced, they reflected that success.

Gottfried was chosen the SEC's coach of the year, the first time an Alabama coach won the award since Wimp Sanderson in 1989. Erwin Dudley, who led the league in rebounding for the second straight season, was voted the SEC's player of the year, an honor no Alabama player had received since Antonio McDyess in 1987. Mo Williams was a unanimous choice as the league's freshman of the year.

"It was a great [regular season]," Gottfried said after the awards had been announced. "But we're not finished yet."

Ahead were the SEC Tournament and a long-awaited return to the NCAA Tournament. As a player at Alabama, Gottfried knew postseason play was the barometer by which good teams were measured. He couldn't wait to see how his own team would fare in the madness of March.

Chapter Two

Arkansas

outheastern Conference basketball was changed forever in Birmingham, Alabama, on the afternoon of March 13, 1992. That's the day Arkansas fans took over the SEC Tournament.

For hours, the basketball-crazy Razorback fans gathered in Birmingham-Jefferson Civic Center, silently multiplying like those feathered protagonists in Alfred Hitchcock's creepy classic *The Birds*, waiting for the right time to strike. Arkansas was to play the second game of the afternoon session, and Hog fans had invaded Birmingham in droves, some without even having secured a ticket or a hotel room. This was to be Arkansas's first postseason tournament game in its new league. After dominating the Southwest Conference for years, the Razorbacks had joined the SEC in the 1991–92 season. Hog fans couldn't wait to crash the party.

"Somebody told me before the game that there were two busloads of people coming down here who didn't have tickets and didn't have a place to stay," Arkansas center Oliver Miller told the *Northwest Arkansas Times* the day of the big game. "I said no way. But they were right. It was unbelievable. Just unbelievable."

That's the reaction long-time SEC fans had midway through the first half of a first-round game between Kentucky and Vanderbilt. As the Wildcats and Commodores played, an Arkansas player, bedecked in the familiar cardinal and white warm-ups, walked through a tunnel and into the arena. He was followed quickly by another Razorback, then another. By this time, Arkansas fans—nearly six thousand strong—had begun to take notice, as a palpable buzz in the arena became a loud cheer before ultimately giving way to the famed Calling of the Hogs. As the Arkansas fans saluted their team with one of the most unique battle cries in college athletics, curious onlookers that had never seen such commotion marveled at the sight.

"I thought that a pretty lady must have walked in the building," then–Kentucky coach Rick Pitino said.

"It was amazing," said SEC associate commissioner Mark Womack, who had been a key figure in the league's expansion efforts. "People just looked around the arena in awe. Nobody had ever seen anything like it."

At least no one in the SEC had seen anything like it. Former Arkansas coach Nolan

Richardson had grown used to the rabid support of Arkansas fans.

"I never will forget that day," Richardson said. "People kept coming up to me and asking me if we always brought that many fans. I said, 'Hell, when we were in the Southwest Conference Tournament, the arena held 17,000, and we'd have 13,000 of our fans in there.' To our fans, the conference tournament is bigger than the NCAAs. They'd save their money all year, take vacation time to come to the tournament. I think when the other fans around the SEC saw our people, it transformed the tournament.

"It used to be Kentucky and a handful of fans from other schools. Most of 'em couldn't care less. They were waiting on who was going to be recruited in football. But when fans at other schools saw what was happening with our fans, they got excited: 'Man, did you see how many fans Arkansas brought?' During that period, I got so many letters from fans at other schools. Most of 'em said, 'Boy, we're glad you all are in the league. It's not just Kentucky any more.'"

The 1992 tournament was a seminal moment in the rise of SEC basketball. When the league's presidents voted to expand in the spring of 1990, the decision seemed driven by football—Florida State and Miami had been the first schools considered, and later Texas and Texas A&M were seen as possible candidates. SEC athletics directors had been in favor of adding four new schools to the ten-team league, and there was talk of building a superconference with as many as sixteen teams.

Foremost among the benefits of expansion—or so it was thought at the time—would be the creation of an SEC championship football game, permissible under NCAA rules if a conference has ten or more teams split into two divisions. When the SEC expanded and divided into Eastern and Western divisions, the championship football game was quickly adopted. The game would be a natural for prime-time television coverage, and a deal with a major network would eventually net the league millions.

The SEC's expansion didn't play out as some might have hoped. Florida State decided to join the Atlantic Coast Conference, and Miami later settled on the Big East. Texas and Texas A&M would eventually become part of another superconference as the Southwest and Big 8 merged into a twelve-team league. When the conference jumping had ended, the SEC wound up with Arkansas and South Carolina, which had left the Metro Conference.

Some may have been disappointed that Florida State or Miami didn't join the SEC, but league officials were elated with the two schools that did. Arkansas and South Carolina are major state-supported institutions that sponsor broad-based and successful athletic programs. As then–SEC commissioner Roy Kramer told the *Birmingham*

News at the time, "We were not interested in becoming a football consortium."

When the SEC announced its choice of new schools, the conventional wisdom was that the league should sit back, see how the new schools work out, and then decide whether to expand again. Ten years after the fact, the SEC was satisfied with its twelve-team arrangement and hadn't formally sought to add more members. And although the pioneering championship football game did become the financial boon everyone assumed it would, basketball turned out to be the primary beneficiary of expansion.

The Razorback fans proved as much during that first post-expansion tournament in 1992.

"Our basketball tournament had been in a situation where we were a thousand tickets away from selling out," Womack said. "When Arkansas and South Carolina were added, it became an instant sellout. It's become a difficult ticket from then on."

Not to be outdone by the upstart newcomers, Kentucky fans—who follow their team with as much fervor as any in the country—began matching the numbers of the Arkansas swarm. Suddenly, venues such as the Birmingham-Jefferson Civic Center weren't big enough for the SEC Tournament. The league would quickly enter into long-term relationships with domed facilities such as the Georgia Dome in Atlanta and the New Orleans Superdome. The tournament moved to the Georgia Dome in 1995 and was played there in five of the next eight years, including three straight years from 1998 to 2000. Attendance for the four-day tournament averaged more than 210,000 from 1995 to 2001, a far cry from such pre-expansion totals of 75,982 at the Orlando Arena in 1992 and 121,851 at Vanderbilt's Memorial Gym in 1991.

"I really believe we gave the SEC a facelift," Richardson said. "Before, it was like 'Well, it's Kentucky, then it's Kentucky, and then Kentucky.' The first year, we went to Kentucky and beat them in Rupp Arena. All of a sudden other people were saying, 'We can do it too.' Sometimes it takes something to open your eyes. Not only that, we were making money. Everywhere we went fans were there. When we would come into town, fans would pack the arena to either watch us get beat or to see what we had that they didn't have."

The Razorbacks acquitted themselves well in their first SEC Tournament, advancing to the semifinals against Alabama and taking part in a remarkable game many think was among the best in the league's history. In a game that featured numerous lead changes and a host of future pros—Alabama's Latrell Sprewell and Robert Horry, Arkansas's Todd Day and Oliver Miller—it took a three-point basket by Alabama's Eric Washington with 1.2 seconds left to give the Crimson Tide a 90-89 victory. The game winner was the only other shot Washington attempted that day.

"This was the championship game," said Day, who scored 39 points. "It won't get any better than this."

The loss ended Arkansas's run of conference championships; the Hogs had won the previous three Southwest Conference Tournaments. But it didn't dampen the spirits of Razorback fans, who continued to make their presence felt in the SEC Tournament, even though, ironically, Arkansas wouldn't win the championship until the much-maligned 1999–2000 team beat Georgia, Kentucky, LSU, and Auburn on successive days to earn an improbable NCAA Tournament berth.

———

Ten years after that raucous calling of the Hogs signaled Arkansas's arrival into its new league, Nolan Richardson, the man whose program had helped transform Southeastern Conference basketball instantly and permanently for the good, was gone. After seventeen years in Fayetteville, during which he took Arkansas basketball to the highest level of the game, the Richardson era came to a sudden and shocking end on March 1, 2002, when he was unceremoniously fired after a series of incendiary public comments he'd made the previous few days.

The first was puzzling. On his weekly television show, Richardson implied that there were limited opportunities for black athletes to enjoy a social life in Fayetteville. Then, in press conferences two days apart, Richardson suggested that Arkansas athletics director Frank Broyles and chancellor John White could buy him out of the remainder of his contract if they weren't happy with the direction the program was headed. In the second press conference, Richardson lashed out at the media, proclaimed himself the best thing going at Arkansas, and lamented about not being able to "play on the same level" as other coaches at Arkansas. The diatribe was taped by local television stations and would be replayed countless times around the country on ESPN, CNN, and other cable networks.

Richardson's comments were made in obvious reaction to a season that had been slowly slipping from his grasp and would end up as the worst in his time at Arkansas. Weeks later, Richardson said in an interview televised by HBO that his motive for speaking out was a "cry for help" to encourage Broyles and White to give him a public vote of confidence.

If Richardson had intended to elicit support from his bosses, he failed miserably. Instead, he managed to insult half the state of Arkansas. After that, White and Broyles insisted, they had no choice but to fire Richardson, giving him the multimillion dollar buyout they eventually decided he had been seeking.

"There has been a lot of damage overall to the program," White told the *Arkansas Democrat-Gazette*.

Richardson, shocked and outraged after his dismissal, made an appeal to University of Arkansas system president Alan Sugg, hoping he might overturn White's decision. After taking several days to deliberate, Sugg allowed the buyout to stand.

A month later, in the first major interview since his departure, Richardson said on HBO's *Real Sports with Bryant Gumbel* that the season had indeed taken its toll.

"I felt an anger inside that had been building, and building and building," Richardson told Gumbel.

How long had Richardson's anger been building? Less than five weeks before his firing, Richardson told this author in a lengthy, wide-ranging interview that, although the 2001–2002 season had been difficult and media and fan criticism hurtful, he had no intentions of leaving Arkansas. Quite the contrary, Richardson seemed stubbornly insistent on keeping his job.

"He's too old. It's time to change. He doesn't have that burning desire any more. I get all that," Richardson said in the interview. "But you know what? The worst way to get rid of me is to want me out of there. I cannot leave anything until I am ready myself. Healthwise, I've never felt better. I run. I've got my horses. I've got my farm. I'm not consumed totally by basketball. Fifteen years ago, my daughter passed away. Life's a lot different for me now. I don't see it the same way. But at the same time, I enjoy basketball more than I used to. I like to teach more now."

Richardson made it clear he didn't just want to log time as he worked toward his eventual retirement. At sixty years old, he still had worlds to conquer and goals to reach.

"I want another [national championship]," Richardson said. "Bad. I've won one. But there are a few guys who have won one. I want to win two before I get out of here. I'd like to be separated from the pack, because that's who I am. You've got John Wooden, Bobby Knight, Mike Krzyzewski, Denny Crum. Those guys won more than one. They're in an elite group.

"I'd like to be in that group. And I think we're back on the verge of having those kinds of people you need to win a national championship. If you're gonna get me, you'd better get me soon. Because pretty soon, you ain't gonna beat me any more. That's how I feel."

From that hopeful, almost defiant stance, voiced during a ninety-minute interview in Athens, Georgia, on January 23, what happened to Richardson to make him say, just a month later after a game at Kentucky, "If they go ahead and pay me my money, they can take the job tomorrow'"? Did Richardson really expect White and Broyles to come to his defense after such a remark?

Whatever frustration and anger Richardson felt didn't just surface during a month-long stretch in the 2001–2002 season. The travails of being a pioneering African-American head coach had left him filled with bitter memories and feelings he couldn't dismiss, despite the passage of time. On many occasions in his Arkansas career, usually during heavily attended press conferences or when he had the attention of a major media outlet, Richardson couldn't resist the urge to voice his feelings.

In 1994, the year he would lead Arkansas to a national championship, Richardson told the *New York Daily News*, "If I was white and I did what I've done here, they'd build statues to me. I'd be Jesus Christ almighty God."

In 1995, another successful year that saw the Razorbacks advance to the NCAA Tournament title game, Richardson, after a homecourt loss to Alabama, referred to media and fan critics as "turds and assholes." He eventually apologized.

Another incident, little known outside Arkansas, involved Wally Hall, long-time sports editor of the *Arkansas Democrat-Gazette*. In a conversation with Hall, Richardson referred to a faction of fans as "redneck SOBs," which Hall dutifully reported. Richardson later said he had called Hall a redneck SOB, not the fans.

The incident started a long-standing feud between Richardson and Hall. Other Arkansas beat writers had grown weary of hearing Richardson when he dusted off his soapbox and ranted, as broadcaster Tim Brando once said, "like an old fire and brimstone black preacher in the deep South."

Richardson's occasional rants did not go unnoticed by his boss. In a memo to Arkansas chancellor John White that was in Richardson's personnel file and released after his dismissal, Arkansas athletic director Frank Broyles expressed genuine concern.

"I have a concern that needs to be addressed," Broyles wrote. "Nolan's occasionally irrational behavior is becoming more frequent and also more severe. In fact, it seems to develop into a mean-spirited, insulting monologue. On virtually every occasion, these episodes of volatile overreaction have been to minor annoyances or misunderstood communication.

"My sincere fear is that in the near future we could have a Woody Hayes or Bobby Knight episode in the making."

The memo was dated November 9, 1995. It took nearly seven years, but Broyles was a prophet.

There was another source of Richardson's frustration. As Richardson later revealed in his HBO interview, his relationship with Broyles had been strained for years, dating back to his first two seasons, when his daughter Yvonne was battling leukemia. Arkansas struggled for a time in that period as Richardson tried to do his job while spending as much time as possible with his daughter, who died on January 22, 1987. The Razorbacks had a losing record in Richardson's first season, prompting Broyles to write Richardson a memo with suggestions for improving the program. Richardson took particular offense to a suggestion that he learn defense from Indiana coach Bobby Knight. But Richardson was more upset that Broyles, in his opinion, couldn't see past the obvious.

"How could you write me a letter telling me all of the things that he expected of me when I'm tending to my kid?" Richardson told HBO. "I'm struggling with my daughter, and there I was being degraded? And [Broyles] knew when I took the job that she was sick. And that just angered me so much. And the only reason he changed a little bit is because we were beginning to win."

Richardson maintained a cold war with Broyles for years, as a series of memos released by the university after his firing illustrated. In 1998, for example, Richardson asked to be fired because he was unhappy over the way equipment from his shoe and apparel contract would be dispersed.

"The more he talked, the angrier he got," Broyles wrote in a memo that was placed in Richardson's personnel file. "He started shouting and said, 'Just fire me and pay me off. I want to be fired.' I said that was ridiculous and that I have no reason to fire him. His comment was, 'Then by my actions I will give you reasons to fire me.'"

Insiders who know both men say Broyles had grown weary of such seemingly minor complaints. And as his 1995 memo clearly stated, Broyles was also afraid that Richardson was a loose cannon that could go off at any time. As it turned out, Broyles's worst fears were realized.

But did Broyles intend to get rid of Richardson? A few coaches in Broyles's tenure have had confrontations with the demanding athletics director. In the summer of 2001, Broyles suggested to White that the university not roll over Richardson's contract (which still had six years remaining). White rolled over the contract anyway.

As late as May 2001, Broyles commended Richardson's work. "Once again, I am pleased with the overall direction of the basketball program," Broyles wrote in a memo dated May 31, 2001.

White, too, was satisfied with Richardson's performance, despite his occasional public outbursts and other faults, not the least of which was the abysmal graduation rate of his players (which would be revealed in an ESPN special report in late February 2002).

In a three-page letter dated August 6, 2001, White wrote to Richardson that he

40

wanted him to stay for "many, many years. That desire is not because I like you and respect you—although I do! Neither is it because I don't want to go through the search process to secure your replacement—which I don't. Instead, my reason for wanting you to be here for many years is quite selfish. It will mean that you are happy—which will mean you are being enormously successful with your program—all of which makes my job so much easier!"

Their private words wouldn't suggest White or Broyles were out to get Richardson. But did Richardson's public conduct in February 2002 make his bosses change their opinions of him?

If Broyles secretly did want Richardson out, did Richardson—who had been criticized by fans and media in recent years as the Razorbacks couldn't measure up to his better teams—finally give his boss enough ammunition to get rid of him? Or did Richardson actually want to leave, as he told some confidants in private? Arkansas made Richardson rich by making him go away. Was that Richardson's intention all along?

Those questions may never be answered.

————

Richardson's final days ended in controversy, but even his harshest critic would have to admit he took Arkansas basketball to a higher level, and in so doing elevated the level of SEC basketball as well.

Arkansas's basketball program was a strong lure for the SEC when it came time to choosing schools that would fit the league's profile for expansion. After conversations with several traditional football schools that eventually didn't lead anywhere, the SEC centered on Arkansas.

"The success that Arkansas had in basketball certainly was a big part of our league taking that next step," SEC associate commissioner Mark Womack said.

The timing couldn't have been better for Arkansas. SEC presidents voted to expand the league in the spring of 1990, just weeks after Arkansas advanced to the Final Four for the first time under Richardson.

Clearly, the program was on the rise under the guidance of Richardson, who had been a winner at every stop in his coaching career. At Western Texas Junior College, Richardson won a national championship in 1980. Switching to Tulsa the next season, Richardson, who brought his best players from Western Texas along, guided the Golden Hurricane to the NIT championship.

Richardson didn't make that kind of dramatic entrance at Arkansas. The poor

41

health of his daughter, who had been diagnosed with cancer before Richardson left Tulsa, had been foremost among his concerns. And former Arkansas coach Eddie Sutton hadn't left much talent behind before leaving for Kentucky in 1985.

The Razorbacks were 12-16 in 1985–86, Richardson's first season. By his second year, Arkansas improved to 19-14 and won a game in the NIT. In 1987–88, Arkansas played in the NCAA Tournament after a three-year absence, losing in the first round to Villanova. A year later, the Razorbacks won an NCAA game. Given that steady improvement, Arkansas seemed ready for a major step upward in 1989–90, Richardson's fourth season.

The Razorbacks had plenty of talent, but just as important to their coach, they were tough and basketball savvy. Years later, when his teams would struggle trying to run his famed "Forty Minutes of Hell," full-court pressing defense, Richardson would speak fondly of the good old days. "Back then, we had basketball players," Richardson said often.

Indeed he did—players such as Ron Huery, a junior in 1989–90. By most accounts, Huery was the most important recruit in the Richardson era.

"Ron Huery was the biggest key of all," former Arkansas assistant Mike Anderson recalled. "He was the first of the multidimensional, versatile guys in our program. He was a guy that a lot of people wanted."

And Huery was also from Memphis, a fertile recruiting ground that Richardson had been eager to invade. Huery, the coach reasoned, could open up a talent pipeline to Tennessee.

Just as Richardson had hoped, other Memphis stars followed Huery's lead. Todd Day, yet another long, lean, perimeter player, was the next Memphis star to arrive in Fayetteville. In 1988–89, he was part of a talented sophomore class that included guard Lee Mayberry and center Oliver Miller. All three had impressive debut seasons, and in 1989–90, they would elevate their games.

The Razorbacks, then still competing in the old Southwest Conference, started 8-2 that season, averaging 104 points per game as they buried every opponent save Missouri and UNLV.

Arkansas made a statement in its first SWC game of the year. At Houston, Arkansas rallied from 18 points down to win 82-78. The Razorbacks started 11-0 in the conference and at that point were ranked No. 3 in the country. Richardson began to think he might have a special team on his hands.

"During this time, I thought we might have a chance to go a long way in the NCAA Tournament," Richardson said in Dudley Dawson's *Razorbacks Handbook*. "Maybe not win it all because Vegas [UNLV] had men and everybody else little boys, but then again, they had to come from behind to beat us at their place."

Richardson had reason to feel confident after the Hogs pulled out a win at Texas. The game appeared lost when Mayberry was called for an intentional foul with fourteen seconds left and the Longhorns ahead, 84-83. Before Lance Blanks could make his two free throws for an 86-83 Texas lead, Richardson got up, strolled past the Texas bench and went to the Arkansas locker room. Was he protesting the official's call in a game televised nationally by ABC? Not exactly.

"I was feeling sick," Richardson recalled in *Razorbacks Handbook.* "I went straight to the bathroom."

Arkansas appeared finished when Texas's Travis Mays stepped to the free throw line with eleven seconds left, but he missed both shots. Oliver Miller grabbed the second miss and tossed the ball to Lee Mayberry, who drained a twenty-five-foot three-pointer to send the game into overtime. Richardson missed the heroics while easing his pain in the restroom.

"I'm waiting for this big roar when they beat us and it never came," Richardson recalled in *Razorbacks Handbook.* "I couldn't figure out what happened, but then our manager came to the door and said, 'Coach, let's go. Lee hit a shot and we're in overtime.' I thought about not coming back since they were doing OK without me."

Arkansas won in overtime.

The Razorbacks finished the SWC season at 14-2, inexplicably losing two games in a row at Baylor and TCU late in the season. But those losses only served as a warning that the postseason was fast approaching. Arkansas won its final three regular-season games, three games in successive days to win the SWC Tournament, and then waded through Princeton, Dayton, North Carolina, and Texas to reach the Final Four.

The Hogs' run ended when Duke overcame a 69-62 deficit and won, 97-83. But Arkansas would extract a measure of revenge from the Blue Devils, beating them in the preseason NIT the next season. A sweeter victory over Duke would come three years later.

In 1990–91, Arkansas was a lame-duck team in the Southwest Conference, having already accepted the SEC's invitation to join. Some SWC coaches didn't think Arkansas should have been eligible for the league championship after its decision to leave. Richardson resented that sentiment and took out his anger on the rest of the conference. Arkansas was 15-1 in its final SWC season, then crushed Texas A&M, Rice, and Texas in the league tournament, scoring an average of 112 points in the three games.

Arkansas fans eagerly awaited the NCAA Tournament and the Hogs responded with three straight wins. They led Kansas by 12 points at halftime of the Southeast Regional championship, but were denied a second straight trip to the Final Four when the Jayhawks rallied for a 93-81 win.

Thus ended Arkansas's sixty-seven-year affiliation with the Southwest Conference. The SEC was next, and though the competition was considerably tougher, the Razorbacks were still a formidable team in 1991–92. Without Todd Day, who had been suspended after two separate transgressions, Arkansas was 9-3 through late December.

Day returned in time for the Hogs' final nonconference game and was in fine form by Arkansas's historic SEC debut. Behind Day's 35 points, the Razorbacks ripped Auburn, 110-91. Arkansas next traveled to Alabama, where it would get a taste of the team that had dominated the SEC's Tournament, having won the championship four times in the previous five seasons. A late charging call that went against Arkansas allowed Alabama to sneak away with a 65-63 win.

Arkansas went through the first half of its first SEC season with a 6-2 record, also losing to Tennessee. But just before that loss to the Vols, the Razorbacks sent a message to the rest of the SEC by going to Kentucky, the league's marquee program, and handing the Wildcats a 105-88 whipping. A crowd of 24,324, then a Rupp Arena record, was on hand to see the Hogs break the Wildcats' twenty-one-game homecourt winning streak.

"We had to come in and prove something," Arkansas center Oliver Miller told the Arkansas press after the game. Mission accomplished.

Jerry Tipton, long-time Kentucky beat writer for the *Lexington Herald-Leader*, recalls being impressed with the attitude the Razorbacks brought to Rupp.

"Arkansas was the only team in the league that came to Lexington fearless," Tipton said. "They came to play and to win. And they looked Kentucky dead in the eye. I always thought that everyone in the league—though different teams challenged from time to time—always showed some sort of deference to Kentucky. Arkansas never felt that. And I always thought it was Nolan's doing."

Arkansas won the SEC's Western Division with a 13-3 record, then played Alabama in a third memorable game of the season, losing in the league tournament semifinals. Southeastern Conference basketball would never be the same.

"Arkansas created more competition among our other schools in basketball," said SEC associate commissioner Mark Womack. "Everybody else began to feel like they had to provide facilities and hire coaches and do things to get their programs to the next level. The arrival of Arkansas was certainly one of the factors that has led to the success our conference began to have in men's basketball."

"I really believe we gave the SEC a facelift," Richardson said. "The biggest facelift probably in the history of any program, I think, was when Arkansas joined the Southeastern Conference. We were playing great basketball at Arkansas. In our first year in the SEC we probably should have been 14-2, but there was a bad call against Alabama, so we could have easily been 15-1 or even 16-0 going into their league when they said we were coming out of a weak league. We went [on the road] and there was no fear because we just thought we were better than they were.

"I saw the following year that recruiting had changed. I used to go on the road and to be honest I didn't see a whole lot of Southeastern Conference coaches out there that much. Whether we didn't run in the same circles might have been the difference, but you would cross paths [with other coaches] a lot. Because of our impact the first year, everybody went to work. Coaches brought in players and basketball became something."

Arkansas might have provided a few lessons about running a basketball program to the rest of the SEC, but there was one area where the school found itself lacking as compared to its new playmates. Even before Arkansas officially joined the SEC, Arkansas athletics director Frank Broyles and Richardson knew they would need a facilities upgrade, despite the fact that for years the Razorbacks' Barnhill Fieldhouse had been one of the most feared places to play in college basketball.

"You don't have memories of the place," former TCU coach Jim Killingsworthy said in *Razorbacks Handbook*. "Just nightmares."

"Undoubtedly the toughest place in the country to play," former Houston coach Pat Foster said.

Former Arkansas coach Eddie Sutton, who took over the program in 1974, had been the catalyst for a two-tiered renovation of Barnhill. Before Sutton would take the job, he extracted a promise from Broyles that the building's seating capacity would be increased from 5,000 to 6,200. Another 2,800 seats were added in 1977.

As Sutton's teams began to win an ever-increasing amount of games and eventually become a perennial NCAA Tournament threat, Barnhill was filled to capacity night after night. With the Hog Wild band intimidating opposing teams by surrounding them during pre-game warm-ups and fans rocking the building with their deafening hog call, Barnhill had an atmosphere matched by few arenas in the country.

In 1990, Broyles and Richardson wanted to keep pace with SEC facilities and increase Barnhill's seating capacity to 10,000. As much a home-court advantage as Barnhill had been, Richardson wanted more—more seats, more fans, more noise.

"We thought if we could get to ten [thousand], we'd be comparable with the SEC schools that had buildings that seated ten, eleven, twelve [thousand]," Richardson recalled.

Broyles thought the upgrade might cost around a million dollars. One day during a conversation with J. L. "Bud" Walton, one of the founders of the Arkansas-based Wal-Mart chain, Broyles mentioned his plans for Barnhill. He was taken aback by Walton's response.

"How much would it cost to build a new arena?" Walton asked. "We need a new arena."

Broyles threw out a number between thirty and thirty-five million dollars.

"Count me in for half of it," Walton said.

Staked to such a huge head start by Walton's donation, Arkansas quickly raised the rest of the money it would take to build a new area. Work for the project began in 1991. Just eighteen months later the gleaming Bud Walton Arena opened with a seating capacity of 19,200.

Rosser International, an Atlanta-based architectural firm, designed the building so it would have more seats in less space than any similar arena in the world. The result was a home-court advantage that quickly took the one the Razorbacks enjoyed at Barnhill to a whole different level. The noise in Walton Arena can at times become deafening, and when the place really gets rowdy, the specially designed spring-mounted floor seems to shake in concert with the reaction of the fans.

Once again, Arkansas had clearly demonstrated to the rest of the SEC how to get things done. Bud Walton Arena created arena envy around the league. Years after its opening, SEC schools were still pouring money into facility upgrades.

Georgia turned to the same company that built Walton Arena to design improvements for its Stegeman Coliseum. In 2001, Ole Miss coach Rod Barnes wanted a provision written into his contract that the school would revamp the Rebels' Tad Smith Coliseum. The same year, Vanderbilt spent twenty-five million dollars on refurbishing its venerable Memorial Gymnasium. And in 2002, South Carolina moved into a new building that was also built by Rosser International and designed with many of the same features as BWA.

The arena was the final ingredient Richardson needed. When he coached at Tulsa, which back then played its games in a downtown arena, Richardson made a prediction to his daughter.

46

"I'd always told Yvonne that if I could ever coach at a school that had its own [on-campus] arena, I could win a national championship," Richardson said.

The Razorbacks took to their new arena as quickly as their fans, who filled it to capacity every game. Arkansas officially opened the building in 1993 with a 93-67 victory over Murray State, but it was officially dedicated in the Hogs' next game, against Missouri. ESPN was on hand to televise the game, which quickly developed into a rout. Arkansas won, 120-68, impressive considering Missouri would later go undefeated in the Big 8 and come within a game of the Final Four.

———

Richardson knew it would take more than an arena to win games. A coach is only as good as his players, and in 1993–94, his team was loaded. The stars were a pair of sophomores, Corliss Williamson and Scotty Thurman. Williamson was a physical presence inside, and Thurman was an outside threat with a knack for making clutch shots.

At guard, Richardson placed his faith in yet another Memphis import, Corey Beck. A rugged competitor with a high basketball I.Q., Beck was the Razorbacks' play-maker. His backcourt partner was Clint McDaniel, like Beck a strong defender. McDaniel was also a perimeter threat.

Arkansas had lacked size in 1992–93, so Richardson remedied that by signing a pair of six-foot-eleven freshmen, Darnell Robinson and Lee Wilson. The Hogs also relied on six-foot-nine junior Dwight Stewart, who was just as likely to shoot from three-point range as he was in the post.

Arkansas's secret weapon was Al Dillard, a shameless three-point shooter who seemed to possess unlimited range. Dillard had a quick release and would hoist a three from anywhere, making him as dangerous a shooter as there was in the country. He made 13 three-pointers against Delaware State, a school record that probably won't be threatened for a while.

Richardson remembers the unique chemistry his team possessed.

"It's funny, those guys were probably as close to one another as you could ever have," he said. "They were very close. And I thought everybody played their role. Everybody gave everything they had."

Arkansas started the season ranked No. 2 in the country, but soon moved to No. 1, a position it maintained off and on for ten weeks. The Hogs got bumped from the top spot after a rugged start in SEC play. Arkansas beat Ole Miss in its opener, but lost, 66-64, at Alabama when Clint McDaniel missed a shot with ten seconds left and

Dwight Stewart couldn't tip in the rebound. Two games later, the Razorbacks lost by a point at Mississippi State and stood at 3-2 in the league, two games behind the 5-0 Bulldogs.

Arkansas wouldn't lose again in the regular season. The twelve-game winning streak included yet another win over Kentucky, the Razorbacks' third straight since they joined the SEC. Kentucky, which had already begun its resurgence under coach Rick Pitino, had played in the Final Four the season before. Arkansas also paid back Alabama, winning 102-81, and Mississippi State, beating the Bulldogs by 18 points in the regular-season finale.

The 1994 SEC Tournament was played in Memphis, and Arkansas started out with an easy quarterfinal victory over Georgia. Next came a rematch with Kentucky. Finally, the Wildcats would have an answer for the Razorbacks, limiting them to 32 percent shooting en route to a 90-78 win.

The loss didn't hurt Arkansas's seeding in the NCAA Tournament. The Hogs were given a No. 1 seed and sent to the Midwest Regional. Two wins over North Carolina A&T and Georgetown earned them a trip to the Sweet 16, where they proceeded to beat Richardson's old Tulsa team and Michigan, then in the middle of its own run, having played in the two previous Final Fours.

In a game attended by President Bill Clinton, the former Arkansas governor and huge Hog fan, Arkansas dispatched the Wolverines 76-68. For the second time in four years, they were headed to the Final Four. Earlier in the day, Richardson was awarded the Naismith Coach of the Year award.

"Never have I had all these things happen in one day—coach of the year, the president comes to the game and hugs you, and you win a trip to the Final Four," Richardson told the press.

Arkansas arrived at the Final Four in Charlotte, North Carolina, with something to prove. Richardson had been telling the Razorbacks all season that, despite the fact they had been ranked No. 1, they hadn't gotten the respect they deserved nationally.

The Hogs made short work of national semifinal opponent Arizona, manhandling the Wildcats' great guard tandem of Damon Stoudamire and Khalid Reeves. The duo combined for just 11-of-43 shooting, including 2-for-22 from three-point range.

Corliss Williamson dominated Arizona inside, scoring 29 points and grabbing 13 rebounds. Arkansas won 91-82.

President Clinton was again in the stands on April 4, 1994, when the Razorbacks played Duke for the national championship. The game was close in the first half, but the Blue Devils opened up a 10-point lead early in the second.

Richardson didn't like what he was seeing, so he ordered the Hogs to accelerate the game's tempo. The Blue Devils had expended a considerable amount of energy in building their lead, and when Arkansas began to play at a faster pace, Duke wore down. Arkansas forged ahead, and late in the game led 70-65. But Duke, which had already won two national championships in the 1990s, wasn't finished. Grant Hill's three-pointer with 1:29 to play tied the score at 70, setting the stage for the most memorable shot in Arkansas history.

As the shot clock ran down, Dwight Stewart threw a pass to Scotty Thurman, who was outside the three-point line. With Duke's Antonio Lang lunging at him, Thurman calmly tossed in a shot that gave the Hogs a 73-70 lead with fifty-one seconds left. Clint McDaniel hit two free throws and Al Dillard another to make the final score 76-72.

At the moment of his greatest professional achievement, Richardson could think only of his daughter.

"As I was walking out of the gym I looked up and said, 'Yvonne, I got you one,'" Richardson recalled. 'I told you if I had a gym, I'd get you one.'

"When I went into the dressing room, the president was waiting for me. Our kids were so elated, but I swear to God, it just totally went by me. I had no more feeling. I was numb. I remember thinking, 'My God, it's anticlimactic.' It's like, there it is, and it's gone. I never will forget that."

With every key player save reserve Ken Biley returning in 1994–95, much was expected of Arkansas, but the Hogs needed a couple of slaps in the face to get going. There had been some talk of Arkansas being capable of going undefeated, which hadn't been done since Indiana won the national championship in 1976.

If the Hogs did have any hopes of an unbeaten season, they were dashed in a hurry. Paired against Massachusetts in the Hall of Fame game, Arkansas came out flat and got buried, 104-80. With the burden of expectations lifted, the Razorbacks proceeded to play as expected. They beat fourteenth-ranked Georgetown in their next game and breezed through the rest of their nonconference schedule.

The highlight came in Hawaii, where Arkansas won the Rainbow Classic, beating Oklahoma, Cincinnati, and Iowa in the process. It was the first time the Razorbacks had won an in-season tournament since 1968.

The SEC portion of Arkansas's schedule started as badly as the regular-season had. Ole Miss, in a sign of things to come, handed the Razorbacks a 76-71 defeat. Arkansas lost three of its first seven league games, which included an 88-70 beating by Alabama. It was the Hogs' first loss ever in Bud Walton Arena.

Better days were ahead. Arkansas beat Kentucky yet again—the fourth victory over the Wildcats in the five games the two had played since the 1991–92 season. Arkansas finished its SEC schedule tied with Mississippi State atop the Western Division standings at 12-4.

In the league tournament, Arkansas beat Vanderbilt and Alabama to set up a rematch with Kentucky in the championship game. The game turned out to be a classic, as once again Arkansas helped usher in a new era for the league. Never before had the SEC played its tournament in a domed stadium. But the addition of Arkansas and its strong fan support necessitated the move to larger facilities.

In 1995, the tournament was played in the Georgia Dome in Atlanta. Previous attendance marks were broken as a record crowd of 30,057 watched the title game.

The huge crowd wasn't disappointed. Arkansas jumped out quickly, taking a 35-16 lead in the first half. But the Wildcats battled back, and had a chance to win with 1.3 seconds left. When forward Rodrick Rhodes went to the free throw line with the game tied at 80, the cause seemed lost for the Razorbacks. But Rhodes missed both free throws and the game went into overtime.

Arkansas again took a seemingly commanding lead. The Razorbacks led 91-82 with 1:39 to play in the extra period, but the Wildcats rallied

Scotty Thurman. *University of Arkansas Sports Information Office*

for an improbable 95-93 victory. The game immediately became a part of SEC lore.

"It was a great college basketball game," Richardson told the media afterward. "I didn't think it would ever end. It's too bad there was a loser in this game."

Kentucky coach Rick Pitino, whose team won its fourth straight SEC Tournament, called the Arkansas-Kentucky rivalry the "best in college basketball. We have tremendous respect and admiration for Nolan Richardson. Our players have tremendous respect for their players. . . . A lot of rivalries are built on hatred. This one is built on respect. That's the type of rivalry that's needed in college basketball."

The first two rounds of the NCAA Tournament were a struggle for the Hogs, seeded No. 2 in the Midwest Region. They had to scramble to slip past fifteenth-seeded Texas Southern, 79-78. Syracuse had Arkansas beaten in the second round, but when guard Lawrence Moten called a timeout his team didn't have after coming up with a loose ball with seconds to play, the Orangemen were assessed a technical foul. The game went into overtime, and Arkansas won, 96-94.

Things didn't get any easier for the Hogs, who needed overtime to get past Memphis in the Sweet 16. A 68-61 win over Virginia in the Elite Eight sent Arkansas back to the Final Four, where the Razorbacks beat North Carolina to set up a championship game against UCLA.

Fate seemed to be in favor of the Hogs' winning consecutive national titles when Bruin point guard Tyus Edney was unable to play. But UCLA rallied behind Ed O'Bannon's 30 points and 17 rebounds and won, 89-78.

Years later, Richardson had fond memories of Arkansas's second straight appearance in the national championship game, even though the Razorbacks couldn't pull off the repeat.

"I remember the '95 team more than the '94 team," Richardson said. "It's funny because second place is something nobody ever remembers, but to me, that was a tremendous accomplishment to almost win them back-to-back. Obviously, I would have enjoyed that more. But the hardest thing in the world to do is put yourself on top and remain there. Getting to '94 was building, and then after getting to the pinnacle, how do you stay there? I remember getting there in '94, but I remember our '95 team that much more."

———

Early in the 2001–2002 season, as Richardson neared his five hundredth career Division I victory, it seemed everyone else even remotely associated with the program thought it was a far bigger deal than he did. His thinking changed on the day the milestone finally figured to be achieved, December 10, 2001. That night, the Razorbacks were scheduled to host UNC Greensboro, prompting Don Haskins, Richardson's coach at UTEP and lifelong mentor, to give his protégé a call.

"If you get 500 victories tonight, it would be nice to enjoy it," the old coach told Richardson. Haskins knew a few things about milestones. The man who had guided his team to an improbable NCAA championship game victory over mighty Kentucky in 1966 had won 719 games before finally retiring in 1999.

"That conversation made me aware of 500, because if it had not been for being able to win on a consistent basis, I would not be the coach at Arkansas," Richardson said after his team put away a surprisingly scrappy Greensboro team. "It is a big deal. [But] the biggest deal is being able to coach this long and to have so many kids and to withstand and be in places that maybe you weren't supposed to be. That's real big to me."

Richardson was alluding to the fact that he was the first African-American coach hired by a major program in the South.

"We don't all play on the same playing field, the field is not level," Richardson told the *Arkansas Democrat-Gazette*. "I've got to be twice as good as the guy next to me. And I know that. I have to put up with and endure those things, so 500, yes it's sweet. Because I've endured it, and I'm going to endure some more."

What exactly did Richardson mean? His struggles to succeed in the predominantly white world of coaching left him with painful memories. In an interview just five weeks before he was fired, Richardson shared some of those memories.

"It started early," Richardson recalled. "I started out as a high school coach in Alvin, Texas, the only mixed high school in the whole state. I had to put up with all kinds of shit. Then I left there and became a junior college coach, and I was the only black coach in the state. I had to be different than the other coaches. Other [white] coaches could yell, scream. I'd jump up to [protest a call] and the officials would tell me, 'Sit your ass down.' I've had them tell me, 'Nigger, get your ass and sit it down.'

"I went through that. I went through it in high school, went through it in junior college. I went through it at Tulsa. I'd heard about a guy who offered the [search] committee at Tulsa one hundred thousand dollars not to hire me. That's documented. It's been written about. When I got in the Southwest Conference at Arkansas, I was the first black coach in a major sport. I'm catching holy hell.

"People look at me and they don't understand. They don't even have a clue. And I'm still surviving. I had to do it twice. I tell our kids you don't get breaks."

Richardson believed that until the end at Arkansas. And though he finally allowed himself to revel in his five hundredth win, Richardson couldn't resist reliving his struggles. And he couldn't stop himself from taking a shot at the NCAA.

"If things are right, I could have reached 500 two years ago," Richardson said. "But they investigated my program. Our ship was low, but we didn't sink."

Richardson was referring to what can best be described as the Sunday Adebayo Debacle.

Adebayo, who transferred to Arkansas in 1995 after two years at a Missouri junior college, was declared ineligible by the NCAA in February 1996. He later transferred to Memphis—where he played what he thought was his senior year in 1997—and then, incredibly, was allowed to return to Arkansas to play a second senior season in 1998.

Sandwiched between Adebayo's tours of duty at Arkansas was an NCAA investigation into the program that claimed the jobs of two employees, scared off numerous recruits from signing with the Razorbacks, prompted the school to self-impose sanctions that included a ban on junior college recruits, and, as Richardson has said many times, prompted a downturn in the program.

After the Razorbacks struggled through a 15-12 season in 1999–2000, some disappointed fans wondered aloud whether Richardson, then fifty-seven, had gotten too old and too complacent to deal with the rigors of his job, particularly recruiting.

Richardson countered that criticism by pointing to the negative effect the NCAA investigation had on his program.

It all began in 1996, when Arkansas deemed Adebayo and Pate ineligible after the NCAA's enforcement staff ruled that the school improperly certified their junior college transcripts. Though Arkansas appealed and vehemently argued its case, both players were forced to sit out the rest of the year. Adebayo was allowed by NCAA rules to transfer to Memphis and be eligible the next season. Pate, one of the best players to ever come from the talent-rich Jackson, Mississippi, area, never resurfaced at another college and spent some time in the old Continental Basketball Association.

The NCAA later began an investigation of the program, an ordeal that crawled along for eighteen months. Arkansas's recruiting suffered concurrently—from 1986 to 1996, the program signed eight McDonald's All-Americans, stalwarts such as Todd Day, Corliss Williamson, Lee Mayberry, and Derek Hood. Richardson and his staff didn't land a single All-American from 1996 to 1999. "There were recruits we thought we could get that we couldn't even get close to because of the investigation," Richardson told the *Arkansas Democrat-Gazette* in 2000.

Just as significant was Arkansas's self-imposed moratorium on junior college players. "Just think," Richardson told the newspaper, "I was at one time a junior college coach, but I couldn't touch a JUCO player for two years. That was tough not to be able to bring in any JUCO kids."

With high-profile players backing off and the junior colleges closed off, Richardson had to take his chances with in-state high school players, kids who had grown up in awe of Razorback basketball but who weren't talented enough to play for Arkansas. Only two of those players wound up making significant contributions.

It was at this point that Arkansas basketball began a steady decline, at least by its own high standards. No longer the swaggering, confident bunch that could go to Kentucky and win, the Razorbacks became fair game for the rest of the conference. In many ways, they were victims of their own success. As other SEC programs began to follow Arkansas's lead and place an emphasis on basketball, the Hogs had become vulnerable. And whereas the Final Four had become a reasonable goal in the early 1990s, later in the decade Arkansas struggled to simply make the NCAA Tournament field.

In 1996–97, the Razorbacks finished 18-14 and 8-8 in the SEC and weren't invited to the Big Dance for the first time in ten years, the first sign of their vulnerability. The next season, Arkansas lost to Division II American University of Puerto Rico. The Razorbacks regrouped and eventually won twenty-four games, including a first-round matchup with Nebraska in the NCAA Tournament.

In 1998–99, Arkansas advanced to the NCAAs again, and again won a first round game. The 1999–2000 team shocked the SEC by winning the league tournament after finishing 7-9 in the West Division. The Hogs didn't last long in the dance, losing a first-round game to Miami. It was the first time in ten NCAAs that Arkansas didn't advance past the first round.

In 2000–2001, Arkansas was good enough to earn an NCAA Tournament berth again but lost in the first round to Georgetown.

By the standards of lesser programs, the Razorbacks' accomplishments the previous four years would have been cause for rejoicing. But not at Arkansas, where the fans were getting restless and the media wondered whether Richardson had retired and not bothered to tell anyone.

———

Nolan Richardson's last season at Arkansas started badly and got worse. In the second round of the Preseason NIT, the Razorbacks lost at home to Wake Forest. The Demon Deacons were talented enough—they would go on to play in the NCAA Tournament—but nevertheless this was a team Arkansas should have handled on its home floor.

After the game, Richardson offered a grim assessment to the media. "Early in the year we were hitting shots, but now it looks like we're one of the worst-shooting teams I've coached in a long time because it's 35 percent every night," Richardson told the *Arkansas Democrat-Gazette*. "I don't care how good your defense is or how hard you board, you're not going to win if you can't hit some shots."

Richardson's summary might have seemed premature and perhaps a bit harsh at the time. Arkansas had played just one other game. But Richardson had been around long enough to know his team. As it turned out, his take on the Hogs' shooting prowess was all too accurate.

That was quickly proven. Though Arkansas managed some decent nonconference wins—at Tulsa, at Memphis—the Razorbacks gave every indication that, compared to some of Richardson's better teams, they weren't going to measure up. For the fourth straight year, Oklahoma handed the Hogs a loss, this one convincingly, and worse, at Bud Walton Arena. Oklahoma State and former Arkansas coach Eddie Sutton also slipped into Fayetteville and stole a win.

Soon Arkansas fans began wondering whether the Razorbacks were capable of beating elite teams.

Arkansas did play well against Illinois in a game at Chicago, but it ended in controversy, and another loss. The Razorbacks' Brandon Dean was called for charging with 5.5 seconds left after scoring a basket that would have given his team a 93-91 lead. The Illini, ranked fifth at the time, escaped with a 94-91 win.

The Razorbacks regrouped by winning four of their last five nonconference games, and seemed ready to make an impact in the SEC after opening league play with wins at Auburn and at home against a good Mississippi State team. Then the Hogs' weaknesses began to catch up with them.

As Richardson had predicted, this would be one of his worst shooting teams. Of even greater concern to Richardson was the fact he couldn't trust his team to run his system. Richardson's pressing defense calls for players to make decisions and for their coach to relinquish a certain amount of control. Richardson seldom felt comfortable doing that.

"We play about two minutes of hell and thirty-eight minutes of what the hell are we doing," Richardson said after his team lost three consecutive SEC games to drop to 2-3 in the league. "It's hard to coach the kind of basketball I enjoy with a group that doesn't have that basketball IQ.

"We've had good athletes and good kids here the last couple of years, but our kids don't ad lib very well. I'll tell 'em, 'Don't shoot the first three you see, go to the basket.' And then they'll go to the basket every single time, because that's the last thing I said. I'll say, 'Son, you had the wide-open three.' And they'll say, 'But you said drive, coach.' They never can seem to figure out to go with the flow."

A loss at Georgia on January 23 extended the losing streak to four, but then Arkansas regrouped by beating then fourth-ranked Florida in an overtime game at home. That win seemed as though it could help reverse the Razorbacks' fortunes, but it didn't. Arkansas would win just three more games the rest of the season.

As the losses mounted, Richardson began to show signs of the strain. After a loss at Tennessee during which the Hogs shot 33 percent, Richardson took offense to an innocent question *Democrat-Gazette* reporter Bob Holt asked about shot selection, and he let Holt know it in front of several other reporters. In private, Richardson began to admit to his inner circle of friends and confidants that the season was taking its toll.

"He told me [after a loss at Ole Miss on February 9] that this was the most stressed he'd ever been, this season," said Mike Nail, Arkansas's radio voice and a long-time Richardson friend. "The reason was he had such high expectations for this team. There had been no continuity or consistency through the year, and he blamed himself for not being able to push the right button, or make the right substitution at the right time or whatever."

It was around this time that Richardson began behaving irrationally. The first sign came on his weekly television show, when he told a startled Nail that Fayetteville wasn't a haven of opportunity for black athletes.

"What he said basically was that he didn't feel like there wasn't any social life opportunities for black players," Nail recalled. "It was something we've heard before but nobody's come out and said it. When he said it, I was thinking, 'Coach, maybe you shouldn't be giving other schools ammunition to recruit against you.' Does something like that cut your own throat? Yes it does."

Indeed, Richardson's off-hand remark was akin to professional suicide. Why would a coach whose livelihood so clearly depends on the recruitment of black athletes want to take a chance on scaring them away? Suffice to say other Arkansas coaches, most notably football coach Houston Nutt, were troubled by the comment.

Of all the words that would leave Richardson's mouth in the next few weeks, those could have been the most damning, but because his television show isn't seen outside the state of Arkansas, they went unnoticed—for a time.

Richardson's next public display of disaffection came after the February 23 Kentucky game. Ten years before, Arkansas went into Lexington and came away with a convincing victory. This time, the Hogs were no match for the Wildcats, losing 71-58.

Before the game, Richardson and Kentucky coach Tubby Smith exchanged pleasantries. In his post-game press conference, Richardson was asked what the two discussed.

Richardson had a few kind words for Smith, who, Richardson said, could commiserate with him like no other coach in the SEC. Both programs are held to the highest of expectations by their demanding fans, a constant source of pressure for both coaches.

Then came the sentence that got Richardson fired.

With no prompting, Richardson blurted out a suggestion for his bosses. "If they go ahead and pay me my money, they can take the job tomorrow."

Pressed to clarify by Arkansas *Democrat-Gazette* reporters, Richardson twice

56

repeated his buyout comment. He didn't explain why he mentioned a buyout in the first place, but did say that the media had been "crucifying" him.

That comment may have been in reference to a column written a few days before by the *Democrat-Gazette*'s sports editor, Wally Hall. Hall questioned whether the five-man 2002 recruiting class that Richardson had been proclaiming as the savior of the program would really have that kind of impact. By Hall's account, the column was "tame."

Arkansas chancellor John White read Richardson's comments in the February 24 edition of the *Democrat-Gazette*. After fielding calls from members of the school's board of trustees who were in favor of granting Richardson's request, White had no choice but to begin strongly considering the possibility of getting rid of an institution.

Arkansas

All-SEC Expansion Era Team

F-Joe Johnson
F-Corliss Williamson
C-Oliver Miller
G-Todd Day
G-Corey Beck
Top Reserves-Scotty Thurman, Clint McDaniel

The next day, Richardson sealed his fate at his press conference before the Razorbacks were to play Mississippi State. He started out lambasting the media, but the longer he railed, the madder he got. Soon, the press conference had turned into a heated Richardson diatribe that dealt with a variety of topics made relevant only because he deemed them so. In overstating his importance as "the biggest thing going" at Arkansas, he managed to alienate his fellow coaches, professors, and administrators. Richardson implied that football coach Houston Nutt used him as a recruiting tool, bringing recruits by to meet him (which hadn't been the case in three years). He closed practice to the media, and refused to take any more calls from the press at his home.

"All I've tried to do is help you do your job," Richardson told the media as he wound down. "I just want you to remember one thing: I did not apply. They thought I was the best man for the job, and I got it. I've applied three times in my lifetime. Where would I go? I say this again, the more you are on my case, the longer I will stay here.

"So maybe that's what you want. Because you know what? Ol' Granny told me, 'Nobody runs you anywhere, Nolan.' I know that. See, my great-great-grandfather came over here on the ship. I didn't, and I don't think you understand what I'm saying. My great-great grandfather came over on the ship. Not Nolan Richardson. I did not come over on that ship. So I expect to be treated a little bit different.

"Because I know for a fact that I do not play on the same level as the other coaches around this school play on. I know that. You know it. And people of my color know that. And that angers me.

"But I've dealt with it for seventeen years. And let me tell you something, I'll deal with it for seventeen more. Because that's my makeup. With that, I've cleared the air. You got questions, ask it. If I choose to answer it, I'll try. I hope we're all on the same page. Thank you."

Richardson had one final exclamation point to his rant. "You can run that on every TV show in America," he said.

The outburst wasn't run on every TV show in America, but it seemed that way the next several days. And Richardson's fate was sealed. Rumors of his impending buyout swirled as Arkansas chancellor John White and athletics director Frank Broyles began the process, contacting everyone of authority in the Arkansas system.

Two days after blasting the media, Richardson seemed resigned to the fact he was gone after Arkansas's game at Mississippi State. He delivered another rambling speech that covered everything from Martin Luther King, Jr., to his work on behalf of charities.

"I don't know whether I'll be the coach here or whether I want to be here," Richardson said in his eighteen-minute talk. "Sometimes where there's smoke, there could be fire. All I can say is I'm the basketball coach at Arkansas right now."

Richardson wouldn't be able to say that much longer. But on February 28, the day after the Mississippi State game, he had apparently changed his mind about wanting to leave.

"I enjoy where I am," Richardson said during the SEC's weekly coaches' teleconference. "I've worked extremely hard. We've got a good recruiting class coming in next year. I had made those promises to the families, and so my interest has always been high in coaching. Tried to stay physically fit. Once I reach that point where I don't like the game anymore, that will be the point where I may decide to step down. At this point, I still love the game."

A few minutes later, Richardson seemed certain about his future at Arkansas.

"I'm going to stay," he said. "I will stay and coach my basketball team and I will stay and receive the kids that are coming to me next year."

Later that morning, White and Broyles went to Richardson's office and met with him for ninety minutes. Richardson was apparently allowed to voice his frustrations, particularly about his relationship—or lack thereof—with Broyles. The two had barely spoken to one another for years.

After giving Richardson his say, White and Broyles offered the beleaguered coach a chance to retire. Richardson refused, though the deal included a buyout of his contract, which still had six years remaining at $1.03 million per year. "I am not going to resign," Richardson was quoted as saying, by Broyles and White. "You'll have to fire my ass."

Richardson's firing was announced the next day.

"The University of Arkansas today exercised the terms of its contract with men's basketball coach Nolan Richardson, concluding his employment with the University, effective immediately," said the official press release. "This action was taken after Coach Richardson expressed his desire, publicly and privately, for the University to buy out his contract and after offering him an opportunity to retire. Under previously agreed-to terms, Richardson could receive five hundred thousand dollars a year during the next six years, a sum totaling three million dollars."

A quote from Broyles served as an epitaph for the Richardson era at Arkansas.

"We are grateful to Coach Richardson for his many contributions to the program over his tenure," Broyles said. "We believe it is time for a change in leadership for the best interests of the basketball program."

With that, the man whose program had helped reshape the Southeastern Conference in the 1990s and for the new millennium was gone. Mike Anderson, who had played for Richardson at Tulsa and served seventeen years on the staff at Arkansas, was put in charge of the program on an interim basis. Even as Anderson tried to pick up the pieces of a shattered season and a shattered era and prepare the Razorbacks for the SEC Tournament, Richardson didn't plan on going away quietly.

Chapter Three

Auburn

A uburn coach Cliff Ellis was in his office on a fall day in 1995 when a call came in that would change the course of his program. On the other end of the line was Julius "Doc" Robinson, a point guard from Selma, Alabama. Auburn had been locked in a struggle with cross-state Southeastern Conference rival Alabama for the services of Robinson, rated one of the top high school point guards in the country.

Robinson was calling to commit to Auburn. Ellis took the news well.

"I shouted out 'hallelujah,'" Ellis recalled. "I was ecstatic. There's no question getting Doc Robinson was big from the standpoint that, here was a top-twenty-five in-state kid who had been highly recruited, and he was a point guard. We felt like we had to have a big-time point guard to help us turn our program around. We told Doc we'd put the ball in his hands for four years. And that's what we did. There's no question he was one of the pivotal players in the SEC in the 1990s."

Robinson was pivotal for two reasons. At the time Ellis was more concerned about what Robinson could do for his team. But he gladly accepted any residual effects Robinson's signing had on Alabama, which suffered through a five-year point guard drought that didn't end until Maurice Williams took the floor in 2001.

"Doc's signing was so key for us," Ellis recalled. "At the time, Alabama had been on top of things. They had signed people like Antonio McDyess and Roy Rogers and Jason Caffey and James Robinson and Jamaal Faulkner. Brian Williams [another blue-chip in-state guard] had signed with them the year before. That probably helped us with Doc. But Doc liked Auburn. He felt comfortable with us."

With a point guard in place, Ellis and his staff thought they could put together a recruiting class that could have a real impact a year or two later. Ellis used some old ties to sign another important player, six-foot-five forward Daymeon Fishback, the Kentucky high school player of the year. Fishback's father had played for Ellis at Cumberland College in the early 1970s.

Next on Ellis's wish list was a center, and he didn't have to look very far. Mamadou N'diaye was practically dropped into his lap.

N'diaye, a seven-footer from Dakar, Senegal, came to the United States in 1995 to attend Maine Central Institute. Though N'diaye's only season at Maine Central was his first playing organized basketball, he proved to be a natural, averaging 13.3 points, 15.6 rebounds and 7.1 blocked shots. The University of Maine had an obvious head start recruiting N'diaye and got a commitment from him and another seven-footer from Senegal, Ndongo N'diaye, who attended a prep school in Connecticut. The two weren't related, but both came to the United States after meeting Maine assistant Mike LaPlante—who was a consultant to the Senegalese national team—at a clinic in Senegal.

Both players signed with Maine in the November signing period. The Black Bears were about to become the scourge of the America East Conference, but before that could happen head coach Rudy Keeling left to take over at Northeastern. LaPlante, who had played for Maine, had hoped to replace Keeling. It seemed as though he had plenty of bargaining power, given his relationship with the N'diayes.

Much to his dismay, LaPlante wasn't hired, so he turned to his friend and mentor, Wake Forest coach Dave Odom, for help finding another coaching job. Odom had been one of Ellis's better friends when Ellis coached in the ACC. Odom knew Ellis had an opening on his staff, and called to recommend LaPlante, whom he had gotten to know well during their days at Howard Garfinkel's Five-Star camps. That was enough for Ellis.

Meanwhile, after LaPlante left for Auburn, the N'diayes successfully petitioned the NCAA for a release from their scholarships. Ndongo N'diaye signed with Providence. And Mamadou N'diaye followed LaPlante to Auburn.

"Coach Ellis knew my background, obviously," LaPlante said. "But there wasn't any guarantee Mamadou could get his release after I got the job at Auburn. Once he got released, we had him down for an official visit. I knew he'd have a comfort zone with me. But he got a chance to see Auburn and to learn about the SEC. He was comfortable with Cliff. Auburn had already had a solid recruiting class. With Mamadou, some analysts ended up ranking it a top-five class."

It took another two years for Ellis and his staff to put the finishing touches on what would become an SEC championship team. In the spring of 1996, Auburn was searching for a scorer and had been on the trail of Jasper Sanks, a Top 100 guard from Columbus, Georgia. But Sanks was an even better football player and eventually signed with Georgia as a running back. Knowing Auburn needed a shooter, Sanks's high school coach told Auburn assistant Eugene Harris about a guard from Roswell, Georgia, who hadn't received very much Division I attention.

"The coach at Columbus Carver told Eugene they'd played Roswell the night before and this kid they had ran circles around Jasper," LaPlante recalled. "He said the kid had 30 points against them and they couldn't guard him."

As luck would have it, Roswell coach Roy Pugliese was another friend of LaPlante's from his days at Five-Star. The player in question was Scott Pohlman, a scrawny, baby-faced shooter who was all set to sign with Pepperdine, but was quickly convinced to switch to Auburn.

"Pepperdine was the only Division I school that offered him," LaPlante said. "I'd seen the kid play that summer and liked him, but a lot of people, including us, had some concerns about his size [six-foot-one, 155 pounds] and if he could guard at the SEC level. Sometimes, looks are deceiving. We all get caught up in whether a kid's big enough or quick enough. But you can't measure heart. We ended up calling the kid 'The Assassin.'"

As freshmen, Robinson, Fishback, and N'diaye help lead Auburn to a 16-15 record in 1996–97. The Tigers won sixteen games and played in the NIT again the next season as Pohlman became a surprising major contributor. In Auburn's first game of the year, against Temple, Ellis brought Pohlman off the bench and he responded with 14 points. Pohlman started the next game and didn't come out of the starting lineup for the rest of his career. He averaged 10.6 points as a freshman.

Before that season began, Auburn signed the final component part that would push the program to the next level a year later.

In 1996, Chris Porter, a six-foot-seven forward from the tiny Alabama town of Abbeville, had been set to join Robinson, Fishback, and N'diaye in Auburn's recruiting class. But Porter was unable to qualify academically and had to play for Chipola (Florida) Junior College for two seasons. Porter, who had grown up watching Charles Barkley star for the Tigers, had always dreamed of playing for Auburn and emulating his hero's accomplishments there. Suffice to say Ellis had no trouble re-signing Porter in 1998.

The two years of junior college had done Porter's game considerable good. He left Chipola as the nation's No. 2–rated junior college player after averaging 24 points and nearly 12 rebounds as a sophomore. Recruiting experts raved about Porter.

"Porter is Auburn's best signee since Charles Barkley," Bob Gibbons said at the time. "He's great. He's one of the top two junior college players in the nation, which makes him like a top-five high school player. He's a major impact player."

Gibbons turned out to be correct. Porter would have a major impact at Auburn, both good and bad.

———

Auburn had enjoyed success in basketball before Ellis arrived, but it was sporadic.

Auburn

The school's record book shows a couple of periods of winning basketball interspersed with extended stretches of mediocrity.

The original glory days of Auburn basketball came in the late 1950s and early 1960s under coach Joel Eaves, the man for whom the Tigers' arena was named in 1987 (the building also took on the name of former Auburn athletic director Jeff Beard in 1993).

Eaves had been at Auburn eight years before his program, always competitive, rose to another level. In 1957–58, the Tigers finished 16-6 overall and 11-3 in the SEC and were ranked No. 16 in the final Associated Press poll. That was the first time in school history Auburn appeared in a season-ending poll. The next year, Auburn finished 20-2 and 12-2 in the SEC. The Tigers wound up ranked No. 8 by the Associated Press and No. 10 by United Press International. But the best was yet to come.

In 1959–60, the Tigers compiled a 19-2 overall record and were 12-2 in the SEC. By virtue of a stirring homecourt victory over Kentucky, Auburn claimed the SEC championship, its first ever.

In those days, the Tigers played their games in the tiny Sports Arena.

"It was an old airplane hangar, painted white," wrote Auburn native Owen Davis in the *Detroit Free Press*, where he is deputy sports editor. "Fans sat on wooden bleacher seats, and the teams sat on wooden benches behind the baselines. Only twenty-five hundred fans could fit inside. But the arena had charm, the way relics do when they symbolize something special. And in the late 1950s and early 1960s, basketball at Auburn was special."

Never was that more true than on a February night in 1960. Kentucky, which had won four NCAA championships the previous twelve seasons under legendary coach Adolph Rupp, was in Auburn for a pivotal SEC game—the Tigers and Wildcats were tied for first in the conference. The game was important enough to be televised, which was a big story unto itself. Auburn had never appeared on TV.

The game came down to the final seconds. With just four ticks of the clock left, Auburn forward Jimmy Fibbe stood at the free throw line for a one-and-one. The Tigers trailed 60-59. Fibbe calmly made both free throws, after which Rupp called two consecutive timeouts. Kentucky would inbound the ball from halfcourt. The ball was thrown in to Allen Feldhaus, who scrambled for the basket with no defender in front of him. But John Hemlinger, Auburn's six-foot-six center, caught Feldhaus from behind and swatted his shot away.

It would be another quarter century before the Tigers would generate as much excitement as the 1960 team had.

Charles H. "Sonny" Smith came to Auburn from East Tennessee State in 1978.

63

With his ever-present smile, quick wit, and innate public relations skills, Smith seemed equipped to handle the rigors of coaching at Auburn, which had slipped into another of its down cycles. The program was on NCAA probation when Smith took over.

Even the easy-going Smith was tested in his early days at Auburn. He'd been warned that Auburn was first and foremost a football school. But he never realized how apathetic its fans could be.

"I wasn't aware of that until I got there," Smith said. "We'd have some games where we'd fill the gym with big numbers, and then some games where nobody would come. I remember beating Kentucky one year when they were No. 1 in the country. We had a [capacity] crowd of 13,500. Two nights later, we played the fifteenth-ranked team in the country, and we drew 2,500. You just never could be sure if the fans were going to come out."

The Tigers had losing records in Smith's first three seasons, but began to show signs of life after Smith recruited future NBA stars Charles Barkley and, later, Chuck Person. Auburn was 14-14 in 1981–82, its first nonlosing season since 1977. By 1983–84, when Barkley and Person were in the starting lineup, the Tigers improved to 20-11, lost by just two points to Kentucky in the finals of the SEC Tournament, and played in the NCAA Tournament for the first time in school history.

Barkley passed up his final year of eligibility and was gone by the 1984–85 season, but Chris Morris, another future NBA player, replaced him in the starting lineup. Smith seemed to have the makings of a program in place, but about midway through the season, he decided he'd had enough. Smith announced his resignation, effective at the end of the season. No one save Smith's wife and assistant coaches knew it at the time, but he was considering a return to East Tennessee State, which was looking for a coach and an athletic director. Smith had secretly spoken with ETSU about taking both jobs.

Smith's decision to leave touched off one of the more dramatic postseason runs in SEC history. The inspired Tigers, who had finished just 16-11 in the regular season, didn't want Smith's career to end. They won four games in as many days to capture the SEC Tournament championship, then beat Purdue and Kansas in the NCAA Tournament to advance to the Sweet 16. The Tigers' run was ended there by North Carolina, but it had so thrilled the masses that Smith was convinced to stay.

Smith returned to his job with newfound energy, and for the first time in its history Auburn became a perennial postseason team. The Tigers played in the NCAA Tournament each of the next three seasons. Led by Person and Morris, the 1985–86 team advanced all the way to the Elite Eight, beating Arizona, St. John's, and UNLV before finally losing to Louisville.

The NCAA Tournament streak reached five years before the program finally bottomed out in 1988–89. That season, the Tigers had another future NBA player, center Matt Geiger, in the starting lineup and were 7-2 through December. A total collapse was in store.

It began when Smith was forced to kick talented junior college transfer Kelvin Ardister off the team. Ardister was averaging 24 points and 11 rebounds when Smith chased him. Two more key players, Mike Jones and Johnny Benjamin, got into trouble with drugs and essentially eliminated themselves.

Auburn won just two more games the rest of the season, finishing 2-16 in the SEC. Smith knew better than to try to pull the program through another dry spell. After the season he received a lucrative offer from VCU and jumped at it.

Smith's instincts proved correct. His replacement, Tommy Joe Eagles, could manage just a 64-78 record the next five years. In 1994, he was fired.

———

Cliff Ellis had accomplished all he could at Clemson. In a ten-year career that began in 1984 at the Atlantic Coast Conference school, Ellis won 177 games and took the Tigers to eight postseason tournaments. In one glorious season, 1989–90, Ellis led Clemson to a 24-8 record, the regular-season ACC championship, and an appearance in the NCAA Tournament's Sweet 16. But that kind of success was short-lived.

The next year Clemson was 11-16. And in Ellis's final four seasons at the school, the Tigers were a combined 17-45 in ACC games. Uncertain of whether he could engineer a dramatic turnaround in a league dominated by powers Duke and North Carolina and populated with several other strong programs, Ellis decided to look for a new challenge in 1994. Auburn athletic director David Housel just happened to have one for him.

Housel had a vision for Auburn basketball.

"My hope and my belief was that Auburn could become a consistent participant in the NCAA Tournament," Housel said. "Auburn's men's basketball program should be among the top sixty-four teams in the country every year."

Housel wanted to send that message when he hired a basketball coach. The coaching search was his first; he had been elevated from associate athletic director just days after the 1993–94 season ended.

"It was a challenge," Housel recalled. "But I wasn't afraid of it. We wanted somebody who was a proven head coach, or an assistant from an upper-echelon program

65

with a history of success."

After a thorough search, Housel offered the job to former Duke assistant Mike Brey, then the head coach at Delaware. Brey took the job, but a few days later changed his mind.

"I didn't know his reasoning then and I still don't know," Housel said. "But I can imagine his decision was based on the fact he perceived Auburn as too great a challenge."

Housel didn't want to take any chances the next time he offered the job. Ellis had informed Housel of his interest early in the search process. After Brey's decision, Housel wanted someone who was undaunted by Auburn's football program.

"Coach Ellis was happy to accept the challenge," Housel recalled. "And we felt comfortable with Cliff. The head coach at Auburn can look at football as a competitor or an ally. If you look at it as a competitor, well, you're not going to win that fight. Cliff could see football as an ally."

Ellis didn't have to be told about Auburn or the immense popularity of its football team.

"I was very familiar with Auburn," Ellis said. "I'd grown up in the Panhandle of Florida twenty miles from the Alabama line. When I was coming up in the 1950s and 1960s, Florida State wasn't much of an entity, and Florida was all the way over in Gainesville. Auburn was probably the biggest big-time school that was closest to our home. The first athletic event I recall seeing was an Auburn football game."

Years later, Ellis had a chance to observe Auburn closely after landing his first Division I head coaching job at South Alabama in 1975.

"I could really see what was going on at Auburn firsthand," Ellis recalled. "And I watched with great interest the Auburn-Alabama rivalry. I was building a program that was dependent upon Alabama and Auburn fans. I started in 1975, and the first graduating class at South Alabama was 1968. So there weren't many alumni to draw from. Most of our supporters were either Auburn or Alabama fans. So I got to know the people and the schools they followed."

The fact that Auburn was a fixer-upper program didn't scare Ellis one bit. He had made a career out of taking jobs that other coaches wouldn't touch.

Ellis was twenty-six when he took his first head-coaching job at Cumberland College, a Tennessee junior college that was 8-18 the season before he arrived. When Cumberland's coach unexpectedly quit just two weeks before the 1972–73 season began, Ellis, then coaching at a Florida high school, jumped into the job with no hesitation.

Cumberland finished 20-5, 34-2, and 24-5 in Ellis's three seasons there.

When Ellis took his first Division I job at South Alabama in 1975, he inherited just five scholarship players. The school's administration, concerned by poor attendance and whether the team could compete in the Sun Belt Conference, was seriously considering de-emphasizing basketball and dropping down to Division II. Ellis dashed that notion after the Jaguars averaged eighteen wins his first four years. In 1979–80, his fifth year, Ellis led South Alabama to twenty-three wins, a No. 10 national ranking, and an NCAA Tournament bid.

Moving to Clemson in 1984, Ellis knew how tough it would be to compete in the ACC, but that didn't stop him from giving the job a shot. In his first season, the Tigers won sixteen games and played in the NIT.

"My challenge in coaching has always been to take the underdog," Ellis said. "South Alabama was a non-entity. Then we get to the NCAA Tournament at a time when only thirty-two teams went, and that whole city [Mobile] was on fire. Clemson was another challenge. Everybody said they couldn't win an ACC championship, but we did."

The downside of coaching at schools that don't have as many built-in advantages as others in their respective leagues is that success can be cyclical. Pleased as he was with the accomplishment of winning an ACC championship, Ellis knew it would difficult maintaining that level of success. Ellis was able to guide the Tigers to seventeen and eighteen victories in his last two seasons. And Clemson played in the NIT both years, reaching the quarterfinals in 1993–94. But in late 1993, Ellis had a feeling it was time for a change.

At the Rainbow Classic in Hawaii, Ellis gathered his family and shared his feelings. With the support of his wife and children, Ellis returned home and, before Clemson's ACC opener against Duke, turned in his resignation. He finished out the season and, before Clemson's final regular-season game, was given an emotional send-off by Tiger fans.

"Leaving Clemson was just something I needed to do," Ellis recalled. "I just felt like things from a support standpoint weren't where they needed to be. I'd had a great run, a run that had never been made before. Ten years at Clemson was unprecedented [for a coach]. And not only did we win a championship, we had a runner-up finish. At Clemson, that was an accomplishment. The ACC was a tough league with great coaches and great teams."

Having left Clemson on his own terms as the winningest coach in school history, Ellis had to figure out what to do with the rest of his life. He had options. Western Kentucky needed a coach to replace Ralph Willard, who had left for Pittsburgh. And Auburn had already expressed strong interest. Ellis could take his pick.

"Western Kentucky was attractive because they had a full team coming back and had basketball tradition for many years," Ellis wrote in his book, *Cliff Ellis: The Winning Edge*. "Auburn was in a better conference, it was near home, and the program needed rebuilding. It was my cup of tea. I said, 'Let's go for the Grand Slam.' That was my immediate thought. The Grand Slam for me would be winning the [league] championship at each school: Cumberland, South Alabama, Clemson, and now, Auburn."

As he had at his other coaching stops, Ellis quickly reversed Auburn's fortunes. The career Grand Slam he coveted would be achieved in short order.

———

Auburn athletic director David Housel might not have realized it at the time, but when he hired Cliff Ellis to coach his basketball team, he was also getting a showman.

Like Sonny Smith before him, Ellis would use his particular talents and personality to charm Auburn fans into going to games. Where Smith used his humor and gift of gab, Ellis drew on a different skill, albeit a long dormant one. In another life, Cliff Ellis was a rock and roll singer.

As a child, Ellis had always sung in church, but he never considered singing professionally until the night in 1964 he was asked to attend a jam session by a group called the Uniques. Ellis was a student at a Florida junior college at the time. He was a huge music fan, so he couldn't wait to hear the Uniques. After the band played a few songs, Ellis worked up the courage to ask if he could sing.

Ellis chose an old Bo Diddley song, "You Can't Judge the Book by Looking at Its Cover." He'll never forget the feeling that shot through his body when he picked up the microphone. The Uniques quickly fell in behind him.

"There was electricity with the band and me," Ellis wrote in his book, *Cliff Ellis: The Winning Edge*. "It was 'tight,' as musicians like to describe it. I was now a lead singer and couldn't let go."

That night Ellis was asked to join the band. For the next several months, the Uniques toured the high school dance circuit, making the princely sum of fifty dollars a night.

Not long after Ellis hooked up with the Uniques, the band was forced to change its name when another group called the Uniques came out with a top-ten hit, "All These Things." Thus was born The Villagers. Ellis would soon evolve into the band's driving force after becoming convinced it should play beach music.

"It wasn't the Beach Boys," Ellis is quick to point out. "I'm talking about rhythm and blues, music that you can dance to. Beach music was popular all along the Gulf

Coast, from New Orleans to Orlando, Florida; the Carolinas; Virginia; and Savannah, Georgia."

Once The Villagers had fine-tuned their sound, Ellis pushed the group to make a record. He had heard about Fame Recording Studio in Muscle Shoals, Alabama, so one day, he picked up the phone. Ellis talked to producer Rick Hall, who encouraged The Villagers to come to Muscle Shoals to record. Ellis didn't know Hall at the time, but he soon would. Hall was one of the architects of the famed Muscle Shoals sound and would go on to produce legendary soul and rhythm and blues artists the likes of Otis Redding, Aretha Franklin, Etta James, and Wilson Pickett.

The Villagers didn't have a record deal, so they were on their own once they arrived in Muscle Shoals. Studio time would cost fifty-five dollars per hour.

It didn't take the band too long to do its thing. The studio tab was just eighty-eight dollars. The Villagers recorded two songs in their first Muscle Shoals session, "Laugh It Off," which was the B side to The Tams' hit "What Kind of Fool," and, in an obvious concession to the times, the Beatles' "You're Gonna Lose That Girl."

Now that The Villagers had a record, Ellis knew it had to get played. Drawing on his lifelong competitive nature, he barged into the studio at fifty-thousand-watt WBAM in Montgomery, Alabama, and asked disc jockey Bill Moody to play the record. Moody agreed to give it a spin.

"Before the record was half over, Bill Moody called me in," Ellis wrote in his book. "He said, 'I don't let people come in here, but do you see all these phone lines?' Every one of the buttons was lit up. People were going crazy over the song. He said, 'Son, you've got a hit.' "

The radio exposure took The Villagers to another level. Soon they were opening for such established acts as Charlie Rich and Roy Orbison and earning six hundred dollars a night. The band played colleges across the South and eventually signed a record deal with Atco.

It wasn't long before The Villagers went back to Fame Recording Studio to record more songs. One day Ellis walked in on a recording session by the great Etta James. Ellis was so elated to be in James's presence that someone tossed him a tambourine and asked if he wanted to sit in. Listen close to James's smash "Tell Mamma" and you can hear Ellis shaking that tambourine for all it's worth.

The Villagers became a regional sensation, charting several hits in the South. But despite the heady times, the band never lost sight of reality. School was a priority.

"Most of us went on to get our college degrees," Ellis said. "We had talked about ending the band when we finished school. And that's pretty much what happened."

In college, Ellis's love of basketball began to overtake his love of music. At

Chipola Junior College, he learned all he could from the school's coach, Milton Johnson. And when Ellis transferred to Florida State, he became friends with Hugh Durham, who coached the Seminoles and, later, the University of Georgia to the Final Four. Ellis studied Durham's playbook and his practices.

When Ellis graduated from Florida State in 1968 and took a job teaching in Niceville, Florida, his singing career was all but over.

"I always knew I was going to coach," Ellis said. "The music business, it just happened. We were having fun. But sometimes I think back to those days. It could have happened for us."

Ellis kept his hand in music over the years, performing with his coaching buddies at impromptu jam sessions and even venturing back into the recording studio. In 1984, Clemson basketball fan Marion Carter surprised Ellis with a phone call.

"I know you as more than just a basketball coach," Carter said. Carter owned a record company and had all The Villagers' old recordings in his personal collection. After a few conversations, Carter compelled Ellis to record some tracks. One, "Love Land," was played on the beach music circuit in 1991. Carter eventually compiled Ellis's songs into a CD. Another song on the disc was "Amazing Grace," which Ellis dedicated to his friend, former North Carolina State coach Jim Valvano, who died of cancer in 1993.

In the summer of 2001, Ellis returned to Muscle Shoals with Alabama Music Hall of Fame director and producer David Johnson and a talented group of session musicians to record another CD. The project later turned into a charitable effort after the September 11, 2001, terrorist attacks on New York and Washington, D.C. Ellis dedicated the Impressions' classic "People Get Ready" to the victims of the attacks and donated some of the proceeds from the CD's sale to the Red Cross.

Ellis has always credited his music career for giving him the courage to command an audience, no small skill for someone who has to lead young men and be entertaining in public-speaking situations. And Ellis's performance background served him well once he got to Auburn. Having spent considerable time on stages, Ellis knew the Tigers needed a better showcase for their games than the dingy arena he inherited. And his days of shamelessly promoting The Villagers would come in handy when it came to attracting fans to see Auburn play.

"I walked into Beard-Eaves Coliseum for the first time and it looked antiquated," Ellis wrote in his book. "The seats were old-fashioned, and the paint was drab. There was no character in the coliseum. The west end-line seats were so far removed from the floor, it appeared binoculars might be needed on certain plays. . . . I immediately started looking for ways to improve the situation."

Auburn eventually put five million dollars into renovating the coliseum, actually reducing the seating capacity and bringing the fans, particularly the rowdy "Cliff Dwellers," Auburn's student section, closer to the floor. The building became much more of a homecourt advantage, which was the first step toward rebuilding the program. By Ellis's fifth season, Beard-Eaves was rocking every night as the Tigers played to record crowds.

———

Had Chris Porter never darkened the door of Beard-Eaves Coliseum, Auburn would still have been a good team in 1999. Ellis and his staff had put in a lot of hard work as they pointed toward the fifth year in their rebuilding effort.

Auburn's strength started in the backcourt. In Doc Robinson, the Tigers had as steady a point guard as there was in the SEC. And Scott Pohlman had become a crafty shooting guard who would work tirelessly for his shot.

Up front, junior center Mamadou N'diaye was progressing better than the Auburn staff could have hoped on his way to becoming a future first-round NBA draft pick. And Bryant Smith, a six-foot-five senior, was probably the best defender in the league, a solid rebounder and decent scorer when called upon.

Behind the frontcourt starters were veterans Daymeon Fishback and Adrian Chilliest. And a recruiting class that included transfer guard Reggie Sharp, freshmen forwards Mack McGadney and David Hamilton, freshman guard Jay Heard, and junior-college forward Adrian Person had given Ellis depth for the first time in his Auburn tenure.

With a solid team in place, all the Tigers needed to jump to a higher level was a skilled power forward. Enter Porter, who had been placed by the Auburn staff at Florida's Chipola Junior College in 1996. Porter had promised to return, and he kept his word. Not that Porter had other schools beating down his door. Surprisingly for a player so highly regarded by the recruiting analysts, Mississippi State was the only other SEC school to offer a scholarship.

When Porter re-signed with the Tigers after his two-year layover at Chipola, he transformed them from a good team to a great team.

"Chris Porter just took us to another level," Ellis recalled. "He was a tremendous athlete—as quick a jumper as I've ever seen. He just did a lot of things that you couldn't teach. He had a quick first step. He knew how to finish. He was an awesome rebounder. He didn't have range to the three-point line, but he had range to about eighteen feet. Chris didn't mind defending. And he came to play. Loved to play. You never worried about him competing."

"Chris Porter was that last piece of the puzzle," former Auburn assistant Mike LaPlante said. "We had gone to the NIT with a group of sophomores the year before. So it's not like we weren't getting better already. But Porter was that athletic component that put us over the edge. His motor just ran faster than everybody else's motor. He was a superstar with a blue-collar mentality."

That blue-collar mentality was Auburn's stock in trade—the Tigers excelled at rebounding and defense. Auburn often punished its opponents on the glass, particularly on the offensive end. And Auburn's defensive pressure was relentless. The basic alignment was a 1-3-1 zone press, with the long-armed Porter in front wreaking havoc. If the Tigers couldn't get a trap and a subsequent steal, they would race downcourt and assume their basic, sticky man-to-man defense.

With depth, Ellis could substitute freely, allowing the Tigers to pressure the ball and crash the boards incessantly.

Auburn's defense was its best offense; the Tigers scored points in bunches in transition that usually began with steals. SEC statistics clearly illustrated the Tigers' strengths. They led the league in scoring, scoring defense, rebounding, rebounding margin, and offensive rebounds.

Auburn warmed up for SEC play by crushing all comers on its cozy, nonconference schedule. There weren't too many challenges, but the Tigers' average winning margin of 29 points was impressive.

After winning its first eight games, Auburn slipped into the ESPN/*USA Today* poll for the first time on December 7. The next week, the Tigers jumped all the way to No. 18 in the ESPN/*USA Today* poll and were ranked No. 19 by the Associated Press. Thus began a steady ascent, in the polls and the national spotlight.

"It was a Cinderella season and story, because no one had us picked anywhere," Ellis said. "Nowhere. We were not in any poll at any time—early in the season. But then we came out of the box fast, and it never stopped."

Once SEC play began, the Tigers—12-0 through December—quickly dispelled the notion that their nonconference record overinflated their talent. The first league opponent was Tennessee, which had been picked to win the Eastern Division. Volunteer coach Jerry Green unwittingly set the tone for the game. A comment he made on one of his post-game radio shows to the effect that Auburn hadn't proven itself against its nonconference schedule somehow got back to Ellis.

Jumping out to a quick start before a sold-out crowd of 10,108, Auburn embarrassed the Vols, 90-62, crushing them on the backboards, 57-30, and forcing 28 turnovers. Porter formally introduced himself to the SEC with 17 points and 13 rebounds.

Afterward, Tennessee forward Vincent Yarbrough summed up the game appropriately. "They beat us like we were an NAIA team," he said.

Four days later, 10,500 fans squeezed into Beard-Eaves as the Tigers, then ranked No. 14, dispatched No. 18 Arkansas, 83-66, improving their record to 14-0. Auburn had proven it could win at home. Next came a road game that would influence the rest of the season.

"By this time people were starting to take notice of us," Ellis recalled. "*Sports Illustrated* had called and said they were sending a reporter to join the team at LSU. If we won that game, they were going to do a major story on us. Talk about pressure."

As Ellis might have predicted, Auburn found itself trailing pesky LSU by 19 points with 10:34 to go. Incredibly, behind 21 second-half points from Porter, the Tigers rallied for a 73-70 victory. *Sports Illustrated* ran its story.

Auburn kept winning, beating Ole Miss on the road and Florida at home to improve its record to 17-0. By January 18, the Tigers were ranked No. 6 in both major polls. Up next was a key game at Kentucky.

Unfortunately for the Tigers, the flu bug robbed them of a chance to give the mighty Wildcats, the defending national champions, their best shot. Doc Robinson, Adrian Chilliest, and Daymeon Fishback were all ill. "We were sick as dogs," Ellis recalled. Robinson tried to play, but was a nonfactor as Kentucky won 72-62.

It was at this point of the season that things could have slipped away. That the Tigers had just suffered their first loss wasn't the worst of their problems. Shockingly, the seemingly dependable Porter was suspended for three games for a violation of team rules. With a game coming up at Alabama, where Auburn hadn't won in fourteen years, it looked as though the Tigers had lost their momentum.

Thanks to some inspired play by a freshman, that wasn't the case. Mack McGadney had originally committed to Indiana during his senior year at LeFlore High School in Mobile, Alabama, but his grandmother, Jessie Mae Feggian, asked him to reconsider the decision. She had raised McGadney and wanted to be able to watch him play. "She said Indiana was too far away," McGadney told the *Birmingham News*. "I guess she predicted something would happen. She said I needed to take care of her."

Feggian never got to see McGadney's finest hour. She died of breast cancer the morning of the Alabama game. McGadney gamely took Porter's place in the starting lineup. Playing twenty-eight minutes, McGadney scored 11 points and grabbed eight rebounds as the Tigers blew past Alabama, 73-58. It was Auburn's second-largest margin of victory ever over Alabama in Tuscaloosa. The Tigers had proven they were a good team with or without Chris Porter.

Auburn won two more times without Porter as McGadney chipped in 15 points and six rebounds in a homecourt victory over Mississippi State and 17 points and six rebounds in a win at Georgia.

Porter returned the next game, but it was two more games before he was re-inserted into the starting lineup. Auburn kept rolling along, winning its school-record twenty-third game against Ole Miss and then clinching its first SEC Western Division championship four days later. When the Tigers traveled to Arkansas for a late-February game, they were ranked No. 2 in the country.

Arkansas got the better of Auburn that day, but neither that loss nor a loss to Kentucky in the semifinals of the SEC Tournament hampered the Tigers' seeding in the NCAA Tournament. In its first trip to the Big Dance in eleven years, Auburn, 27-3, was seeded No. 1 in the South Regional.

Sent to Indianapolis, Auburn coasted in its first-round game against sixteenth-seeded Winthrop, winning 80-41. Up next was a considerably tougher test against Oklahoma State.

Trying to earn their first Sweet 16 trip since 1986, the Tigers rode there on the scrawny shoulders of Scott Pohlman, who scored a career-high 28 points, including a late jump shot and two free throws that sealed a win over the Cowboys.

With the win, Auburn advanced to a familiar spot—the University of Tennessee's Thompson-Boling Arena. The opponent was Ohio State.

The Buckeyes' talented backcourt tandem of Scoonie Penn and Michael Redd would prove too much for the Tigers. Penn, the Big Ten Player of the Year, scored 26 points, 19 of them in the second half, and Redd added 22 in as the Buckeyes won, 72-64, en route to the Final Four. Porter played his best game of the tournament with 15 points and 11 rebounds, but fouled out with less than two minutes to play. Auburn's great ride was over.

"That was a great season," Ellis said. "We won twenty-nine games. We won the SEC West for the first time. We were a No. 1 seed in the NCAA Tournament. But what was most pleasing to me was that our team had no experience in those kinds of situations. And we never folded."

The Tigers had every reason to expect another extended run in the NCAA Tournament in 1999–2000. Porter, who was chosen the SEC's Player of the Year and made numerous All-American teams after averaging 16 points and nine rebounds, resisted the temptations of the NBA draft and returned for his senior season.

The only key player missing from the year before was Bryant Smith, but two *Parade* All-Americans, forward Marquis Daniels and guard Jamison Brewer, had been recruited as replacements. *Sports Illustrated* went so far as to proclaim Auburn its pre-season No. 1 team; the cover of its annual preview edition featured Chris Porter. Some fans joked about the *Sports Illustrated* cover jinx. Little did they know what was in store for the Tigers.

The Tigers didn't appear to be too hexed in the first two months of the season, rolling to a 16-1 record. They started the season ranked No. 3 in the Associated Press poll, and, despite a loss to Stanford in their third game, maintained a top-five ranking through mid January.

Despite its record, Auburn didn't seem to be nearly as dominant as it had been the season before. Porter, convinced he had to show NBA scouts his perimeter skills, seemed to focus too much on three-point shooting and not enough on his strengths. The loss of Bryant Smith had taken away a defensive stopper Auburn had relied upon and seemingly couldn't replace.

Still, when the Tigers went to Ole Miss for a January 19, 2001, game, they were ranked No. 4 in the country. Given that lofty status, Auburn had become a target in its own league. The Rebels' Tad Smith Coliseum would not be the easiest place to preserve a top-five ranking. True to form, Ole Miss, which had become difficult to beat at home under coaches Rob Evans and Rod Barnes, played inspired basketball in handing the Tigers a 79-77 overtime loss. When the game ended, Rebel fans stormed the floor.

Three days later, Tennessee added to Auburn's woes, gaining a measure of revenge for the beating the Tigers had administered a year earlier with a 105-76 win.

Auburn was reeling a bit, but regrouped with five wins in its next six games. At 9-3 in the SEC, the Tigers seemed in good shape to win a second straight Western Division championship, but the season was about to take a shocking turn for the worse.

Knee troubles might have cost the Tigers a win in a February 22 game at Alabama. Daymeon Fishback had already been nursing a bad knee, and early in the first half, Mamadou N'diaye strained the medial collateral ligament in his left knee. Without two key contributors, the Tigers battled, but lost, 68-64. A day later, forward David Hamilton announced he was leaving the team to return to his home in California because of the death of his grandfather. With N'diaye ailing and Hamilton gone, the Tigers' post play suffered.

The worst was yet to come. Five days after the loss at Alabama, Auburn traveled to Florida for a key game that would be televised by CBS. At Auburn's shoot-around the day before the game, beat writers could clearly see something was amiss with Chris Porter.

"Chris got called off the practice floor by Cliff," recalled Neal McCready, then working for the *Birmingham Post-Herald*. "They spent the whole practice on the opposite ends of the floor on cell phones. The beat writers didn't know what was going on, but the next day I kept looking for Porter in warm-ups. He wasn't there. By that time, [Auburn sports information director] Chuck Gallina was passing out a release that said Chris was suspended indefinitely for a violation of team rules. We all assumed drugs, but then we were told it wasn't drugs."

If there is a scarier word to a college basketball coach than "drugs," it's "agent." Every coach who has a player with the potential to play professionally warns him against the dangers of consorting with agents while he still has eligibility. There have been numerous instances, in the SEC and around the country, of players having been convinced by outside parties to turn professional only to be overlooked in the NBA draft. Having given up their college eligibility, those players often have to scramble to find work, traveling overseas to play or catching on with a minor-league team.

Ellis had feared something might be amiss with Porter when, two weeks before the Florida game, Porter had requested a meeting. Porter told Ellis his mother needed money to be able to stay in her home. Ellis couldn't give Porter money, but he offered some advice.

"My advice to Chris was to try to handle the situation within his family," Ellis wrote in his book *Cliff*

Julius "Doc" Robinson. *Auburn University Athletic Media Relations*

Ellis: The Winning Edge. "I told him that he would be soon free of this kind of problem. In two months, he would have had few worries about money. I suggested that he go to his family and investigate appropriate ways to handle the problem—arrange a loan or get legal advice."

Unbeknownst to Ellis, Porter handled the problem on his own. Earlier in the season, David Hamilton had introduced Porter to Nate Cebrun, a representative for Las Vegas–based agent Robert J. Walsh. That meeting proved costly.

Cebrun, through a third party, Colleen Preiss, arranged to provide two cash payments, one of five hundred dollars, the other, two thousand, to Porter. When Porter accepted the money, he was in violation of NCAA rules. And Walsh, Cebrun, and Preiss were in violation of Alabama's Athlete Agent Regulatory Act. More than a year later, Walsh was convicted and given a one-year suspended sentence and two years probation and was ordered to pay twenty thousand dollars in restitution to Auburn and to suspend his agent's license with the NBA.

When Auburn officials learned Porter had been given money by an agent, they immediately suspended him. An appeal to the NCAA to have Porter reinstated was denied.

Without Porter, the Tigers were beaten handily at Florida. And in a game that would determine the SEC West championship, Auburn lost at home to LSU on March 1. That was a bittersweet day for Porter, who, despite his suspension, was honored during Auburn's Senior Day sendoff.

Auburn lost its season finale at Arkansas, its fourth straight defeat. After contending for the division championship all season, the Tigers finished at 9-7 in the SEC West, three games behind 12-4 LSU.

"It was disappointing," Ellis recalled. "We had a chance to win our second straight division title, but [the suspension] took that out."

Auburn rallied without its star. Behind Fishback's 20 points and 14 rebounds, the Tigers somehow managed to beat Florida in the quarterfinals of the SEC Tournament. The next day, Auburn got past South Carolina in overtime. Few would have predicted the Tigers could play their way into the tournament championship game and have a chance to salvage their season and their pride.

Arkansas proved to be too much to handle for the second time in a week. The Razorbacks, who had struggled during much of the regular season, had to win the tournament to earn an NCAA Tournament bid. After winning three games in three days, they weren't going to be denied. Arkansas won, 75-67, but Auburn could still look forward to the NCAA Tournament.

The Tigers were seeded seventh in the Midwest Regional and paired against tenth-seeded Creighton in the first round. Auburn held off a furious rally and hung on to beat the Bluejays, but their reward was a second-round game against No. 2 seed Iowa State. It was in that game that the loss of Porter finally caught up to the Tigers, who couldn't contain Iowa State power forward Marcus Fizer. Auburn lost, 79-60, and a season that had begun with such promise ended in disappointment.

After the game, Ellis had an emotional meeting with his seniors. The group of N'diaye, Robinson, and Fishback had led Auburn basketball back from another dark period, leading the Tigers to a pair of NIT trips and two NCAA Tournament appearances.

"It was a great run," Ellis said. "Despite the way it turned out, with all that happened to us, it was a great run."

Unfortunately for Porter, his troubles were not over. Drafted in the second round by the Golden State Warriors, Porter seemed to be establishing himself as an NBA contributor in the 2000–2001 season, starting thirty-five games and averaging 8.6 points and 3.7 rebounds. But Porter's old demons resurfaced. He was arrested in Dothan, Alabama, in August 2001 after being stopped for a minor traffic violation. Police found cocaine and marijuana in his car.

Golden State unloaded Porter in late October 2001 in a multiplayer deal with the Charlotte Hornets. The Hornets' management warned Porter that his first slipup would be his last. When Porter missed his flight from Oakland to Charlotte the day after the trade, he was gone. He spent the 2001–2002 season playing in obscurity for the Dakota Wizards of the Continental Basketball Association. In a testament to the great skills he seemed intent on wasting, Porter led the Wizards—thought to be a second-tier CBA team before he arrived—to the league championship.

Despite the burden that Porter placed on Ellis and the disappointment he left in his wake at Auburn, Ellis has steadfastly refused to be critical of his former player.

"Any time a guy plays for me, he's like a son," Ellis said. "And I'm going to treat him like a son. The things you say to a son are in private, not a public thing for everybody to see. I've told Chris the way I feel about some of the things that happened. He knows where I stand. But with all the positive things he did for Auburn, he will not be forgotten."

———

The front cover of Auburn's 2001–2002 media guide got a little bit ahead of itself. Emblazoned next to a picture of Cliff Ellis was a logo, complete with a pair of Tiger eyes staring menacingly ahead, that said "500 Wins." The logo was in reference to the fact that Ellis was nearing the 500-win milestone as a Division I coach. The cover's designer couldn't have been blamed for assuming Ellis would bag that five hundredth win sometime in 2002. The Tigers had averaged just a fraction under twenty wins in Ellis's seven previous seasons on the job. And Ellis needed just fourteen to reach the magic number. No one could have envisioned Auburn winning fewer than fourteen games, even though the program went through a slight downturn in 2000–2001 with the loss of Mamadou N'diaye, Doc Robinson, Daymeon Fishback, and Chris Porter.

Auburn ended up 18-14 and 79 in the SEC, but still managed to play in the NIT.

Unfortunately for Ellis, his chance to win No. 500 in 2002 was doomed before the season began. Make that six months before the season began.

Ellis and his assistant coaches became concerned about the 2001–2002 season on May 14, 2001. That's the day sophomore point guard Jamison Brewer came into the office and told Ellis he was declaring for the NBA draft. Ellis was stunned. Brewer was the only true lead guard on the Tigers' roster, and he wasn't just any point guard. A third-team All-SEC pick in 2000–2001, Brewer had led the Tigers in assists, rebounds and minutes played and was second in steals. At six-foot-five, he had grabbed 7.2 rebounds a game, the third-leading average among guards in the country. Brewer wasn't much of a shooter, but when Auburn needed a basket, he had an uncanny way of getting it himself or finding a wide-open teammate.

Suffice to say Brewer would have been a vital part of any success Auburn had in 2001–2002. Someone could have come into Ellis's office on May 14 and told him they were taking one of his lungs and he'd have accepted that easier than the news of Brewer's imminent departure.

"I was shocked," Ellis said. "The NBA scouts had been around here all year, but [Brewer's] name was never there. Then in the middle of May he decides to put his name in the draft. When the middle of May comes, what can you do? Who's available? You can't fault the kid, I'm happy for him, but you'd like a little heads up. I never got the heads up."

Brewer's decision placed the Auburn staff in full panic mode as the coaches scrambled around to find a replacement. Assistant Charlton Young, who formerly worked at Northeastern, had heard about a player named Lewis Monroe, who had been released from his scholarship at Duquesne after a coaching change there and was looking for a place to play. In the summer of 2001, Monroe, from Madison, Wisconsin, was something of a commodity and was being recruited by, among others, Wisconsin and Houston. "The kid had options," said Alabama assistant Shannon Weaver. "Anybody who was point guard needy at the time was looking at him."

Monroe took a visit to Auburn, liked the place and agreed to sign. But Ellis wasn't sure Monroe was the answer. Ellis's search for a point guard would become the story of his worst season at Auburn.

Monroe's early-season progress was severely hampered after he injured his back in practice, and Ellis considered redshirting him. Making matters worse, five-foot-ten senior Lincoln Glass, who had transferred from junior college the year before and played well in spots while backing up Brewer, had been suspended by Ellis for academic reasons. Glass would return by December 16, the start of the second semester, but the Tigers would have to survive their early-season schedule with either an untested freshman or a converted wing player at the point.

Enter the versatile Marquis Daniels. As a freshman in 1999–2000, the six-foot-six Daniels played small forward, doing some of his best work in postseason play while filling in for the suspended Chris Porter. A year later, after teammate Mack McGadney went down with a season-ending knee injury, Daniels moved to power forward, averaged a team-high 15.7 points and seven rebounds, led the SEC with 2.2 steals per game, and earned third-team all-league honors.

In his third year, Daniels, obviously a handy guy to have around, faced his greatest challenge. In a late November 2001 game against McNeese State, an unheralded but potentially dangerous bunch that would go on to play in the NCAA Tournament, Daniels found himself as the starting point guard, a position he hadn't played since high school.

With Daniels at the point, Auburn managed an 8-3 record in nonconference games. And two of the losses—to Rutgers and Louisiana Tech—were by one point. So the Auburn staff had reason to hope the Tigers could scrape through the SEC season, steal another seven or eight victories, and earn an NIT bid. But the lack of a proven point guard wasn't the Tigers' only problem.

By January 2002, it had become apparent Mack McGadney, who had played so well earlier in his career, hadn't recovered from a serious knee injury suffered the year before. McGadney had been averaging a double-double when he tore his anterior cruciate ligament in the eighth game of the 2000–2001 season. He would never regain that form, played sparingly in SEC games, and eventually left the team.

"Mack just never made it back," Auburn assistant Shannon Weaver said. "His situation was very similar to Jeremy Hays at Alabama [who had injured his knee in 1999 and couldn't return in 2000]. To be able to walk or run or play basketball is one thing. To play SEC basketball is another."

In the Tigers' SEC opener against Arkansas, the Razorbacks forced 20 turnovers, 8 of them by Daniels and Lincoln Glass. Auburn committed 16 turnovers, 7 by Daniels and Glass, in its next game, a loss at Ole Miss.

Somehow, Auburn managed to beat then No. 14 Alabama in its third SEC game, but the Tigers collapsed after that, losing six games in a row. The Marquis Daniels point-guard experiment ended after Auburn got whipped, 82-59, at Tennessee. In the Tigers' next game against Mississippi State, Monroe moved into the starting lineup.

And though the Tigers lost, he showed promise, handing out 8 assists and making just 2 turnovers in twenty-nine minutes.

"That was a big decision I had to make with Lewis," Ellis said. "Marquis had been playing out of position. Monroe had gotten hurt early and didn't play much in the non-conference season. I had to decide. Do I get him a medical redshirt or do I go ahead and throw him in there? In practice I thought he could do it, so I said, why not?"

Two games later, Ellis made what seemed like an even more drastic decision, starting four freshmen and junior college transfer Derrick Bird against Georgia. When the revamped lineup, which included freshmen Monroe at point guard, Dwayne Mitchell at shooting guard, Marco Killingsworth at power forward, and Brandon Robinson at small forward, battled seventeenth-ranked Georgia—literally—and won, Ellis thought he was on to something. The young Tigers had hung tough in the game's closing minutes, when a fight between Auburn's Kyle Davis and the Bulldogs' Steven Thomas marred the proceedings.

Auburn

All-SEC Expansion Era Team

F-Chris Porter

F-Marquis Daniels

C-Mamadou N'diaye

G-Wesley Person

G-Doc Robinson

Top Reserves-Jamison Brewer, Bryant Smith

"Our older guys were plodding along," Weaver said in explaining the youth movement. "We decided to throw our kids in there. One thing we learned during the year was how much experience meant in this league. We decided we're not going to be in the same position next year, having to rely on a lot of young guys. We were going to get them the experience and let them take their lumps. And we were going to keep playing them come hell or high water."

"I did the same thing with Doc Robinson and that group," Ellis recalled. "At Clemson, I did the same thing with Dale Davis and Elden Campbell. Sometimes, at schools like Auburn and Clemson, that's what you have to do. You take a group of young guys and you play them and you let them take a bath. That's how they learn and get tougher."

When the "Tiger Tots," as sports information director Chuck Gallina began calling Auburn's freshmen, upset Ole Miss in their next game, Ellis had hopes of pulling out an NIT bid. But Auburn closed out the regular season with losses in four of its last five games. The Tigers finished 12-15 overall and 4-12—last—in the SEC West. A first-round matchup against Florida in the SEC Tournament didn't seem too promising.

Ellis wasn't sad to see the regular season end, given all that had happened from the start of practice in mid October to the final game in early March. Three players—

81

Marin Bota, Abdou Diame, and Mack McGadney—quit the team. Two were kicked off, Glass after he'd returned from a suspension, and Diame after he quit, then had a change of heart and returned. Injuries had limited the effectiveness of several players, notably McGadney and starting center Kyle Davis, the SEC's top shot blocker.

"This was as an unfortunate year of circumstances as I've had," Ellis said. "We had so many things go wrong we couldn't control. It was the first year I had where it didn't go the way you'd like for it to go, but you couldn't control it. Sometimes that just happens. Everybody goes through that time where it doesn't go your way. You want to think you're a magician, that you can fix it. Then things happen so fast, you can't control them."

As tough as his twenty-seventh year as a Division I coach had been, Ellis, at fifty-six years old, couldn't wait to get started on his twenty-eighth season. He was under no pressure from his bosses to get the program back to a post-season tournament.

"Lord no I'm not feeling any heat," Ellis said a day before Auburn played Florida in the SEC Tournament. [The Auburn administration] is excited about these young guys. They've been real supportive of me. They know what it's like in the SEC. Sometimes during the course of a season, you get knocked down, and in this conference, it's tough to get back up. But we'll be back."

Chapter Four

Florida

O n September 11, 2001, the day America's view of the world changed forever, Florida coach Billy Donovan was on a plane headed for Boston when terrorists attacked the World Trade Center in New York.

"The captain gets on [the public address system] and said there had been an attack on the World Trade Center," recalled Donovan, who was on the first leg of an extended recruiting trip. "Then he gets back on and says every flight in progress must land at the closest airport immediately."

In Donovan's case, the nearest airport was in Buffalo, New York. When Donovan's plane landed, he turned on his cell phone in time to receive a call from his wife.

"I said, 'What is going on?'" Donovan recalled. "She explained it. I said 'Wow.' I was absolutely blown away. Being from New York and having worked on Wall Street, I can't tell you how many people I knew who worked in that area. It was a sad, sad day. An unbelievable day."

As stunned as he was by the day's tragic events, Donovan knew he couldn't stay in Buffalo. His famous work ethic wouldn't allow that much idle time. All flights had been grounded, so Donovan did the only thing he could. With an in-home visit scheduled in Dallas in a few days, Donovan rented the last car available in the Buffalo airport and set out for Texas.

"I drove twenty-five hundred miles," Donovan said, laughing at the recollection. "I drove from Buffalo to Philadelphia to North Carolina to Atlanta to Dallas. It was from Tuesday to Saturday. I tried to change home visits along the way on the phone. Trying to reschedule home visits is just like a nightmare. People have stuff going on, you're trying to coordinate times. It was a fiasco.

"Finally I just said, 'You know what, I'm going to just get in the car for four or five days and drive this thing, do what we need to do, and then get back home and regroup and go from there.'"

Unfortunately for Donovan, his marathon drive was all for naught.

"I drove all that way, and the kid committed to another school," Donovan said. "That's how impressed he was I drove from Buffalo to his house."

Donovan doesn't typically make twenty-five-hundred-mile treks to recruit, not by car anyway. But his willingness to do so when he'd had good reason to take a few days off speaks volumes about the man.

When Florida athletic director Jeremy Foley hired Donovan in 1996, it was precisely for the reason illustrated by that drive from Buffalo to Dallas. If Florida's basketball program were ever to thrive on a consistent basis, it needed a coach willing to outwork the opposition. Foley found his man in Billy Donovan.

How did Foley know Donovan, just thirty years old in the spring of 1996, could handle all the demands that would be placed on him at Florida, a program that had enjoyed but a taste of postseason success in its long history? Foley had proof. For Donovan, albeit at a different level, had already demonstrated he could revive a sagging program.

———

Searching for a basketball coach in the spring of 1994, Marshall athletic director Lee Moon decided that any potential candidate had to have two qualities. "I wanted somebody with energy," Moon recalled. "And a sense of urgency. That was my big catch phrase. I had to have a guy who understood what it took to win, and someone who could get there in a hurry."

Moon's own sense of urgency was understandable. Starting with the 1990–91 season, when Dwight Freeman took over for Dana Altman as the Thundering Herd's coach, the program began a gradual decline. West Virginians love their basketball, but by the 1993–94 season, when Marshall finished 8-19, Herd fans had become disinterested, as their declining numbers at home games clearly demonstrated. Dwindling attendance, as any athletic director knows too well, doesn't make for a healthy bottom line.

Appointing himself a committee of one, Moon conducted his search the right way. Knowing he couldn't attract a head coach with Division I experience, Moon narrowed his search to assistants at elite programs. Three candidates quickly emerged—Dan Dakich of Indiana, Mike Brey of Duke, and Billy Donovan of Kentucky.

Once Moon identified his candidates, he traveled to each school, went to practice, watched games and talked to everyone he could, especially players, about the particular coach he was visiting.

When Moon's travels were completed, one candidate had emerged as the frontrunner. "Billy Donovan really impressed me," Moon recalled. "He was so bright eyed. And his work ethic . . . When I started checking and talking to people, I found out he was relentless as far as game preparation. Then I watched him on the sidelines. [Kentucky coach Rick] Pitino had a strong staff, but when players would come off the floor, Billy was the guy they went to. Almost always. I remember riding on an elevator with a couple of players, and they had nothing but great things to say about Billy. 'He knows the game,' one of them said. That stood out in my mind."

There was another thing that stood out about Donovan—his age. At twenty-eight, he had been a full-time assistant for just four seasons, a graduate assistant for one. In assessing Donovan's merits, Moon had to decide whether Donovan was experienced enough to run his own program.

"When I first met Billy, I thought, 'My God, he's young,'" Moon recalled. "But I had hired Dana Altman when he was twenty-nine. My whole deal is that it's not the number of years of experience, it's the number of experiences in the years. Billy had seen how coach Pitino did things. He'd played for coach Pitino and seen how he'd built Providence into a success story, and seen it from the other side of the fence. When he came to Kentucky, I just thought that at that level, he had learned what the sense of urgency was all about."

Moon was right, for Pitino, knowing his young protégé would one day become a head coach, heaped an inordinate share of responsibility on Donovan. Before the 1993–94 season, Donovan was promoted to associate coach.

"People talked about my age at that time," Donovan recalled. "Years-wise I was twenty-eight. But I think with coach Pitino, I just got so much stuff thrown at me. He challenged me and was very demanding. It was tough. But what he did for me, he forced me to coach.

"One of the things a lot of coaches do sometimes is put their assistants off to the side and just say recruit. And they don't get to coach. I got thrown into the mix. [Kentucky assistant] Ralph Willard leaves, and now I'm handling preparation and putting together scouting reports. Coach Pitino said, 'I don't want you coming to me with a scouting report of what the other team's plays are. Any person can watch a film and write down what plays are. I want to know how we're stopping them.'

"That forced me to think at a completely different level than I ever thought of before. All of a sudden he's got me thinking like a head coach. I remember times he'd say, 'I'm gonna go recruiting. Take my radio show for me.' I'd do his show, and I'm twenty-six, twenty-seven years old. He'd say, 'I've got to go do this, take practice. Do this, do that.' It really helped accelerate my learning curve."

Donovan didn't have to deliberate long when Moon called to offer him the Marshall job. Donovan had the blessing of Pitino, who by that time had a pretty good history of developing coaches. Already, Ralph Williard (Western Kentucky), Tubby Smith (Tulsa), and Herb Sendek (Miami-Ohio) had left the Kentucky staff for head-coaching jobs.

"Rick always felt like you should stay with him only three or four years because of the intensity level," Donovan recalled. "He wanted fresh guys in there. And he wanted his guys to move on. He helped a lot of us get our starts as head coaches."

When Donovan signed on at Marshall, he became the youngest Division I coach in the country. The work he did in quickly transforming the program was befitting a veteran coach.

Things were so bad at Marshall, and the Thundering Herd's roster so depleted, that when the team took a preseason trip to Spain, assistant coaches John Pelphrey and Donnie Jones had to play. Donovan had just seven scholarship players.

There was never a doubt which system Donovan would run as a head coach. Pressing, shooting three-pointers, and dictating tempo like the best of Pitino's Kentucky teams, Marshall started 10-3 overall and 3-0 in the Southern Conference in 1994–95, Donovan's first season. At that point, the Herd's lack of bodies began to catch up with them. Marshall lost five straight games. His team reeling at 10-8, Donovan began to wonder, and to worry.

"The first thing going through your mind is you start questioning yourself," Donovan said. "I didn't want to make excuses like these weren't my guys or I had just seven scholarship guys. I remember talking to the kids and telling them they were at the same stage they were a year ago and the year before that.

"I told them, 'I'm gonna be honest with you. If it continues the way it's going and your career ends here, you guys are going to be looked at as the problem. Because the previous coach lost his job. People are gonna say you guys are the problem, not me. It all depends on how you guys want to end it.'"

Inspired by Donovan's candor, the Herd regrouped and won eight straight games. Marshall finished the year 18-9 and erased several school records in the process, setting standards in three-pointers in a game (17) and a season (253). Marshall led the Southern Conference in scoring, and in a direct correlation, paced the league in attendance. Marshall's increase in attendance from the season before led all Division I schools. Donovan was already paying dividends.

In 1995–96, Marshall was 17-11, and the program had officially been declared rebuilt. Donovan's handiwork had already begun to attract attention.

———

In the spring of 1996, Florida athletic director Jeremy Foley found himself in much the same situation as Lee Moon two years before. The difference was that Foley hadn't had to fire his basketball coach. Lon Kruger was given a great bailout opportunity by Illinois and took it. Ironically, Kruger wasn't able to build on the Gators' improbable Final Four appearance just two years before, and the program, instead of staying at a high level, had started to decline.

That puzzled Foley, who couldn't understand why Florida couldn't have a consistent basketball program.

"When Lon Kruger told us he was leaving, I immediately went to the president [John Lombardi]," Foley recalled. "At that time, I'd been here twenty years. It was the same old stuff being said about Florida. 'Florida can't be a basketball school. Football dominates. There's no basketball commitment.' It was stuff I was tired of hearing.

"I was around when we hired Norm Sloan and Lon Kruger, who had been successful head coaches at other places. They had pockets of success at Florida. But when they left, people said Florida couldn't be a basketball school. Nothing had changed. I wanted to change that."

Foley eventually decided he didn't want to make a conventional hire. In other words, he didn't necessarily want to seek an established coach from another school. Sure, if Duke's Mike Krzyzewski had called him wanting the job, Foley would have changed his strategy in a second. But Coach K didn't call, and neither did any other big-name coaches. The fact that Lon Kruger, widely respected as a bench coach, couldn't capitalize on a Final Four appearance was scary to potential candidates.

"I said, 'This time, we're going to do something different,'" Foley recalled. "'We're not going to hire an established guy'—we'd been that route before. We needed someone who wasn't intimidated by football, a guy who was going to come up here and make a mark for himself. We were going to find an up-and-comer. That was the plan from the get-go."

Like Moon did two years before, Foley called Kentucky athletic director C. M. Newton and basketball coach Rick Pitino to talk about Billy Donovan. Encouraged by what Newton and Pitino had to say, Foley's next step was to call Marshall and ask for permission to speak with Donovan. When permission was granted, Foley set up a meeting.

"When I first met him, I knew he was exactly what I was looking for," Foley said. "After four hours I felt like I'd known him all my life. And if I liked him, I felt like players, coaches, fans, and parents would, too. Rick Pitino said he'd never had a harder worker than Billy Donovan. I knew it was going to take a lot of work to get things done."

Even before Foley hired Donovan, he heard from critics who were under the mistaken impression Florida could attract any coach it wanted. Donovan was too young, the doubters said. Why should Florida have to settle for an inexperienced head coach? "Some people said we took a risk," Foley said. "But what was the risk? People said we couldn't be a basketball school anyway. What did we have to lose? I felt Billy would bring something different to the table."

What sort of program had Donovan inherited from Lon Kruger? To be sure, it was in far better shape than the one Kruger inherited from Don DeVoe, by way of Norm Sloan, in the spring of 1990.

The late 1980s and early 1990s represented the best of times and the worst of times in Florida's basketball history. Under the direction of Sloan—in his second tour of duty at Florida after a stopover at North Carolina State that included winning the 1974 national championship—the Gators enjoyed an unprecedented run of success from the 1986–87 season to 1988–89.

Led by guards Vernon Maxwell and Andrew Moten and brash freshman center Dwayne Schintzius, Florida finished second in the SEC standings in the 1986–87 season and advanced to the NCAA Tournament for the first time in school history.

Florida handily defeated North Carolina State and Purdue in the first two rounds of the NCAAs. And the Gators might have had a chance to go farther had Schintzius kept his mouth shut after the win over the Boilermakers.

Asked to assess Florida's Sweet 16 matchup with Syracuse, Schintzius told the press how he planned to dominate Rony Seikaly, the Orangemen's center. Apparently Seikaly took offense to that. He responded with a career-high 33 points and nine rebounds as Syracuse defeated Florida, 87-71. Schintzius scored six points.

That wasn't the first time Schintzius's words or actions got him into trouble, but somehow, Sloan managed to harness him for two more seasons. The Gators finished second in the SEC again in 1987–88 and again played in the NCAA Tournament, beating St. John's in the first round.

In 1988–89, Florida won its first SEC regular-season championship and advanced to the NCAA Tournament yet again, only to lose in the first round.

As good as things were on the court, the program suffered off the court from a lack of discipline that led to numerous problems. The worst involved Vernon Maxwell, who, it was later discovered by the NCAA, accepted money from an agent in 1987.

At the time, NCAA investigators were swarming Florida; rules violations had also been uncovered in the football program. The investigation turned up another situation involving Maxwell. In 1987, Sloan used university funds to send Maxwell to a Boston Celtics' camp. In NCAA parlance, that was a classic example of an improper benefit.

Hoping to soften the blow that they knew was coming from the NCAA, Florida president Robert Bryan and athletic director Bill Arnsparger asked/forced Sloan to retire in late October 1989.

"I regret very much the events that have occurred today," Bryan said when Sloan's departure was announced. "However, I believe what has occurred is in the best interests of the university's athletic program and the university as a whole."

Bryan was right. The NCAA's sanctions against Florida, announced in late September 1990, weren't as severe as they might have been had Bryan not encouraged Sloan to go away. Florida lost two scholarships in 1991–92 and another the next season. All mention of the Gators' NCAA Tournament participation in 1987 and 1988 was stripped from the record books, and the school had to return its share of money earned in the 1988 tournament. There were no postseason tournament or television bans.

Two days after Sloan stepped aside in 1989, Florida brought in Don DeVoe, who had been fired at Tennessee just months before, to serve as interim coach. Livingston Chatman, Florida's All-SEC forward, quit the team immediately. Schintzius—who by that time had become a first-team All-SEC pick—stayed around, but was a constant pain in DeVoe's backside. He quit in January 1990 after DeVoe insisted he get a haircut.

Predictably, Florida finished 7-21. DeVoe couldn't skip town fast enough when the season was over. Before he left, DeVoe expressed doubts Florida could hire a coach with enough character, talent, and guts to pull the program from the mire into which it had sunk.

———

DeVoe was wrong. Somehow, Florida managed to convince Kansas State coach Lon Kruger that taking the Florida job and turning the program around would look good on his resume.

Kruger had played at Kansas State and did an excellent job after returning to his alma mater as head coach. In 1990, his final season, Kruger coached the Wildcats to a fourth-place finish in the Big 8, no small accomplishment considering the three teams that finished higher—Oklahoma, Kansas, and Missouri—were all ranked No. 1 in the country at some point in the season.

By all accounts, Kruger was a solid coach, and better still for Florida and its tar-

89

nished reputation, a solid citizen.

"He's not a good choice," ESPN analyst Dick Vitale said after Kruger was hired. "He's a great choice. I was shocked when I heard it. I didn't think Florida would be able to get such a quality coach under the circumstances."

Within a year, Kruger had the fragmented Gators believing they were one big happy family. On the court, Florida players were suddenly diving for loose balls and actually listening to their coach. At one point in the SEC portion of their schedule, the Gators were 7-7. They lost their last four games, but still finished in sixth place in the conference, up from ninth the season before.

As much as Kruger accomplished on the court, he did more off it, signing two players who would become central figures in his rebuilding program, guard Dan Cross and center Andrew DeClercq.

In 1991–92, the first season of SEC expansion, Kruger had the Gators prepared. Cross, a big-time scorer in high school, was converted to point guard "to shake things up a little bit," Kruger said at the time. That turned out to be a shrewd move. Cross's play at the point and the instant success of DeClercq, who started every game and made the SEC's All-Freshman team, were keys to a turnaround season for Florida.

Another key was the play of junior forward Stacey Poole, who had come to Florida as a *Parade* and McDonald's All-American in 1988 only to be plagued by an uncanny succession of injuries. Overcoming two torn Achilles tendons and a torn anterior cruciate ligament suffered during his first two seasons, Poole would lead the Gators in scoring and rebounding.

Besides Poole, another veteran presence was guard Craig Brown, a shooting guard with a knack for making clutch baskets.

With such a solid nucleus, the Gators finished second in the SEC's new Eastern Division with a 9-7 record and were 19-14 overall.

Returning to postseason play for the first time in two years, Florida advanced all the way to the Final Four of the NIT, where it lost to Virginia. The program was back.

In 1992–93, Florida again finished 9-7 in the SEC East, good this time for third place, and made a return trip to the NIT, losing to Minnesota in the first round. The Gators finished 16-12.

Cross, Brown, and DeClercq were again stalwarts for Florida. And in the summer of 1993, another star began to emerge. Dametri Hill, a six-foot-seven, 290-pound sophomore center who had averaged just one point per game the season before, attracted some attention during the Gators' barnstorming tour of Australia, averaging 15.3 points and 8.6 rebounds.

Hill's performance was no fluke, as he proved during Florida's 10-2 start to the

1993–94 season. Matched against Oklahoma State center Bryant "Big Country" Reeves in the Rainbow Classic, Hill scored 23 points. The next night Hill, guarded by Louisville center Clifford Rozier, scored a career-high 28 points. This from a player who had accounted for all of 17 points his freshman season.

Hill helped lead Florida back to the top of the SEC in 1993–94. The Gators finished with a 12-4 record in league play, tied Kentucky for the Eastern Division title, and advanced to the finals of the SEC Tournament, where they lost to the Wildcats.

At 25-7, Florida had more than earned its first trip to the NCAA Tournament since 1989. And the Gators made the most of it.

Florida's first tournament game gave no indication of things to come—the Gators struggled to a 64-62 victory over James Madison. Florida, seeded third in the East Regional, needed Cross's running one-hander with 7.2 seconds left to escape with a win.

Cross was a hero again in the Gators' second-round victory over Penn, scoring 22 points. That earned Florida just the second trip to the Sweet 16 in school history, and the Gators didn't squander the opportunity. Brown's three-pointer with 1:09 to play in overtime staked Florida to a 62-58 lead over Connecticut, and the Gators hung on for a 69-60 win.

By this time, the nation was beginning to pay attention to Kruger's band of over-achievers. In the East Regional finals against Boston College, Brown knocked down three straight three-pointers in the game's final five minutes, lifting the Gators from six points down to three ahead. They won 74-66 and were headed to the Final Four.

Duke ended Florida's great run with a 70-65 victory, but there was no denying the job Kruger had done in reviving the program. Much to his disappointment, Kruger wouldn't be able to build on his success.

In 1994–95, Florida, without the departed Craig Brown, finished 17-13. A year later, the Gators ended up 12-16 and a puzzling 6-10 in the SEC. How did Florida fall from its lofty pinnacle so quickly and so drastically?

"There was some frustration from Lon," Florida athletic director Jeremy Foley recalled. "He worked very, very hard. He was hoping to build on that Final Four momentum. But it didn't happen for whatever reason. Two years removed from the Final Four we've got a losing record. But that wasn't due to lack of effort or caring. It just wasn't working. That was frustrating for him and frustrating for us. Change is good sometimes."

Some program insiders insist recruiting was the answer. Kruger and his staff were unable to mine talent-rich Florida consistently enough. When Vince Carter, a gifted forward from Daytona Beach and a future NBA superstar, spurned the Gators to sign

91

with North Carolina, Kruger was disappointed and perhaps convinced it was time to move on.

Kruger got that opportunity in the spring of 1996, when long-time Illinois coach Lou Henson retired. Eager for a return to his Midwestern roots, Kruger jumped at the chance to coach in the Big Ten.

Kruger's departure only convinced critics that Florida, long known as a football school, was capable only of occasional success in basketball. Foley didn't believe it.

"I didn't buy the argument that we can't be consistently good in basketball, because we'd been good in every other sport," Foley said. "Why not basketball? I had to find a coach who shared the belief that we could be among the elite in basketball. We wanted somebody to build a foundation here."

———

When Donovan took over at Florida in 1996, he knew what he was up against. Too many well-meaning friends reminded him of the situation he was inheriting.

"When I first got to Florida, that's all anybody wanted to talk about," Donovan recalled. " 'You've been put in an unfair situation.' 'The talent's down.' My response to that was, if I'm going to talk about that, I shouldn't have taken the job. I understood what I was stepping in to. That's why I signed a six-year deal. But I wasn't going to make any big deal out of what I had to work with."

Donovan knew of Kruger's frustration over Vince Carter and was determined to change the way Florida high school players viewed the program. Donovan wasn't afraid of the success of Florida's football team, which, under the direction of coach Steve Spurrier and his high-octane offense, won the national championship in 1996. In fact, he viewed football as a great recruiting tool.

Donovan, with assistant coach Anthony Grant in tow, spent his first two and a half weeks on the job traveling Florida's highways.

"We drove from Pensacola to Miami, up and down the state," Donovan recalled. "Just meeting people and coaches. We talked to coaches with really good programs, guys who coached former Florida players. We met with coaches who might not necessarily have had players we wanted to recruit at that time. I felt we needed to put up a border around the state and recruit Florida first. If you go back and look at it, Norm Sloan won the SEC championship in 1989, and of the fifteen scholarship players they had on the roster, thirteen were from the state of Florida."

It took a while for Donovan to convince the state's better players to take a chance on Florida.

"In the beginning, it was hard," Donovan recalled. "We lost Alvin Jones [to Georgia Tech], Myron Anthony [to Kentucky], and Keyon Dooling [to Missouri]. But then we got Brent Wright and Major Parker. Then we signed Udonis Haslem, Ted Dupay, and Justin Hamilton. We signed some very, very good players from our state. And if we had other holes to fill, we went elsewhere."

Donovan was hired too late to recruit, so his first team at Florida consisted of players he inherited. Kruger left behind the makings of a good backcourt in Greg Williams and Eddie Shannon, but Florida was weak in the frontcourt, especially after junior LeRon Williams, who didn't buy into the gospel according to Donovan, decided to transfer to South Carolina. Donovan did eventually get a lot of mileage from six-foot-eight sophomore Greg Stolt, who, before his career was finished, would become Florida's all-time leading three-point shooter.

The Gators finished 13-17 and 5-11 in the SEC in Donovan's first season.

"That was as fun a time as I've had in coaching, although we really couldn't compete with the better teams in the league," Donovan recalled. "Those kids gave me everything they had. They weren't the most talented group, but I'll say this about Lon Kruger. Not one of those kids was a bad kid. They were all great people."

Donovan brought in some reinforcements for the 1997–98 season. Jason Williams, a flashy, cocky point guard who had played for Donovan at Marshall, regained his eligibility after sitting out the season as a transfer. With Williams leading a revved-up offense, the Gators averaged 80 points per game. But Williams, who had his eye on the NBA, was a constant source of aggravation to Donovan. Twenty games into the season, Donovan had to kick Williams off the team. Later that year Williams was chosen by the Sacramento Kings in the first round of the NBA draft. He was the seventh overall selection.

If Donovan couldn't count on Williams, he found out quickly he could depend on Major Parker and Brent Wright, two freshmen who helped Florida establish an in-state recruiting base. Neither Wright, from state power Miami Senior High School, nor Parker, from Fort Lauderdale, were stars, but they became solid contributors in their four seasons.

Even without a full season's work from Jason Williams, the Gators showed improvement, despite dropping another notch in the SEC East standings and finishing sixth with a 6-10 record. But in a game that would foreshadow the future, the Gators went to Kentucky and pulled off an 86-78 upset of the eventual national champions. Donovan's mentor Rick Pitino had departed for the Boston Celtics by then, but the win was nevertheless a landmark for Florida's program and a sign that Donovan had the Gators headed in the right direction.

A win over Auburn and a loss to South Carolina in the SEC Tournament left the Gators with a 14-14 record, which was good enough to earn an NIT bid. Florida lost to Georgetown in the first round, but a trend had been established. The Gators were about to become a perennial postseason tournament team.

Immediately before and after that season, Donovan and his assistant coaches established another trend. Florida was going to become a national player in the recruitment of top talent, which would have a disruptive effect on the status quo of college basketball's established powers. That much would soon be evident by Florida's pursuit of Mike Miller.

Even while Donovan was still at Marshall, he and assistant coach John Pelphrey identified a skinny junior high player from Mitchell, South Dakota, as someone who might fit into their system. For the next four years, as Mike Miller was turning himself into a *Parade* and McDonald's All-American, Donovan kept an eye on Miller, who would grow to six-foot-eight and, because of his vast array of skills, prompt comparisons to Larry Bird.

By 1997, Donovan thought Miller was a breakthrough recruit.

"I remember the first conversation I had with Mike Miller," Donovan said. "He says, 'Coach, everybody keeps telling me how great I am. I don't feel like I'm great. What do I have to do to get better?' When I heard that, I said, 'I don't care how hard we have to work. This is the guy I want.'"

Donovan, undaunted that Miller was also being recruited by every top program in the country—most notably Kansas and Kentucky—recruited Miller relentlessly. Some thought a little too relentlessly. Kansas coach Roy Williams accused the Florida staff of breaking NCAA rules by making improper and excessive contact with Miller. He shared his feelings with the NCAA, which eventually conducted an inquiry. No improprieties were found.

"I felt like we needed to be innovative in recruiting," Donovan said. "I was gonna do different things. And the different things that I did, it rubbed people the wrong way. I'm never ever going to jeopardize the University of Florida, my family, or anything and do something that is wrong. If you ask our compliance people of all the sports what coaching staff calls them the most asking questions, they would probably say the basketball staff.

"My thing was just trying to be innovative. My first two years at Florida, I couldn't just sit there in the stands [during the summer evaluation period] with Mike Krzyzewski and Roy Williams and those guys. Maybe Roy Williams can sit in the stands and watch a kid play and the kid is wooed and wowed that Roy Williams is there. I was thirty years old. I just got the job. Some kid is not wooed and wowed because Billy Donovan is sitting in the stands.

"So to me it's about relationships and building a relationship with a kid. That's the only way we can do it."

The time Donovan and his staff put in with Miller paid off. He resisted the overtures of other schools and turned a deaf ear to friends, family, and other coaches when they questioned whether Florida could ever become a consistent power in basketball.

"People said I was selling the kid a pipe dream," Donovan recalled. "But you know what? I never thought about it as a pipe dream. I tried to sell Mike Miller on something I believed in."

Donovan's sales pitch worked. In the fall of 1997, Miller, who could have picked any school in the country, signed with Florida. Asked by an *Orlando Sentinel* sports writer to explain his decision, Miller was brief and to the point.

"A lot of people around here still don't understand why," Miller said. "But they will."

Gary Munsen, Miller's coach at Mitchell High School, thought Donovan and Pelphrey, who was just twenty-nine at the time, used their strengths to perfection.

"They sold their youth, their enthusiasm, and their work ethic, which was like none I'd ever seen," Munsen told the *Orlando Sentinel*. "It was very impressive."

Along with Miller, Donovan sold other players on his dream. Florida's 1998–99 freshman class, for the first time in years, was top-heavy with in-state players. From Cape Coral, Donovan signed guard Teddy Dupay, the state's Mr. Basketball and the all-time leading scorer in Florida history. Dupay was the first recruit to cast his lot with Donovan, committing in his sophomore season. Some thought Dupay, at a stocky five-foot-ten, bore an uncanny resemblance to Donovan. And Dupay was a competitor, just like his future coach. The pairing of Dupay and Donovan, some Gator fans believed, was destiny. Donovan's old high school coach from New Jersey, Frank Morris, also coached Dupay after moving south.

Other Florida high school stars followed Dupay's lead. Guard LaDarius Halton, runner-up for Mr. Basketball, came from New Smyrna Beach. And the Miami pipeline Donovan opened the season before with the signing of Brent Wright produced again, this time delivering center Udonis Haslem. Like Brent Wright, Haslem played at talent-rich Miami Senior.

Donovan's first major recruiting class was ranked among the top five in the country by some analysts and would jump-start a run of success unprecedented in Florida's history. But he hadn't heard the last of questions and criticism directed toward his recruiting practices.

———

After such noted coach-comedians as Auburn's Sonny Smith, Alabama's Wimp Sanderson, and Georgia's Hugh Durham filtered out of the SEC in the early 1990s, the league's basketball annual media day gradually transformed from Comedy Central to C-SPAN, from a-laugh-a-minute to all business. In 1998, South Carolina coach Eddie Fogler did his best to liven up the proceedings. When he finished talking about his team, Fogler had another subject he wanted to discuss.

"The new gig, you want to hear the new gig?" Fogler asked the gathered media. "Let me bring the new gig to your attention. This is a beaut. Tell it like it is. The worst thing that can happen to me is they fire me.

"The new gig is, and it's legal but is it ethical? You guys judge. The new gig is financial managers that put together summer trips. The new gig we had this summer was we had a money manager take ten high school players to France for ten days.

"Two of the kids are freshmen at two different schools, a couple of the kids are already committed or are open to go to those schools. One kid, who is really good, was really being recruited by one of those two groups, and his AAU coach happened to make that trip. Wow. And you know the real interesting part? The guy who put the trip together is a former basketball player in the SEC and the school he was helping in the SEC wasn't even the school he went to. I think [Rick] Pitino called him a disgrace to Kentucky basketball.

"I'm not mentioning names. Think about that gig. That is incredible. The other youngster they were trying to get to go that school went to another school, but he came close. They got an official visit."

Fogler didn't have to mention names, for it was obvious whom he was talking about. The trip to France was sponsored by Bret Bearup, an Atlanta-based financial planner, former Kentucky player, and friend of Donovan's. Three future Florida players made the journey with Bearup—Mike Miller, Brett Nelson, and Matt Bonner.

Donovan was told of Fogler's comments by the media. Suffice to say he wasn't thrilled. By that time, Mike Miller's recruitment was a sore subject to him. Donovan assumed Fogler's diatribe was sparked by his long-time association with Kansas coach Roy Williams. Fogler and Williams worked together on Dean Smith's staff at North Carolina.

"Do you think it was directed toward Florida? OK then," Donovan said after being asked to respond to Fogler's comments. "My thing is, why not come out and say it? He is asking you guys to put two and two together. Why not come out and say it? Obviously I am very, very disappointed and resent the things that Eddie Fogler said.

The thing that bothers me more than anything else is that he doesn't have enough class and enough courtesy that, if he is going to throw out things like that, to at least use my name and the University of Florida. On his behalf, it shows absolutely no guts. . . .

"Prior to the comments he made, I had no problem with Eddie Fogler. I do have a problem with him now."

The incident sparked a cold war between Fogler and Donovan and once again cast Donovan's recruiting practices in a negative light, even though Bearup's trip didn't break any NCAA rules.

"Bret and I are friends," Donovan said. "That's the thing that people don't understand. Besides that every college coach in the country knows Bret. Every coach in the country talks to Bret. But I have a different relationship with him. We both grew up in Long Island. I knew him as a player. And then when I was coaching at Kentucky [in 1991], we took his brother Todd as a transfer [from Utah State]. Bret and I talked a lot about Todd. Bret liked me and respected me.

"After he went into his business and running those overseas trips and I got the job at Florida, he called me. Matt Bonner committed to us and Bret called me and said he'd like to invite Matt to go on the trip. Brett Nelson—who I'd known since he was in the seventh grade—was already coming to our place and he made the trip. All of a sudden, the people's perception was I placed guys on the trip and Bret worked his magic and got them to come to Florida.

"But I don't think Bret's doing anything for any schools. Bret's made those trips for his own personal career. He's a financial planner. Why would Bret Bearup upset another coach? It doesn't make any sense to him. People can draw whatever conclusions about Bret Bearup. People say they don't like what he does. I'm not going to pass judgement on him. For Bret to be around a lot of players, that helps what he does."

More than three years after the fact, any ill will Fogler and Donovan might have had toward one another had died down.

"I'm not saying I was right or wrong on that issue," said Fogler, who in 2002 was enjoying life away from the sidelines as a scout for the Utah Jazz and Philadelphia 76ers and as a television commentator. "I questioned the ethics. I didn't say it was illegal. I questioned whether it was ethical. I asked the media to decide whether that situation was ethical.

"I have great respect for Billy Donovan. There are not five coaches in America better than Billy Donovan. He does a fabulous job. And his concepts are years ahead of others."

In the summer of 2001, Donovan and Fogler got together to talk basketball. No mention was made of Bret Bearup, Mike Miller, or trips to France.

"I think I made a mistake of attacking Eddie Fogler at the media day," Donovan said. "I think I lost my cool there; I was wrong for doing that. Maybe I felt defensive, that somebody was attacking my integrity. Looking back on it, I was wrong to say anything. When I met with Eddie [in the summer of 2001], that situation never came up. I think if Eddie would have had a problem with me, he's the type of guy that would say, 'No, I'm not meeting with you. I don't appreciate what you do.' But I don't think he felt that way."

———

If opposing coaches tried to keep Mike Miller away from Florida because they were afraid he'd help transform the program, they were right. With Miller leading them in scoring, the Gators took another step forward in 1998–99, finishing with a winning SEC record (10-6) for the first time since 1993–94. After picking up their twentieth victory in the SEC Tournament, the Gators had built a strong enough resume to return to the NCAA Tournament. The country was about to find out how far Florida basketball had progressed under Donovan's leadership.

The Gators were seeded sixth in the West Regional and sent all the way to Seattle, where their first-round opponent was Penn. Behind Brent Wright's 15 points and 12 rebounds and 15 points from Miller, the Gators won, 75-61, and advanced to a second-round matchup against Weber State.

Greg Stolt, who scored a school-record 26 points, and Ted Dupay were the heroes as Florida won, 82-74, in overtime. Dupay hit a huge three-pointer with 58.9 seconds to play in regulation that put the Gators ahead, 67-66. Then in overtime, Dupay's three-point play with 2:01 left gave Florida a 75-71 lead. And his two free throws with thirteen seconds left secured the victory.

The trip to the Sweet 16 would be just the third in school history.

Paired against giant-killer Gonzaga, which was forging a reputation of its own, the Gators put up a good fight. The game was close throughout; there were fourteen ties or lead changes in the second half. It took Casey Calvary's tip-in over Wright with 4.4 seconds left to give Gonzaga a 73-72 win.

The loss was devastating to the Gators, but Donovan knew he'd gotten about as much from his young team as he could have hoped. If Florida were to take another step forward, Donovan reasoned, he had to shore up a few weaknesses.

Donovan already had a head start to his second great recruiting class when he signed the best player to come from West Virginia since Jerry West. That was a tough tag for Brett Nelson to live up to, but he brought it on himself. When Nelson averaged 29.4 points per game for St. Albans High in 1997, he became the first sopho-more in West Virginia history to lead the state in scoring. That sort of thing tends to attract attention, which Nelson received in abundant supply throughout his high school career.

Donovan could thank his brief stopover at Marshall for helping him land Nelson. Nelson, fresh out of the seventh grade, attended Donovan's first summer camp at Marshall. Nelson's talent wasn't hard to spot. Donovan made a mental note not to forget the skinny youngster.

Nelson wouldn't forget Donovan, either. In early June 1998, two months before his senior season at St. Albans, Nelson committed to Florida.

Udonis Haslem. *Ron Irby*

Nelson, generally considered one of the top ten players in the country by most recruiting analysts, would help solidify the Gators' backcourt. In the spring of 1999, Donovan needed to solidify his front-court as well. Florida hadn't been a good rebounding team, and Donovan was eager to solve that problem.

Donovan didn't have to look too far for help. Donnell Harvey, of Shellman, Georgia, was generally considered the top high school player in the country. And he lived just four hours away from the Florida campus.

Harvey was a six-foot-eight forward with a ninety-inch wingspan, a blue-collar work ethic, and a knack for rebounding. After Harvey completed his senior season at Randolph-Clay High School, he was chosen the Georgia Player of the Year and *USA Today*'s player of the year, he won the Naismith Trophy (given to the nation's top high school player), and was a first-team *Parade* All-American.

"I've never seen anybody like him at the high school level," recruiting analyst Dave Telep told the *Orlando Sentinel*. "All he does is rebound, and he's very proficient at it. There's no reason to think it'll be any different in college."

Signing Harvey would not be easy. Auburn had been rumored to be the leader for his services, and Georgia, behind new coach Jim Harrick, got into the hunt despite a late start. Once again, Donovan and assistant coach John Pelphrey teamed up to present their pitch. Harvey liked what he heard.

"Something special is about to happen at Florida," Harvey told the *Orlando Sentinel*. "I want to be a part of it."

When Harvey signed with the Gators, it sent shock waves around the SEC. How had Donovan taken Harvey out of the grasp of Auburn and away from home state Georgia? Donovan's critics, fueled by the erroneous contention that he bent rules to sign Mike Miller, assumed Florida bent a few more to land Harvey.

Though Auburn coaches later said they had been outworked by Donovan and thought Harvey's recruitment was clean all the way, Donovan's reputation was beginning to take a beating.

"I'm on the road recruiting in July and hear comments like, 'Florida's recruiting him. You ain't getting him. That's a buy job,'" Donovan said. "That bothers me, but I hear the same thing about some other schools in our league. But I would never repeat that. I know how that feels. It may not be true. Unless I recruit against one of those schools and someone told me flat out that a kid got paid, I'm not gonna sit there because somebody else said something and spread it around."

Along with Nelson and Harvey, Donovan brought in another key recruit. Matt Bonner, a six-foot-ten forward from New Hampshire, had been recruited by North Carolina, Duke, Kansas, and Virginia and was a consensus Top 30 player. Once Donovan locked onto Bonner, he didn't care what other schools were involved.

"I went up to New Hampshire and spent seven straight days watching the kid work out," Donovan said. "I said there's no way he's not going to be a great player. He had all these schools after him, but I just thought the worst thing he could do was tell me no. I about killed myself trying to get involved with Matt Bonner. The same with Mike Miller and Brett Nelson. I knew I had to get guys that loved to play the game and wanted to get better. I needed the gym rats."

Donovan's band of gym rats exceeded even his expectations in the 1999–2000 season as Miller's game continued to evolve, Udonis Haslem became a low-post scoring

100

force, and Ted Dupay, Kenyan Weaks, and Nelson provided perimeter scoring. Donnell Harvey began the season as a starter, but lost his job after returning to Georgia at the New Year's break because he was homesick. Still, he averaged 10 points and a team-high seven rebounds a game.

For the fourth straight season under Donovan, the Gators increased their SEC victory total. This time, they finished 12-4 and tied with Kentucky and Tennessee for the top spot in the Eastern Division, and with those two teams and LSU for the overall regular-season championship.

Florida lost a second round SEC Tournament game to Auburn, but entered the NCAA Tournament as the No. 5 seed in the East Region. The Gators didn't know it as they prepared first-round opponent Butler, but their trip to the Big Dance was going to be a long one.

Were it not for the heroics of Mike Miller, the Gators would have been sent packing after one round. Butler had Florida down 56-49 with 4:17 to play, but rallied to force the game into overtime after two clutch free throws by Udonis Haslem.

Florida had to have a little luck to win in overtime. Butler was ahead 68-67 and had LaVall Jordan at the line for two free throws with 8.1 seconds to play. Jordan missed both shots, giving Florida a chance to win. Miller took the ball from Dupay, slid into the lane between two defenders, and let fly with a shot that went down as time expired. His place in Florida basketball lore was secured.

"I decided in my mind I wanted us to lose the game because of me, or I wanted us to win the game because of me," Miller told the *St. Petersburg Times*. "The play isn't really designed for me, but I don't think Ted [Dupay] had much of a choice. I kind of ran toward the ball. I kind of took it from him."

Florida had no problem in the second round, beating Illinois and former Gator coach Lon Kruger behind 19 points and nine rebounds from Miller and double-figure scoring efforts from Ted Dupay, Brett Nelson, and Udonis Haslem. Nelson, who had struggled at times in his freshman season, had been improving markedly. His 16-point effort against the Illini was a sign of things to come.

So was Florida's victory over top-seeded Duke a sign of things to come. When Donovan took the Florida job, his sights were set on Kentucky, Duke, Kansas, and North Carolina—the game's established powers. Some people laughed when Donovan proclaimed his program capable of attaining elite status.

No one was laughing when the Gators took out the Blue Devils behind 15 points from Nelson. With 5:39 left, Florida trailed, 74-69, but the Gators outscored Duke 18-4 the rest of the way for an 87-78 win. The regional finals and Oklahoma State were next.

Florida wouldn't have to rally to beat the Cowboys. The Gators led by 17 points in the second half and held on for a win that sent them to their second Final Four in six years.

Another established power fell by the wayside in the national semifinals, as Nelson led the way again, scoring 13 points in a 71-59 victory over North Carolina. Florida became the first team since 1986 to beat both Tobacco Road powers, Duke and North Carolina, in the same NCAA Tournament. Michigan State would be the Gators' opponent in the national championship game.

Florida's run was finally stopped by the Spartans, a veteran team led by guard Mateen Cleaves. Though Haslem scored 27 points to establish the Florida's inside scoring, the Gators shot just 28 percent from three-point range and lost to the Spartans 89-76.

Donovan looks back at Florida's NCAA Tournament accomplishments in 1999 and 2000 with pride. He was as surprised as anyone by the run to the championship game and the Gators' school-record twenty-nine victories in 2000.

"I thought when Dupay, Miller, and Haslem got to be juniors and the other guys were a little older, we ought to start turning the corner here a little bit," Donovan recalled. "I never envisioned that those guys would make the impact they made as freshmen. Their freshman year we went to the Sweet 16, and their sophomore year we went to the national championship game and won the SEC. I thought it would take four years for us to start getting competitive and make a run in the NCAA Tournament. It happened a lot quicker than I thought. It had to do with those kids."

———

After the 2000 NCAA championship game, the media was ready to proclaim Florida a budding dynasty. But Donovan's program got derailed twice in the off-season. First Miller announced he would give up his final two years of eligibility and declare for the NBA draft. A few weeks later, Donnell Harvey followed suit. Donovan didn't think either player was ready for the NBA, but he didn't stand in their way. Both were chosen in the first round of the 2000 draft.

"Once Mike and Donnell left, we go from being a top-three [pre-season] pick to maybe not being in the top twenty," Donovan said before the 2000–2001 season began. "I still feel we have a really good team. But we go into the season with a different feel about ourselves."

Florida would have to survive with just ten scholarship players. That situation drove Donovan and his staff in their recruiting efforts. They didn't want to get caught short in subsequent years. By September 2000, the Florida coaches put the finishing touches on a recruiting class most experts were already calling the best in the country. Florida gained commitments from center Kwame Brown and forwards James White and David Lee, all of them *Parade* and McDonald's All-Americans.

The hard work of Donovan and his staff on the recruiting trail was beginning to play dividends. Now, Florida could reasonably expect to do battle with the top programs in the country for the best high school talent and come away with its share.

The 2000–2001 season wasn't as eventful as the previous year had been. Florida, which finished 24-7 and 12-4 in the SEC, did manage to tie Kentucky once again for the league's Eastern Division and overall championships. Haslem became the league's most feared low-post scorer, Nelson moved into the starting lineup and Ted Dupay, the scrappy little guard, won even more admirers than he had already by returning to action twenty days after back surgery.

Postseason play wasn't as kind to the Gators. They lost to Ole Miss in the semifinals of the SEC Tournament and then, after beating Western Kentucky in the first round of the NCAAs, they were ousted by Temple.

By that time, the Kwame Brown Watch had begun.

———

Donovan couldn't have been blamed for looking ahead to the 2001–2002 season, when recruits Brown, James White, and David Lee would join the Gators. But almost from the time Brown committed to Florida, Donovan was also fearful, at least in the back of his mind, that the talented big man would turn pro.

Donovan had never coached a center with Brown's combination of skills. Quick and agile, Brown could run faster and jump higher than most players his size. He could shoot with either hand. Best of all, he was a defensive force. Brown's high school coach in Brunswick, Georgia, Dan Moore, told the *Gainesville Sun* when Brown committed that his star player "could change the game at the collegiate level," if he committed himself to Donovan's player development program.

Donovan couldn't wait to get Brown on campus. And Brown assured Donovan several times in the months after he signed that he would definitely show up in the fall of 2001. Donovan made several trips to Georgia and felt reasonably sure Brown would make good on his promise, but it wasn't to be.

Waiting until the final days before the NBA deadline to declare for the draft, Brown announced he was turning professional. Family was at the heart of his decision; Brown's mother was unable to work because of chronic back problems.

"You couldn't blame the kid for wanting to help out his family," Donovan said.

"Family should be the most important thing in anybody's life. But sure, it was a disappointment not getting to work with Kwame. We could have helped him get better. And he would have made us better, too."

———

Before the season began, Donovan would be disappointed again, this time by a player already on the Gators' roster. In the spring of 2001, a story began circulating around Gainesville that a Florida student had gotten involved with a local bookmaker. Eventually the local media reported that the student was Teddy Dupay, the tough-minded guard who was all but Donovan's alter ego.

Florida athletic director Jeremy Foley quickly began an investigation, and though no details were given, Dupay was suspended on September 7.

"I understand that I have violated NCAA rules," Dupay said during a press conference announcing his departure. "And I take full responsibility for those actions. I put myself into situations that I should not have put myself in, and I'm paying the price for that."

According to a criminal complaint filed days after Dupay's dismissal, the district attorney named Dupay as an uncharged co-defendant along with a former roommate who admitted to placing bets on games. The complaint alleged that Dupay provided his roommate with inside information on whether the Gators could cover a point spread and that Dupay took a portion of winnings.

Dupay denied that charge, but Florida officials wanted to take a proactive approach to the situation.

"The thing about Teddy's situation, there was no proof," Donovan said. "That's what became very difficult. I was not privy to all the police reports and information Jeremy Foley was. Jeremy kept me out of it. He said, 'Trust me on this. I would never do anything to hurt a player here, but this is a problem. If we don't step in as an institution, the NCAA probably will.'

"So the university made a ruling. I had to support the decision of the school, but I've also got to support the kid. He's got nowhere to turn. It was sad. Teddy is a great kid. And he had to pay a very dear price."

Dupay dropped out of school and played wherever he could in the fall of 2001 and the winter of 2002. He started out on a Nike Elite team that played Big Ten schools in preseason exhibitions. Dupay later switched to the ABA's Phoenix Eclipse until the team stopped paying him. He eventually wound up playing for a Venezuelan pro team.

Donovan kept in touch with Dupay as much as he could. Donovan wanted his former player to finish his degree—Dupay needed just six hours—and pursue his dream of becoming a coach.

"He would be a great coach," Donovan said. "I need to help him do that. I want to help him get his feet back on the ground."

———

Donovan wasn't too thrilled about entering the season without his most experienced guard and a center that might have been a difference maker. And he couldn't help but wonder how strong his team could have been had Dupay, Brown, Mike Miller, and Donnell Harvey all stayed around.

The competitor in Donovan would have liked to take a shot at all comers with a team so talented. But Donovan never mentioned the critical loss of personnel, at least not to the media or, especially, his players.

"Coaches always ponder what could have been," Donovan said. "But I was not going to use Teddy or Kwame as an excuse. I start talking about those guys, and now what I'm saying is we can't win. What kind of message am I sending to my team?

"To me, coaching is taking the hand you have and putting your team in a position to win."

Florida
All-SEC Expansion Era Team
F-Mike Miller
F-Matt Bonner
C-Udonis Haslem
G-Dan Cross
G-Brett Nelson
Top Reserves-Andrew DeClerq, Donnell Harvey

That's exactly what Donovan did in his sixth season at Florida. If Dupay wasn't going to be around to run the point, that duty would be handed to Justin Hamilton. If Donovan couldn't put a front line of Miller, Brown, and Harvey on the floor, he would make sure Udonis Haslem and Matt Bonner took their games to another level.

Bonner in particular elevated his game and became an All-SEC player as the Gators, as had been the case the previous season, played shorthanded, three scholarship players below the NCAA limit of thirteen.

Despite the loss of personnel, preseason pollsters were kind to the Gators, who began the season ranked No. 5 by ESPN/USA Today and No. 6 by the Associated Press. Florida started by avenging its loss to Temple in the NCAAs, beating the Owls in the IKON Coaches vs. Cancer Classic. But in the same tournament the next night, the Gators lost to a young Arizona team that had seemingly been depleted after four 2000–2001 starters left for the NBA.

That game convinced Donovan, who had feared the Gators were overrated, that he was right. Still, Florida wouldn't lose again for more than two months, reeling off fourteen straight wins. The streak was ended by an upstart Georgia team, which came to Gainesville without center Steven Thomas, who had been suspended. The Bulldogs outplayed the Gators in the game's all-important closing minutes, a fact that concerned Donovan. That concern was justified.

In their next two games, the Gators failed to perform in the clutch, losing by two points in overtime at Arkansas and by two points to Kentucky. That game was in Gainesville, and might have been Florida's most critical loss in SEC play.

The Gators regrouped with four straight wins, but lost three of its last five games. Kentucky's 70-67 victory in the season finale cost Florida a first-round bye in the SEC Tournament.

Asked to sum up the regular season, Donovan did so with his usual positive spin. Teddy Dupay and Kwame Brown didn't enter into his assessment.

"It was a good regular season," Donovan said before the Gators' first-round SEC Tournament game. "We had some chances at Kentucky and Alabama and at Arkansas to really put ourselves in position to be right there with Alabama [as the SEC overall champion]. But that didn't happen. But all those games were on the road. To win in this league on the road is tough. For us, playing in the SEC, to be 21-7 with our non-conference schedule, I'm pleased.

"RPI-wise this league is No. 1 in the country. I'm hoping those experiences will be very, very good learning experiences and ending up helping us."

Unfortunately for Donovan and the Gators, their experiences in close games wouldn't help them in March. For the second straight year, postseason play would be unkind to Florida.

Chapter Five

Georgia

I t was nearly an hour after his team had beaten Tennessee in a key Southeastern Conference game in early January, and Georgia coach Jim Harrick was still on the floor of the Bulldogs' Stegeman Coliseum, glad-handing fans and well-wishers, talking to the press, and just trying to absorb and appreciate all that was going on around him.

The game itself had given Harrick reason enough to go home and sleep like a baby, a luxury of which college basketball coaches are often deprived, depending on the outcome of a game. On this night, the ending couldn't have been scripted any better for Georgia or more conducive to a good night's sleep for its coach. The game had been a typical Southeastern Conference matchup—two talented teams going at one another for forty minutes, taking punches and throwing some, leaving nothing on the floor. Georgia had led much of the way, but when Tennessee's Ron Slay buried a three-pointer with 15.3 seconds to play, the score was tied at 70. The Bulldogs called time with 11.3 seconds to set up a final shot.

Harrick called a backdoor play complete with single and double screens, but as Georgia point guard Rashad Wright raced down the floor, he saw his teammates weren't getting into position fast enough. Instead of wasting precious time, Wright drove the lane, hoping to slip past the Volunteers for a layup. But when a Tennessee player stripped Wright of the ball, it looked as though the game was headed to overtime.

Typical of the way the Bulldogs' seemingly improbable season had transpired to that point, two Georgia players, Chris Daniels and Ezra Williams, were in position to get their hands on the ball. Knowing something had to be done quickly, Williams commanded Daniels to let him have the ball, stepped back past the three-point line and let fly with a high-arcing jumper that swished through the net as time expired.

The shot touched off bedlam on the floor as Williams, his arms raised high, turned and saluted the Georgia student section before being mobbed by his teammates. Coupled with the Bulldogs' victory at Kentucky three nights earlier, this latest win would finally serve notice to the country that Georgia, which had been picked to finish fifth or sixth in the SEC's Eastern Division, had defied those predictions and had become one of the nation's elite teams. The victory was the Bulldogs' fourteenth against two losses. A day later, they would turn up in the national rankings for the first time since a one-week stay the season before. Experts around the country hailed Harrick for doing perhaps the best coaching job in Division I. Few could dispute that contention, considering Harrick began the year with just seven scholarship players, nearly all of them unproven sophomores.

"It's been fun," Harrick said. "My wife and I were talking about that the other day. This is so rewarding. The rewarding part is in that just three years, we're there. This hasn't been a traditional basketball school. Too see the crowd and the excitement in the state of Georgia. . . . I'm having fun here. The people appreciate you."

Even before the Bulldogs' great start to the 2001–2002 season, Harrick had considered the Georgia job his career mulligan. Having been unceremoniously fired in 1996 from his beloved UCLA, where he remains the only Bruin coach since the great John Wooden to have won a national championship, Harrick stayed out of coaching for a year before resurfacing at Rhode Island for the 1997–98 season. Harrick, who led the Rams to the NCAA Tournament's Midwest Region finals in his first season, wouldn't be in Rhode Island long.

In 1999, Georgia athletic director Vince Dooley, badly in need of an experienced coach, put in a call to Harrick. A move to the competitive SEC appealed to Harrick, and he accepted the job. He flew to Athens for a press conference, but after returning to Rhode Island, he had a change of heart. Georgia's antinepotism rule would have prevented Harrick from hiring his son Jim, Jr., as an assistant. Harrick, intensely loyal to family and friends, was prepared to give up the job that meant so much to his career comeback.

The story goes that if Dooley, who had been on a trip with his grandson, had brought his Rolodex with him, Buzz Peterson, then coach at Appalachian State, would have been offered the Georgia job. But by the time Dooley returned to Athens, Harrick had changed his mind again, after being convinced by his family that he should jump at the chance to coach in the SEC. This time, he assured Dooley his commitment to Georgia was firm.

In the aftermath of the 'Dogs' big victory over Tennessee, Harrick recalled that day and was glad he'd come to his senses about leaving Rhode Island.

"Not very many guys leave a place like UCLA, get recycled, and come back to a school like this, in a conference like the SEC," Harrick said.

At 63, Harrick was indeed getting a second chance that few college coaches who get fired or resign amid a scandal ever do. His 1996 ouster at UCLA brought a shocking and disappointing end to a successful eight-year tenure. Just two weeks before the season began, university chancellor Charles Young fired Harrick for falsifying an expense report and then trying to cover it up. Harrick had entertained a group of thirteen people, including recruits Earl Watson and brothers Jarron and Jason Collins, for dinner. NCAA rules were broken when, in addition to the three UCLA players who were hosting the recruits, Harrick paid for meals for two more of his players, Charles O'Bannon and Cameron Dollar. When confronted by UCLA athletic director Pete Dalis, Harrick said Dollar and O'Bannon weren't part of the group. A UCLA investigation revealed that Harrick asked assistant coach Michael Holton, who was at the dinner, to misrepresent the facts.

Harrick admitted to the wrongdoing, but thought Dalis had been looking for a reason to get rid of him, even though the program was on as good a foundation as it had been since Wooden won his last of ten national championships two decades before.

The pain of his departure from UCLA hadn't left Harrick when he finally reported for duty in Athens. Though he had enjoyed a nice run at Rhode Island—coaching the Rams to the NCAA Tournament's Elite Eight in 1998—Harrick looked at the Georgia job as an opportunity to make a point. Sixteen games into the 2001–2002 season, Harrick's point was well taken. After having inherited a program that began a downward spiral during the two-year coaching tenure of Ron Jirsa, Harrick turned around Georgia's fortunes so quickly and with seemingly so little talent at his disposal that even his harshest critics had to admire the job he'd done. As for his friends, no one who knows Harrick well was all that surprised about Georgia's start.

"I'm not surprised only because I worked with Jim for seven years," said Alabama coach Mark Gottfried, an assistant to Harrick at UCLA from 1988 to 1995. "He's very, very good at what he does. What he's really good at is looking at what he has, figuring out what they need to do and who needs to do what, and then shaping them into a team."

"Jim Harrick can flat-out coach," said former Citadel, East Tennessee State, and North Carolina State coach Les Robinson, who grew up with Harrick in West Virginia. "When you can win at Pepperdine, UCLA, Rhode Island, and Georgia— four uniquely different schools—that's special. You're talking about four different sets of circumstances and four different challenges. Jim's met them all."

True enough, Harrick didn't need a program the likes of UCLA, with all of its great tradition and championships, to help him showcase the coaching skills he had spent a lifetime refining. A football school that had enjoyed only sporadic success and interest in basketball would do nicely.

The third time proved to be the charm for James Holland. While an assistant coach at San Diego State in the mid-1990s, Holland had gotten to know Harrick, then coach at UCLA. Harrick, whose son Jim, Jr., was also an assistant on the San Diego State staff, would occasionally drive over to watch the Aztecs play. He always found time to talk basketball with Holland. Holland made it a point to speak to Harrick when the two crossed paths on the recruiting trail.

When Lorenzo Romar left UCLA after the 1995–96 season to take the top job at Pepperdine, Holland talked to Harrick about joining his staff. But Harrick eventually hired former UCLA player Michael Holton. Holland understood, and vowed to keep in contact with Harrick. As it turned out, had Holland been hired at UCLA, he wouldn't have worked for Harrick, who was fired before the 1996–97 season began.

"We talked even more after that," Holland recalled. "You got to see a different side of his personality than you saw when he was the head coach at UCLA. I felt we had developed a special bond."

When Harrick was hired at Rhode Island, he again talked to Holland about a job on his staff. But again he hired a former UCLA player, Larry Farmer.

"I could understand from the professional side of it," Holland said. "Jim was trying to re-establish things at Rhode Island. He had to go with somebody he knew. And I didn't have any ties to the Northeast."

Harrick didn't forget Holland, and when he left Rhode Island for Georgia in 1999, he put in a call to Holland, who by that time had become associate head coach at San Diego State.

"We had spoken at the Final Four earlier," Holland said. "I let Jim know that I'd still be interested in working for him. When he called to offer me a job at Georgia, it didn't take me very long to say yes. Working for Jim was something I'd always wanted to do."

The move turned out to be beneficial for both men, and for Georgia basketball. Harrick needed an assistant who didn't have to be told what to do. And Holland, whose basketball travels had taken him away from his North Carolina roots most of his adult life—he even spent a year after college touring with the Harlem Globetrotters—wanted to get closer to home. There was an added benefit that Holland saw in working for Harrick. With an eye toward being a head coach some day, Holland wanted to learn from a master of the craft.

Harrick was hired at Georgia in early April, so he started in full recruiting scramble mode as he tried to restock Georgia's roster. The Bulldogs had sustained heavy graduation losses, and worse, figured to lose first-team All-SEC pick Jumaine Jones, a six-foot-seven sophomore who eventually decided to declare for the NBA draft. Georgia needed some frontcourt players, but Harrick was hired too late to have a serious chance at Donnell Harvey, a power forward from Shellman, Georgia, who was considered by some the top high school player in the country. Harvey eventually signed with Florida. Several other top recruits in the South had already signed or committed.

Given Georgia's pressing needs, Harrick eventually decided to go with a quick fix and signed two junior college players, Anthony Evans and Shon Coleman. With his frontcourt fortified, Harrick, who had already hired Holland and retained Michael Hunt from the previous Georgia staff, instructed his assistants to think about the future. Harrick's goal was to mine the state of Georgia for talent. For years, Georgia high school stars had consistently turned up on other SEC rosters. Harrick wanted to change that. The players Holland and Hunt uncovered would form the nucleus of the surprising 2001–2002 team.

"This is a great recruiting base," Harrick said. "The whole state of Georgia. Georgia is much like Southern California in terms of the talent produced here. When I got here, we wanted to put a fence around the state, to keep in-state kids at home to play for the University of Georgia."

"We wanted to make an effort to recruit kids in-state," Holland said. "That hadn't been a strength, for whatever reason, for a long, long time. We had heard there wasn't a great relationship between the state's high school coaches and the University of Georgia. We were trying to bridge that."

Hunt, a native Georgian, already had his recruiting territory staked out. Holland, who had coached previously at Murray State and South Carolina, knew his way around the state, too. One of the first calls he put in was to Lee Hill, coach at Statesboro High School.

"I asked him about Kwame Brown [a rising junior from Brunswick, Georgia, who later signed with Florida, then skipped college and was the top pick in the 2001 NBA draft]," Holland said. "I wanted to get a head start on him and wanted Lee to tell me who I should contact."

Eventually, the conversation turned to point guards.

"I asked him who the best point guard in the state was," Holland recalled. "A lot of coaches will recommend their own guys, and Lee said he had a guy who might be the best point guard in the state. You're wary sometimes when a coach pumps his own player, but Lee had several good point guards play for him over the years. I trusted his judgement."

The point guard Hill recommended was Rashad Wright, who was largely unnoticed because he didn't play for one of the major AAU teams in Georgia, the Stars or the Celtics. Both are based out of Atlanta. It didn't help Wright's cause that, in the summer before his senior year, he suffered an Achilles tendon injury that kept him out of

111

the Peach Jam, an annual tournament in Augusta, Georgia, that is attended by scores of college coaches.

"Rashad was a sleeper," Holland said. "The impressive things to me were that he had size and he'd always played the position. He wasn't an off guard we were going to have to convert, which rarely works. And his brother was Marko Wright, who'd played at Cincinnati, so he had good bloodlines."

Holland went to see Wright during the latter's senior season and came away impressed. "He jumped, handled the ball, he passed the ball," Holland said. "His team was winning. You walk away and you wonder what's wrong with him, why hasn't anybody noticed him? I brought some tape back to the office, and that was the first reaction coach Harrick had."

Holland did some background checks on Wright and, much to his delight, found nothing negative. "We decided he was solid," Holland said, "and we signed him. You never know how tough a kid is until you get him, but the first thing we learned about Rashad was that he was very coachable and wanted to get better."

With a point guard, albeit an unheralded one, in the fold, the Georgia staff went looking for frontcourt help.

An obvious place to start looking was the AAU circuit. The Georgia Stars, one of two powerful teams based out of Atlanta, were loaded with talent. Kwame Brown stood out, as did Larry Turner, a six-foot-eleven athlete who, like Brown, was heading into his junior year. Hidden between those two players was the unsung hero of the Stars, six-foot-eight, 235-pound Steven Thomas.

"We saw every game the Stars played when we could get out on the road," Harrick said. "We kept noticing that the coach would take Kwame Brown out, put him back in. Take him out, put him back in. Thomas never came out. That coach knew something."

"We saw Steven play a lot," Holland said. "Whereas Brown and Larry did it with flash and dunks, Steven did it with defense and rebounding. He just always ended up with 12 points and 11 rebounds. And he guarded people like Tyson Chandler and Eddy Curry and didn't back down. He played hard, worked hard. He was a guy we felt like you just can't go wrong taking."

The only other upper-level Division I school to show interest in Thomas was Auburn. Like Wright, Thomas had played for a smaller school and wasn't widely known. His AAU experience helped, but ultimately, it was only because the Georgia coaches looked past Brown and Turner. (Georgia went back for Turner the next year, but he was academically ineligible for the 2001–2002 season and wound up at a prep school.)

"On a team by himself, Steven might have been recruited a lot heavier," Holland said. "But he was on a team with a number of talented guys. It wasn't just Kwame and Larry. You had Gerald Riley, who went to Georgetown, and Marvin Lewis, who signed with Georgia Tech. You really had to know what you were looking for."

Thomas wasn't ranked anywhere close to the top one hundred high school recruits nationally—one service listed him No. 254—but the Georgia coaches knew his background. Thomas was Carrollton High School's all-time scoring leader, having produced 2,087 points in his career. It was obvious to Holland and Hunt that Thomas could do more than dirty work.

"We watched a lot of tape," Holland said. "We noticed Steven could shoot the foul line jump shot. And we found out there was a toughness about him."

"I can remember sitting in a gym in Augusta, watching Steven play," Hunt said. "I looked over at James, and we kept asking each other, 'What's wrong with this kid?'"

Holland and Hunt eventually decided nothing was wrong with Thomas. Now all they had to do was convince Harrick to take a chance on the big man.

Two years later, after a December 2001 victory against Georgia Tech, Harrick thought back to the conversation he had with his assistants about Thomas. Thomas had just scored a career-high 24 points, grabbed nine rebounds, blocked two shots and made two steals. "[Holland and Hunt] had to convince me to take Thomas," Harrick said. "I didn't think he was quite good enough, but they did."

Jim Harrick. *UGA Sports Communications/Bill Smith*

The Georgia staff would sign one more building-block recruit for the 2000 class. Chris Daniels, a six-foot-seven forward from Georgia basketball hotbed Albany, had earned considerably more attention than Wright or Thomas. He hovered near the top one hundred of a lot of recruiting analysts and his final list of schools included Tennessee and a pair of ACC teams, Georgia Tech and Florida State.

Harrick liked what he saw of Daniels in AAU competition, paying particular attention to his defense. Holland and Hunt liked Daniels's versatility.

"He was a do-it-all guy on his high school team," Holland said. "He was a six-foot-seven guy who played inside or out on the wing. Teams would press his high school team, and he'd bring it up some. He was a utility-type guy who did a little bit of everything."

To top it all off, Daniels actually wanted to play for Georgia, despite the hard times the Bulldogs endured in Harrick's first season when they were 10-20. "I just felt comfortable going to Georgia," Daniels recalled. "I wanted to be a part of rebuilding the program."

The only flaw Georgia coaches could see in Daniels was his jump shot.

"It was a little unorthodox," Holland said. "Initially, that was a concern, because we thought that if he ever got into a shooting slump, we wouldn't be able to help him out of it because his shot was unorthodox."

Eventually, the numbers added up in Daniels's favor.

"He'd have games where he was 13-for-16, 15-for-17," Holland said. "He'd step out and hit some threes. After a while, we realized that he knew what shots to take, and when to take them."

Two years later that was even more apparent as Daniels was a huge factor in the Bulldogs' surprising success. Despite his slender frame, Daniels became one of the SEC's top rebounders because of his willingness to relentlessly pursue the basketball. And he could score, too. When Daniels put together a 21-point, 14-rebound, 4-assist, 3-blocked shot night against South Alabama in a mid-December 2001 game, the Georgia staff knew he had arrived.

"He creates matchup problems for people," Holland said. "He's a perimeter guy, even though he plays the post. And the kid's a warrior."

Along with Ezra Williams, a Top 100 player from Marietta, Georgia, who had been recruited by Ron Jirsa's staff in 1998, Harrick had the makings of a lineup that would shock the SEC in 2002. But he couldn't have foreseen that when the Georgia staff wrapped up its recruiting efforts after the 1999–2000 season. And he couldn't have known the Bulldogs were going to get some more help from a pair of brothers who wanted to come home.

————

Jarvis and Jonas Hayes, who transferred to Georgia from Western Carolina in 1999 and sat out the 2000–2001 season, are identical twins. Born five minutes apart, the six-foot-six, 200-pound sophomore forwards would be impossible to tell apart if Jarvis didn't shave his head and Jonas hadn't spent a bit more time in the weight room, bulking up his biceps. The brothers are fiercely loyal to one another, to the point where they insisted that they played college basketball together, even if the school they chose was a mid- or low-major Division I program.

114

"We're inseparable," Jonas said.

"Our bond is unbreakable," Jarvis said.

Despite that close bond, the brothers couldn't remember ever being able to read one another's thoughts, or feel one another's pain—at least not until an early December game against Minnesota in Athens.

Thanks in large part to a swarming defense, the Bulldogs jumped all over their visitors from the Big Ten. Georgia built a 19-6 with 12:33 to play and looked to be in command until play stopped at around the ten-minute mark. As Georgia fans looked on in stunned silence, Jonas Hayes ran screaming toward the Georgia bench, then dove onto the floor in obvious pain, his legs flailing wildly.

Unbeknownst to his teammates at the time, Jonas had suffered a bizarre injury when a Minnesota player threw a two-handed pass to a teammate. As he released the ball, his hands came down on top of Jonas's left finger, causing his bone to pop through his skin. Not a compound fracture, this injury, as Georgia sports information director Tim Hix quickly informed the media, was an "open dislocation."

Jarvis did his best not to look at his brother as he writhed in pain, but the injury clearly affected his play in the first half. "I just wasn't in the game after my brother got hurt," he said. "I was out of it."

At halftime, instead of going with the team to the locker room, Jarvis headed to his brother's side. "I saw they were stitching him up," Jarvis said. "It made me sick to my stomach. It was so weird. Tonight, for the first time, I could feel his pain. When I saw him on the ground, I just said, 'Oh man.' And then my finger started hurting. It was an odd feeling. Growing up, people always asked me if I could feel his pain. I always said no. But tonight I actually did. I was running around holding my finger. It's true. I can feel his pain."

Jim Harrick noticed Jarvis Hayes's reaction after he returned to the locker room.

"He went in there and saw his brother and he was very emotional," Harrick said. The canny old coach knew he could capitalize on that emotion.

Early in the second half, Jarvis Hayes tossed in an eighteen-foot jumper. Harrick knew he was back.

"He came back and hit his first one," Harrick said. "So we called the next one inside."

Hayes scored.

"Then we called the next one off a screen."

Hayes knocked down a three-pointer.

"Then we called the next one off the wing."

Hayes swished another three.

When the outburst was over, Georgia led, 57-36, and the game was essentially over. This wasn't the first Georgia victory directly attributable to the Hayes twins, and it would be far from the last. But it clearly demonstrated that in this package deal, Harrick landed a couple of players whose physical skills were exceeded only by their emotions and their amazing bond, traits that, in the heat of a game, can be as important as making jumpers or grabbing rebounds.

And to think the Hayes boys didn't start their career at Georgia.

After making it clear in 1999 that they wanted to play together in college, the twins, who are from Atlanta, didn't have many offers to sift through. Jarvis was considered the better prospect and perhaps could have signed with Georgia or another upper-major school. But when he insisted on playing with Jonas, the only schools that offered scholarships to both players were Western Carolina, Mercer, and Jacksonville State.

That struck Harrick as odd, especially after he saw the twins play in the Georgia North-South All-Star game in the summer of 1999. Harrick, who had replaced the deposed Ron Jirsa as Georgia coach two months earlier, had gone there to see his freshman recruit, Ezra Williams, play, but came away impressed with the Hayes brothers.

"Jarvis was far and above the best player on the floor that night," Harrick said. "I came back and asked my assistant, Michael Hunt [who has served on the previous Georgia staff under Jirsa], why hadn't they taken him. And he told me [Jirsa] didn't want to give both of them a scholarship."

"I wanted to take them," Hunt recalled. "My thinking was you can never have too many good in-state kids. But the thinking with coach Jirsa was probably that we'd already signed Ezra and we had D. A. Layne ahead of them. Maybe he thought there wasn't room."

Jarvis Hayes took Jirsa's decision hard, much more so than his brother. "I was almost in tears when I found out Georgia wasn't going to recruit me," he said. "I didn't know what it was."

"Coach Jirsa came to a couple of our games in high school," Jonas Hayes said. "But then he stopped coming. I wasn't as disappointed. We knew we were going to play somewhere together."

That somewhere turned out to be Cullowhee, North Carolina, home of the mighty Catamounts of Western Carolina. Cullowhee, nestled next to the Great Smoky Mountains, is in a beautiful setting, but it's a tad remote. One former Western Carolina coach, Steve Cottrell, said he survived there by recruiting players who loved to hunt and fish. Another ex-Western coach, Benny Dees, made it a point to recruit junior college players. "By time they realize there's nothing to do [socially] here, they've got one year left and it's too late to transfer," Dees said.

116

The Hayes twins made the best of their brief stay at Western Carolina. Jarvis averaged 17.1 points and 5.4 rebounds and was chosen the Southern Conference Freshman of the Year. He was the first freshman in forty years to lead that league in scoring. Jonas averaged eight points and five rebounds and shot 63 percent from the floor. He also proved that, like his brother, he could handle upper-major competition by scoring 20 points against Northwestern, then coached by the maniacally defensive-minded Kevin O'Neill.

None of this was lost on Jim Harrick.

"I kept watching [Western Carolina's] scores and saw how many points [the Hayes brothers] were scoring," Harrick said. "I knew what they were doing, and I kept thinking how much they could both have helped us. I mean, we won ten games my first year here. What are you talking about?"

Imagine Harrick's delight when, after Western Carolina cleaned house in early 2000, firing coach Phil Hopkins and his staff, he received a call from James Hayes, the twins' father.

"He says, 'Coach, I've got these two boys and they want to come home and play for Georgia,'" Harrick said. "I said, 'James, you've got two scholarships. Get 'em up here. I'll take 'em right now.'

"I didn't hesitate one second. It's funny. We have a big, huge recruiting budget. I mean *huge*. We go all over the country looking for players. And I get a phone call. We don't spend ten cents recruiting these guys."

Harrick did call Western Carolina and made sure the twins had obtained their release. Georgia was free to sign the brothers, who didn't even consider another school after making the decision to transfer.

"It was a dream come true," Jarvis said. "Growing up, playing in the backyard, we used to dream about us playing together on the same team at a big-time university."

"I thought about being a Bulldog," Jonas said. "It's a dream come true to share that with my brother. We're like best friends. It's a special relationship, and to be able to play together at Georgia, it's unbelievable."

"It's a marriage made in heaven," Harrick said. "They wanted to come home. They're as happy as can be, their parents are happy, and the head coach is real happy."

The twins sat out the 2000–2001 season as redshirts, but showed Harrick in practice that his faith in taking both brothers was more than justified. While the prognosticators predicted a gloomy year for Georgia in 2001–2002, Harrick, who had seen the Hayes brothers in practice every day the season before, knew he had a couple of secret weapons to unleash on the SEC. Jarvis in particular.

"A lot of times in practice I said to myself, 'Wow, this guy [Jarvis] is playing great,'"

Harrick recalled. "Last year, the second unit beat the first unit nearly every single day. I'd get on the first unit, but I really knew why they got beat. It was because of him."

In the fall of 2001, after the brothers had regained their eligibility, Harrick said that Jonas, not his higher-flying brother, was the best player in practice.

"They're great kids and can both play," Harrick said. "It's funny that one's a perimeter player and one's an inside player. Jarvis is a fiery guy. He can do things on his own, go get his shot, and he's a splendid athlete. Jonas is more happy-go-lucky and he's a system player. He comes off screens. He does what he's supposed to do. He's a great shooter to fifteen feet. People don't realize that. But they're going to."

Jonas began to prove his worth after his brother injured his right knee in a late-November practice. Jarvis had gotten off to a great start, scoring 40 points in an exhibition and averaging nearly 16 points through the first three regular-season games. He scored 19 points and grabbed seven rebounds in an upset of nationally ranked Georgetown in the Hall of Fame Tip-Off Classic and was chosen the game's MVP. Hayes went for 19 again in a win over Georgia Southern. Then came the knee injury, and when it happened, the Georgia coaches and players feared the worst—that Jarvis had torn his anterior cruciate ligament. An MRI revealed the injury was far less serious—a sprained medial collateral ligament. Hayes was supposed to miss two to four weeks.

When Jarvis went down, Jonas filled in admirably, leading the Bulldogs with 14 points and eight rebounds as Georgia defeated pesky Samford, and scoring 17 points in a win over Colorado. But Jonas injured an ankle in the Colorado game. Not surprisingly, without the services of both twins, the Bulldogs lost their first game of the season, to Georgia State.

Jarvis returned two weeks ahead of schedule to play against Minnesota, and Jonas was back, too, only to injure his finger on the freak play.

"It was agonizing," Jonas said. "The worst thing I've ever felt. When they were trying to pop it back in, it wouldn't go at first. I was biting on something, or somebody. I don't know what. It's funny, my brother and I keep getting hurt. We're the most injured people on campus."

The brothers' teammates made sure to point out how brittle the twins had been. In practice the next day, redshirt forward Damien Wilkins, a North Carolina State transfer and nephew of former Bulldog great Dominque Wilkins, gave Jonas some serious grief, perfectly imitating his scream, dive, and kick routine of the night before. The players had a big laugh, but Jonas just absorbed it all with a smile. If he was going to get hurt and made fun of, better it be in Athens than Cullowhee.

118

Georgia fans have come to look on Harrick's first season as an aberration. The Bulldogs, who had appeared in post-season play the previous four seasons, took a drastic tumble to 10-20 in 1999–2000. That team sorely missed three key seniors from the season before: guards G. G. Smith (the son of former Georgia coach Tubby Smith), Ray Harrison, and Michael Chadwick.

Harrick might have been able to absorb those losses and still put a decent team on the floor had sophomore Jumaine Jones not decided he would rather sit on the bench of an NBA team than refine his skills for another season in college. And Harrick might have been able to overcome the loss of Jones had Ezra Williams been declared eligible by the NCAA.

The debacle involving Williams's eligibility irks Harrick to this day. Williams, a six-foot-four shooting guard, was by far the best player signed by former coach Ron Jirsa, who was on Tubby Smith's staff for two seasons and replaced the latter when he left for Kentucky in 1997. Williams was a consensus Top 50 player coming out of Marietta High School, where as a senior he averaged 26.5 points and led the Blue Devils to the 1999 Class AAAA state championship. Williams's exploits in the state tournament—he scored 38, 29, and 29 points in the three games—weren't lost on Harrick when he took over for Jirsa, who had been fired after a 15-15 disappointment that ended with a loss to Clemson in the 1999 NIT. Harrick had to dust off his recruiting spiel for Williams, who didn't take the news of Jirsa's departure well. For a time, he considered asking for his release and transferring to another school.

Williams was convinced to honor his scholarship to Georgia, but he eventually fell victim to his own honesty, barred by the NCAA from playing his freshman season.

Ironically, Williams's high school academic record had been cleared by the NCAA Clearinghouse, this despite the fact he hadn't passed the science portion of the Georgia High School graduation tests.

Three days before the fall 1999 semester, Williams shared that information with university officials. Technically, he wasn't yet a high school graduate, but he was allowed to enroll in classes at Georgia. Williams couldn't participate in preseason drills with the team until the matter was resolved.

Georgia appealed Williams's case to the NCAA, which took until December 6 to decide that Williams—who had taken and passed the Georgia's high school science test on November 15—wasn't eligible. Georgia appealed a second time, only to be denied again. The bad news didn't come until the first week in January. In denying the appeal, the NCAA said Georgia should have taken Williams out of classes in the fall semester so he could have preserved eligibility for the spring semester.

Harrick was angry throughout the appeal process, but avoided blasting the NCAA. When the NCAA refused to relent after Williams's second appeal, Harrick went off.

"The NCAA reared its ugly head and crucified another student-athlete by nailing him to the cross," Harrick told the *Athens Banner-Herald*. "Here's a young man who is absolutely, unequivocally eligible. Now if the school made a mistake, then punish the school. But the young man did everything adults asked him to do. To punish the kid is unconstitutional."

Though Williams was disappointed by the NCAA's ruling, he decided to stay at Georgia, even though he had to pay his own way in the spring semester. As a non-qualifier he could have been recruited by another school. The full benefits of Williams's decision to stay wouldn't be known for another two years.

Williams might have made a difference and prevented some of Georgia's 20 defeats in 1999–2000, but he resigned himself to watching games from the stands and having sophomore eligibility the next season.

In 2000–2001, Williams gave Georgia fans a glimpse of what they had missed the year before. He scored 23 points in his college debut against Georgia State, and two games later produced 21 against Indiana State. But rookie mistakes began to crop up in games against Utah and California, where he was shut out. In SEC games, Williams also started strong, scoring 30 points against Auburn, 18 against Ole Miss, and 24 against Florida in the Bulldogs' first three games. Again, Williams tapered off as his jump shot went AWOL. Though he finished as Georgia's second leading scorer, Williams shot just 41 percent from the field and 29 percent from three-point range. His assists (71) barely outnumbered his turnovers (69).

The Georgia coaching staff acknowledged that Williams's forced season on the sidelines a year earlier had hurt his progress.

"Any time you take a year off, especially when you were as young as Ezra was, it hurts you," Georgia assistant James Holland said. "There's a certain speed in high school you play at, and then the game speeds up when you get to college. Things happen so much quicker. Ezra lost that natural transition by having to sit out. Not only could he not play, he couldn't practice."

Harrick understood all that, but there were times when he seriously considered asking Williams, whose work ethic the coach questioned, to leave.

"I was ready to throw him off," Harrick recalled. "He wasn't doing what he needed to do on or off the floor. He was overweight. He was out of condition. I just hated him at the end of that year. And he brought it on himself."

Before Harrick could run Williams off, he began to come around. The catalyst was a first-round game in the 2001 SEC Tournament. The Bulldogs were desperately trying to earn an NCAA Tournament berth, but lost to LSU, which at the time seemed a crippling blow. Williams blamed himself. With thirty seconds to play Williams threw the ball away on an in-bounds play. He compounded the problem by fouling LSU's Collis Temple III, who hit two free throws that gave the Tigers the lead. Georgia guard Rashad Wright missed a shot at the buzzer that could have won the game.

"I put a lot of pressure on myself after that," Williams said. "It made me want to focus myself mentally and do whatever I could to become a better player and a better person."

"Ideally, you'd like that switch to go on in a young person's head at age nineteen," Harrick said. "You want them to do what you want, and you want them to do it now. Sometimes it takes until a kid's twenty or twenty-three until the switch goes on. I think Ezra woke up after last year and realized he wasn't doing the right thing."

Williams got serious about his basketball, but still needed some none-too-gentle prodding from Harrick to get his academic affairs in order. Williams had a chance in the summer of 2001 to earn eighteen credit hours and be on pace to graduate in four years, which, under NCAA rules, would allow him to regain his lost year of eligibility.

The summer didn't start off well for Williams. He took a trip to Mexico with a group of students from Georgia

Jarvis Hayes. *UGA Sports Communications/Bill Smith*

and earned nine credits. But he left the trip early, incurring Harrick's wrath.

"He bolted out early on that Mexico trip," Harrick said. "When he came back, I told him he was going to have to sign a contract, or I wouldn't send him to Washington, D.C., which was another trip he wanted to go on. He'd embarrassed me, and I got mad at him. I told him he couldn't continue to do this, and that I couldn't win with guys like him."

Williams took Harrick's urging to heart and was a model citizen on the Washington trip. "The first day he was up there he met [Alan] Greenspan and fell in love with it,"

Harrick said. "He also talked to congressmen, went to the Treasury, visited the FBI. He loved it, was on time, did his work, and the teacher praised him."

In addition to his game and his academics, Williams worked on his body. After his first season, Williams allowed himself to swell to 245 pounds. Before he showed up for fall practice in 2001, he was down to a solid 218.

"In the off-season, I really worked hard on my weaknesses," Williams said. "I just came back and dedicated myself to the team."

Williams's work was evident as his junior season began. He scored 26 points against Furman in the Bulldogs' opener, then scored at least 20 in five of his next seven games. Williams cooled off a bit after that, but remained one of the SEC's leading scorers. In the second week of January, he showed the country how far he had progressed, scoring 20 points—with six three-pointers—in an upset win over Kentucky in Lexington, and 22 more against Tennessee. Williams made five three-pointers in that game, including the game winner as time expired.

"Last summer, Ezra turned the corner and grew up a little bit," Harrick said. "I haven't had to say a word to him since. He's been one of our leaders."

———

At Georgia, just like at every Southeastern Conference school save Kentucky and Vanderbilt, football is the primary focus of the fans, and it always will be. But indicative of the changing times in the SEC has been the willingness of Georgia officials to change coaches if they thought the basketball program wasn't going in the right direction. More specifically, the NCAA Tournament is Georgia's goal, and a failure to get there cost two good men their jobs in the 1990s.

Hugh Durham had served Georgia faithfully and successfully for seventeen seasons, taking over in 1978 and producing fourteen winning seasons and ten trips to postseason tournaments, five NITs and five NCAAs. The highlight of Durham's tenure in Athens was the Bulldogs' appearance in the 1983 Final Four, which came, ironically, the year after Dominique Wilkins left for the NBA.

The Final Four might have been the high point in Durham's career, but it wasn't Georgia's last taste of postseason play. Even as late as 1991, the Bulldogs played in the NCAAs, but the program began a gradual downturn after that. Georgia was 15-14 in 1991–92 and 1992–93, and slipped below .500 the next season at 14-16. Durham began taking some heat because his team was floundering despite the presence of a strong 1993 recruiting class that included forwards Carlos Strong and Shandon Anderson, center Terrell Bell, and guard Pertha Robinson. So heralded was that group of recruits that some fans and recruiting analysts referred to it as the "Fab Five II," an unfair reference to the great early-1990s Michigan class that included Chris Webber and Jalen Rose.

There wouldn't be any Final Four appearances in this Fab Five's future. The best the group could do in Durham's tenure was an 18-10 record and a trip to the NIT in 1994–95. Given the disappointment of the previous three seasons, that represented progress, but it wasn't enough to save Durham's job. He was forced out, and a national search began to find a replacement.

It didn't take long for the search to center on Tulsa coach Tubby Smith. Kentucky athletic director C. M. Newton strongly encouraged his Georgia counterpart, Vince Dooley, to take a look at Smith, who had served for two seasons as an assistant on Rick Pitino's staff at Kentucky. Newton had given Smith a ringing endorsement when the latter was hired at Tulsa, and he didn't disappoint. In four seasons at Tulsa, Smith produced a 79-43 record. In his last two seasons, the Golden Hurricane was 23-8 and 24-8 and each time advanced to the NCAA Tournament's Sweet 16.

Though Smith loved Tulsa and could have stayed there the rest of his career, the prospect of returning to the South and coaching a team in the SEC appealed to him.

"I bet I turned down five jobs, five good jobs, while I was the coach at Tulsa," Smith said. "I always said that if I was going to change jobs, I was going to go to a place where they would give you the time and the resources, and coach Dooley offered that."

Smith didn't go into the situation blind. He was well aware of Georgia's recent history. When Durham led the Bulldogs to the 1990 SEC championship, Smith was a Kentucky assistant. Smith knew what would be asked of him if took the Georgia job.

"Getting to the NCAA Tournament was a big key," Smith said. "[Durham] had been there for seventeen years. He won the SEC in 1990. I'm thinking 'What do I have to do?' The answer was the NCAA Tournament."

Dooley eased any concerns Smith might have had by offering him a multiyear contract. Smith went quickly to work, importing his Tulsa staff of Mike Sutton, Shawn Finney, and Ron Jirsa to Athens. There was little time to recruit, but Smith was able to add a couple of players to the roster, including his son G. G., an all-state guard in Oklahoma, and Michael Chadwick, a six-foot-five all-stater from Georgia.

Smith started the 1995–96 season with a veteran team that had, by most anyone's standards, underachieved. The nucleus of Strong, Anderson, Robinson, and Bell— hailed by some recruiting experts as the No. 1 class in the country three years before—was ready and willing to listen to whatever Smith said. The Bulldogs jumped out to a 10-1 start in the nonconference portion of their schedule, only to flounder in the first half of Southeastern Conference play, losing six of their first eight games.

123

"Any time you go into a program, there's got to be an adjustment period because you're instituting a new system," recalled Sutton. "We got off to an OK start because of the nonconference schedule, then we struggled in the league. Coach [Smith] did a really good job of bringing them back around."

Georgia rallied with a 7-1 record in the second half of the SEC schedule, and finished second to Kentucky in the Eastern Division at 9-7. A win in the SEC Tournament was enough to get the Bulldogs into the NCAA Tournament for the first time since 1991. Smith had accomplished his mission, but he was far from finished. Georgia beat Clemson and Purdue in the NCAAs and lost by two points in overtime to Syracuse, which would eventually play in the championship game, losing to Kentucky. That got Georgia fans excited.

"It was a great first year," Smith said. "It was just a matter of getting the right people in the right spots. We had eight seniors on that team, and we had some talent. It was just a matter of getting everybody in tune to what we were trying to do."

Smith and his staff had to rebuild the next year, signing nine new players, four of them from junior college. Georgia actually signed another recruit, Radoslav Nesterovic, a seven-footer from Slovenia who was still playing for the NBA's Minnesota Timberwolves in 2002, but he never made it to Athens. "I think some other schools signed him, too," Sutton recalled.

With junior college transfers Lorenzo Hall and Derrick Dukes playing key roles and sophomores Chadwick, G. G. Smith, and Raymond Harrison forming a potent starting perimeter group, the Bulldogs were even better in Smith's second year. They served notice of that by winning the Rainbow Classic in December, beating Maryland in the championship game. Georgia finished with a better SEC record (10-6) than the year before and created a stir by winning three straight games and advancing to the finals of the SEC Tournament. The Bulldogs ran out of gas in the championship game, losing by 27 points to Kentucky, and that might have carried over to the first round of the NCAA Tournament, where they were upset by Tennessee-Chattanooga in the first round.

Georgia fans couldn't have known then, but that game was to be Smith's last.

For several seasons, Kentucky coach Rick Pitino had been approached by NBA teams hoping to lure him back into that league, where he had coached the New York Knicks before moving to Lexington. Pitino wasn't interested, at least not until the Boston Celtics came calling. When he agreed to take the job in the spring of 1996, Kentucky athletic director C. M. Newton, who had been so instrumental in shaping Smith's career, extended an offer to come to Lexington.

Georgia athletic director Vince Dooley had done everything in his power to keep

Smith in Athens, signing him to six-year contract extension after the 1995–96 season. But that wasn't enough. For Smith, Kentucky was an opportunity too good to pass up.

After Smith left for Lexington, Dooley once again conducted a national search. But he eventually settled on Smith's former assistant Ron Jirsa, who had been the choice of several Georgia players, including G. G. Smith, who promised not to follow his father to Kentucky. Recruit Jumaine Jones, a six-foot-eight blue-chipper from Georgia, also agreed to honor his scholarship if Jirsa got the job.

While the hiring of Jirsa, by all accounts a kind and decent person, might have mollified Georgia players and recruits, it sent the program into a three-year downturn. Jirsa had never before been a head coach, and following Smith's act in his first season was difficult. In 1997–98, the Bulldogs slid to 7-9 in the SEC, and though they reached twenty victories with a run to the Final Four of the NIT, no one associated with the program was satisfied.

Things were even worse the next year. After three years of playing against G. G. Smith and Ray Harrison, SEC coaches figured out how to neutralize them. And Georgia's offense had become predictable; one league coach said he didn't bother to scout the Bulldogs because their offense consisted of getting the ball to Jones and letting him freelance.

Georgia's overreliance on Jones caused some in-fighting on the team, and the results were predictable. The Bulldogs finished 6-10 in the SEC, their worst finish in ten years. At 15-14 overall, they barely scraped into the NIT, but only after Jirsa overruled his players, who had voted overwhelmingly not to accept an NIT bid.

The Bulldogs' first-round opponent was Clemson, but they would have to play on the road. When Dooley and Georgia president Michael Adams drove to the game together, some program insiders feared the worst.

The game proved to be a debacle, as the Bulldogs, who didn't want to be there in the first place, got run out of Clemson's gym by 20 points. Some say Jirsa's fate was decided well before the game ended. Twenty days after Dooley had given him a vote of confidence, Jirsa was gone.

"I'm sure everybody would give somebody the right to change their mind," Dooley said at a press conference where he announced Jirsa's ouster. "What I said at the time, I meant. I also said that the season is not over yet. And that's exactly what happened. I was hoping at the time it would be much better. As it turned out, it was worse."

The decision crushed Jirsa, who didn't think two years was enough to prove what he could do. Years later, Jirsa's old boss Tubby Smith was still disappointed about Dooley's abrupt decision.

"Coach Dooley and I disagreed on that," Smith said. "It takes a while for a [for-

String Music

mer] assistant coach to establish his philosophy and his rapport. You've recruited kids, now you have to coach them. That's probably the toughest thing to do in sports—to be elevated."

Though Dooley claimed he was "hurt by [Jirsa's] hurt," after the firing, there was one thing that made him feel worse. And that was the prospect of the Bulldogs sinking any deeper in the SEC. To get the Bulldogs back on track, Dooley knew he needed a coach who was a proven winner. After hiring a coach with too little experience, Dooley would go out and find one with a wealth of experience.

———

In Jim Harrick, Dooley found the polar opposite of Ron Jirsa. Whereas Jirsa had never been a head coach at any level before taking over at Georgia, Harrick, sixty when he replaced Jirsa, had run successful programs at every level. From Los Angeles's Morningside High School in 1970 through Pepperdine, UCLA, and Rhode Island, Harrick had been a winner. A full-blown disciple of John Wooden, Harrick had taken what he learned from the Wizard of Westwood at clinics, camps, and numerous private meetings, mixed it with the defensive principles of Pete Newell, sprinkled in his own homespun personality, and came up with a system.

The system lent itself to the college game. In Harrick's first season at Pepperdine in 1979, he took the Waves to the NIT. He led Pepperdine to four NCAA Tournaments and an NIT before he left for UCLA in 1988.

Harrick coached the Bruins to the NCAA Tournament in each of his eight seasons. The obvious highlight was the 1995 national championship. UCLA, 31-2 that season, conjured memories of the Wooden years for the Bruins' long-frustrated fans.

Despite his considerable accomplishments at UCLA, Harrick's career there ended badly. Out of coaching for one year, Harrick was eager to, as he put it, be recycled into the system. His chance came when Al Skinner left Rhode Island for Boston College in 1997. Again, Harrick worked quickly, taking the Rams to the Elite Eight in 1998. The next season, Rhode Island again advanced to the NCAA Tournament. The Rams' first-round loss to Charlotte was Harrick's last game at Rhode Island. Days later, Vince Dooley came calling.

Harrick was intrigued by the Georgia job and readily accepted Dooley's offer. But after showing up in Athens for a press conference, Harrick flew back to Rhode Island, where he quickly had second thoughts.

"I went back home and I quit," Harrick recalled. "I quit because I couldn't bring my son. I also had my other son in Rhode Island, and he was married and had two

126

kids. I was so emotional at the time.

"But eventually, all three of my boys got together and told me, 'You made a commitment. You always told us if you make a commitment, you've got to honor it.' And they thought Georgia was a terrific opportunity. To come from where I came from and get a chance to coach in the Southeastern Conference."

Luckily for Harrick, Dooley was away from his office and couldn't start his search for a coach until a day after Harrick changed his mind. By that time, Harrick had committed himself to Georgia, and Dooley took him back.

Harrick's waffling didn't endear him to Georgia fans at first. And the UCLA debacle had dealt his credibility a serious blow. But Harrick brought a renewed sense of enthusiasm and a high energy level to Georgia. It took all the energy Harrick could muster to begin the rebuilding process.

He didn't say so publicly, but Harrick was appalled at how low the talent level had slipped, just two years after Tubby Smith had led the Bulldogs to a No. 3 seed in the NCAA Tournament.

Harrick shudders to think about if he hadn't out-recruited Tennessee for Anthony Evans and Kentucky for Shon Coleman. The two junior-college big men reinforced Georgia's front line and helped Harrick squeeze out ten victories in 1999–2000. But Georgia had also lost twenty games. Harrick and his staff knew they had a lot of work ahead of them.

Blending his unheralded recruiting class with Coleman, Evans, and guard D. A. Layne, Harrick might have turned in his best coaching job in 2000–2001. Despite the fact the Bulldogs played the nation's toughest schedule, they won sixteen games. Georgia finished 9-7 in the SEC's Eastern Division, which was enough to convince the NCAA Tournament selection committee the Bulldogs belonged. With Georgia's invitation Harrick joined some elite company, becoming only the third coach in history— along with Eddie Sutton and Lefty Driesell—to coach four schools into the NCAAs.

Georgia lost its first-round game to Missouri, but the groundwork for a program had been set.

———

No one, not even Jim Harrick, could have forecast Georgia's 2001–2002 season. In nearly every preseason poll, the Bulldogs had been picked to finish fifth or six in the SEC East. There didn't seem to be too much to like about the Bulldogs. Their entire front line from the season before had departed along with leading scorer D. A. Layne, who made a terrible decision to give up his final year of eligibility and declare for the

NBA draft. He wasn't taken. Making matters worse, Harrick's entire recruiting class was ineligible. Center Larry Turner wound up in a prep school, and guard Jarrod Gerald went to a military school and eventually signed with South Carolina. Guard Mike Dean was cleared to play in December, but by that time had missed preseason conditioning and two months of practice.

"I thought fifth or sixth was about right," Harrick said. "You look at the division. You've got Kentucky and Florida, which you know are going to be good. South Carolina's got a huge front line and Dave Odom to coach them. I thought they'd get a piece of the action. And Tennessee was talented. I figured we'd be lucky to just get ahead of Vanderbilt."

Georgia did just a little better than that. Despite a regular-season ending loss at Tennessee, the Bulldogs finished tied with Kentucky atop the SEC East with a 10-6 record. Since the SEC split into divisions in the 1991–92 season, only one school had failed to win or tie for a division championship. That was Georgia.

The Bulldogs' season was full of surprises, starting with their second game. The ease at which Georgia dispatched nationally ranked Georgetown in the Tip-Off Classic gave notice of things to come. The Bulldogs won three straight games after that to go 5-0, but without the Hayes brothers, who were both injured, they lost to Georgia State.

When the twins returned to the lineup, Georgia defeated Minnesota and Georgia Tech before embarking on a road trip that would take the Bulldogs to Mobile, Alabama; Malibu, California; and Honolulu, Hawaii. Along the way, Georgia won four straight games, finally losing to Rainbow Classic host Hawaii on the Rainbow Warriors' home court. At that point of their journey, the Bulldogs were worn out.

Despite the loss, Georgia entered SEC play on a high note after fashioning an 11-2 record in nonconference games. League play would bring a dizzying assortment of highs and lows.

Georgia began its SEC season with a home-court victory over Vanderbilt. Next up was a game at Kentucky, where the Bulldogs hadn't won since 1985. If the rest of the conference wasn't aware of Jarvis Hayes, it quickly discovered him after he scored a career-high 30 points in Georgia's 88-84 upset victory.

"This is exactly the reason I transferred to Georgia," a jubilant Hayes said after the game. "To play teams like Kentucky, Arkansas, and Florida."

Next came the Bulldogs' stirring last-second victory over Tennessee. By this time, the rest of the SEC knew Georgia, with a 3-0 SEC record, would have to be reckoned with. Little did anyone know the first of a series of suspensions was about to derail the Bulldogs' progress.

128

Even before the season began, Harrick had taken some criticism for signing guard Tony Cole, a well-traveled junior college transfer who arrived with a questionable past. Cole, originally from Baton Rouge, Louisiana, had either been homeless or lived in a foster home most of his life. His mother had spent years in a mental institution. And Cole didn't get to know his father, Elasko Burrell, until ninth grade. Two years later, Burrell was killed in a construction accident.

Without a family, Cole was often left to his own devices and forced to find shelter wherever he could. There were many nights he waited until the custodians in LSU's Pete Maravich Assembly Center left so he could sleep there. Not surprisingly, Cole's high school career was a journey. He started at Baton Rouge's Glen Oaks High School, then had brief stops at four other schools from California to Maine. Harrick found out about the jet-quick, five-foot-eleven guard from former LSU coach Dale Brown and signed Cole at Rhode Island in 1999.

Cole was never admitted to Rhode Island, and after Harrick left for Georgia in 1999, it didn't appear the two would hook up again. But Cole got that chance after playing for the Community College of Rhode Island in 1999 and Wabash (Illinois) Community College in 2000. In need of another point guard, Harrick once again turned to Cole.

Considering that Harrick had already received criticism for signing the equally troubled and well-traveled Kenny Brunner in 1999, the signing of Cole was questioned by some Georgia fans and the media. Why take a chance?

Harrick wondered that, too, as he gradually learned the quirky Cole wasn't going to be easy to coach. Cole was unreliable off the court, wild and unpredictable on it.

"I take it as a challenge to coach difficult kids," Harrick said. "He takes it beyond."

So why did Harrick put up with Cole? "My son [Jim, Jr.] said he'd never seen me take things like I have from Cole," Harrick said. "But if I sent him home, he'd have no place to go."

Harrick tried as hard as he could to channel Cole's ability. Sometimes he succeeded, such as the night Cole scored 21 points in eighteen minutes in the win over Pepperdine. But while Harrick marveled at Cole's talent, he also hoped the player could stay out of serious trouble.

By January, Cole had alienated most of his teammates. Only the kind-hearted Steven Thomas spent any time with him, which proved to be hazardous to Thomas's well being. On January 12, Cole and Thomas were accused of rape by a Georgia student. Harrick suspended both players.

The loss of Cole wouldn't hurt that much, but without Thomas the Bulldogs didn't have enough manpower to beat Alabama, even though the game was played in

Athens. The 77-72 loss and Thomas's uncertain status seemed likely to derail the Bulldogs' progress, but Harrick's scrappy team had some more surprises in store.

No one who follows college basketball would have taken a bet that Georgia could have gone into Florida's O'Dome, without Thomas and with just six scholarship players available to Harrick, and won. But behind 23 points from Jarvis Hayes and 19 from Williams, the Bulldogs pulled off an 84-79 upset. For the second straight game, Jonas Hayes came up big in relief of Thomas. Hayes scored 14 points and grabbed 14 rebounds against Alabama, and followed that with 14 points and 4 rebounds against Florida.

Georgia won one more time without Thomas to improve its SEC record to 5-1. Thomas was eventually reinstated after Georgia officials uncovered evidence of his innocence. Cole, too, was reinstated, but never played for the Bulldogs again.

Ironically, after Thomas's return, Georgia lost two straight games, at Vanderbilt and South Carolina. Thomas found his stride in the Bulldogs' next two games, though, scoring 16 points and grabbing seven rebounds in a homecourt win over Ole Miss, and collecting game-high totals of 21 and 10 rebounds in a big win at Mississippi State. That was the first time the Bulldogs won in Starkville since 1991.

"I'm mentally back," Thomas told the *Athens Banner-Herald*.

No sooner did Georgia regain the services of Thomas than it lost him again after a wild game at Auburn during which Thomas was ejected for fighting and Harrick was tossed after drawing two technical fouls for protesting an offensive foul called on Chris Daniels. Thomas's ejection meant he would automatically miss the Bulldogs' next game against Florida.

Georgia's loss at Auburn paled in comparison to the one suffered that day by Ezra Williams. As Williams walked off the bus after the Bulldogs' return from Auburn, his cell phone rang. The call was from his mother, who told Williams his beloved older brother Antwonne had been shot and killed.

Numb with grief, Williams retreated to his room, where he briefly considered suicide. "I seriously thought about killing myself," Williams told the *Athens Banner-Herald*. "Just so I could be with him. That's how much I missed him."

Somehow Williams found the courage to play when the Bulldogs played host to Florida three days later. Antwonne Williams had always attended Georgia home games. In the first half, Williams avoided looking at his brother's empty seat in the stands. But in the second half, a wave of sadness gripped him. He spent the rest of the game on the bench, with a towel draped over his head. Williams's numbers for the evening reflected his distress: 3-for-14 from the field, 1-for-11 from three-point range.

Not surprisingly, Georgia, with Williams grieving and Thomas again on the sidelines, lost 85-70 to Florida, dropping its overall record to 18-7 and its SEC record to 7-5.

130

Another suspension would add to the Bulldogs' woes in their game against Kentucky four days later. Chris Daniels was ordered by the SEC to sit out the first half, the result of an elbow he threw at an Auburn player two games before. Though the incident escaped the attention of the officials, it was pointed out to the SEC by another league school. Some believed it was Kentucky.

Without their most versatile player, the Bulldogs managed a 32-32 tie at halftime. Then, with Daniels playing all twenty minutes of the second half, Georgia pulled out a win that all but assured the Bulldogs—19-7 overall and 8-5 in the SEC—an NCAA Tournament bid.

Georgia padded its Big Dance resume with two consecutive wins during which Rashad Wright provided late-game heroics. In a 55-54 win at LSU, Wright's jump shot from the left wing provided the margin of victory. In an 82-75 overtime win over South Carolina in Athens, Wright's three-pointer with 5.4 seconds left tied the score, and the Bulldogs took charge in the extra period.

The victory boosted Georgia to 21-7 overall and 10-5 in the SEC. A regular season–ending win at Tennessee would have given the Bulldogs the outright Eastern Division championship. But it wasn't to be. Despite taking an 18-point halftime lead, Georgia couldn't hang on, losing 71-63. Williams, who seemed to lack his early-season fire after the death of his brother, had another poor shooting day, going one for ten from the field.

Georgia
All-SEC Expansion Era Team
F-Jumaine Jones
F-Jarvis Hayes
C-Carlos Strong
G-Shandon Anderson
G-Litterial Green
Top Reserves-Ezra Williams, D. A. Layne

Despite the loss, Georgia managed to tie Kentucky and Florida for first place in the East. And because of its first season sweep of Kentucky since 1987, the Bulldogs won a tiebreaker, which meant they earned a first-round bye into the SEC Tournament.

After the game, a clearly exhausted Harrick wasn't too disappointed.

"I can't be," he said. "If you'd told me in October that we'd have shared the conference championship and been ahead of Florida and Kentucky, I'd have thought you were crazy. It's been a great ride. We played solid basketball all the way through. Jarvis Hayes was a missing piece, but Ezra Williams matured. Steven Thomas and Chris Daniels got so much better. And frankly I never dreamed Rashad Wright could give us the kind of play at point guard that he has. I'm so proud of this team. They pleased me more than I could have imagined."

Chapter Six

Kentucky

After the final broadcast of a legendary career spent recounting Kentucky basketball games on the radio, Cawood Ledford took time to reflect on his thirty-nine years behind the microphone.

It was March 28, 1992, and Ledford had just witnessed what some believe was the greatest college basketball game ever played. Ledford's beloved Wildcats had come out on the short end of the score in their East Regional championship game against Duke, thanks to a miraculous last-second shot by the Blue Devils' Christian Laettner. But as Ledford neared the final sign-off of his life, he took a moment to thank Kentucky coach Rick Pitino and his determined, overachieving team.

Why did Ledford, the man for whom the floor at Kentucky's famed Rupp Arena would be named in 2001, feel compelled to express gratitude to Pitino and the Wildcats?

"They brought this program back from the dead," he said.

To best understand what Ledford meant, to fully comprehend how remarkable Pitino's resurrection project was, it's necessary to look back a few years to a couple of events that shook the program to its core.

The first came in 1985, when a team of reporters from the *Lexington Herald-Leader* interviewed thirty-three former Kentucky players and convinced them to speak on the record about cash payments they had received during the tenure of Joe B. Hall, who coached the Wildcats from 1972 to 1985. These payments, the newspaper said, came in various forms through boosters who bought tickets from players, overpaid them for jobs, or simply stuffed cash into their hands or pockets before or after games.

After the *Herald-Leader* published its findings in a series of articles, many of the players recanted their statements. But the series—which would later win the Pulitzer Prize—had already instigated an NCAA investigation.

The NCAA dug around for a couple of years, but couldn't corroborate the newspaper's findings. And the *Herald-Leader* refused to turn over its collection of taped interviews with Kentucky players. With no hard evidence and players suddenly changing their stories, the NCAA couldn't levy any sanctions against the school.

132

Kentucky got off lightly with a reprimand for not cooperating with the investigation. Hall resigned in 1985 and was replaced by Eddie Sutton, a respected coach who had taken two other schools, Creighton and Arkansas, to the NCAA Tournament. Sutton had actively campaigned for the Kentucky job and thought he could accomplish great things there. But his four-year tenure would be remembered not for any great success the Wildcats had on the court, but for dissension and scandal off it.

Sutton's first year in Lexington gave no indication of what was to come. In fact, it turned out to be one of the greatest in school history. With a team that had finished 18-13 and 11-7 in the SEC in Hall's last year, Sutton turned in a remarkable coaching job in 1985–86. Squeezing everything he could from a team that lacked a true center and a strong bench, Sutton guided the Wildcats to a 32-4 record. Kentucky was 17-1 in the SEC, easily winning the regular-season championship over runners-up Alabama and Auburn, which finished 13-5. And the Wildcats also won the SEC Tournament.

Kentucky's great season carried over to the NCAA Tournament, where the Wildcats defeated Davidson, Western Kentucky, and Alabama to advance to the Elite Eight. The Wildcats' run was ended there by an old nemesis, SEC rival LSU, but the future looked bright. True, some long-time Wildcat fans that fondly recalled the days of Adolph Rupp's up-tempo style didn't fancy Sutton's defensive-oriented, grind-it-out philosophy. But those thirty-two wins couldn't be denied. Kentucky hadn't won that many games since the 1948–49 team finished 32-2 and won the school's second consecutive NCAA championship.

Good things were happening off the court as well. Kentucky won a major recruiting battle with North Carolina for the services of home-state superstar Rex Chapman, a prep All-American from Owensboro, Kentucky. Though Michael Jordan called Chapman on behalf of the Tar Heels, Chapman signed with Kentucky, much to the delight of Wildcat fans that viewed him as a latter-day Pete Maravich. Sutton took that comparison a step beyond. "I would call him a combination of Pete Maravich and Jerry West," Sutton said.

Chapman—dubbed the Boy King or King Rex by his adoring fans—had a game worthy of his hype. Chapman had that rare combination of great leaping ability and a good outside shooting touch. He was also a flashy passer and was fearless when he took the ball to the basket. With such a flamboyant, wide-open style, it was inevitable that Chapman would clash with Sutton. And clash they did.

In 1986–87, Chapman's freshman season, the Wildcats couldn't measure up to their performance of the year before, especially without forward Winston Bennett, who injured his knee in the preseason and wouldn't play.

Though Chapman averaged 16 points per game, Kentucky finished 18-11. And the

133

Wildcats' trip to the NCAA Tournament was a short one; they were knocked out in the first round by Ohio State. Late in the regular season, Chapman felt compelled to publicly dispel rumors to the effect that his presence had caused conflict between him and veteran guards Ed Davender and James Blackmon.

Chapman averaged 19 points in 1987–88, his last year in Lexington. And the Wildcats, lifted by the return of Bennett and the addition of high school All-Americans Eric Manuel and LeRon Ellis, returned to the form they showed in Sutton's first season, winning twenty-seven games, the SEC regular-season championship, and the SEC Tournament. Kentucky advanced to the Sweet 16 of the NCAA Tournament.

Despite the outward signs of success, the program was beginning to unravel from within. A rift had developed between Sutton and Chapman. Sutton, who preferred a disciplined offense, openly criticized Chapman's shot selection, using the media to voice his frustration. Chapman thought the matter should be resolved in private.

A picture taken after a home-court loss to Auburn in early January 1988 spoke volumes about the cold war between player and coach. The picture showed Sutton and Chapman seated at a table for the post-game press conference. Sutton's face is buried in his left hand. Chapman is staring blankly into space.

After the season, perhaps because of his strained relationship with Sutton, Chapman disappointed Kentucky fans by announcing he was foregoing his final two seasons of eligibility and declaring for the NBA draft.

Chapman had another reason to consider leaving. In April 1988, the news broke that an Emery overnight package containing one thousand dollars, sent by Kentucky assistant coach Dwane Casey and earmarked for the father of Kentucky recruit Chris Mills, had come apart in an Emery warehouse, revealing its contents.

The NCAA, which only months before had announced its wrist slap of the Kentucky program stemming from its investigation after the *Lexington Herald-Leader* stories, quickly began another probe.

This time, the evidence was irrefutable. And in the course of the NCAA's investigation, other rules violations were revealed, most notably that Kentucky coaches had helped Eric Manuel cheat on his college entrance exams.

Sutton and his assistants denied all charges, but the NCAA, determined after not being able to find any violations despite the *Herald-Leader*'s groundwork in 1985, forged relentlessly ahead, realizing it had the proof it needed this time around.

Sutton's final season in Lexington was shrouded by the growing scandal, and the Wildcats finished 13-19. It was Kentucky's first losing season in sixty-one years.

Before the year ended, Kentucky athletic director Cliff Hagan, who had been a star player for the Wildcats in the early 1950s, resigned. C. M. Newton, then-basketball coach at Vanderbilt and a Kentucky graduate, agreed to return to his alma mater as athletic director. In a compelling coincidence, Newton's Vanderbilt team ousted Kentucky from the SEC Tournament, ending the Wildcats' season and Eddie Sutton's coaching career. Sutton resigned nine days after that loss, on March 19, 1989. And on April 1, Newton took over at Kentucky and began cleaning up a mess of epic proportions.

"The eleven-month period between the discovery of the Emery package and the end of the 1988–89 season was without question the bleakest in UK's long and illustrious basketball history," wrote Tom Wallace in his book, *Kentucky Basketball Encyclopedia*. "Never had the program come under such intense scrutiny, and never had the stakes been higher."

―――――

Years later, Newton recalled his motivation for jumping into the maelstrom that had become Kentucky athletics.

"Things were in total disarray," Newton said. "Going through the NCAA issues that were there. The coach had just been released. They were about to receive serious sanctions by the NCAA.

"I had no interest in being an athletics director. I wanted to coach basketball. And we had it going good at Vanderbilt. But I was convinced by people I respect that I was not only wanted as the AD at Kentucky, I was needed. It was my school and pretty screwed up. The need part was more significant to me than the wanted part.

"So I decided I was going to end my [coaching] career at age fifty-nine. I left a lot of income on the table as a coach to become the AD and also left a good team. The team that I left a year later won the NIT.

"To me it was important to come to my school and see if we couldn't get the thing straightened out. I felt like if we could get the right coach and make the right decisions early, we could come back rather quickly. If not, I feared we'd go the way UCLA did after coach [John] Wooden retired, go through several coaches, drift around and come back some day."

Newton's first choice to replace Sutton was Pat Riley, then coaching the Los Angeles Lakers. Riley had been a member of one of Kentucky's most beloved teams, "Rupp's Runts," that reached the 1966 NCAA championship game, where it lost to Texas Western. Newton was hoping he could entice another one of Kentucky's own to help him rebuild the program.

Riley chose to stay in the NBA, but Newton was undaunted. He quickly switched to New York Knicks coach Rick Pitino, who had forged his reputation in the college ranks, taking an unheralded Providence team to the Final Four in 1987. But Pitino didn't want to discuss the job until after the Knicks' season had ended.

Newton kept trying. He interviewed Arizona coach Lute Olson and Seton Hall's P. J. Carlesimo, but both of them, perhaps wary of the impending NCAA sanctions that hung over the program, declined Newton's offer.

On May 19, 1989, the worst fears of Kentucky fans were realized when the NCAA handed down its punishment. The Wildcats were placed on three years' probation, which included a ban from post-season tournaments the first two years. The NCAA also barred Kentucky from television appearances and took away scholarships, limiting the program to a total of three in the 1989–90 and 1990–91 academic years. The three games in which Eric Manuel took part in the 1988 NCAA Tournament were stricken from the record books. And the SEC presidents voted to strip Kentucky of its 1987–88 league championship.

As severe as those penalties were, they might well have been worse had Kentucky not cooperated with the NCAA's investigation. The forced departures of Cliff Hagan and Eddie Sutton were also a positive factor in the school's behalf.

"Because of the nature of the violations found in this case, the committee seriously considered whether the regular-season schedule of the men's basketball program should be curtailed in whole or in part for one or two seasons of competition," the NCAA's ruling stated. "In the judgement of the committee, the nature of the violations found would justify such a penalty. However, this case was also evaluated in the light of the university's actions to bring itself into compliance."

Kentucky may have avoided the NCAA's dreaded "death penalty," but the program was nevertheless dealt a crippling blow. After the sanctions were announced, several key players quickly abandoned the sinking ship. Chris Mills, whose recruitment had been at the heart of the scandal, left for Arizona. LeRon Ellis transferred to Syracuse. Guard Sean Sutton left for Purdue, only to wind up at Oklahoma State when his father was hired there in 1990. And Eric Manuel, banned by the NCAA from playing for one of its member schools, finished his career at an NAIA school, Oklahoma City College.

Most of the handful of players who remained were either from Kentucky or had ties to the state. John Pelphrey, Deron Feldhaus, Richie Farmer, and Sean Woods would one day be proclaimed heroes for their loyalty and their efforts in rebuilding the program.

Newton, meanwhile, made sure he kept the lines of communication open with Pitino.

"I want to give it my best shot," Newton recalled. "I had been amazed with what Rick had done with the Providence team. The style of play was exciting and I thought would be popular with our fans. And I had reason to believe Rick was interested in

136

getting back into college with the right setting.

"We just exerted some patience until his season was over and made a real strong run at him."

Hampering Newton's search was a story that appeared in the *Lexington Herald-Leader* detailing Pitino's involvement in rules violations that led to the University of Hawaii being placed on probation when Pitino was an assistant there in the mid 1970s. Pitino offered to withdraw his name from consideration, but Newton, convinced that his background check of Pitino had revealed the true character of the man, wouldn't hear of it.

On June 2, 1989, Rick Pitino was announced as the new head coach at Kentucky. Given the state of the program, not even the most loyal Kentucky fan expected a quick turnaround. Most anticipated Pitino's rebuilding efforts would take up to five years. They were about to be surprised, even though Pitino boldly gave the fans a look into the future on the day he was hired.

"We will overcome all the obstacles and make Kentucky's basketball tradition rich again," Pitino said. "I think the University of Kentucky will get turned around in a very short time with me as the coach."

If that sounded a tad arrogant, well, Pitino had some hard numbers to back it up. At twenty-five years old, Pitino landed his first head-coaching job, at Boston University in 1978. In the two seasons before Pitino's arrival, the Terriers won seventeen games. In Pitino's first season, they were 17-9. Pitino's five-year record at the school was 91-51.

After a two-year stint as an assistant for the New York Knicks, Pitino returned to college coaching at Providence in 1985. The Friars were 11-20 the year before Pitino arrived. In his first season, Providence finished 17-14 and played in the NIT. The next season, the Friars were the darlings of the NCAA Tournament as they advanced to the Final Four. One of the stars of that team was a young guard named Billy Donovan, who would later rejoin Pitino as a Kentucky assistant.

After Pitino's great season at Providence, the Knicks again lured him away, this time with an offer to become head coach. The Knicks' two-year record before Pitino's arrival was 71-175, the worst in the NBA. In his first season, the Knicks were 38-44 and landed a spot in the playoffs. New York finished 52-30 and won the NBA's Atlantic Division in Pitino's second year.

"Turning negatives into positives has been the theme of my coaching career," Pitino said after he took over at Kentucky.

His best rebuilding job was ahead of him.

Pitino inherited just eight scholarship players in 1989–90, none of them taller than six-foot-seven. Only two of the holdovers from the ill-fated Eddie Sutton regime had contributed significantly the season before. Derrick Miller, a six-foot-five senior guard, had averaged nearly 14 points. And six-foot-seven junior Reggie Hanson started twenty-nine games and averaged nearly 10 points.

The rest of Pitino's motley crew included Deron Feldhaus and John Pelphrey, a pair of six-foot-seven forwards and Kentucky natives; six-foot Richie Farmer, who had been a Kentucky schoolboy legend; and guards Sean Woods and Jeff Brassow.

Assisting Pitino in his first season was a coaching staff that would go down as one of the best in the game's history. Billy Donovan, who had starred for Pitino at Providence and played one season with the Knicks, signed on as a graduate assistant. Tapping his East Coast connections, Pitino hired Ralph Willard, who had been a successful high school coach in New York, and Herb Sendek, an assistant on Pitino's staff at Providence. In need of an assistant with some experience recruiting the South, Pitino turned to his new athletic director C. M. Newton for help. Newton knew just the person.

Tubby Smith remembers the day he first heard from Pitino.

"I'd never even talked to Rick," said. "I'm at the Black Coaches Association function in Dallas. He calls the house and my wife answers. She calls me and she's excited. 'Hey, Rick Pitino from Kentucky just called. Kentucky. Oh Tubby, we've got to go.' She was ready for a change.

"But I was perfectly happy. I've always been happy everywhere I've been. I was with [South Carolina head coach] George Felton, and we had it going there. We were winning, going to the NCAA Tournament. We had Brent Price. We were rolling. I could have stayed in Columbia.

"But I called Rick. He didn't know anybody in the Southeast. He needed a recruiter, someone who knew the territory. He brought in Herb Sendek and Ralph Willard, but those were East Coast guys. I kind of had tentacles in the South. That was a big help. Coach Newton knew that.

"At the time I had to make a decision. You make decisions for many reasons. They were personal at the time. I finally decided I needed a change. Sometimes God brings things to you, decisions like that, for a certain reason. I'm just glad I made the decision that was best at the time for me and my family. It was career altering. Unbelievable."

Unbelievable would be a good word to describe Pitino's first season in Lexington. Despite the Wildcats' personnel limitations, he made a decision early that Kentucky would play the up-tempo brand of basketball he favored, complete with pressure defense and liberal use of the three-point goal. If eight players were going to survive in that system, they would have to be in shape.

"Knowing that his thin troops were far from ready to play his up-tempo, all-out, pressing style of play, Pitino turned his pre-season conditioning into a Marine-type boot camp," Tom Wallace wrote in *Kentucky Basketball Encyclopedia*. "There were 5 A.M. practices. The weight training program, under the guidance of Rock Oliver, was brutal, driving the players to the very edge of endurance. Pitino's goal wasn't limited to developing physical toughness—he wanted his players mentally tough as well."

Fortunately for Pitino, his new charges were willing. Most had grown up in Kentucky and were living a dream to wear the uniform of the mighty Wildcats. Given that chance, they weren't about to let the proud old program down.

Pitino didn't ask his players for any more commitment than he was willing to give himself. With so much ground to make up, Pitino and his staff worked hard. Eighteen-hour days were commonplace.

"It was intense in that you had to be committed," Tubby Smith recalled. "You had to work your tail off. The head coach has to be the guy who sets the pace, sets the tone. Rick set the tone with his work ethic and his intensity and his focus. You feed off that and pick up on it."

Pitino's first team quickly found its way into the hearts of Kentucky fans everywhere. Firing three-pointers with abandon—a staggering 810 for the season—and smothering opponents with full-court defensive pressure—the Wildcats set a school record with 309 steals—Kentucky was the surprise of college basketball. In their first nine games during which they were 6-3, "Pitino's Bombinos," as they were dubbed in the press, scored 100 or more points five times. As Pitino said, Kentucky, despite its crippling shortage of manpower, wouldn't back down.

That much was evident in a 150-95 loss at Kansas, a rout that began a feud between Pitino and Jayhawk coach Roy Williams. Despite the increasingly lopsided score, Pitino kept the Wildcats pressing throughout the game.

It was safe to say the SEC wasn't ready for the team Kentucky had become under Pitino. The deliberate style of Eddie Sutton had been replaced by an aggressive, up-tempo assault. The Wildcats didn't care about their limitations. They went after every opponent with a maniacal fervor, pressing on defense and firing away from the three-point line. Amazingly, Kentucky finished 10-8 in SEC play, a record that, had it counted, would have placed the Wildcats in a tie for fourth place.

Kentucky's most impressive victory all season came at home against LSU, which was loaded with talent. The Tigers had their massive twin towers of Shaquille O'Neal and Stanley Roberts and scoring machine Chris Jackson, but they weren't enough to hold off Pitino's Bombinos, who won 100-95. Richie Farmer came through in the clutch, hitting six free throws in the final 1:05 that preserved the victory.

Kentucky finished 14-14 overall. Before the season, Cawood Ledford predicted Kentucky would win eight games. If the Wildcats won as many as 10, the legendary announcer said, Pitino should be chosen national coach of the year.

"It was an amazing season," recalled John Pelphrey, now the head coach at South Alabama. "I can remember people doubting us. They said the players that were left at Kentucky [when Pitino took over] weren't very good. That in itself was a huge motivating thing for us. We didn't want to be remembered as the guys who were at Kentucky when Kentucky was bad. So we bought into coach Pitino's philosophy. From day one he'd look at us in terms of the things we could do, not in terms of things we couldn't do."

Billy Donovan, who would later take charge of his own program in his twenties, just as his mentor Pitino did, has fond memories of the 1989–90 season.

"The coaching job coach Pitino did that first season was incredible," Donovan recalled. "Beating LSU with Chris Jackson, Stanley Roberts, and Shaquille O'Neal, going 14-14 when people said we weren't going to win more than eight games . . . .

"We had guys who were in-state Kentucky kids, that were good solid players, not the kind of guys who were going to take you to the next level. Coach Pitino has a way of finding places for people to play if you can shoot the basketball. That group could really, really shoot. And they had a great basketball IQ. Coach has been good through the years at dealing with guys who aren't superstars and dealing with guys who are hungry and want to overachieve. Like myself when I was playing for him. John and Daren Feldhaus and Richie Farmer, those guys bought into what coach was teaching. And he gave them tremendous confidence."

Despite the promise the Wildcats showed in their first season under Pitino, the Kentucky coaching staff was still having trouble convincing good players to sign. But in Pitino's first recruiting class, one blue-chip player took a chance. Jamal Mashburn came from the Bronx as one of the top ten players nationally. The six-foot-eight, 230-pound forward with the skills of a guard was a breakthrough recruit in Pitino's rebuilding efforts.

"Mashburn brought all-around skills and physical presence to a team that had an abundance of heart, character, intelligence, and mental toughness," wrote Tom Wallace in *Kentucky Basketball Encyclopedia*. "He was the first 'Pitino-type' recruit, a super athlete who could run the floor, shoot, pass, and defend."

Billy Donovan remembers a conversation between Pitino and Mashburn when the latter was making his official visit.

"I remember a comment that Jamal made," Donovan said. "Coach says, 'Jamal, why do you want to come here and play? All I've heard is you're lazy, you don't work hard, you don't play hard, and I'm the complete opposite. Why would you want to come here?' And he said, 'Because I have talent and I know that's what I need. I need to play for you to get it brought out of me.' I thought that was a pretty mature statement by a kid who said I am a little lazy, I need to be pushed."

Besides Mashburn, none of Kentucky's other four newcomers would make much of an impact in Pitino's second season. By Kentucky's high standards, the Wildcats would still be undermanned and outmatched physically. Pitino was careful not to tell them that.

———

If there were any doubts about Pitino's ability to revive Kentucky basketball, they were quickly erased in the 1990–91 season. The Wildcats beat Penn, Cincinnati, and Notre Dame to open the year 3-0, and in their fourth game they handled Kansas, 88-71. Only a year before, the Jayhawks had blown Kentucky out of their gym.

Kentucky lost its next game at North Carolina after squandering an 81-77 lead late in the game. No one realized it at the time, but a trend had begun to form. In Pitino's first season, the Wildcats were 1-10 on the road and 0-2 in neutral sites. Even in losing to the Tar Heels, the Wildcats showed that, inspired by the confidence Pitino had given them, they could perform away from Rupp Arena. In subsequent seasons, Kentucky would become the best road team in the SEC.

Kentucky lost another nonconference game to arch rival Indiana, but jumped out to a 16-2 record. The Wildcats finished their season 22-6, 14-4 in the Southeastern Conference, and ranked ninth in the Associated Press poll. But the NCAA probation put a damper on the year. Postseason play was out of the question, and though Kentucky had the best record in the SEC, as it states in the school's record book, it wasn't eligible for the league championship.

That didn't stop the Wildcats from having a little fun. After they beat Auburn in their regular-season finale at Rupp, Kentucky players and coaches cut down the nets. In another year, the NCAA sanctions finally over, the Wildcats would be cutting down nets again. Only this time, the SEC had to recognize the accomplishment.

———

The decade that's the focal point of this book begins with the 1991–92 season for two important reasons. First, that was the year the conference expanded by taking in Arkansas and South Carolina. Second, it was the year Kentucky basketball regained its customary spot atop the SEC standings. Both events led to the remarkable growth of SEC basketball as the ten other schools did all they could to keep from getting left in the dust of the Wildcats and Razorbacks.

With Arkansas—which had played in the 1990 Final Four and would win the national championship in 1994—in the league and Kentucky dominant after some rare lean seasons, the SEC had two flagship teams, one in each of its new divisions.

Arkansas made its presence felt quickly, going into Rupp Arena and coming away with a victory in that first season of expansion. And Kentucky served notice that it had returned with a vengeance, winning the SEC's first Eastern Division championship and the first league tournament with the twelve-team format.

In the first decade of expansion, the Wildcats once again became the barometer by which other SEC schools would measure their programs. During that span, Kentucky won or tied for eight SEC Eastern Division and five overall championships and won the SEC Tournament eight times. And even when the Wildcats didn't win a championship, they almost always figured into the equation. Every year, it seemed a given that Kentucky's last home game would be a factor in the league race.

That run of success began in 1991–92, when Kentucky, still not appreciably strengthened through recruiting over Pitino's first team, won the SEC East and the tournament championship. In hindsight, it seems absurd that critics dared question Pitino's recruiting during that period, but they did. One obviously misguided Kentucky television personality went so far as to go on the air and suggest the Wildcats had better start cheating if they wanted to remain a player on the national recruiting scene.

Pitino scoffed at the notion that his recruiting was substandard, even though his class, which included rail-thin forwards Aminu Timberlake and Andre Riddick, junior-college transfer Dale Brown, and Missouri transfer Travis Ford, wasn't highly regarded by recruiting analysts.

"Kids having their names in publications doesn't mean a hill of beans," Pitino told *Blue Ribbon College Basketball Yearbook* in 1991. "In Kentucky, there's way too much emphasis put on names. . . . Contrary to what the media says and the so-called experts say, I think we had a very good recruiting year [in 1990–91]. We don't look at it as failure. We look at it as fertilizer."

Pitino was right, for he and his unheralded band of players took his rebuilding efforts to another level in 1991–92. And along the way they made a little history. Two events told the story of a season in which the Wildcats finished 29-7 and came within two seconds of playing in the Final Four.

The first was Kentucky's epic battle with Duke in the NCAA Tournament's East Regional finals. The Wildcats had blown past Old Dominion, Iowa State, and

Massachusetts to get to the final against Duke, the No. 1 seed and defending national champions.

The Blue Devils, with All-Americans and future NBA players Grant Hill and Christian Laettner and heady point guard Bobby Hurley, were a formidable team, but Pitino's preseason words about recruiting rankings being overrated rang true. Battling Duke's roster full of McDonald's All-Americans to the bitter end, Kentucky's group of mostly in-state country boys nearly pulled off the impossible. With 2.1 seconds to play in overtime, the Wildcats led Duke, 103-102, after Sean Woods's miracle bank shot in the lane. The Blue Devils would have to go the length of the court to score a game-winning basket.

Hill inbounded the ball for the Blue Devils. He lofted a perfect pass to Laettner, who caught the ball unimpeded as the Wildcats' John Pelphrey and Deron Feldhaus seemed to back away. Laettner took one dribble, turned, and calmly tossed in a seventeen-foot jumper. Duke won 104-103.

Years later, Pelphrey said he was in a dreamlike state during those fateful final ticks of the clock.

"Where I was on the floor, I was the safety," Pelphrey recalled. "I didn't have a man. I was playing the basketball and we were five on four. If that situation happened tonight, that's the way I'd play. Five on four is much better.

"The thing that's so amazing about the last play wasn't the fact that Laettner hit the shot—he was ten for ten from the field and ten for ten from the foul line in the game. He didn't miss. The amazing thing was the throw and the catch. I'm standing there, playing the ball, taking steps actually backwards. And the ball is curving as it's in the air. I think I'm gonna catch it. Laettner comes up from the baseline, and he's being guarded by Daren. We're both six-seven, and this guy—a lot of guys lie about their height—but he's a legitimate six-eleven, huge. Freakin' huge.

"Essentially what happened was, the bigger guy won out. At that moment in time, I thought I had both hands on the basketball. It was so real to me. And he took it out of my hands. [In reality] I never got a hand on it. He caught it, staggered back a little bit, shook his shoulders. I'm thinking, 'Where is the horn?' When he turned it loose, you had a feeling it was going down.

"It all happened so fast. From the time we left the huddle to the time the ball hit the floor, it was like, 'Wait a second. Let's go back and do this again.'"

In looking back at the play years after the fact, former Kentucky assistant Billy Donovan—who would go on to head-coaching success at Florida—defended Pitino's decision to not guard Hill.

"So much was made whether to put a guy on the ball or not on the ball," Donovan said. "I think the right decision was to put a guy off the ball. Mashburn had fouled out. Martinez had fouled out. We were playing with John Pelphrey and Feldhaus who were six-seven. Laettner was six-eleven and Hill six-nine. We didn't want to get caught with them throwing the ball long and Laettner catching the ball and getting it inside and scoring. We went with a safety back there to help.

"When he caught the ball it was as though our guys were afraid. Almost like, 'Go make this shot to beat us, but we're not gonna foul you and put you at the line.' When he made it, it was devastation. But sometimes you lose games like that and the next year it makes you that much hungrier."

Nine years later, after having coached the Boston Celtics and returned to college coaching at Kentucky's hated rival Louisville, Pitino was reluctant to talk about his days at Kentucky. But after a miraculous win over Tennessee in December 2001 that included a last-second shot that brought back memories of the Duke game, Pitino couldn't help but reference Laettner's miracle play.

The Cardinals, behind 70-64 with thirty-six seconds left, hit three three-point shots in roughly thirty-four seconds and took a 73-72 lead. After Louisville's final basket, Tennessee had 1.8 seconds to throw the ball the length of the floor and get off a shot. The Vols' Marcus Haislip actually got a clean look at the basket and tossed up a shot that barely missed, but the Cardinals had been prepared for the play. In a reversal of his strategy in the Duke game, Pitino put a man on Tennessee's inbounder.

"You see, I can learn," Pitino told the media.

Once he got on the subject, Pitino relived those final two seconds against the Blue Devils. His mistake, Pitino said, wasn't in failing to put a man in Grant Hill's face. His mistake was telling Pelphrey and Feldhaus not to foul Laettner.

"That was where I cost us the game," Pitino said.

The pain of the loss to Duke, as Donovan said, would stay with the Wildcats in the 1992–93 season and drive them to success. But before the book was closed on 1991–92 and the players who had made Kentucky's dramatic turnaround possible, a special ceremony for the Wildcats' departing seniors was conducted at Rupp Arena.

"I got there early that night," Pelphrey recalled. "I remember doing a radio show and from where I was sitting, all I had to do was raise my head and I would have seen four banners up there [in the rafters]. I never looked up. And I was there for an hour. Not once did I look up. I think the good Lord wanted to have happen what happened.

"So we go out there, and we're all on the floor sitting in our chairs, with our backs to the banners. We'd seen coach Newton retire other jerseys—he had kind of a way that he did it. 'It's my privilege,' and stuff like that. When he started that routine, I thought back to when Dan Issel, Kyle Macy, and all those guys had their jerseys retired. I had watched that.

"So when he started, I turned and looked and there were four blue banners up there covered up. I turned around and said to Daren [Feldhaus], 'They're gonna retire our jerseys.' He said 'No way.' I said, 'Turn and look.' He said, 'I can't.' It was fairy-tale land. Growing up in that state, you hope and dream to have a chance to play there. You don't dream of getting your jersey retired because of all the great players that went before you.

"There were players that were far greater than I who don't have their names up there. It's almost embarrassing sometimes. Because I know the heritage of the guys who built that place before us. But I have special feelings. People ask me where I played, there's no hesitation. I stick out my chest. I played at Kentucky. That means something to us. It was a special feeling to put that jersey on."

Newton's words during the ceremony said much about the job Pitino had done in rebuilding Kentucky basketball, thanks to the remarkable contributions of John Pelphrey, Daren Feldhaus, Richie Farmer, and Sean Woods. The foursome would be forever known as "The Unforgettables."

"Today, our program is back on top, due largely to four young men who persevered, who weathered the hard times, and who brought the good time back to Kentucky basketball," Newton told the crowd in Rupp Arena. "Their contributions to UK basketball cannot be measured in statistics or record books."

———

Not that he felt any great pressure to do so, but Pitino finally got the critics off his back about recruiting as Kentucky headed into the 1992–93 season. After losing all the Unforgettables, Pitino had to reload. He and his assistants scoured the country for talent, and with the NCAA probation over and the program on the upswing, Kentucky was suddenly an easy sell again.

From New Jersey, the Wildcats signed Rodrick Rhodes, a versatile forward who was ranked the No. 1 high school player in the country by *Basketball Times* and *Basketball Weekly* and was a consensus top-five pick among recruiting analysts.

Kentucky went to Tennessee and plucked that state's best prospect away from SEC rivals Tennessee and Vanderbilt. Tony Delk, a McDonald's All-American, consensus Top 20 player, and the Tennessee Class AAA Player of the Year, led the state in scoring with a 38.6 points per game average. In one game his senior year, Delk scored 70 points. Pitino called Delk the best three-point shooter he had ever signed.

In West Virginia, the Wildcats found Jared Prickett, a six-foot-nine forward considered the best big man to come from that state in decades.

145

The last piece of the puzzle was center Rodney Dent, a six-foot-ten junior-college transfer who originally signed with Georgia.

Walter McCarty, a *Parade* All-American from Indiana, was also a part of the recruiting class, but wouldn't become eligible until the 1993–94 season. The six-foot-nine McCarty was considered the best big man in the Midwest.

Paired with holdovers such as Travis Ford, the transfer guard who finally emerged in his junior season, the new players would give Pitino a formidable team. Ford, who had battled injuries in his first season in Lexington and was a nonfactor, emerged as Kentucky's leader. Pitino told the *Lexington Herald-Leader* that, for a time, he didn't hold much hope for Ford ever helping the Wildcats.

"When he first got here, I would have traded him for any street-corner player," Pitino said. "He was a tough little kid. He was always respectful. He always did what you said, but I called him Eddie Haskell because he'd say, 'Sure, coach, anything you want.' Then, I knew as soon as left, I'm sure he'd say, 'I'm going to get him.'

"He just pouted a lot. He slammed the basketball, made faces, made excuses. Now, he's totally the opposite. I kid him about it now, but without him, we'd be up a river."

In his junior season, Ford averaged 13.6 points, led the Wildcats in assists, and became the first Kentucky player to make more than 100 three-pointers in a season.

Dragging the talented but inexperienced group of newcomers alongside, Ford led the Wildcats to an 11-0 start in 1992–93. That gained Kentucky the No. 1 ranking in the country for the first time since 1988. The program was all the way back.

Kentucky compiled a 23-3 record in the regular season, finishing second in the SEC Eastern Division behind an unusually strong Vanderbilt team. But the Wildcats would make their mark in the postseason. They won the SEC Tournament as Ford was chosen most valuable player, and earned a No. 3 seed in the NCAA Tournament's Southeast Regional. They made short work of Rider, Utah, Wake Forest, and Florida State, beating the four by an average of 31 points to claim the Final Four berth that had been taken from their grasp the season before.

Once again, Ford shined. After he scored 26 points against Wake Forest, Ford earned rave reviews from Demon Deacons coach Dave Odom, who called him "the most underrated guard in the country." Ford scored 19 points in the regional final against Florida State, prompting the Seminoles' future NBA guard Charlie Ward to call Ford "another Mark Price."

Ford earned regional MVP honors.

Kentucky's great run ended in the national semifinals, as the Wildcats lost to Michigan and its famed "Fab Five" recruiting class that included Chris Webber and Jalen Rose. But the Wildcats would be back in the Final Four.

146

Billy Donovan remembers a comment Pitino made after the Michigan game.

"It was one of the greatest things I ever heard him say," Donovan recalled. "He looked at our kids and said they were going to be a better recruiting class than the Fab Five. I said, 'Coach, you've got to be kidding me. You're talking about Chris Weber and Jalen Rose and all those guys.' He said, 'Billy, those guys will stay two years. Our guys will stay four and they'll all end up becoming great players.'"

———

Pitino would prove to be a prophet. But it took a while for his prediction to come true. In 1993–94, the Wildcats finished 27-7, tied for the SEC East title with a 12-4 record, and won the league tournament. But they were bounced from the NCAA Tournament in the second round by Marquette.

A year later, Kentucky finished 28-5 and made a clean sweep of SEC honors, winning the Eastern Division, the overall championship, and the tournament. Wildcat fans will never forget that epic 1995 championship game against Arkansas. The addition of Razorbacks and the resurgence of Kentucky had placed such an unprecedented demand on tournament tickets that the SEC had to move it to a larger facility. In 1995, the tournament was played in the Georgia Dome, where 30,057 people witnessed Kentucky's thrilling victory over Arkansas. The Wildcats trailed by 19 points in the first half and 91-82 in overtime but still managed to win as they helped shepherd SEC basketball into a new era.

Kentucky earned a No. 1 seed in the Southeast Regional, but its bid for the Final Four fell short after a loss to North Carolina in the regional finals.

Pitino's reconstruction of Kentucky basketball came full circle in the 1995–96 season. By that time, all his original staff had left the program to become head coaches— Ralph Willard at Western Kentucky, Tubby Smith at Tulsa, Herb Sendek at Miami of Ohio, and Billy Donovan at Marshall—a tribute to the job he'd done. Every athletic director of a struggling program in the country wanted to tap into the Pitino magic.

As Pitino had predicted, the nucleus of his first strong recruiting class stayed intact for four seasons. The only casualty was Roderick Rhodes, who struggled to live up to his high school clippings, clashed with Pitino, and ultimately transferred to Southern Cal.

Rhodes wasn't missed. In addition to the senior duo of Tony Delk and Walter McCarty (fellow senior Jared Prickett sat out the season as a redshirt), Pitino had his strongest team yet. Mark Pope, a transfer from Washington, shored up Kentucky's inside play. Antoine Walker, a gifted, versatile forward from Chicago, had proven his worth as a freshman in the 1995 SEC Tournament, winning MVP honors. Jeff Sheppard, a talented

147

shooting guard, had been voted the team's most improved player in 1994–95.

To that talented mix Pitino added two exceptional newcomers. Derek Anderson, a six-foot-five forward, had transferred from Ohio State the season before and impressed Pitino during his redshirt season. "He really knows how to play," Pitino said at the time. "He sees things others don't see."

Freshman forward Ron Mercer was also a key addition. Signed after a hard-fought recruiting battle with his home-state schools Vanderbilt and Tennessee, Mercer was considered by many the nation's top freshman. Former Kentucky star Rex Chapman proclaimed Mercer as the school's best recruit in thirty years. Howard Garfinkel, Pitino's mentor from his days at the famed Five Star Camp, proved to be a prophet when, after Mercer signed with Kentucky, he said, "I personally think the 1995–96 season is over. I think Kentucky is a lock with [Mercer]. He's that good."

So too was Kentucky.

"Few teams in UK history can come close to matching this one in terms of quality depth at all positions," wrote Tom Wallace in *Kentucky Basketball Encyclopedia*. "Throughout the season, rival coaches and basketball commentators said that UK's second five could easily have been a Top 10 team. . . ."

Kentucky lived up to all its advance billing. The Wildcats lost their second game of the season to Massachusetts, but wouldn't lose again until the finals of the SEC Tournament, when Mississippi State, en route to a Final Four appearance, would handle the Wildcats, 84-73. In between those losses, Kentucky dominated the SEC in a way that hadn't been seen in decades. With a 16-0 record in league play, the Wildcats became the first team since Alabama was 14-0 in 1956 to go undefeated. In winning all of its eight SEC away games, Kentucky extended to twelve its winning streak on the road over a two-year period. As competitive as the SEC had become by that time, twelve consecutive road wins was a major deal.

The Wildcats won twenty-seven straight games in 1995–96. A key cog in the winning streak was previously unheralded Anthony Epps, who started at point guard the season before but lost the job after six games. Kentucky had recruited freshman Wayne Turner to put some heat on Epps, who responded with his best season.

The loss to Mississippi State in the SEC Tournament didn't derail the Wildcats' momentum, but it did get their attention. They showed no mercy in the NCAA Tournament's Midwest Regional, pounding San Jose State, Virginia Tech, Utah, and Wake Forest by an average of 28 points. The win over Wake Forest lifted Kentucky to its second trip to the Final Four in Pitino's seven seasons.

Paired against the University of Massachusetts in the national semifinals, Kentucky gained revenge with an 81-74 win behind Tony Delk's 20 points.

That set up a championship game match against Syracuse. The Wildcats were just too strong for the Orangemen, as Delk scored 24 points and freshman Ron Mercer came off the bench for 20. Kentucky's 76-67 victory gave the school its sixth national championship and first since 1978. The program had come light years from the mess Pitino inherited in 1989.

"NCAA sanctions for academic fraud and sending money to a recruit's father prompted *Sports Illustrated*'s 'Kentucky Shame' cover in 1989," wrote Jerry Tipton in the *Lexington Herald-Leader*. "When he became UK coach in June 1989, Pitino promised a future [*Sports Illustrated*] cover of Kentucky cutting down the nets at a Final Four. 'We're like the Packers,' Pitino said. 'The university is what we're all about, but this is the team that belongs to the state of Kentucky, the Commonwealth of Kentucky. And we're very excited we represented them for a national championship.'"

After the season, Kentucky fans went through some anxious days as the New Jersey Nets tempted Pitino with an offer to take their head-coaching job. Several NBA teams had tried and failed before to lure Pitino away. But the Nets came after Pitino with a staggering offer. In addition to a reported thirty-million-dollar contract, Pitino was offered a percentage of the franchise. Suffice to say he had to do some serious soul searching as he pondered that. By early June, Pitino still hadn't announced his decision.

Ultimately, a golfing trip to Ireland that Pitino took with about thirty Kentucky alumni proved to be the deciding factor, as he chose to stay put.

"When I left [for Ireland], I was ninety-nine percent sure in my mind I was going to take the job," Pitino said at a June 3, 1996, press conference. "If I had made the decision right away, I'd be the coach of the New Jersey Nets. I was able to get away, without any pressure at all, and make a clear-cut decision. By waiting, I realized that after spending seven years [in Kentucky], you don't decide at the snap of a finger to leave something that has made you so happy."

Once again, Kentucky fans could breathe easier. Rick Pitino was still the Wildcats' coach. But he wouldn't be much longer.

———

Kentucky lost a ton of firepower from its national championship season. Antoine Walker—who left after just two seasons—Tony Delk, and Walter McCarty were all first-round NBA draft picks. Mark Pope, who had also used his eligibility, wasn't drafted, but eventually played in the NBA.

In a testimony to how well things were going in the latter stages of Pitino's tenure, Kentucky was still loaded with talent. Pitino had a great perimeter rotation, with Ron

Mercer, Derek Anderson, Allen Edwards, Anthony Epps, Jeff Sheppard, and Wayne Turner. Jared Prickett—once called "Larry Bird without a jump shot" by Pitino— returned from his redshirt year. Scott Padgett, a six-foot-nine forward from Louisville, finally gained eligibility after a year of trying. And Kentucky filled a hole in the middle by signing freshman center Jamaal Magloire to team with previously little-used Nazr Mohammed.

Kentucky lost its 1996–97 season opener to Clemson but then won fourteen straight games. During that streak, the Wildcats won the Great Alaska Shootout and also took out Purdue, Indiana, Notre Dame, and Louisville.

The streak was stopped in SEC play in an early January game at Ole Miss. Two games later, against Auburn, Kentucky's chances to win another national championship might have been dashed when Derek Anderson tore the anterior cruciate ligament in his right knee and was lost for the season.

To their credit, the Wildcats regrouped from that setback. They didn't win the SEC East after being swept by eventual champion South Carolina, but did claim the SEC Tournament championship for the fifth time in six years. As the No. 2 seed in the West Regional, Kentucky breezed through Montana, Iowa, St. Joseph's, and Utah en route to its second straight trip to the Final Four. A win over Minnesota set up a championship game matchup with Arizona.

With a healthy Anderson, Kentucky might have been able to win its second championship in a row. There had been some talk that Anderson, who dedicated himself to rehab, would try to play in the game. And Pitino did reward him with a token appearance to shoot free throws. But without Anderson at full strength, the Wildcats lost to Arizona, 84-79.

In the minds of Kentucky fans, that loss didn't compare to the ones the program suffered after the season. First, Ron Mercer decided to give up his final two years of eligibility and enter the NBA draft. Then in early May, Pitino shocked Big Blue fans everywhere by announcing he had finally been offered an NBA job that appealed to him.

"I felt if Rick would leave for pro basketball, the only job he'd take would be the Boston Celtics," former Kentucky athletic director C. M. Newton recalled. "I didn't concern myself much with other pro teams that came after him. And I really didn't think he'd be interested in coaching at another college team. When the Celtics called, I began thinking seriously about who I wanted to hire [to replace Pitino]."

That decision wouldn't rest solely with Newton, but part of the terms he negotiated when he took over as athletic director was that he could be a committee of one when it came to hiring coaches. Newton's search to replace Pitino wasn't very taxing. All he had to do was pick up the phone and call Tubby Smith.

Smith, who had served on Pitino's first staff at Kentucky, had by this time made a name for himself as a head coach, taking Tulsa and then Georgia to the NCAA Tournament's Sweet 16.

"I knew him as an assistant," Newton recalled. "I'd recommended him to Rick. When he'd been on our staff here he performed well and we helped him get the Tulsa job. Then, when Georgia needed a coach, I recommended him to [athletic director] Vince Dooley. Vince hadn't even heard of him. I told Vince, 'I'll tell you this. If you hire [Smith] and if Rick should ever leave, he'll probably be one of the few people I'll be coming after.' Vince wasn't surprised when I made the call."

Newton had been one of Smith's biggest supporters through the years.

"I was impressed by his work ethic and knowledge of basketball," Newton said. "He had demonstrated a unique ability and I followed his career very closely. I had seen how he went into Tulsa and Georgia, took other coaches' personnel and won immediately. I knew that was tough, because I had to do it twice in my career. Some people can go in there and handle those players and handle that situation. Some can't.

"Tubby had demonstrated he could do that. He had immediate success at Tulsa and the same thing at Georgia, where it was a tough thing to follow Hugh Durham. But Tubby got those players to buy into his system.

"I felt like at Kentucky that as good as we had been, our fan base was not going to tolerate a down year. We were left with some carryover players, but we also lost a lot. I wanted someone who I felt could come in and take Rick's players—who were so committed to Rick, so dedicated to him—and get them to buy into a new system and get them to play."

Smith, who had just signed a new contract with Georgia, was flattered by Kentucky's interest. But at first he wasn't sure he was interested.

"We had turned down a number of jobs at Georgia," Smith recalled. "People were saying to me, 'Tubby you're going to get the Kentucky job.' I'm thinking, 'Why would they hire me at Kentucky?' Coach Newton had never talked about it. Never once. I never even thought about it. I didn't think Rick would leave, and I kept thinking that right up until the time he left.

"A half an hour after they have Rick's press conference, my phone rings. It was the first time I'd talked to coach Newton about the job. I was probably more surprised than anybody. I remember going to my staff and my wife and saying, 'I've got to make another decision.' I'd moved my family eight times in twenty-five years of coaching. I've got G. G. [his oldest son] playing for me. Saul [his middle son] has just committed to me to come to Georgia. I've got [youngest son] Brian in school at Athens, and a beautiful home. I just signed a new six-year extension at Georgia. It wasn't an easy decision. It wasn't an easy decision at all."

It took a little prodding from Pitino to bring Smith around.

"Rick called me and said, 'Tubby are you out of your mind?'" Smith recalled. "'You've gotta take this job. Are you out of your freakin' mind?' He thought I was kind of hesitant about it. That call was a big key. He said, 'You don't have to worry about me. I'm gonna help you. They have wonderful people. You'll do great there.' After that, there was a calm that went over me. Don't say no right away. Make the right decision. Two days later I'm flying up there and meeting with coach Newton."

On May 12, 1997, just six days after Pitino announced he was leaving for the Celtics, Tubby Smith was hired as Kentucky's new basketball coach.

The move was almost universally applauded, but one strong voice in Lexington's black community wondered aloud whether Smith would be welcomed with open arms by the people of Kentucky.

"It will be hard enough for a white coach to follow Pitino," wrote *Lexington Herald-Leader* columnist Merlene Davis in an open letter to Smith. "It will be an awesome responsibility for a black one. I can hear racists throughout the commonwealth agreeing with this letter. Others who are more enlightened will say I have become so indoctrinated into this racist system I am just like my oppressors.

"All of that may be true. But I sincerely fear for your safety and the safety of your family if you agree to become head coach. I am not interested in using you as a social symbol or as proof of what the black man can accomplish given the opportunity. Nor am I interested in seeing you transformed into a lightning rod for this state's bigots."

Before Smith took the job, he was faxed a copy of Davis's column.

"At first when I read it, I was thinking that I'd been through civil rights," Smith recalled. "I was in school when the riots were going on. I remember when Martin Luther King was killed and how upset I was and wanting to be a part of the riots. But I also grew up in a household, a Christian home with love and understanding and care, and taking people for who they are, not what they are. My dad taught me not to judge a man by the color of his skin from day one. Most people are that way.

"[Davis] was scared, worried, like most minorities are. But when I considered every aspect of the Kentucky job, I drew from another thing my dad taught me: Never be afraid to step out there."

Just in case he'd forgotten how serious Kentucky fans take their basketball, Tubby Smith got a gentle reminder by way of his radio show in the fall of 1997, just as he was about to begin his first season as head coach of the Wildcats.

"I remember this guy calls in—it's my first show—and he said 'Coach, you can stay here as long as you want, as long as you beat Indiana, beat Louisville, and win the national championship,'" Smith recalled.

Smith thought nothing of the comment until his final radio show of the season. It was just days after he'd led the Wildcats to the national championship.

"The same guys calls me back," Smith said. "And he said, 'Coach, you did alright. Two out of three ain't bad.' I'd won the SEC championship, beat Indiana, and won the national championship. But we lost to Louisville that year. I told the guy, 'Two out of three isn't good enough, is it?'"

With that, Smith's honeymoon period, if he was even given one, was officially over in Kentucky. During the 1998–99 season, just months removed from winning an NCAA title, Smith would be bombarded with criticism when the Wildcats didn't live up to their demanding fans' expectations. All Kentucky did that season was win the SEC Tournament and advance to the Elite Eight of the NCAAs. In subsequent years, Smith's son Saul—who had the unenviable task of playing for his father—would become a focal point for abuse from fans who thought his presence prevented Kentucky from getting a real point guard. That gave fans an entrée to criticize Smith's recruiting, which meant he had no safe haven even when the Wildcats weren't playing games.

"It's difficult, because it never goes away," Jerry Tipton, long-time Kentucky beat writer for the *Lexington Herald-Leader*, said in explaining the pressure on the head coach at Kentucky. "It's always there, twelve months a year. Expectations of some sort—winning games or recruiting a certain guy or making sure nobody gets caught using a fake ID going into a bar. Everything goes back to the coach.

"[Former Marquette coach] Al McGuire said it best years ago when it was rumored he was going to be the next Kentucky coach. He said he didn't want the job. His reason was that being the Kentucky coach is like being Wilt Chamberlain. You can never hide. Which is true. No matter where you go. People are watching you out of the corner of their eye."

———

As C. M. Newton knew he would, Tubby Smith took another man's program and made it his own in 1997–98. The makings of another strong team were in place. Jamaal Magloire and Nazr Mohammed were a formidable duo at center. Wayne Turner was a solid point guard. Scott Padgett, with his inside-outside game, was poised to become the Wildcats' go-to scorer. And Allen Edwards had been around the program for four years. He knew what to do.

So did Jeff Sheppard, who redshirted the season before because Kentucky was so deep at the perimeter positions.

There was also a solid class of newcomers. The impact player of the group was Heshimu Evans, a transfer from Manhattan who had been an all-conference player for the Jaspers. Forward Myron Anthony, center Michael Bradley, and guard Ryan Hogan made up the freshman class along with Saul Smith, who had followed his father from Georgia.

Under Smith's leadership, the Wildcats would play a slightly different style than they did under Pitino. Smith didn't discard the full-court pressure favored by Pitino, but he put a lot more emphasis on defense in the halfcourt. Mental toughness was stressed. Rebounding was as important as breathing.

The Wildcats quickly adapted. They breezed through their nonconference schedule at 11-2, losing only to Arizona and Louisville. Kentucky reclaimed the SEC East and overall championships with a 14-2 record, then went to Atlanta, once again the site of the SEC Tournament, and won the championship in convincing fashion. In the title game, Kentucky bashed South Carolina, 86-56. The talk among sports writers after the tournament was that the Wildcats were looking good, good enough to be a huge factor in the NCAA Tournament.

Five days after the SEC Tournament, the Wildcats headed back to the Georgia Dome as the No. 1 seed in the NCAA Tournament's South Regional. They beat South Carolina State and Saint Louis for their eighth and ninth consecutive wins. UCLA would be next in the Sweet 16.

The Bruins didn't have a chance. Kentucky raced to an early lead, shot 54 percent for the game and won 94-68. Duke, the No. 1 seed in the regional, stood in the way of a trip to the Final Four.

For a time, it looked as though the Blue Devils had Kentucky's number again. They led by as many as 17 points, but Kentucky rallied and won, 86-84. Wildcat fans who had suffered so much after Christian Laettner's shot in 1992 finally had their revenge.

"I didn't understand how strong the Duke ties were until we beat them," recalled Kentucky assistant Mike Sutton. "That was like catharsis when we came back and did that. That was a big deal."

Kentucky's Final Four appearance would be its third straight, and fourth of the 1990s. The team that had come to be known as the "Comeback 'Cats" would make things interesting.

Stanford, Kentucky's opponent in the national semifinals, took a 46-36 lead in the second half, but Kentucky, as it had done so many times during the season, rallied to take a 72-68 lead with 1:17 left. Stanford managed to tie the game to send it into overtime, where the Wildcats quickly took command with a five-point lead.

154

The Cardinal rallied again and cut Kentucky's advantage to 79-78, but Jeff Sheppard's clutch three-pointer put the Wildcats ahead to stay. They won 86-85.

The championship game against Utah was more of the same. The Utes took a 41-31 halftime lead, and this time, the odds seemed stacked against Kentucky. No team in championship game history had erased a halftime deficit so big and come back to win.

Smith's defensive philosophy proved to be the difference. Kentucky bore down in its halfcourt defense in the second half. At one point, Utah missed eleven straight shots, allowing the Wildcats to pull away.

Any doubts about Smith's ability to keep the train rolling at Kentucky ended with that game—at least until the next season. In guiding the Wildcats to a 35-4 record, Smith became the first coach to win a national title in his first season at a school since Cincinnati's Ed Jucker in 1961.

Far from letting that lofty accomplishment change him, Smith put the national championship in the back of his mind, to be savored at another time in his life.

"I don't think about it," Smith said. "It'll probably be put in perspective once I'm done. History always has a way of correcting things or putting them in the proper perspective."

C. M. Newton, who had been hired to clean up Kentucky's basketball program and make it a winner again, looks back with pride on Smith's national title.

"He won the championship that year when nobody thought that would be possible," Newton said. "He did a tremendous job with that team. And he's done a tremendous job since."

———

As Smith came to find out, there was only one bad thing about winning the national championship in his first season. By setting the standard so high so quickly, Smith had taken the already enormous expectations of Kentucky's rabid fans and multiplied them times two.

Kentucky had won two of the last three national championships, very nearly winning three in a row. It was going to be difficult for anyone, even Pitino, to sustain that kind of success. Sure enough, in each of Smith's next three years, the Wildcats achieved just a little bit less.

In 1998–99, Kentucky was 28-9 and advanced to the Elite Eight. The next season, the Wildcats were 23-10 and won just a single NCAA Tournament game before being eliminated. By 2000–2001, when Kentucky finished 24-10 and could "only" advance to the Sweet 16, some fans were hypercritical of Smith and longed for the good old days of Rick Pitino. To some, even the national championship Smith's first team won was tainted, having been done with Pitino's players.

A succession of injuries, transfers, off-the-court problems, and even the death of a star recruit plagued the program in Smith's third through fifth seasons on the job.

Kentucky took a huge hit through graduation as Smith started his third season, but he expected to lose Wayne Turner, Scott Padgett, and Heshimu Evans. What he didn't expect was that Michael Bradley, who had started every game in 1998–99, and guard Ryan Hogan would transfer.

Already down to eleven scholarship players, Kentucky lost two more during the course of the season, after recruit Nate Knight transferred and starter Desmond Allison was charged with DUI. Under Kentucky's zero-tolerance alcohol policy, he was suspended for a full season. He didn't return.

Every program in the country deals with such problems, but at Kentucky, where the expectations are higher and the program is under intense and constant scrutiny, they're magnified. When in 1999–2000 Kentucky started 4-4 against a brutal schedule and dropped out of the major polls for the first time in ten years, some Wildcat fans thought the program was in ruins.

To his credit, Smith rallied his undermanned team to a 23-10 record. But Kentucky's early ouster in the NCAA Tournament didn't go over well. By this time, fans were heaping an inordinate amount of blame on Saul Smith, the coach's son and the Wildcats' starting point guard.

Kentucky got off to a poor start in 2000–2001, but again, the schedule was a monster—St. John's and UCLA to open the season in the Coaches vs. Cancer Classic, plus North Carolina, Georgia Tech, Michigan State, and Indiana, all in the first five weeks. After eight games, the Wildcats were 3-5, their worst start since 1975–76. If someone who didn't know anything about basketball had listened to a radio talk show, they might have gotten the impression that Saul Smith was the anti-Christ.

To the credit of both Smiths, Kentucky shook off its poor start and won twenty-four games. Along the way Tayshaun Prince and Keith Bogans became stars. The Wildcats won the SEC Eastern Division and overall championships and the league tournament and advanced to the Sweet 16 of the NCAA Tournament before being beaten by Southern Cal.

Tubby Smith isn't quite sure how he'll remember his first four years at Kentucky, during which he had the added pressure of coaching his son.

"Saul accomplished some things," Smith said. "We averaged twenty-eight wins a season in his time there. He finished eleventh in steals all-time [at Kentucky] and ninth in assists. And he didn't start a game until his junior and senior year.

Tayshaun Prince. *Clay Jackson*

"If we could have kept that group together—Ryan Hogan, Michael Bradley, and some of those guys—we'd have won more, but we didn't. Saul was the only senior on a team that had seven freshmen and four sophomores and was playing the toughest schedule in the country. I thought to myself, 'People don't care. They don't see that.' All they see is that he's your son.

"But Saul was able to deflect attention from a lot of our players. Saul was able to draw all of that to him and it allowed Tayshaun to have a great year, it allowed Keith to have a great year. It didn't phase him. Oh, I'm sure it bothered him some. Sometimes it wasn't deserved. But I was always his biggest critic. He was my point guard. And not only was he my point guard, he's my son. So he's getting a double dose. Anything the people said, that's like water off his back. Because I'm hammering him every day. Not just as my point guard, but as my son. Can you imagine that pressure?"

Smith, who had also coached oldest son G. G. for two seasons at Georgia, made a decision after Saul's career was finished. His youngest son, Brian, who helped lead Lexington Catholic to the 2002 state championship, was a legitimate Division I prospect in 2002–2003. Smith didn't plan on coaching him.

"I wouldn't put Brian through it," Smith said. "Each kid has a different personality. I'm not sure Brian can handle it. Saul could handle it. For four years, he did the right thing. He was a great ambassador for Kentucky basketball."

Smith was feeling good about his team and his job in the spring of 2001. After considerable thought, leading scorers Tayshaun Prince and Keith Bogans decided not to test their marketability in the NBA draft and would return to school. Without Prince—the SEC Player of the Year in 2000–2001—and Bogans—a second-team All-SEC pick—Kentucky would have been a decent team. With them, the Wildcats figured to be a great team.

Some early preseason polls even placed Kentucky among the top two or three teams in the country. After the 2000–2001 season, during which Smith received torrents of criticism and the Wildcats were bumped out of the NCAA Tournament in the Sweet 16, he was glad to once again have a team that figured to be strong enough to contend for a national championship.

Smith had another reason to feel secure and confident after signing the multimillion-dollar contract that was offered when South Carolina made a serious attempt to hire him away. His spirits lifted and financial well-being secured with the new deal, Smith felt confident and was eager for the new season to begin.

And then Jason Parker blew out his knee.

The injury to the six-foot-nine, 260-pound sophomore was freakish. Playing in a pickup game with some of his teammates in late June, Parker attempted to plant his right leg to receive a pass. With no more pressure than that, the anterior cruciate ligament in his knee came apart—the injury would be diagnosed as a complete tear.

"This is a very tough loss for us," Smith said at the time. "Jason is a big part of our team, and we were expecting him to make even greater contributions. Now it looks like we could lose him for the entire season."

The loss of Parker caused Kentucky's stock to plummet as the Wildcats fell out of the top five in most polls. But Parker didn't wallow in self-pity. He dedicated himself to rehab and there was even talk he would be ready to play in January.

Then the unthinkable happened. Before the start of Kentucky's first practice of the season—Big Blue Madness—Parker, waiting to be introduced to the crowd, re-injured his knee in the Wildcats' locker room.

"Jason is just devastated right now," Smith said as Parker's injury was announced to the media. "He was doing exceptionally well in his rehabilitation and was on track to return to our team later in the season. He was horsing around with a couple of the other players and he said he just stepped, planted, and rotated on that knee. It was a freak accident."

Smith couldn't know it at the time, but Parker's second injury was a harbinger of a difficult season to come, as difficult a season as Smith had faced as a head coach.

———

The score sent shock waves throughout the SEC: Western Kentucky 64, Kentucky 52. It was the Wildcats' 2001–2002 season opener, and the game was played in Rupp Arena. "They outplayed us in every phase of the game," Smith said. "I am very disappointed in our effort. I am still looking for something positive in this game."

Smith never did find anything positive about the Western Kentucky game. "Team Turmoil," as the Wildcats would come to be known by the media, was off to a rocky start.

To its credit, Kentucky quickly shook off that loss, winning six straight games. Included in the streak was a win over North Carolina that was the eighteen-hundredth victory in Kentucky history. Fittingly, Kentucky was the first team to reach that milestone.

Duke ended the Wildcats' winning streak, but the game was well played. The Blue Devils needed overtime to squeeze out a 95-92 win, which was encouraging to Smith and Kentucky fans.

The Wildcats regrouped with wins over traditional rivals Indiana and Louisville.

The latter game, played at Rupp, marked the return of Rick Pitino to Lexington. Ironically, Pitino couldn't turn around the struggling Boston Celtics franchise. Eventually deciding he'd had enough of the NBA, Pitino left the Celtics during the 2000–2001 season. He wouldn't be unemployed long. Pitino's name was quickly linked to various college jobs, including UNLV, Michigan, and Louisville. Wildcat fans were saddened and outraged when Pitino chose to replace long-time Louisville coach Denny Crum.

Smith recalls the day he first learned Pitino was interested in Louisville. Kentucky was playing at Florida in a late-2001 SEC game.

"I think he came in for a visit just to tell me he was thinking about taking the Louisville job," Smith said. "That's the first time I heard it from his mouth. He said 'What do you think?' I said, "Rick you're the best coach available. Why wouldn't they consider you? You don't have to worry about me. I love you man.'

"But I also told him he had to be careful. I said, 'You know the people in Kentucky aren't going to like it. It's not gonna go over well.' It wasn't a real lengthy conversation. By that time I think he had pretty much decided. I think he was trying to let me know what was going on."

In 2001, it so happened that the annual Louisville-Kentucky game was scheduled for Rupp Arena. When Smith took the floor, Kentucky fans voiced their appreciation of him, chanting his name. Pitino pulled a fast one on the crowd and entered the court on Kentucky's side of the floor. By the time anyone realized he was courtside, the edge had been taken off his much-anticipated arrival.

The game didn't match its hype, as Kentucky hammered Louisville, 82-62.

Pitino and Louisville wouldn't go away, however. When center Marvin Stone didn't return from his Alabama home after the Christmas break, Smith, tired of dealing with the troubled player, kicked him off the team. Stone had been Kentucky's best post defender, and his loss would soon be felt.

Stone eventually decided to transfer to Louisville, a choice that struck Smith as odd. At first, Kentucky refused to release Stone from his scholarship, but eventually Smith decided he didn't want to stand in Stone's way.

"It just adds more fuel to the flame," Smith said of the Kentucky-Louisville rivalry. "The flame is always burning. Everything is going to be compared now that Rick's there. Recruiting will be a war. The games will be tough. And this situation with Marvin just escalates it."

Kentucky entered conference play at 9-2, and looked to be in control of its SEC debut after taking a 21-2 lead at Mississippi State. But the Bulldogs—who trailed 40-24 at halftime—rallied to win, showing the rest of the league that Kentucky could be

Rick Pitino. *Clay Jackson*

beaten. Four days later, Georgia traveled to Rupp Arena and stole away with an 88-84 win, its first in Lexington since 1979.

All of a sudden mighty Kentucky was 0-2 in the SEC. And of course, the fans were howling.

But things are never as bad as they seem, not at Kentucky. The Wildcats eventually won a share of the league championship despite a litany of off-the-court problems that took their toll on the players, coaches, and fans. Particularly frustrating to Smith was the erratic behavior of guard Gerald Fitch, who had joined the starting lineup as a freshman the year before and gave the Wildcats a lift with his steady play. Fitch was suspended once after a brief skirmish with teammate Cory Sears and again after he and teammate Erik Daniels tried to get into a Lexington nightclub with fake IDs.

The latter offense came just days after a no-holds-barred team meeting, during which players and coaches spoke candidly as they tried to prepare for the stretch run in February and March. Apparently, Fitch and Daniels hadn't been paying attention.

Smith dealt with various other squabbles throughout the season. Freshman Rashad Carruth, recruited to help the Wildcats' occa-

Kentucky
All-SEC Expansion Era Team

F-Jamal Mashburn
F-Antoine Walker
C-Nazr Mohammed
G-Ron Mercer
G-Tony Delk
Top Reserves-Travis Ford, Scott Padgett

sional woeful outside shooting, pouted all season about a lack of playing time and was even suspended for a game. ESPN cameras captured Smith jumping all over freshman guard Adam Chiles in a game against Tennessee. During another game, Smith also had words with and eventually benched Keith Bogans, whose junior season was a disappointment.

As tough as it was, Smith didn't let the season get the better of him. After five years he had learned some survival skills. Part of coping with the job is realizing how important basketball is at Kentucky.

"The program is bigger than life to a lot of people," Smith said. "It's a way of life, and I'm in the eye of the storm, all the time. But you know what? Sometimes that might be the safest place to be."

Smith might not have thought that after the SEC Tournament. But when the Wildcats, defying expectations and ruining office pools everywhere, made a surprisingly competitive run in the NCAA Tournament, the eye of the storm would be safe again.

Chapter Seven

LSU

hen John Brady was hired in April 1997 to replace Dale Brown as LSU's basketball coach, he couldn't wait to get started. Coming from tiny Division I school Samford, Brady knew this move to the Southeastern Conference was a major step. Far more attention would be placed on him and his program as fan and media scrutiny would increase tenfold. The pressure to win, and win right away, would be greater.

Aware of the major rebuilding task ahead of him, Brady didn't want to waste a second getting his system established and the makings of a program in place. Soon after hiring his first assistant, long-time friend Kermit Davis, Brady gathered the eight players he had inherited from Brown into the Tigers' locker room. Brady's first speech to his new charges was stern and to the point as he laid down some rules. Going to class would be mandatory and study halls required. Weight lifting and conditioning would become a priority. The new head coach's word was law, no questions asked.

When he was finished, Brady asked his players if they thought they belonged at LSU. Two of them walked out immediately. As Davis remembers, the meeting went quickly downhill from that point.

"John asked another kid, 'Do you think you belong at LSU?'" Davis recalled. "He said, 'Well, I don't know.' John said, 'You're done.' Another kid looked at John kind of funny. John said, 'You're done.' The kid had LSU shorts on, and John told him he didn't deserve to wear the LSU uniform. So he dropped his shorts right there and walked out in his boxers."

Brady looked at Davis and then counted the bodies left in the room. Four players stared back at him.

"Coach," Brady said to Davis, "Now what do we do?"

Davis's reply was classic. "John," Davis said, "maybe we shouldn't have any more meetings."

From that shaky beginning, things only got worse for Brady and LSU. Brady only thought he knew how difficult rebuilding would be. Not long after he arrived, he found out things would be far tougher than he could have dreamed.

Because of NCAA rules violations that occurred while Brown was still coach, Brady's career at LSU would begin under major penalties. The sanctions included a one-year post-season tournament ban and—far worse—a substantial reduction in scholarships.

LSU basketball had fallen on lean times in the latter stages of Brown's career—in 1996–97, his final season, the Tigers finished 10-20, by far their worst record in Brown's twenty-five seasons in Baton Rouge. LSU had won no more than twelve games in each of the previous three seasons, finishing all of them with losing records.

How had LSU basketball deteriorated to that point? For years, Brown, in his own inimitable style, had the program rolling. Outspoken, emotional, and offbeat, Brown guided the Tigers to their best stretch in school history.

From 1977 to 1993, the Tigers didn't have a losing season. During that time LSU won twenty or more games ten times, won four SEC regular-season championships—the last in 1990–91—and a league tournament championship. LSU advanced to the NCAA Tournament's Final Four twice, in 1981 and 1986. Players the likes of Shaquille O'Neal, Chris Jackson, Randy Livingston, Durand Macklin, Howard Carter, DeWayne Scales, Ronnie Henderson, Ethan Martin, John Williams, and Stanley Roberts passed through the program.

To Brown, his most memorable accomplishment might have been his success against Kentucky, long the SEC's marquee program. In Brown's career, the Tigers got the better of the Wildcats twenty times, ten times when they were ranked among the top ten teams in the country. Beating Kentucky, recalls Brown, was his primary goal when he arrived at LSU. That, and drumming up some interest in the program.

Ironically, when Brown was hired in 1972, the program wasn't that far removed from what had been its most memorable era ever. No player in the history of the SEC, and few in the history of college basketball, was as exciting to watch as the Tigers' Pete Maravich. From 1967 to 1970, the "Pistol," set scoring records that will never be broken. Maravich—coached by his father, Press—averaged 44.2 points in the eighty-three games he played in three seasons. He set NCAA records for scoring average and career points (3,667) and established school standards in several statistical categories.

In the 1969–70 season, Maravich was voted the national player of the year after averaging 44.5 points. As prolific a scorer as Maravich was, he was an even better passer. As a senior Maravich also handed out 192 assists, an average of more than 6 per game.

Almost single-handedly, Maravich sparked an intense interest in basketball at LSU, where football had always been number one in the hearts of fans. Largely because

Maravich had proven basketball could become big in the Deep South, LSU built a new arena, which opened for play in 1971. Fittingly, the building was renamed the Pete Maravich Assembly Center in 1988, the year Maravich died of a heart attack at age forty.

Despite the best efforts of Maravich, LSU never got a sniff of the NCAA Tournament in his three seasons. The closest the Tigers got was the NIT, in his senior year. The Tigers were 22-10 that season, but after Maravich left for a future in pro basketball, the program slid back to the depths from which it had briefly escaped. In Press Maravich's last two seasons, LSU was 14-12 and 10-16.

Maravich was forced out in 1972. By that time, the Tigers were in their new arena, but playing to sparse crowds of less than 2,500. Something had to be done to rekindle interest in the program.

Carl Maddox, then LSU's athletic director, conducted a nationwide search to find a replacement. He tried hard to hire Bob Boyd, then the coach at Southern Cal, but Boyd wasn't ready to leave the West Coast. Years later, after having switched to Mississippi State, Maddox did lure Boyd to the SEC.

Unable to hire the established head coach he wanted, Maddox turned his attention to promising assistants, eventually narrowing his list to three candidates. Bill Guthridge, who would later succeed his long-time boss Dean Smith at North Carolina, was a finalist. So was Gale Catlett, who later became a successful head coach at Cincinnati and West Virginia.

The final candidate was Dale Brown, then an assistant coach at Washington State. Brown had earned a reputation of being a great recruiter at Utah State as an assistant to Ladell Anderson. When Anderson left to coach the Utah Stars of the old American Basketball Association, Brown fully expected to replace him. But after Utah State instead hired T. L. Plain, the head coach at Transylvania University, Brown quit.

Years later, Brown described his final seconds as a Utah State assistant in his book *Tiger in a Lion's Den: Adventures in LSU Basketball.*

"I got up from my chair and I said to the athletic director, 'Let me just say something. The only way you could have hurt my family more would have been to take me to mid-court at halftime and cut my guts out in front of ten thousand people in the area. I quit," Brown wrote.

That flair for melodrama would surface often in the years to come, sometimes serving Brown well and other times not so well.

After he left Utah State, Brown scrambled around and found an assistant's job at Washington State, where he lasted all of one season. Ironically, he would have been offered the top job there after head coach Bob Greenwood was fired, but Brown refused. Greenwood had done Brown a good turn by hiring him when he didn't have a job. Brown didn't want Greenwood to think he had helped force him out.

Unbeknownst to Brown at the time, his name had already been circulated at LSU. Joe Dean, Sr., who would later become athletic director at his alma mater, played basketball at LSU in the late 1940s and early 1950s. After a stint in the military and a season playing semi-pro basketball, Dean returned to Baton Rouge and went to work as a sales representative for Converse. In those days, Converse had a monopoly on the shoe market in college basketball, and Dean got to know just about every coach in the game.

Dean had crossed paths with Brown several times before and was struck by Brown's intensity and his passion. Thinking that Brown had the right stuff to rekindle interest in LSU basketball, Dean went to Maddox.

"I knew he was a dynamic salesman, a promoter," Dean recalled. "And I also knew that, although coaching ability was important, it was all about players. LSU had been one of those schools that would hire a football coach who helped out a little bit with basketball. Or a good X and O guy who had no clue about marketing a program or recruiting. LSU would be lucky to get a couple of players here and there. Bob Pettit was a local guy. Pete Maravich came with his father.

"I knew Dale's background. He'd been at Utah State. In those days, they battled UCLA to get out of a [NCAA Tournament] regional a couple of times. They had players. I knew Dale was the reason. When the LSU thing developed, I went to Carl Maddox and told him to give Dale a call. He did, and the next day Carl called me and asked 'Is this guy for real?' I told him, yes, I thought he was."

Thus began the Dale Brown era at LSU. It's safe to say that LSU might not have been prepared for the sheer force of Brown's personality. And Brown definitely wasn't prepared for LSU.

"Joe told me when I took the job you'd sweep the floor, sing the national anthem, and introduce your own team," Brown recalled. "I thought that was a little embellished, but it turned out to be true. On the first day of practice, we had to sweep our own floor and put the backboards up; they didn't know basketball started on October 15. The interest level in the program was zero. We had to generate our own interest."

Brown proved to be a pioneer in marketing his own program. Together with assistants Homer Drew and Jack Schalow, Brown blanketed the state of Louisiana, sometimes handing out packets that included purple and gold basketball nets, business cards, and a poem written by Drew's wife, Janet. "This is a net from the purple and gold for a sport that will never grow old," the poem read.

Janet Drew's prose was accurate. Though there were some lean years in Brown's quarter century in Baton Rouge, particularly in his final seasons, LSU basketball did-n't get old. Brown saw to that. Whether it was taking his players to a Louisiana prison in an effort to motivate them, feuding with Indiana coach Bob Knight and the NCAA (which Brown once called "Gestapo bastards"), rushing the court to help defend the mammoth Shaquille O'Neal from the elbows of an opposing player, or waxing philo-sophic to the media about an endless array of esoteric subjects, Brown was never dull.

Former Georgia coach Hugh Durham pegged Brown perfectly during one of the SEC coaches' annual pre-season meetings with the media. In the middle of discussing his team, Durham was interrupted when an air-conditioning unit switched on with a deafening roar. Durham didn't miss a beat. "That's Dale Brown's spaceship taking off," Durham said in his nasal twang.

If Brown occupied a place in his own galaxy, that was fine by LSU fans, as long as the Tigers kept winning. As other SEC coaches know all too well, though, if a coach stays too long at one place, an inevitable downturn occurs. Brown staved off that downturn for twenty-one seasons. In fact, at the dawn of SEC expansion, which begins the focal point of this book, LSU was still playing at a high level. The Tigers, behind 1991 national player of the year Shaquille O'Neal, were 21-10 and 12-4 in the SEC in 1991–92 and 22-11, 9-7 the next season. LSU advanced to the NCAA Tournament both years.

In 1993–94, the decline began, perhaps triggered by a knee injury to LSU's most heralded recruit ever.

Before the 1993–94 season, Brown and his staff thought they had pulled a coup when they signed Ronnie Henderson and Randy Livingston, two exceptionally gift-ed guards. Henderson, a cousin of former LSU star Chris Jackson, was thought to be the best player to ever come from talent-rich Mississippi. One recruiting analyst called him "the closest thing to Michael Jordan in his [1993 recruiting] class."

Livingston was even more highly regarded than Henderson. The New Orleans native scored more than 3,000 points in his high school career and was a two-time *Parade* national co-player of the year. After Henderson and Livingston played in Magic Johnson's all-star game in the spring of 1993, Johnson said they were the best guards he'd seen since Isiah Thomas. Other recruiting analysts said that LSU had signed the best backcourt ever in one class.

Livingston never got to prove whether the recruiting gurus were right. While work-ing out at a summer camp, Livingston tore the anterior cruciate ligament in his right knee. Livingston tried as hard as he could to rehabilitate the injury, but ended up red-shirting in the 1993–94 season. And LSU finished 11-16 overall and 5-11 in the SEC, which dropped the Tigers to fifth place in the Western Division.

"I learned a lot of things," Brown said after his first losing season since 1976 was over. "I'm a lot more sensitive to losing now. I had more or less taken victory for granted. I had just taken for granted that no matter what kind of talent I had, I'd win twenty games and go to the NCAA Tournament."

Brown couldn't have imagined it at the time, but those days were over. Livingston returned to the court in 1994–95 and was showing signs of living up to his promise. But knee problems continued to plague him. He was involved in a car accident and suffered a fracture in his right knee cap. Then, in a game against Arkansas, Livingston drove to the basket and collapsed in pain. This time, his knee cap was broken. Livingston underwent four surgical procedures to correct his various knee troubles.

LSU, predictably, tanked again at 12-15 and 6-10 in the SEC. It was at this point that Brown began to admit LSU hadn't done a good job recruiting in the early 1990s, save for landing Livingston and Henderson. After nearly thirty years of chasing high school athletes, Brown was beginning to get weary of the process, and it showed.

"I guess the older you get there's less dignity in recruiting," Brown said. "You used to be able to visit with the high school principal and the high school coach and the player's family. It got to where there were so many variables—AAU coaches had more power and influence with a player than his high school coach. So-called friends of the family would show up at the house when you were trying to recruit a kid. They were parasites. You had to deal with them. I really used to love recruiting, but that changed toward the end of my career."

Brown proved as much by walking out of several in-home visits with prospects. One such incident stands out in his mind.

"[Assistant coach] Johnny Jones was presenting our pitch to this kid," Brown recalled. "He was yawning, looking at his watch. He took a book out of the book case. I knelt down beside the kid and said, 'You haven't looked at coach Jones once. You're not interested in LSU. And we're not interested in you.'"

With that, Brown stalked out of the house, leaving a startled Jones behind.

LSU's problems came to a head in the 1995–96 season. Livingston, frustrated because of all his knee problems, quit after thirteen games. Deuce Ford, a talented transfer from Memphis, tore an anterior cruciate ligament and was lost for the season. Even Henderson, who had been forced to carry the load the previous two years, broke down physically.

The Tigers finished 13-17 and 4-12 in the SEC. The Tigers were quickly ousted from the SEC Tournament, losing to South Carolina in the first round. Brown was emotional at his post-game press conference and talked as though he intended to resign. When Mark Bradley, a columnist for the *Atlanta Journal-Constitution*, asked

168

Brown what seemed like a logical question about stepping down, the sixty-year-old coach snapped at him. "You don't know me very well," Brown said.

———

When a head coach makes changes on his staff, that's often a harbinger of bad things to come. Before the 1996–97 season, Brown's last at LSU, he brought in former Mississippi State coach Bob Boyd and former LSU player Ricky Blanton. Their presence couldn't alter the downward path of the program.

Nor could the presence of Lester Earl, LSU's most decorated recruit since Livingston and Henderson. Earl was from Baton Rouge and was a *Parade* All-American. It seemed only natural that he would sign with the Tigers. Brown felt a sense of obligation to sign Earl, even though, as he said years later, he wasn't particularly impressed with him.

"I really didn't want him," Brown recalled. "He was twenty years old coming out of high school. He couldn't shoot, couldn't pass. I was almost forced into recruiting him because he was a local product."

Had Brown let Earl slip away, he would have been crucified by LSU fans and the media. As it turned out, Brown's instincts about Earl had been correct. Earl and Brown lasted all of one semester together. After numerous confrontations with Earl, Brown kicked him off the team in December 1996. Earl later announced he would transfer to Kansas. LSU fans, disappointed that Earl wasn't the savoir of the program, thought they had heard the last of him.

They hadn't.

The Lester Earl fiasco might have finally convinced Brown it was time to try something else. He had considered retirement before, after each of the Tigers' Final Four appearances. Each time, Brown couldn't make himself leave the game he loved. But those were the glory days of LSU basketball. And they were long past.

Brown knew that the day in late 1997 he went to see athletic director Joe Dean.

"He came to my office and said, 'You know, I have lost my enthusiasm for begging an eighteen-year-old kid to come here to school.'" Dean recalled. "I said, 'That's not good.' I think pressure was starting to build, like it did with [Arkansas coach] Nolan Richardson [in 2002]. We went out to dinner that night, and I said, 'I would never fire you. What you've done here is remarkable. And you deserve some slack.' But I told him I don't want him to get hurt or get embarrassed. I wanted him to go out in style. And he began to think and talk more and more about leaving."

Not long after Earl announced his departure, so did Brown. His timing allowed officials at the eleven other SEC schools to set up a farewell tour. At each of the Tiger's eight league road games that season, Brown was honored, given gifts, and wished well by previously hostile fans.

"It was a very humbling experience, particularly at Kentucky," Brown recalled. "Their fans were the most vocal in their appreciation of me. I was sort of a thorn in their side. I think the fans appreciated we were able to compete with Kentucky. But the whole league was appreciative. It surprised me. Because I'd been so outspoken. Our team chaplain told me one time that every time I was involved in controversy I always led with my heart instead of my head. You can manage your head better than you can your heart. That might have gotten me into trouble."

Brown's final season wasn't as well scripted as his departure. Not since Press Maravich's first year in 1966 had the Tigers lost as many as twenty games. Fittingly though, LSU won Brown's last home game, after which the school honored him a final time. At the SEC Tournament, Brown threw a party for the media, handing out commemorative key chains and trading old war stories with the press. Any hard feelings Brown might have had toward a particular writer were forgotten.

In his twenty-five seasons, Dale Brown had taken LSU basketball full circle. After the glory years of Pete Maravich were over, Brown breathed life into the program. And when his own glory days ended, Brown knew it was time to step aside.

———

With interest in LSU's basketball program waning in an era where it was on the rise at every other Southeastern Conference school, LSU athletic director Joe Dean had to hire a coach who could, as Brown did a quarter century before, generate some enthusiasm. Coaching ability was important, to be sure, but the way Dean saw it, he had to hire a coach with some name recognition that Tiger fans could rally around.

Dean's first call went to Iowa State coach Tim Floyd. Floyd had done a good job keeping the Cyclones competitive in the rugged Big 12. And as a former coach at the University of New Orleans, he knew his way around Louisiana and the Deep South.

"Tim had always told me he wanted to come back to the South," Dean recalled. "He was from here—his dad had coached at Southern Mississippi—and enjoyed it here. So I called him and offered him the job. We went back and forth a little bit. He kind of got blinded by money. Those things happen. So I started talking to him about quality of life, how it was cold where he lived, and the food was bland. Anything I could think of to remind him about living down here."

Floyd didn't give Dean an answer that day. It was a couple of more days before

Dean heard from Floyd again. Dean had thought the delay was a bad sign. "Then he calls me," Dean recalled. "He's in a hotel room in College Station, Texas; they were playing Texas A&M. "When he left Ames [Iowa] it was a little bit below thirty degrees. When he got off the plane in College Station, it was sixty-eight degrees. All of a sudden it hit him. And he says, 'I need to take your job.'"

Suffice to say Dean was excited, but his enthusiasm turned to disappointment a few days later when Floyd changed his mind. By that time, the Chicago Bulls had begun a courtship with Floyd. "He told me he had to wait and see how that turned out," Dean said.

With Floyd out of the picture, Dean approached Texas Tech coach James Dickey, who had been an assistant coach in the SEC at Kentucky. Dickey wasn't interested.

Choice number three was Ole Miss coach Rob Evans, who thought long and hard about jumping from one SEC Western Division school to another. Ultimately, Evans's devotion to his players kept him in Oxford.

By this time, Dean was in full scramble mode. He had some conversations with Oregon coach Jerry Green but ultimately thought the fit wasn't right. A few weeks later, Green ended up in the SEC anyway, at Tennessee. Phil Martelli of St. Joseph's was a hot name that Dean considered, but Martelli had spent his entire career in Philadelphia and had no ties to the South.

Dean wasn't sure which direction to go when a call from his son, Joe, Jr., helped him see the light. The younger Dean had been a Division I head coach and an SEC assistant and was then working in private business in Birmingham, where he couldn't help but notice the great coaching job John Brady was doing at Samford.

"I told my dad that of everybody left he had a chance to get, in my opinion the best guy to come in there and do that job was John Brady," Dean recalled.

It just so happened that Joe Dean, Sr., had Brady's resume on his desk. Brady had taken the liberty of sending it a few weeks earlier.

Dean knew about Brady—who had taken Samford to Baton Rouge the year before and beaten LSU—and was aware of his background. But the closer Dean looked over Brady's resume, the better Brady began to look.

"John had all the qualifications," Dean, Jr., said. "And he had a lot of the background that fit the LSU job. Dad's biggest concern was could he sell a no-name guy to the LSU people. I said, 'The bottom line is you want somebody who will work and do the job and win.' Dad was in a position where he could take some heat, so he started looking real seriously at hiring John."

"The more I thought about it, the more I just thought John could do the job," Dean, Sr., recalled. "You never know hiring football and basketball coaches. It's not easy.

But I just had a real comfort level with John."

———

John Brady prepared all his life to be the head basketball coach at LSU. Playing in the mid 1970s for McComb (Mississippi) High School and Belhaven College for coaches with contrasting styles, Brady learned that there was more than one way to win a basketball game. That knowledge would come in handy twenty years later, when he went to war in the rugged SEC with an outmanned crew of overachievers.

"My high school coach [Bobby Nelson] was a real tough-minded guy," Brady recalled. "And he instilled that in you. He wanted you to be competitive. And he loved to get after you. We were a fast-breaking team that played man-to-man defense."

In college, Brady had to adjust to a polar-opposite style.

"I went from high school, where I was the only white guy on the team, to Belhaven, a team that was all white," Brady said. "Instead of running and pressing, we're playing a match-up zone defense and a motion offense. We didn't fast break at all. That's where I learned patience."

After college, Brady began his coaching career in typical fashion, serving as a graduate assistant coach for Mississippi coach Kermit Davis, Sr. It was there where Brady struck up a friendship with Davis's son, who played point guard for the Bulldogs.

After a year at Mississippi State, Brady left for Crowley (Louisiana) High School, where he was the head coach for five seasons. By his fourth year, Brady was chosen the Louisiana Class AAA Coach of the Year.

In 1981, Brady returned to Mississippi State to work for Bob Boyd. That was another learning experience.

"Bob was another guy who understands how to play the game with different types of players," Brady said. "He was one of the best communicators I've ever been around. He could verbalize the game. He could explain a play and players could see it in their minds. That's how good he was. He taught me to communicate with players and how to teach the game."

Brady worked with Boyd for four seasons. And after Boyd left, Brady worked another four years at Mississippi State for Richard Williams. Brady helped recruit a future SEC championship team and also learned more of the game's finer points from Williams, regarded as one of the better tacticians in the SEC.

After his time at Mississippi State, Brady's apprenticeship was all but finished, but he had one last stop to make.

In 1990, Brady left Mississippi State for New Orleans to work for Tim Floyd. As he had at his previous stops, Brady absorbed all he could of a different philosophy.

"Tim Floyd was all about playing hard and tough, rebounding and playing defense," Brady recalled. "He's in the old Hank Iba mentality. I was really fortunate to have learned the game from a wide range of coaches. It made me a more well-rounded coach."

In 1991, Brady was ready for his first head-coaching job. In Brady's six seasons at Samford, the Bulldogs became known as the Princeton of the South, running the patient motion offense Brady had learned in college with some new wrinkles added, making use of precise cuts and screens, and taking full advantage of the three-point shot. Like Princeton, Samford became a giant killer in its own right, as its win at LSU in 1996 would attest. The Bulldogs were a pesky team upper-level Division I schools were wary of playing. Samford won conference championships in 1996 and 1997, Brady's final two seasons.

Brady's Samford training would serve him well at LSU, where for his first five seasons, the Tigers would almost always be short-handed or physically overmatched.

———

Weeks after he arrived at LSU, Brady learned the program was being investigated for recruiting violations associated with Lester Earl. The story at the time was that former Dale Brown assistant Johnny Jones had given Earl cash as an inducement to sign with the Tigers.

"I had no idea," Brady recalled. "If I'd known, I'd have been more adamant about a contract extending through probation."

Though Brady was concerned about the NCAA investigation, he put it out of his mind. After that first room-clearing meeting he had with his new team, Brady needed to go find players. The only two holdovers from the Brown regime that could play were Maurice Carter, a streak-shooting junior guard, and Rogers Washington, a junior forward. Brown's staff had signed one freshman, guard Renaldo Bratton.

"We had to find some people who could help us in a hurry," said Kermit Davis, Jr., then Brady's senior assistant. "So we went the junior-college route. For as late as we got started, we actually signed some pretty good kids."

LSU signed five junior college players, including two guards, Willie Anderson and DeJuan Collins, who would step in and become major contributors.

The Tigers started the 1997–98 season by winning seven of their first ten games.

They opened SEC play 0-3, but then beat Auburn and Florida back-to-back. The upset of the Gators had been televised by ESPN.

Any momentum the win over Florida might have created was quickly dashed by some key injuries. That became a common theme in Brady's first five seasons in Baton Rouge. First, Washington injured a knee. Then, after a practice skirmish between Collins and redshirt Brian Beshara, disaster struck. The disagreement carried over to the locker room, and Collins broke his hand trying to punch Beshara.

The Tigers didn't win a game the rest of the season.

"We finally had our team right," Davis said. "We thought things were going on. Then we lose ten straight."

LSU finished 9-18, 2-14 in the SEC. Brady was disappointed, and in the back of his mind dreaded the outcome of the NCAA's investigation. But he believed better days were ahead. He just wasn't sure when.

Like he had with Kermit Davis, Jr., Brady turned to his Mississippi State connections to complete his staff. When Brady was an assistant there, the Bulldogs' point guard was Butch Pierre. After his playing career was over, Pierre joined the State staff as a graduate assistant and worked with Brady. He left in 1986, and wouldn't see much of Brady for the next ten years.

"But we always stayed in touch," Pierre recalled. "When he was at Samford and went to LSU and won, I was one of the first to call him."

After leaving Mississippi State, Pierre gained a reputation as a solid recruiter. He put together some talented classes in his eight seasons at Louisiana-Lafayette, and when he left there for Charlotte in 1996, he continued his success, helping recruit a class ranked among the top ten in the country for coach Melvin Watkins.

Brady had often talked about one day hiring Pierre. When Brady landed the LSU job in 1997, he quickly called his old friend. Brady didn't have to waste a lot of time convincing Pierre to come to Baton Rouge. A Louisiana native, Pierre was eager to revisit old contacts and work his recruiting magic in his home state.

Pierre didn't arrive at LSU empty-handed. From his days at Louisiana-Lafayette, Pierre had been aware of Jabari Smith, a six-foot-eleven, 250-pound center from Atlanta. When Pierre left for Charlotte, he kept in contact with Smith.

"I had known about Jabari for a long time," Pierre recalled. "When he didn't qualify out of high school, he went to junior college. Jabari was the kind of kid you stay in touch with. I thought he was a [future] pro. I knew back then. He just had some

174

minor problems academically and he was a little immature. I thought he was overlooked to a certain degree. I figured once I got to LSU, we'd have an opportunity to
get him."

Pierre was right. Smith knew that Pierre had followed his career from the beginning, even after it was obvious Smith couldn't sign a Division I scholarship out of
high school.

"Jabari committed to us without even taking an official visit," Pierre said. "We
went into his home and he committed right then. He appreciated the fact I'd stayed in
touch with him." With Smith in the fold, Brady had the first component part to an
SEC championship team.

LSU's next target would be a little tougher to land. Stromile Swift, an athletic six-
foot-nine forward from Shreveport, Louisiana, was one of the most talented players
to come from that state in years. A *Parade* and McDonald's All-American who was
generally considered among the top five players in the country, Swift was a deadly
scorer in the post area because of his athleticism and quickness. He was also a good
rebounder and prolific shot blocker. Brady knew that if he wanted to establish a program at LSU, he had to sign the best high school players from Louisiana. Signing
Swift would set a positive tone.

The LSU coaches thought they would have a tough time prying Swift away from
Georgetown. It had always been Swift's dream to play for Hoya coach John
Thompson. Michigan was also in the picture. And Swift had even considered jumping straight to the NBA. Because he had options, Swift delayed his decision until the
spring of 1998.

Brady knew he couldn't compete with the NBA's dollars if that's the direction
Swift was leaning. All he could offer was the promise that LSU's offense would be
centered around Swift. He also pledged to give Swift a chance to prepare for the NBA
by showcasing his perimeter skills along with his inside game.

"We just had to convince him that the stage was as big at LSU as it was anywhere
else," Pierre said. "That had been illustrated by Chris Jackson and Shaquille O'Neal.
The other thing about Stromile was that he needed a family atmosphere and personal attention. He needed LSU as much as we needed him."

Pierre was in the office the day Swift committed to LSU.

"I took the call," Pierre said. "Pumped wasn't the word. The whole staff went
through the roof. We all knew he was a program changer."

"It was unbelievable the day Stromile committed to us," Davis said. "John and
Butch Pierre did a great job with that kid. Everybody said it was a done deal, he was
going to Georgetown to play for John Thompson."

Along with Swift, LSU signed three other recruits who would help shepherd the program through some tough times. Jermaine Williams, Collis Temple III, and Brad Bridgewater all placed their faith in the Brady regime, and at the mercy of the NCAA, which was still investigating the program.

"You can imagine people were telling those kids about what the NCAA was going to do to the program," Davis said. "All those kids did not sign national letters. They signed an SEC letter, which wasn't binding. You go the whole summer not knowing whether they'd show up. It was tough."

Not every player LSU recruited could get past the threat of NCAA sanctions. Brandon Dean, a stocky, athletic guard from Monroe, Louisiana, wanted to play for Brady, but eventually signed with Arkansas.

"We worked him hard," Davis recalled. "We thought he could be a great player, and he went on to prove that. But he just couldn't pull the trigger. It was the uncertainty of the sanctions."

Two days after LSU's first game of the 1998–99 season, on November 18, 1998, the NCAA dropped its hammer on LSU. The infractions committee found during its investigation that an LSU booster had given Lester Earl approximately five thousand dollars in cash. That was the major violation uncovered, but there were other minor ones as well. The NCAA also determined that free medical care had been given to Earl's brother Louis and that former LSU assistant Johnny Jones had made an excessive amount of phone calls to Earl during the recruiting process.

The NCAA stopped short at accusing LSU of the dreaded "lack of institutional control," a charge that usually carries with it harsh penalties. Given that, the sanctions LSU got slapped with seemed excessive. In addition to a postseason tournament ban in 1999, LSU was stripped of two scholarships for each of the next three years. The school was also limited to giving just four scholarships total in 1998–99 and 1999–2000.

"I was shocked, stunned," Brady recalled. "In essence, what the NCAA determined was that somebody gave a young man five thousand dollars. They'd had cases of academic fraud and a lack of institutional control in football and basketball at other schools, and our penalty was more severe. Johnny Jones never missed a beat [he later worked as an assistant at Memphis and Alabama before taking the top job at North Texas]. Dale Brown retired. Lester Earl got a year back and kept playing ball. And we took the hit.

"It would seem to me if there were no sanctions against Johnny or Dale, and they let Earl keep playing, what was done wrong? What did I do?"

Brown, often critical of the NCAA during his career, thought there was a motive behind the penalties that went beyond rules violations.

"I would not want to sound like Mr. Paranoid," Brown said. "But it was a witch hunt. The penalty was not LSU, it was Dale Brown. It was a tremendous injustice, no question about that."

Brown claimed to have known nothing about the booster giving Earl money.

"They had sent [Lester Earl] to a doctor, a guy who owned a lot of businesses," said former LSU athletic director Joe Dean. "Periodically, he would give players jobs. Then the kid cries on his shoulder and, to make a long story short, the doctor gave him cash."

"[Earl] went to the guy and asked him for an advance," Brown said. "He said his mother was about to be evicted from her home and his brother was in the hospital. Any decent human being would want to help out someone in that situation."

As critical as he was of the NCAA's penalties, Brady couldn't quite bring himself to believe that the NCAA wanted to send a message to Brown.

"I've been asked many times did the NCAA get back at Dale Brown because of all his banter over the years," Brady said. "I would hope not. To be that petty . . . I would hope the NCAA isn't that petty to get back at someone by hurting someone else."

Why was the NCAA so hard on LSU? An explanation was given in a statement released by the NCAA when the sanctions were announced.

"The violations centered on the recruitment and retention of a high-profile prospective student-athlete, with a prominent representative of the institution's athletics interests providing substantial cash to the prospect on several occasions," the NCAA's statement said. "In its report, the committee noted that this case is exceptional, not because it might have been an inadvertent accumulation of smaller violations, but because athletics department personnel and representatives of LSU's athletics interests so completely departed both from institutional expectations and NCAA rules in recruiting a premier prospect."

As disappointed as he was over the NCAA's decision, Brady had a more pressing concern in the fall of 1998. Stromile Swift hadn't yet received a qualifying standardized test score, and it meant he would miss the fall semester.

Even without Swift, the Tigers managed to win eight of their first nine nonconference games. Swift finally gained eligibility two games into the SEC schedule. His entry into college basketball was slow, and his impact wouldn't drastically reverse LSU's fortunes in conference play. But Swift showed signs of his talent. He blocked

String Music

eleven shots in a game at Alabama, a record in the Crimson Tide's Coleman Coliseum. Against Arizona in a mid-February game, Swift scored 24 points and grabbed nine rebounds.

Despite Swift's steady improvement, LSU struggled in SEC games. Making matters worse, injury problems continued to plague the Tigers. Senior guard Willie Anderson blew out his knee with more than half the league schedule to go. "He was probably the most important guy on our team in terms of leadership," assistant coach Kermit Davis recalled.

LSU finished 12-14 in the regular season and 4-12 in the SEC. It was the Tigers' fourth straight last-place finish in the league's Western Division.

Because of NCAA sanctions that prohibited LSU from playing in a postseason tournament, the SEC had to make a decision on whether to allow the Tigers to play in its own tournament. Though it didn't seem likely, LSU, by winning the SEC Tournament, could have wasted the league's automatic bid to the NCAA Tournament.

LSU didn't learn its postseason fate until a week before the SEC Tournament, when the SEC announced the Tigers would be allowed to play.

"We didn't know until four days before the SEC Tournament was to begin we were going to be able to go," Brady recalled. "That's how crazy it was. We went the whole year with no SEC Tournament, nothing on the horizon. That was tough."

Brady's second season ended in the Georgia Dome in Atlanta with a 97-75 loss to Florida in the first round of the SEC Tournament. Typical of the way the year had gone for Brady, he was stopped from going on the court before the game by a security guard that didn't recognize him. Brady had to pull out a credential in order to join his team.

"That's bullshit," Brady said to a reporter as he walked to the court. "Do you think Dale Brown would have had to show a pass? That guy didn't even know who I was."

A year later, Brady wouldn't have to suffer the indignity of not being recognized. Everyone would know about him, and his team.

In assessing their personnel needs for the 1999–2000 season, Brady and his assistants didn't have to agonize too long. For one thing, they would have only two scholarships at their disposal. And their needs were obvious. With future NBA draft picks at the center and power forward positions and as many as three players capable of playing small forward, all the Tigers lacked were guards.

The LSU coaches didn't have to look far for a point guard. In the 1998–99 season,

Torris Bright was the leading scorer in the metro New Orleans area, averaging 33 for Slidell High School. But Brady wasn't interested in Bright because of his scoring average. What intrigued Brady was Bright's assist average (nine per game) and his size. At six-foot-four and 205 pounds, Bright was an industrial-strength point guard.

Butch Pierre, the LSU assistant who focused on Bright's recruitment, was convinced Bright could handle the point in the SEC.

"Everbody thought Torris was a two guard," Pierre recalled. "But I thought he could play point, and I kind of persuaded John that he was the one we really needed. Torris was a big-time scorer in high school, but he was also unselfish. He could have easily averaged 40 points a game. He was the type of kid who really wanted to win and he really wanted to play with Stromile Swift. John took my word on him."

Bright signed with LSU in the spring of 1999. Soon to follow was another big guard, a player who became available in May, which is fairly late in the recruiting process. Lamont Roland started his college career in 1996 at Ball State, where he averaged 13 points and four rebounds as a freshman and was chosen the Mid-American Conference's Newcomer of the Year.

That taste of success convinced Roland he could play at a higher level of Division I, so he left Ball State and headed to a Kansas junior college. In his only season there, Roland was chosen the national junior college player of the year, and just as he'd hoped, he had his pick of big-time schools.

Roland eventually decided on Connecticut, but a transcript problem held him up. That gave Davis, who had been recruiting Roland, a chance. Davis convinced Roland to visit LSU.

"He signed on the visit," Davis recalled. "He just loved the place. He was an absolute perfect fit for what we needed, because he was tough and could defend."

Luckily for LSU, Brady had added another freshman in the November signing period, just days before the NCAA sanctions were handed down. Ronald Dupree, a Top 100 recruit from Biloxi, Mississippi, would eventually become an All-SEC player.

"If you live on the coast in Mississippi, it's almost like you follow LSU," Davis said. "Ronald had a lot of familiarity with us, and we had watched him since he was a sophomore. He's a smart kid—he wanted to major in electrical engineering—and he narrowed it down to LSU, Georgia Tech, and Syracuse. But his mom wanted to see him play and Biloxi is two hours and fifteen minutes from Baton Rouge. It was just a great break for us."

_____

With just nine scholarship players on its roster, LSU started the 1999–2000 season by winning its first thirteen games. That was reason enough for Brady and his coaches to feel encouraged. But besides the winning streak, there was another trend taking shape before their eyes that got them excited. Stromile Swift was starting to dominate.

In his abbreviated freshman season, Swift wasn't able to practice with the team until January. That meant he missed preseason conditioning and several months of weight training. Stamina was a problem, and there were times when Swift was outmuscled in the post.

All that changed in Swift's sophomore season. Once he got into optimum physical condition, he became a force. Even his coaches were stunned to watch him work.

At a tournament in Hawaii, Swift scored 21 points and grabbed eight rebounds against Oakland, went for 33 points and 13 rebounds against Wyoming, and scored 19 points to go with five rebounds against Fresno State as the Tigers won the championship.

"It was the most unbelievable thing," recalled Davis. "Other teams wouldn't leave the tournament after their games were over just to watch him play. He was dunking balls right and left, rebounding, blocking shots, all the things you expected him to do. He was finally getting his strength into his game. He just went off. That's when a lot of NBA scouts starting noticing."

The Tigers beat Oklahoma State in their second-to-last nonconference game, and then handled Alabama in their SEC opener. At 14-0, LSU was the surprise of the league and beginning to receive some national attention, showing up in the Associated Press poll on January 3, 2000, at No. 21.

The Tigers' momentum was quickly dashed when they lost three straight league games to Tennessee, Florida, and Vanderbilt. But no sooner were LSU's doubters agreeing that the tough SEC schedule had brought the Tigers back to reality, they rebounded with three straight wins.

The last, an 86-60 pounding of Arizona in a nationally televised game, proved that, against all odds, Brady and his staff had brought LSU back from the grave in which it had been buried the previous six seasons. And it proved without a doubt that Swift was the real deal.

Swift burned Arizona's front line of future NBA draft picks for 29 points and nine rebounds. He looked so good that his coaches started to worry.

"Stromile just kept making shots," Davis recalled. "We looked at each other on the bench and said he needs to quit making those shots."

By that time it was too late. NBA scouts had locked on Swift and would follow his trail the rest of the season.

Though the dramatic elevation of Swift's game had attracted considerable attention, LSU was far from a one-man show. Jabari Smith was playing his way into becoming a first-round NBA draft pick, teaming with Swift to give LSU the toughest low-post tandem in the conference. As LSU assistant Butch Pierre had predicted, Torris Bright proved he could handle the point, taking charge of LSU's offense and making timely shots when the need arose. And Lamont Roland justified his junior college press clippings.

LSU won ten straight games to close out the regular season. In three of those games, Roland was the leading scorer.

Even freshman Ronald Dupree was able to showcase his considerable skills. In the Tigers' biggest game of the season, Dupree scored 16 points in a win at Auburn that clinched the SEC's Western Division championship and took the title away from the defending champions on their own court.

With a win over Ole Miss in their regular-season finale, the Tigers, who finished the regular season 24-5, had done what no one thought possible before the season began. After finishing in last place in the West for four straight seasons, the championship was theirs. LSU also tied with Kentucky, Tennessee, and Florida for the overall SEC championship. And as an added bonus, the Tigers were ranked tenth in the country in the AP poll, eleventh in the ESPN/*USA Today* poll.

"It was rewarding," Brady recalled, "For us to have gone through what we'd gone through with the loss of scholarships, then to take a team with nine scholarship players and win the West. A lot of hard work went into it."

LSU earned a first-round bye into the SEC Tournament and won a quarterfinal game over Vanderbilt when a new hero, sophomore Collis Temple III, came off the bench and scored 20 points.

Next up was Arkansas, which LSU had beaten twice in the regular season. The Razorbacks came into the tournament on a mission. With no other chance to gain entry into the NCAA Tournament, Arkansas knew it had to win the SEC championship. LSU turned out to be the Hogs' third victim in as many days.

A familiar face did most of the damage to the Tigers. Arkansas guard Brandon Dean, a Louisiana native who might have gone to LSU were it not for the impending NCAA sanctions, scored 20 points, including the go-ahead basket with twenty-one seconds left, in a 69-67 Arkansas victory.

Ousted from the SEC Tournament, the Tigers could still look forward to the NCAAs. On Selection Sunday, they were elated to learn they'd earned a fourth seed and would play in the West Region. It was LSU's first trip to the Big Dance since

1993.

It took Brian Beshara's three-pointer with 17.8 seconds to play to lift the Tigers past first-round opponent Southeast Missouri State. Brady was happy just to survive and advance; the win was LSU's first in the tournament since 1992, when Shaquille O'Neal blocked a tournament-record 11 shots against BYU.

LSU didn't have nearly as difficult a time in its second-round win over Texas. The game was tied at 60 with three minutes to play, but the Tigers scored six straight points to assume control. Beshara was again a hero as his steal and two free throws capped the run. And Swift blocked a dunk attempt by Texas center Chris Mihm that would have tied the score at 62.

"There's not a better story in college basketball this year than LSU," Brady told the media after the game. "Now, maybe nationally, people will recognize what we've been through, and what these young people have done."

LSU advanced to its first appearance in the Sweet 16 since 1987, but the Tigers' postseason run was stopped cold by Wisconsin, a gritty defensive-minded team that had finished sixth in the Big Ten but would advance to the Final Four. LSU committed 23 turnovers against the withering Wisconsin defense that limited Swift to five shots and 12 points.

Though Brady and his team had hoped for a trip to the Final Four, their season was still one for the ages. LSU had won twenty-eight games and lost just six, won an SEC title when it had been picked to finish last, and played in the Sweet 16. Brady was a much-deserved winner of the SEC's Coach of the Year award, Bright was co-freshman of the year, and Swift co-player of the year.

Unfortunately for the Tigers, their success would prove to be short-lived.

———

The fate of LSU's 2000–2001 season was essentially determined in mid May 2000, when Swift decided to declare for the NBA draft.

"I always loved LSU and planned to come back, but I heard so much about where I would go in the draft, I decided I had to find out what was there for me," Swift told the Associated Press. Swift was later chosen second overall by the Vancouver Grizzlies.

Brady understood Swift's decision, though he knew what it would mean for his team. With the NCAA-imposed scholarship limitations still in place, LSU couldn't recruit a replacement, even though it made an appeal after Swift turned pro.

"We appealed to the benevolent NCAA," Brady said before the season began. "But

182

Stromile Swift. *teamcoyle*

they turned it down. They sent me a letter and said the only way we could get a scholarship back was if a player passed away. It was just another sensitive, understanding gesture by the NCAA toward the LSU basketball program."

Brady had just one scholarship available after having signed Torris Bright, Lamont Roland, and Ronald Dupree the season before. That was used on guard Jue Michael Young, but he was later ruled ineligible.

Once again LSU would have to compete in the rugged SEC with a threadbare roster—this time Brady was down to six scholarship players. The Tigers' numbers became even smaller in preseason practice when center Brad Bridgewater blew out his knee and was lost for the year.

LSU rallied around its solid group of perimeter players. Dupree, Collis Temple, Jermaine Williams, Bright, and Roland gave the Tigers some firepower, if not a lot of size or strength under the basket. Returning to the offense of his Samford days, Brady used a four-out, one-in motion, and it was like old times, the Tigers screening, cutting, and racking up points from the perimeter.

LSU got off to an 11-1 start in nonconference games. The schedule wasn't the toughest, but the LSU coaches were confident heading into SEC games. But in the conference opener against Alabama, the injury curse struck again when Roland, after making a steal, blew out his knee.

Down to five scholarship players, LSU won just three more times the rest of the season. The Tigers were competitive in most of their games, but almost always wore down by the thirty-minute mark. LSU finished 13-16 and 2-14 in the SEC. Having gone from last place in the SEC's Western Division in 1998–99 to first place the next season, the Tigers returned to the bottom in 2000–2001. It was a dizzying ride for Brady.

"The scholarship limitations took their toll on us," Brady said. "It doesn't show up the first year or so, it shows up the third, fourth, and fifth seasons when you haven't been able to replenish your team in a normal way. It makes it almost impossible to sustain growth. Your team becomes so limited in numbers that the five or six quality players you have really have to play well every night for you to have a chance."

———

Brady and his staff made such good choices on the players they were able to sign that LSU might have been able to withstand the NCAA sanctions without any significant downturns if it had any luck at all. But academic problems, injuries, and defections to the NBA took their toll.

All three problems conspired against the Tigers in 2001–2002. Just like the season before, LSU's fortunes took a turn for the worse just before the NBA draft. Kedrick Brown, a six-foot-seven forward from a Florida junior college, signed in the fall of 2000, and Brady was touting him as a talent capable of putting the program back on pace. But Brown never made it to LSU. Though Brady never saw it coming, Brown declared for the NBA draft and was taken as the eleventh pick in the first round by the Boston Celtics.

"I was in total shock," Brady recalled. "Kedrick Brown was the first junior college player in the history of the NBA draft to be taken in the first round. And it has to be my guy. After all the things that happened to us, we think we've got it turned. I would have loved to put Ronald Dupree and Kedrick Brown in there together and see what we could have done. But Kedrick never comes to school. That hurt us."

Brown wasn't the only junior college player Brady counted on but didn't get. Six-foot-nine forward Shawnson Johnson was supposed to help shore up the Tigers' weak inside game, but couldn't gain eligibility because he hadn't

LSU
All-SEC Expansion Era Team
F-Stromile Swift
F-Ronald Dupree
C-Shaquille O'Neal
G-Ronnie Henderson
G-Torris Bright
Top Reserves-Jabari Smith, Collis Temple III

graduated from his junior college. Before the season started, Brady was down to nine scholarship players. He hoped the Tigers would have better luck staving off injuries than they had in his previous seasons.

That wasn't meant to be. JueMichael Young missed nearly all of the Tigers' non-conference games after breaking a bone in his left foot. Collis Temple, who along with Dupree and Torris Bright had become the Tigers' stalwarts, sprained his right ankle in mid December and the injury never healed. Temple gamely tried to play, but he was ineffective. Eventually, doctors discovered a ruptured tendon in his foot. Again, Temple tried to play, but by February he was finished. He later underwent surgery to repair the tendon and reconstruct his ankle.

Rather than resign himself to yet another losing season, Brady dug deep and somehow kept his team competitive. The Tigers were 10-3 in nonconference games. Then, in their season opener at Alabama, they took the eventual league champions to the final seconds before losing, 76-74. Clearly, LSU was not giving up.

"There's one thing about John," said LSU assistant Kermit Davis. "He gets knocked on the ground and the next day he comes in the office and says, 'It's a new day. What can we do to bounce back?' We can have an injury, and the next day, he's asking what can we do to get our team back. That's the biggest thing I've seen about John. It's his resiliency. He can take licks and jump back into the fire."

Riding Ronald Dupree, who would become a second-team All-SEC pick, and surprising freshman guard Antonio Hudson, LSU battled through its conference schedule. After the decent nonconference start, Brady hoped the Tigers could win five SEC games so they could have a shot at the NIT. League win number five came in late February over defending Western Division champion Ole Miss. And an insurance victory over Auburn followed four days later.

The Tigers entered the SEC Tournament with a 16-13 record and their NIT bid secure. Brady, who despite NCAA sanctions, injuries, and defections to the NBA, had taken LSU to two postseason tournaments in his first five years. He looked back with pride on the program's resilience.

"We've done a good job bringing respect back to the program," Brady said. "Our kids play hard and we've got good players—we just need to get more of them. Only time can take care of that.

"It's been tough. There's one of two ways you can look at it. You can sit back and feel sorry for yourself, but that's just negative thoughts that don't help the situation you're in. Or you can take care of what's at hand and make sure you keep your competitive nature. For the most part, we've done that better than a lot of people expected."

Chapter Eight

Mississippi State

R ichard Williams was in a jam. It was a week before the July recruiting period in 1990, and the Mississippi State coach had just learned his top assistant, John Brady, was leaving to go to New Orleans. The loss of Brady, who would go on to become a successful head coach at Samford and LSU, could have been a huge blow for Williams, especially because his departure came so close to the all-important period when coaches were allowed to go on the road and evaluate talent.

Fortunately for Williams, Brady had recruited his own replacement. In the spring of 1990, Rick Stansbury, a brash, confident farm boy from Kentucky, had left his assistant's job at Austin Peay in search of a greater challenge. He had been acquainted with Brady through their occasional meetings on the recruiting trail. When Mississippi State had an opening for a third assistant, Brady recommended Stansbury.

"John came to me and said he had a guy who would take the job for one year," Williams recalled. "I didn't know Rick Stansbury. John said if I hired Rick, he was going to bring a seven-footer with him from Florida. I brought Rick in, liked him, and hired him. Sure enough, he had a seven-foot kid named David Dean that was going to come with him. But he never made grades and went to junior college. He wound up at Ole Miss."

Stansbury was on the job less than a month when Brady left.

"It was a week before [the July recruiting period]," Williams said. "I had nobody to put on the road. So I gave the job to Rick. He worked so hard, I kept him out there."

Stansbury's one-year gig turned into two years, and then three. By his sixth year, Stansbury had helped Williams recruit a team that would reach heights no one could have predicted when Williams took over a dismal program from Bob Boyd in 1986. After Stansbury helped bring forward Dontae' Jones into the fold before the 1995–96 season, he made a prediction.

"He told me that with Dontae' we had a Final Four team," Williams recalled.

"And Richard said I was crazier than hell," Stansbury said.

But Stansbury, who would go on to replace Williams in 1998, wasn't crazy.

"At Austin Peay, we were one free throw away from the Sweet 16, and the team that beat us [Providence] went to the Final Four," Stansbury said. "Now we're talking about Mississippi State, which has got great facilities and is playing in the best league in America. Why can't you compete for the national championship?"

Stansbury proved to be a prophet. In March of 1996, as the Bulldogs boarded a plane that would take them to the Final Four, Williams looked back at his assistant. "He smiled at me," Stansbury recalled. "And then he said, 'Rick, you were right.'"

Mississippi State's surprising ascension to the Final Four was a landmark occurrence in the history of Southeastern Conference basketball. In a two-year span that began in 1994 when Florida and Arkansas played in the Final Four, four SEC teams reached that coveted pinnacle. In 1996, there had been talk of an All-SEC national championship game, because Kentucky, under coach Rick Pitino, had also advanced to the Final Four. That dream matchup never materialized, but the SEC's reputation as a basketball conference had been solidified. That reputation would grow throughout the rest of the decade.

———

Richard Williams was a math teacher by trade. For seventeen years, even while he was learning to coach basketball, Williams always viewed himself as a teacher first.

"I think my teaching background has been a tremendous help in my coaching," Williams told the *Memphis Commercial-Appeal* in 1996. "When you teach math as I did for seventeen years, you have to prepare lesson plans, you have to prepare for the questions the kids might ask you. In my mind, that's what coaching is—it's teaching. All good coaches are teachers."

Williams first realized that during his frequent visits to Mississippi State practices when he was an undergraduate there in the 1960s. The Bulldogs' coach then was the legendary Babe McCarthy, who had presided over the glory days of Mississippi State basketball. Between 1959—the last season of the great center Bailey Howell—and 1963, the Bulldogs won or tied for four SEC championships.

Williams had always admired McCarthy, but he never thought about becoming a coach until he started keeping statistics for a junior high school team in Natchez, Mississippi. That job convinced Williams he wanted to be around the game. From 1967 until 1984, Williams rose through the coaching ranks in his home state, first at two junior high schools, then at a pair of high schools. He made his first step to the next level in 1979 when he took over at Copiah-Lincoln Junior College in Wesson, Mississippi. Then, in 1984, he was hired as a part-time assistant at his alma mater by then-coach Bob Boyd.

Boyd's five-year tenure was nearing an end by the time he hired Williams. Despite the presence of future NBA star Jeff Malone, the Bulldogs weren't very good in the early 1980s. Malone's SEC-leading 26.8 scoring average was a key element in the Bulldogs' 17-12 showing in 1982–83, MSU's first winning season in four years. But when Malone, the school's all-time leading scorer, left for the NBA, the program slid back into decline.

In 1984–85, the Bulldogs were 13-15 and 9-9 in the SEC. The next year, the bottom fell out of the program as MSU was 8-22 overall and 3-13, good for last place, in the SEC. Boyd resigned after that season, but before he left, he recommended Williams for the job.

Charlie Carr, then athletics director at Mississippi State, wasn't sure about Williams, who had never coached at a Division I school before returning to Starkville to work for Boyd. Besides that, Carr thought he could hire a big-name coach. But after a lengthy, fruitless search, Carr realized he was wrong. There weren't many takers for a job at a supposed football school in a rural Mississippi town. The program had suffered six losing seasons in the previous seven. In the twenty-two years between McCarthy's departure in 1964 and Boyd's in 1986, six coaches had tried and failed to rekindle McCarthy's late 1950s–early 1960s run of success. The Mississippi State job was considered a coach's graveyard.

Once Carr realized that, and after he got to know Williams and learn of his enthusiasm for the school and the state of Mississippi, his choice became clear. At forty years old, Williams, who had taught math most of his adult life, became the head basketball coach at his alma mater.

"I got the job because no one else wanted it," Williams said. "The program was not in good shape, even coach Boyd would tell you that. I remember the night I was named the coach. I was watching *SportsCenter* on ESPN and Dick Vitale came on and said it was the toughest Division I coaching job in America. I knew it was a hard job. But I grew up in Mississippi and graduated from Mississippi State. That was the only Division I job I ever wanted or ever tried to get. It was my dream job. When Charlie hired me, I didn't even ask what I was going to get paid."

Williams had a plan for rebuilding the program. He retained the hard-working Brady as his lead assistant and hired Julius Smith as his other full-time assistant. Their charge was to beat the bushes of Mississippi to find players. Williams, who had coached at every level of competition in the state, knew some players were out there.

"When I coached at South Natchez high school, I kept up with Alcorn State, which was about forty miles up the road," Williams recalled. "Alcorn's coach was Davey Whitney, and he had been taking Mississippi kids and beating people with them for years. They had gone to the NCAA Tournament and won some games, beat

Mississippi State in the NIT. I decided that if I ever got the job at Mississippi State, I was going to recruit Mississippi kids. Even before I got the job, M. K. Turk was recruiting kids at Southern Mississippi and winning. So basically all I did was copy Davey Whitney and M. K. Turk."

The Bulldogs' first full recruiting class was loaded with in-state players, players who would eventually breathe life back into the program. There was Cameron Burns of Flora, a six-foot-seven forward, guard Tony Watts of Rolling Fork, and six-foot-six forward Greg Carter of Forest. Guard Doug Hartsfield came from Utica and forward Carl Nichols from East Flora.

"Those are the kids we built our program on," Williams said. "In a way, coach Whitney was a victim of his own success. A lot of those kids we signed might have gone to Alcorn State or maybe Jackson State. But we convinced them we had more to offer in terms of the league we played in, and the publicity. It made sense to me, and it must have made sense to them, too."

Slowly, Williams coaxed some life back into the program. The Bulldogs were 7-21 overall and 3-15 in the SEC in Williams's first season, but doubled those win totals the next year. By 1989–90, the Bulldogs won sixteen games, played in the NIT, and began showing signs of becoming competitive again in the SEC. The next season, State was the surprise of the league, putting together a 20-9 record that included a 13-5 SEC mark. That earned the Bulldogs a share of the league's regular-season championship and the school's first NCAA Tournament bid since 1963. Williams became the first coach in State history to take the Bulldogs to more than one postseason tournament appearance.

The two stars of the 1990–91 SEC championship team were Burns, who averaged 16.9 points and 6.1 rebounds, and Carter, who averaged 15.4 points and 7.8 rebounds. Another key player was Watts, the son of former NBA guard Donald "Slick" Watts, and also a double-figure scorer.

As successful as Williams had been signing in-state players, he felt frustrated by the big ones that had gotten away. Mississippi has long been an underrated breeding ground for high school talent, producing the likes of Chris Jackson (LSU), Antonio McDyess (Alabama), Othella Harringon (Georgetown), Ronnie Henderson (LSU), and Litterial Green (Georgia). When Williams hired Rick Stansbury in 1990, he realized that Burns and Carter had but one season remaining. To keep the program at a high level, Williams wanted to stem that flow of in-state blue-chip talent that had been finding its way to other schools. That would be Stansbury's primary job.

When Mississippi State fans look back at the decade of the 1990s and recall the players who helped revive the program, the name of Bubba Wilson might be overlooked, which is understandable. Wilson's name barely shows up among the school's all-time statistical leaders. But there's no overemphasizing the six-foot-eleven center's contributions to the program. Wilson was the first in-state player signed by Williams's staff who was highly regarded nationally. Before he left to take an assistant's job at New Orleans, John Brady had laid the groundwork for Wilson's recruitment. When Brady left, Ricky Stansbury and Robert Kirby took over.

"Bubba was a top-ten player nationally," Stansbury said, "a kid we thought we could get. It came down to us and Kentucky."

"Bubba was the breakthrough recruit," said Kirby, who served as an assistant for Williams, left in 1993 for the University of Houston, and eventually returned to Mississipi State in 1998. "He was a *Parade* All-American and everybody was recruiting him."

Unfortunately for Wilson, he would never live up to his billing after suffering a serious knee injury his senior season at Stone County High School and missing all but one game.

"He tore up his knee on a Tuesday night," Stansbury said. "And we signed him in the hospital on Wednesday morning. He never totally recovered. Never was the same player at all."

Wilson's contributions transcended anything he was able to accomplish on the court. By resisting the overtures of Kentucky—at that time a program on the rise under coach Rick Pitino—as well as several other high-level schools, Wilson stood out as an example for other blue-chip Mississippi high school players to follow. If Wilson could take a chance on Mississippi State, trust that the program could compete in the SEC and play in the NCAA Tournament, then others could, too. For the next several years, Stansbury preached the gospel of Bubba Wilson when he traveled the back roads of Mississippi. He found several willing converts to the cause.

In 1992, Mississippi State struck again when yet another Mississippi *Parade* All-American, six-foot-four shooting guard Vandale Thomas of Monticello, signed with the Bulldogs. Still another key player in that class was Marlon Dorsey, also a six-foot-four guard and first-team All-State pick from Shelby, Mississippi. Neither Thomas nor Dorsey would make significant contributions during their MSU careers, but they helped keep the in-state talent flow streaming toward Starkville.

The next year, the makings of an NCAA Tournament team were put in place. A key ingredient was Erick Dampier, a rugged six-foot-eleven center from Lawrence

County High School in Monticello, Mississippi. The MSU staff put in a lot of work to sign him.

"You couldn't count the hours Rick spent recruiting Erick," Williams recalled. "He got to know everybody in Monticello, everybody close to Erick, and got them on our side. The only official visit he made was to us."

"Erick was a Mississippi kid all the way," Stansbury said. "We just made him understand where his roots were."

Two other newcomers on the 1993–94 team were junior-college transfers. Power forward Russell Walters had originally signed with Alabama, where he sat out the 1991–92 season. But the Mississippi native eventually left Tuscaloosa for Jones County (Mississippi) Junior College. After one season there, he signed with the Bulldogs. Joining Walters from the junior-college ranks was T. J. Honore, a point guard who would take over running Williams's offense.

At the same time it was mining in-state talent, Mississippi State got lucky with some out-of-state players. Forward Marcus Grant was coaxed out of Georgia. Guard Darryl Wilson had played in the shadow of the University of Alabama at South Lamar High School in Kennedy, Alabama, where he led the state with his 37.8 scoring average and was chosen Mr. Basketball his senior year. Stansbury latched onto Wilson after getting a tip from an unlikely source.

"Ralph Radford was an assistant at Auburn and Ralph and Rick were buddies," Williams recalled. "He'd recruited Darryl, but Auburn wasn't going to take him because he was going to be a partial qualifier. But Ralph really liked Darryl and told Rick we should try and sign him."

Williams and Stansbury couldn't figure out why Alabama wasn't interested in Wilson. They found out later.

"After we signed him, [Alabama coach] Wimp Sanderson called Richard and told him the kid couldn't play at all," Stansbury said. "The rest is history."

After the 1990–91 team claimed a share of the SEC's regular-season championship, Williams's next two teams could manage just a 12-20 record in league games. But in 1993, the Bulldogs regrouped to 18-11 and 9-7 in the SEC and played in the NIT for a second time under Williams. The leaders of that team were Dampier, who earned second-team All-SEC honors as a freshman, Honore, who locked down the point-guard job, and Wilson. Wilson, who sat out for academic reasons his freshman year, was particularly impressive as a first-year sophomore, leading the Bulldogs in scoring with a 16.2 average and setting a school record for three-pointers made (67) and attempted (181). The best was yet to come.

In 1994–95, the program took another step forward, this time claiming a share of the

SEC's Western Division championship and winning twenty-two games. Mississippi State advanced to the NCAA Tournament and made the most of its trip, beating Santa Clara and Utah to advance to the Sweet 16. The Bulldogs lost to eventual national championship UCLA, but they had given their fans a preview of the next season.

———

As they looked toward the 1995–96 season, Richard Williams and Rick Stansbury thought their team was lacking one key ingredient to make another run at the NCAA Tournament. The Bulldogs badly needed a forward who could score. They didn't have to go too far to find one.

Dontae' Jones had been the ultimate hard-luck kid at Stratford High School in Nashville, Tennessee. The six-foot-seven Jones was by no means unintelligent, but academic problems dogged him his entire high school career. He was ineligible as a sophomore, and again at the beginning of his junior season. Once he regained eligibility, Jones suffered a knee injury and was lost for the season. When Jones was again ruled ineligible his senior season, he quit school and went to work at a Kenny Rogers Roasters restaurant. Jones might have had a long career in the fast-food business had the Nashville police not intervened.

In an effort to keep young adults off the streets at night, the police created a midnight basketball league. Jones quickly became the scourge of the league, earning MVP honors and changing his way of thinking.

"I knew I didn't want to work 9 to 5 the rest of my life," Jones told the *Memphis Commercial-Appeal*. "I knew I wanted to do something I liked."

Enter Kendall Stephens, who had been working as a sports information director at Tennessee State, located in Nashville. Stephens persuaded Jones to earn his general equivalency diploma. That enabled Jones to enroll at Northeast Mississippi Junior College. Northeast coach Mike Lewis had learned of Jones from Stansbury, who had been tipped off about the player by a friend who witnessed Jones's exploits on the playgrounds of Nashville.

Jones was an instant star at the junior-college level. As a freshman, he averaged 25.2 points and 11.2 rebounds. A year later, he increased those averages to 28.7 and 13.3. Williams and Stansbury didn't have to agonize over a recruiting spiel to lay on Jones.

"Our selling pitch to him was easy," Stansbury recalled. "We had just gone to the Sweet 16. We told Dontae' that we had everybody returning and we only needed a power forward. We told him we'd have an opportunity to compete for the national championship. The way it turned out, that's exactly what happened. He was that missing link that got us over the hump."

Jones bought Stansbury's pitch and signed with Mississippi State, but before he could hope to play Division I basketball, he had to get his academic affairs in order. At times during his career at Northeast, that looked hopeless. He ran countless sets of sprints for missing classes. Eventually, Lewis assigned Jones a tutor.

"The tutor told me that Dontae' knew how to do the work," Lewis told the *Commercial-Appeal*. "He just needed motivating."

Jones needed more than motivation the summer before he left for Mississippi State. He needed a miracle. Jones was way behind in his academic requirements and would need to pass thirty-six hours to become eligible.

During the spring and summer of 1995, Jones passed twenty-one hours at Northeast Mississippi and earned fifteen more through correspondence courses from Southern Mississippi.

Such an accomplishment by anyone, let alone someone who had struggled academically since high school, seemed impossible to a lot of coaches, administrators, and media around the SEC. Some were openly skeptical and critical. But as suspicious as Jones's sudden academic enlightenment might have seemed, the NCAA uncovered no wrongdoing after checking into the situation. Seven years after the fact, Stansbury still bristled at the suggestion that Jones didn't do the class work. And the skeptics still don't believe it.

"Dontae' took advantage of a rule that no one else knew how to do," Stansbury said. "It wasn't a gray area; there wasn't a rule saying you couldn't do that. It never was a question of Dontae's ability. Did I pass the classes for him? Did I go to school for him? Talk to people at Northeast. He went to class. The NCAA checked it over with a fine-tooth comb. The SEC checked it over with a fine-tooth comb."

Regardless of what anyone thought of how he became eligible, Jones did, and he would go on to make an impact. That impact wasn't limited to the court. The NCAA later passed a rule—dubbed the "Dontae' Jones rule" among coaches—that limited the number of summer school hours a student-athlete could use for eligibility purposes.

———

With Jones eligible, Williams could put a talented, well-balanced team on the floor. He had plenty of size at his disposal in Erick Dampier and Russell Walters. Dampier, at six-foot-eleven and 265 pounds, was the premier defender in the SEC, able to clog the lane and alter shots with his long arms. Offense wasn't his forte, but he still managed to average 14.6 points and shoot 54 percent from the field as a junior.

"The key guy on that team was Dampier," Williams recalled. "He gave us a chance to win every game because he was such an intimidator defensively in that lane."

The six-foot-ten, 230-pound Walters wasn't asked to contribute a lot offensively, but he was the team's blue-collar guy who loved physical play and wasn't afraid to do the dirty work.

At 220 pounds, Jones, recruited as a power forward, had the luxury of playing the small-forward position. It wasn't a reach for Jones, who had the ability to bang inside or step outside and make three-pointers.

The Bulldogs also had some good guards. Marcus Bullard, a six-foot-three sophomore, had been a big-time scorer in high school but was converted to the point, where he made a lot of turnovers but also a lot of assists and steals. And he shot 40 percent from three-point range. Darryl Wilson was the Bulldogs' scariest weapon; as a senior he had smashed the school record for three-pointers and had led the Bulldogs in scoring, averaging nearly 19 points.

Mississippi State didn't have a lot of depth, but Bart Hyche, a freshman guard who was a two-time player of the year in Alabama, filled in at the backcourt positions along with former walk-on Whit Hughes. And Mississippi State kept its streak of signing blue-chip in-state big men going by bringing in six-foot-ten, 250-pound Tyrone Washington of Indianola. Washington was chosen a *Parade* All-American in his senior season at Gentry High School.

Mississippi State was highly regarded in the preseason, as their No. 9 ranking in the first Associated Press poll attested. Their first "Midnight Madness" practice was televised by ESPN2. And season tickets were selling at record numbers. Now all Mississippi State had to do was produce.

Though Jones had been hampered by a stress fracture in his foot suffered in the preseason, the Bulldogs started strong, winning their first four games and rising to No. 8 in both major polls. Then came a humbling, last-second loss to Arkansas Little Rock, which might have gotten a little inside knowledge about Mississippi State from coach Wimp Sanderson, who had been at Alabama for thirty-two seasons, the last twelve as the Crimson Tide's head coach.

The Bulldogs regrouped and won their next six games, including two in a row to start the SEC season. But then came a humiliating, 74-56 home-court loss to Kentucky during which Mississippi State committed 28 turnovers, nine of them by Jones, who didn't start the next game against Alabama. The Bulldogs lost that game and, after a win over Ole Miss, lost two straight to Arkansas and South Carolina.

195

Those losses saddled the pre-season favorites to win the SEC's Western Division with a 3-4 league record.

During that disappointing stretch, Jones struggled to adapt to Division I basketball. Whereas he had the green light to shoot in junior college, often putting up thirty shots a game, Jones had been asked to buy into a team concept at Mississippi State. And he was also required to play defense.

"He wasn't nearly so hard to coach as people think," Williams recalled. "It was hard to get him to understand that there were other good players on the team, and that

he didn't have to do it all. And he had to learn to guard people."

Williams had to keep a tight rein on Jones, especially after he learned the player was fond of cutting class. That earned Jones more than his share of 6 A.M. workouts, which were particularly brutal.

"I'll never forget one day I went into the weight room and Dontae' was sleeping," Williams said. "I went over to him and asked him what was wrong. He used to call himself 'Kid,' and he told me, 'Coach, Kid tired.' I told him if he got himself to class, he wouldn't have to do the 6 A.M workouts. He said, 'Coach, you win. I'm not missing any more class.' Dontae' was really a smart kid. He just didn't like going to school and he made no bones about it."

Dontae' Jones. *Mississippi State Athletic Media Relations*

After several attitude adjustment seminars, Jones began to find his way. The Bulldogs won five straight games, including a huge victory at Oklahoma. Darryl Wilson scored 32 points and grabbed 11 rebounds in that CBS-televised game, which put Mississippi State back in the Associated Press poll at No. 25. Though they lost two more SEC games, the Bulldogs wound up winning the Western Division with a 10-6 record and earned a first-round bye in the league tournament in New Orleans.

The Bulldogs breezed past Auburn and Georgia, their first two opponents, setting up a rematch with Kentucky. The Wildcats had won 27 straight games and 26 straight over SEC teams. They were going for their fifth straight SEC Tournament championship and were a 22-point favorite over Mississippi State.

None of that mattered to the Bulldogs, who were playing with the attitude that they had nothing to lose. Led by Jones, who scored 28 points and grabbed 11 rebounds, Mississippi State upset Kentucky, 84-73. Now 22-7, the Bulldogs were seeded No. 5 and would play VCU in the first round of the NCAA Tournament's Southeast Regional.

That game—played at the RCA Dome in Indianapolis—turned out to be a classic example of the tournament adage "survive and advance." The Bulldogs seemed in control until Dampier got into foul trouble. The Rams quickly took advantage of Dampier's absence by getting the ball to six-foot-seven, 240-pound forward Bernard Hopkins. With 8:12 to play, VCU tied the score at 40.

At that point, Williams had no choice but to put Dampier back on the floor. He sealed off the low-post area defensively, and Wilson took control offensively, scoring 12 of State's last 16 points. The Bulldogs were elated to sneak out with a 58-51 win.

"At this time of year, it's not a beauty contest," Williams told the media. "So we're certainly happy with the win."

Mississippi State's next opponent was a scary one. During much of the twenty-nine-year career of Princeton coach Pete Carril, no one wanted to play the Tigers in the NCAA Tournament. With its deliberate offense that took advantage of screens, precise movement, backdoor lay-ups, and three-point shots, Princeton often gave more talented teams fits. In their first round game, the Tigers knocked out defending national champion UCLA.

Making things worse for the Bulldogs was the fact Carril had announced his retirement. His team knew that every game in the postseason could be his last. The Tigers had every reason to be motivated.

Unlike many teams before it, Mississippi State made short work of Princeton, winning 63-41 by powering the ball inside to Dampier, who scored 20 points on ten-of-twelve shooting, and Jones, who finished with 11 points. "UCLA didn't pound it inside," point guard Marcus Bullard told the *Jackson Clarion-Ledger*. "We didn't want that to happen to us. We didn't forget about the big guy [Dampier]. When he's posted up and he's screaming at you to throw him the ball, it's kind of hard to forget about him."

From Indianapolis, the Bulldogs would travel to a familiar place—the University of Kentucky's Rupp Arena—for the regional semifinals. The opponent would be No. 1–seeded Connecticut, which came into the game with a 32-2 record and No. 3 national ranking.

The Huskies had a talented guard tandem of Ray Allen, a first-team All-American, and Doron Sheffer, but Wilson set out to prove that the Bulldogs had a decent backcourt, too. He hammered home his point by draining seven three-pointers and scoring 27 points.

Despite Wilson's second-highest scoring game of the season, the Bulldogs—who led most of the game—had to hold their breath at the end. Sheffer made a three-pointer to cut the State lead to 58-55 with thirty-eight seconds left. The Bulldogs turned the ball over on their possession, giving UConn a chance to tie the score. There didn't seem to be any doubt who would take the last shot for the Huskies. Allen got what seemed like a good look, but Russell Walters alertly switched off a high-post screen and lunged at Allen, who missed. "I knew he was going to shoot it," Walters told the *Clarion-Ledger.* "I got up in his face and contested the shot pretty good. It threw him off."

State's 60-55 victory set up a regional final matchup with Cincinnati, and the Bulldogs weren't to be denied as they revved up their defense for a 73-63 win. The Bearcats were held to a season-low 33.8 percent shooting. The 63 points were 17 below their season average.

Dontae' Jones was the Bulldogs' offensive star, scoring 23 points and grabbing 13 rebounds to claim regional MVP honors. For the first time in school history, Mississippi State was headed to the Final Four.

Suffice it to say the town of Starkville had never seen such commotion. It seemed as though everyone in town wanted a ticket.

"This is wild," Jones told the *Clarion-Ledger.* "When we got back Sunday night, it was like a mini-riot on campus. They were shaking cars and things like that. The folks around here are having fun. They've never experienced something like this, and neither have the players. It's just exciting for everybody right now."

The Final Four in 1996 was played in the Meadowlands in East Rutherford, N.J. Mississippi State couldn't be blamed for heading east thinking it could win the national championship. The Bulldogs were 8-0 in March and had won fifteen of their last seventeen games, including a resounding win over Kentucky, which had also advanced to the Final Four. SEC officials were ecstatic at the prospect of an All-SEC Final.

Before that could happen, there was the little matter of Mississippi State getting past Syracuse, which had advanced as the No. 4 seed from the West Regional. The Orangemen, like the Bulldogs, had considered themselves underdogs and had to fight and scrape their way to the Meadowlands. Syracuse desperately wanted to give its coach, Jim Boeheim, a national championship; he had been denied in 1987 on Indiana guard Keith Smart's now legendary jump shot in the final seconds.

State's magic ended against Syracuse, which frustrated the Bulldogs into 21 turnovers with its tricky 2-3 zone defense. Things might have turned out differently if State hadn't hit four three-pointers early in the first half for an 18-10 lead.

"I think sometimes when teams hit their first couple of outside shots they think it's going to be easy," Boeheim told the media after the game. "They think they can make threes, and sometimes they take more threes than maybe they would like in that situation."

The Bulldogs ended up hoisting 28 three-pointers and made 11, but Wilson hit three of those in the final minute after the Orangemen had built a 16-point lead. The comeback was too late to make a difference, and Syracuse won, 77-69.

After the game, a deflated Williams told his team to remember the journey that had taken it to the brink of the national championship.

"The wins are great," Williams told the *Memphis Commercial-Appeal.* "But to see this group of people grow together and become a team was a very rewarding experience. They came from different backgrounds and grew to like each other, maybe even love each other."

Rick Stansbury, who had come to Starkville in 1990 thinking he would be leaving the next year, knew how fortunate he was to have been involved in a Final Four run. What he couldn't know at the time was that the Bulldogs wouldn't even make it back to the NCAA Tournament until 2002, his fourth year as head coach.

"I had an opportunity to experience something a lot of good coaches and a lot of good players never get the opportunity to," Stansbury said. "And we did it at Mississippi State. No one can ever take that from us. Ever."

———

After the Final Four, Mississippi State scrambled to put a new contract—complete with a hefty raise—in front of Richard Williams. Ironically, the Bulldogs' success didn't whet his appetite for more.

"I'd thought about leaving earlier in the year," Williams said. "We were struggling and the expectations were really high. We had lost to Kentucky and I was really getting blasted because we weren't playing well. People were on me about the way I was handling Dontae'. So finally, I said to myself, 'It's just not worth it. I'm tired. I'm done.'"

Mississippi State athletic director Larry Templeton changed Williams's mind with a new contract.

"I'd never made a lot of money," Williams said. "The contract was good for Mississippi State. So I said I'd try and do it again. But I told Larry and Rick at the time that Rick was going to get a lot more opportunity to do things."

In hindsight, Williams might have wished he had stayed with his original inclination to retire. Erick Dampier, as many Bulldog fans feared, declared for the NBA draft, giving up his final year of eligibility. The move was a good one for Dampier, who turned out to be a lottery pick. He was chosen No. 10 by the Indiana Pacers.

Dontae' Jones had also considered the NBA, but wasn't as certain about the move as Dampier had been.

"But Dontae' got some bad advice," Stansbury recalled. "He had an agent buy him a truck, and once he did, he was done. After that, he decided he didn't want to leave school, but it was too late."

Jones was chosen as the No. 21 pick in the first round by the New York Knicks, but he never played in New York. The next season he was traded to the Boston Celtics, where he averaged 2.9 points in fifteen games. That was the extent of his NBA career.

"Dontae' needed another year [in college]," Stansbury said. "It was a shame, because he was really a great kid. He got a bad rap because of the summer classes he took before he got here. People said he was a dumb kid and he was lazy. But he really wasn't. He was a pleasant kid to be around."

Jones eventually went to Italy to play and managed to forge out a nice career while drawing a six-figure salary.

"He's making some money doing what he loves," Stansbury said. "The difference is if he'd have stayed in college, he would still be in the big leagues. He's an example of how agents can mess you up. We educate our kids about agents constantly."

Without Dampier and Jones, Mississippi State's fortunes underwent a rapid reversal. The Bulldogs were 12-18 overall and 6-10 in the SEC in 1996–97. The next year was even worse; though State was 15-15 overall, the league record was a woeful 4-12. Not long after the season, Williams decided he had had enough. He retired on March 12, 1998, and a day later, Stansbury was announced as his replacement.

Rick Stansbury prepared his whole life to become a college basketball coach. Born in the basketball hotbed of Kentucky, he couldn't help but be drawn to the game. Once he was, basketball took a serious hold on him.

"Basketball was my life," Stansbury recalled. "When most of the other kids were out on Friday and Saturday night, going on dates, having fun, partying, I was playing basketball on an outdoor court. We'd play till twelve, one, two o'clock in the morning. That's all I ever wanted to do. Basketball was what I was most comfortable and happy with."

Stansbury wasn't blessed with great size or athleticism, so he had to work to become a star at Meade County High School in the late 1970s. He did so with the support of his parents, who followed his career with great interest.

"My mom and dad never missed a game, from junior high to high school to college," Stansbury said. "My dad worked for Ford. He drove an hour and a half to work each day. We also owned a big farm. So for him it was work, work, work. But he never missed one of my games. Sometimes he'd drop mom off after a game and go right to work. He wouldn't even sleep."

Stansbury eventually landed a scholarship to Campbellsville (Kentucky) College, where he played for Lou Cunningham and got to know Lou's son Phil, who eventually became a graduate assistant at Mississippi State in 1991. Nine years later, Stansbury would bring Cunningham back to Starkville.

After his college career ended in 1981, Stansbury joined the staff at Campbellsville as a student assistant. A year later, Stansbury moved to Cumberland (Kentucky) College, where he learned from another respected NAIA coach, Randy Vernon.

The next season, Stansbury was on the move again after landing his first Division I job at Austin Peay. Stansbury relied on some help from a couple of friends to get that job—Vernon and Lake Kelly, who had worked together at Austin Peay when Kelly was the Governors' head coach in the early 1970s, recommended him. Howard Jackson was Stansbury's first boss at Austin Peay, but when Jackson got fired after just one season, Kelly was convinced to return.

Stansbury stayed at Austin Peay from 1985 to 1990, when he made his move to Mississippi State. As Williams's chief recruiter, Stansbury helped change the perception of Mississippi State, especially as it related to in-state recruiting. For years, other SEC schools—and assorted high-level programs such as Louisville and Georgetown—raided Mississippi for many of its marquee high school players. Stansbury, with the blessing of Williams, made it his personal quest to stop that talent flow.

"Rick Stansbury and [former Ole Miss coach Rob Evans] were the two that started bringing about the change," recalled Wayne Brent, an Ole Miss assistant coach who coached Jackson, Mississippi, powerhouse Provine High School from 1992 to 1998. "You started seeing their faces in Jackson all the time. Before those two, you just didn't see the coaches from the major [in-state] universities as much. Rick and Rob came to the inner city in Jackson and laid the groundwork. They started making inroads with the high school coaches. That's when the best talent in Mississippi started staying in-state."

Williams can remember the first July recruiting period Stansbury worked and how impressed he was with his new assistant's work ethic.

"Nobody will outwork Rick Stansbury," Williams said. "If you think you can, you're crazy. In the recruiting process, I didn't feel like my strength was going out and doing the day-to-day thing recruiting. I wanted people on my staff who could do that. John Brady could do that. And Rick could do that. A great philosopher once said 'A wise man is a man who knows that he knows not.' It was easy for me to put Rick in charge of recruiting."

Given his role in rebuilding the program, it was logical that Stansbury would get the first chance to replace Williams.

"It's something you always dream about," Stansbury said. "Growing up in Kentucky, you follow the SEC. To be able to coach in that league is an incredible thrill."

Stansbury felt no particular pressure in taking over for Williams. For the previous two seasons, Williams had turned many of his duties over to Stansbury, preparing him for the future.

"I let him do the scheduling," Williams recalled. "He broke down tape and scouted our opponents. He was in charge of recruiting. I was trying to prepare him to be a head coach."

"From that standpoint, it was an easy transition for me," Stansbury recalled. "And as far as pressure, there's no greater pressure anyone can put on me than what I put on myself. I wasn't worried about that."

Stansbury prepared himself for his new job as best he could in the off-season. But something unforeseen, something for which he could not prepare, intervened during pre-season practice, making his debut as the Bulldogs' head coach bittersweet.

In the fall of 1998, Stansbury's mother Norma became ill during a cruise. When the trip was over, she went to a hospital, where doctors decided to operate on her gall bladder.

"It was the second day of practice," Stansbury recalled. "Her sister called, and I told her I'd take my cell phone to practice with me, so I could find out how the surgery went. I was worried, but she was only sixty-three. She'd never been sick a day in her life. During practice, I got a call. Her sister told me that the doctor said we've got less than twenty-four hours to get the family there. Something had gone wrong with the surgery."

Stansbury hurried to his mother's side. "I got there that night," he recalled. "She was talking fine, but she didn't know what was fixing to hit her. In three or four hours, her kidneys shut down. They put her on a respirator."

Stansbury visited his mother several times in the next three weeks. "I was trying to coach my team, but I was still going to be with my mom," he said. "That last two or three weeks, there wasn't much to be done. But I wanted to be there."

On November 17, 1998, Stansbury's first game as a head coach was scheduled against Arkansas-Pine Bluff in Jackson, Mississippi. That afternoon, Stansbury received a call from his father. "He told me they were unhooking the respirator," Stansbury said. "I went to the game thinking she'd already passed away."

Stansbury's emotions were understandably mixed after the Bulldogs' won and made his opening game a successful debut. But a phone call from his dad lifted his spirits.

"He told me mom didn't pass away until 7:15 that night," Stansbury said. "After my first official game got started. It's as though she wanted to hang on. It's amazing how it happened."

Stansbury devoted his first season to his mother. Many times after losses, when his outlook on life was gloomy, he thought of her.

"She was so inspirational," Stansbury said. "When I got this job, it was a dream come true for her, too. For her not to be able to realize it was painful to me. But I think about my mom all the time. She'll always be a part of me. I wouldn't be where I am today without my mother and father. Not even close. I owe it all to them."

Stansbury's first season began in sadness and ended with disappointment. The Bulldogs were 18-13 in the regular season and 8-8 in SEC games, giving Stansbury hope they could earn an NCAA Tournament bid with a strong showing in the league tournament. State responded, disposing of Vanderbilt and Tennessee in the first two rounds. But in the third round, the Bulldogs lost in overtime to Arkansas.

Still, in his post-game press conference, Stansbury expressed confidence that the NCAA Tournament selection committee would see fit to include his team. He turned out to be wrong. The Bulldogs settled for an NIT bid, and Stansbury hoped for a home game. But State was dispatched to Fort Collins, Colorado, where it was quickly ousted from the tournament by Colorado State.

By leading the Bulldogs to twenty wins, Stansbury became the winningest rookie coach in school history. He had proven his worth as a head coach, but Stansbury's first season had left him spent emotionally.

———

Disappointed as he was by the NCAA Tournament snub, Stansbury didn't stay that way for long. He had the makings of a good team returning, despite the loss of Tyrone

Washington, who was picked in the second round of the NBA draft by the Houston Rockets. And just to make sure the Bulldogs' nonconference schedule wouldn't be a sticking point with the tournament selection committee again, Stansbury significantly upgraded by adding, among others, Texas and Stanford.

Stansbury thought he had the team to handle a tougher workload because of the addition of a newcomer, a player so gifted Stansbury devoted much of his waking life for four years recruiting him. Jonathan Bender was a slim, six-foot-eleven athlete who had the whole package of skills. Stansbury first learned about Bender in 1995, when he was still an assistant to Richard Williams and Bender was a gangly freshman at Picayune (Mississippi) High School. "Somebody had told me about the kid, so one day I just stopped in to see him," Stansbury said. "He was in a P.E. class. He must have been about six-eight at the time and probably didn't weigh a buck twenty-five. But I could just see it. He was long and athletic. And he could shoot the basketball."

Stansbury was hooked. He saw Bender, even at that early stage of his development, as a difference maker. For the next four years, Stansbury made Bender his top priority.

"I spent four years of my life with that kid," Stansbury said. "In all the recruiting situations I've been in, there's not a kid I spent more time with. People have no idea how much time I put in. I'd work on it all day, and then I'd work on it at home. At night, when I laid my head down on the pillow, I wasn't thinking about my wife— and I had just gotten married—I was thinking about Jonathan Bender. I know that's sick, but that's the way it was. I was absorbed with it."

All Stansbury's effort wasn't in vain, or so he thought on October 26, 1998, when Bender—who had become a consensus top-ten player in the country—cancelled a visit to Kentucky and committed to Mississippi State. Suffice it to say Stansbury was elated. Bender made it official a few days later during the NCAA's early signing period. Stansbury couldn't be blamed for thinking about his second season in Starkville before his first had even begun.

"With Bender coming in," Stansbury recalled, "I thought we could be as good as anybody."

Stansbury never got to find out if he was right. As Bender's senior season at Picayune progressed, he began to get some serious attention from NBA scouts. Stansbury was concerned, but thought Bender was committed to attending college, at least for a season or two. Then came the 1999 McDonald's All-Star game, during which Bender broke Michael Jordan's eighteen-year-old record by scoring 31 points.

"All of a sudden it just blew up," Stansbury said. "Jonathan had done something better than Jordan. The media got a hold of it and things changed. The kid kept saying he wasn't going, he wasn't going. Then he got some advice to go."

Bender kept Stansbury waiting and hoping until May 14, the day before the NBA's deadline for high school or college players to declare for the draft. When Stansbury found out Bender was headed to the pros, he was crushed.

"I was devasted, deflated," Stansbury said. "For two weeks, I literally crawled in a hole. It wasn't just a normal recruiting situation. It was my heart and soul. There aren't many kids you recruit for four years, but this kid was a four-year process. Jonathan was the first [high school] player in history who had signed with a college and was qualified academically to turn pro. And it happened to me. At the eleventh hour."

Stansbury couldn't fault Bender for his decision. Bender was chosen as the No. 5 pick in the draft by the Toronto Raptors and then traded to the Indiana Pacers. "I hold nothing against the kid," Stansbury said. "He's a great kid. And he made the right decision for him. But for us—we've never had a kid with his ability. Ever. I was in my first year as a head coach, and I'd gotten him to sign with Mississippi State. The things he could have done for this program. . ."

Once Stansbury emerged from his funk, he knew he had to put Jonathan Bender behind him. There would be other players to recruit, other battles to wage. Stansbury didn't know it at the time, but another of those battles was almost upon him.

———

When SEC coaches talk about how tough it is to recruit against other league schools, they often sprinkle pugilistic terms into the conversation.

"In this league you've got to put on the boxing gloves," Alabama coach Mark Gottfried said. "It's very competitive. A lot of times we're recruiting the same kid. This is not a league for guys that are soft and get their feelings hurt easily. You've got to have some backbone and be willing to handle comments here and there and move on and do your job."

"Recruiting in the SEC is a war," Rick Stansbury said. "It's all about recruiting. You've got to have players to compete at this level. In the SEC, you're always going against other schools in the league to get those players."

No two league schools are located closer together than Alabama and Mississippi State. A mere eighty miles separates the two campuses, so it isn't surprising that the Bulldogs and Crimson Tide have squared off over talent many times over the years. Alabama has recruited some star players from Mississippi—Derrick McKey, James Robinson—and Mississippi State has taken its share from Alabama, notably Darryl Wilson and Mario Austin.

The recruitment of Austin is the most recent example of how rancorous recruiting can get between Alabama and Mississippi State and between SEC schools in general. Austin first committed to Alabama—or at least that's what his self-proclaimed advisor said—and then changed his mind and signed with Mississippi State.

Austin, a massive, skilled center, comes from the small town of York, Alabama. York sits on the Mississippi-Alabama border and is within an easy drive of Tuscaloosa or Starkville. Once Austin began playing basketball in earnest in his soph-

omore season at Sumter County High School, it didn't take long for Alabama and Mississippi State to take notice. In his sophomore season, Austin—who was six-foot-nine and 250 pounds even then—and Sumter County won the Alabama Class 4A championship. A year later, Sumter County won the championship again, this time behind a 24-point, 12-rebound, five-blocked-shot performance by Austin, who was chosen the tournament MVP.

Austin had improved markedly between his sophomore and junior seasons, attributable in large part to his participation in AAU basketball. A team based in Birmingham, the Alabama Ice, picked up Austin and paired him with Gerald Wallace, who hailed from Childersburg, Alabama, and would become the No. 1 high school recruit in

Richard Williams. *Mississippi State Athletic Media Relations*

the country by the time he was a senior at Childersburg High School.

The combination of the hulking Austin and Wallace, an athletic slasher, was hard to beat. In 1999, the Ice won the AAU championship as Austin was chosen a first-team AAU All-American. During the course of their travels around the country, Austin and Wallace became close friends and decided to play together in college.

From that point, the story of Gerald Wallace and Mario Austin becomes less clear. In August 1999, Alabama Ice coach Kenny Harris called a press conference to announce that Wallace and Austin had committed to Alabama. Harris's news was strange, for two reasons. First, it was announced to the media via an e-mail from

Adidas America. The fact that a shoe company was publicizing a press conference for high school players touched off alarm bells with a lot of people. The other oddity about the press conference? Austin didn't show up.

When Stansbury learned of the press conference, he quickly got on the phone to Austin. "All I was concerned about was what the kid was saying," Stansbury said. "He had to make the decision, he and his mother. And they were saying it wasn't true. He didn't want to go to Alabama. That was something Kenny Harris tried to shove down his throat."

Mississippi State assistant coach Robert Kirby had feared that would be the case after his first conversation with Harris.

"I called him to ask about some of his kids," Kirby said. "And he said, 'Listen, it's over. Gerald Wallace and Mario Austin are both going to Alabama.' He said he was in charge of Mario's recruitment."

Kirby passed that news bulletin along to Austin's mother Deborah, who wasn't pleased with the thought of an outsider controlling her son's destiny.

"She told me that he [Harris] hadn't bought the first Pamper, hadn't changed the first dirty diaper," Kirby recalled. "Mario was her son, and momma was in control."

Thus Austin's decision to bypass the press conference. The way Stansbury and his staff saw it, Austin's recruitment was wide open.

"We worked Mario extremely hard," Kirby said. "For us, it was a question of finding out who was close to him up there [York]. Once we sat down and talked with mom, we found out who was in charge. Mario didn't want to go far from home. He's a homebody, a momma's boy."

Austin wound up visiting only two schools—Alabama and Mississippi State. He visited Starkville last, and after he committed to the Bulldogs, he never heard from Wallace again. And some Alabama fans in his hometown weren't too happy with Austin's choice, either.

"A lot of people back home turned their back on me," Austin said. "But I didn't let that get me down. As long as I had my family around me, that's all I needed. My mom and grandfather helped me make my decision. I didn't want to go to Duke or St. John's or some school way off. I just wanted to go to a place where my mom could see me play, and where I felt comfortable. For me, that was Mississippi State."

"Once we got Mario to visit our campus, it was a natural," Stansbury said. "He didn't have to go far from home. Mario's a Starkville-Mississippi-type person. That's why it was a perfect setting for him. He was used to walking on grass, not concrete. Starkville gave him an opportunity to walk on that grass. Plus we had an opportunity for him to step in and play right away."

Wallace, who signed with Alabama but stayed just one season before heading to the

NBA, would cross paths with Austin one more time before their high school careers ended. Austin averaged 23.9 points and 15.9 rebounds and was chosen a second-team *Parade* All-American in his senior season. And Wallace, as expected, was a consensus pick among recruiting analysts as the top high school player in the country and had begun attracting a horde of NBA scouts to his games. On February 18, 2000, Childersburg and Sumter met in the Alabama high school playoffs. Austin scored 21 points, grabbed eight rebounds, and blocked five shots, but it wasn't enough to keep Childersburg from winning, 51-50, behind 28 points, 19 rebounds, and six blocks from Wallace.

Austin couldn't get to Mississippi State fast enough as far as Rick Stansbury was concerned. In Stansbury's second season in Starkville, the Bulldogs were 14-16 overall and 5-11 in the SEC. Unlike the year before, there would be no mystery about the Bulldogs' postseason destination. In March, the closest they got to the NCAA Tournament was their television sets.

Stansbury had plenty of reinforcements coming in for the 2000–2001 season. In addition to Austin, who was the first McDonald's All-American to play for Mississippi State (Jonathan Bender would have been the first), Stansbury also signed guard Timmy Bowers from Gulfport, Mississippi. Bowers had been chosen Mississippi's player of the year in his senior season at Harrison Central High School.

Stansbury also recruited some help for his bench. Reaching out to an old friend, Stansbury hired Phil Cunningham, the son of his college coach, away from Georgia State. Cunningham started his Division I coaching career at Mississippi State as a graduate assistant in 1991, and later spent five years working for the venerable Lefty Driesell at James Madison and later Georgia State.

Austin didn't take long to justify his high school reputation. In the Bulldogs' season opener against California in the Preseason NIT, he scored 16 points and passed for four assists. Despite Austin's auspicious debut, Stansbury brought him along slowly behind junior Robert Jackson, starting him just five times in thirty-one games. He went on to average 7.9 points and 3.6 rebounds.

While Austin was developing, Mississippi State was returning to the form it showed in Stansbury's first season. The Bulldogs' 8-2 regular-season record included a win over Arizona. State struggled in SEC play, though, losing four of its first six games. The Bulldogs eventually sunk to 4-8 in the league, but regrouped with three straight wins over Auburn, Vanderbilt, and LSU. As it turned out, that stretch enabled

State to land an NIT bid, making Stansbury just the second coach in school history to lead the Bulldogs to more than one postseason tournament.

Mississippi State received a home game and played in-state rival Southern Mississippi in the first round, winning 75-68. All that win earned the Bulldogs was a road trip to Pittsburgh, but when they won there, they were sent back to Starkville to play host to Tulsa.

Tulsa came into the game with a lot to prove. A home-court loss to Hawaii in the finals of the Western Athletic Conference Tournament had kept the Golden Hurricane out of the NCAA Tournament, so this was a team on a mission. And though he didn't say so publicly, Tulsa coach Buzz Peterson had something to prove, too. He was on the short list for the job at Tennessee, and in the back of his mind, he wanted to impress the school's selection committee.

The game was entertaining. The Bulldogs never led in the second half, but they managed to tie the score at 75 with 21 seconds left on a lay-up by Austin. Tulsa went back ahead when guard Greg Harrington tossed in a five-foot jump hook with 2.6 seconds left. It didn't seem as though State had a chance to get off a shot, but guard Derek Zimmerman got free from the right side for a three-pointer that swished through the nets. Unfortunately for the Bulldogs, the game clock had expired, and Tulsa walked away a 77-75 winner. The last play had transpired so quickly that Stansbury charged the referees and demanded they check ESPN's monitor to make sure Zimmerman's shot hadn't been too late. A quick review of the tape proved it was.

Though the Bulldogs were that close from a trip to New York and the NIT finals in Madison Square Garden, there were those who wondered about the state of the program under Stansbury's leadership. Before the start of the next season, at least two basketball publications claimed that Stansbury, who would be in the last year of a four-year contract, was in trouble if he didn't coach the Bulldogs into the NCAA Tournament in 2002.

———

Neither Austin nor Mississippi State rested on their laurels after the 2000–2001 season ended. Austin, who had played his freshman season at 285 pounds, stayed on campus all summer and dedicated himself to a weight training and conditioning program. He lost thirty pounds, which would eventually enable him to become more mobile and play more minutes.

Stansbury and his staff, meanwhile, were prowling the junior college ranks for some immediate help, trying as hard as they could to find a lead guard to team with

Derek Zimmerman in the backcourt. Assistant coaches Phil Cunningham and Robert Kirby were in the chase for two good ones who eventually signed with Big 12 schools. The two coaches had even secured a commitment from first-team junior-college All-American Terrell Ross, who had led Allegany College of Maryland to a runner-up finish in the national championship tournament. But Ross's coach compelled him to sign with Texas, which had lost guard Roosevelt Brown—who transferred because of a lack of playing time—and needed a replacement.

Cunningham and Kirby tried to convince Ross he'd be doomed playing behind prep All-American T. J. Ford, who had already signed with Texas.

"In the end, he was too good a kid to go against his junior college coach," Cunningham said. Ross averaged six minutes a game in his first season at Texas, while Ford became the Big 12 Freshman of the Year and led the nation in assists.

If the State staff was disappointed by the loss of Ross, it was encouraged by the late acquisition of six-foot-ten Michal Ignerski, who Cunningham had recruited while at Georgia State. Ignerski didn't speak a word of English when he came to the United States in time for the 1999–2000 season, so the Georgia State staff sent him to Bacone College in Oklahoma.

"I'd heard about the kid from Rich Sheubrooks, who ran the Nike Eurocamp," said Cunningham, who left Georgia State for Mississippi State in 2000. "He told me the kid reminded him of Tom Gugliotta—he was a big white kid who could run, jump, and shoot the ball well."

Ignerski played well in his only year at Bacone before following coach Jimmy Voight to Eastern Oklahoma Junior College to play his sophomore season. Voight had been loyal to Georgia State and had encouraged Ignerski to sign there, but when the player made his official visit in the fall of 2000, he decided against it.

"What happened was he'd been in the U.S. for a year watching ESPN and all those games," Cunningham said. "He wanted to play for a major conference."

Ignerski had begun to attract some Big 12 and Big Ten attention, but he was interested in Mississippi State.

"It was tough on me," Cunningham said. "I think coach [Lefty] Driesell and everybody at Georgia State got upset with me and thought I was behind everything. But Iggy had known I went to Mississippi State and had followed us."

When Ignerski signed with the Bulldogs, they gained the unexpected gift of a starting power forward with some genuine basketball skills.

"Mississippi State has traditionally been very athletic," Cunningham said. "But Iggy added a lot of skills for our team. Plus he's athletic himself. He's not like this big, slow white guy who can only shoot the three."

Despite the hard off-season work put in by Austin and others, and despite a recruiting class that brought in reinforcements such as Ignerski and seven-foot freshman Marcus Campbell, the media didn't think too much of Mississippi State's chances in 2001–2002. Most preseason publications picked the Bulldogs to finish last in the SEC's Western Division. Some went so far as to proclaim that Stansbury, in the fourth year of his contract, was on the dreaded "hot seat."

"Who the hell writes this stuff?" Stansbury asked before the season began. "How do they get their information? No one talked to me about it."

As if to vindicate their coach, the Bulldogs started out strong, tying a school record by winning their first eleven games. But even that accomplishment was tainted— instead of handing out praise, the experts bashed Mississippi State's schedule, which was filled with several mid- to low-major Division I teams. The first real test would come against Cincinnati in a late-December game, and when State lost, 90-56, critics of Stansbury and the schedule weren't surprised.

The Bulldogs regrouped from that pounding, beating Richmond, Illinois-Chicago, and Tulane to head into the SEC season 13-1. Their first league game would be a test—mighty Kentucky was coming to Starkville.

The Wildcats threatened to blow the game open early, jumping out to a 22-1 lead in the first nine minutes. By halftime, things had gotten only slightly better; Mississippi State trailed 40-24. "It was on the borderline of me saying 'Guys, we've got to go out here and play for pride,'" senior forward Marckell Patterson told the *Jackson Clarion-Ledger.*

Stansbury assured the Bulldogs at halftime that they had nothing to lose in the second half. "Nobody expected us to win at that point," he told the media later.

Inspired by Stansbury's urging to play loose, State rallied in the second half, slowly trimming Kentucky's lead. With 2:57 to play, Patterson's three-pointer gave the Bulldogs their first lead at 61-59. Kentucky fought back to reclaim a 65-62 lead, but the Bulldogs had one last chance to tie and send the game into overtime.

It wasn't the play that Stansbury drew up, but Austin, who had already established himself in pre-conference games as the Bulldogs' go-to scorer, cemented that status and etched his name into Mississippi State basketball lore. With 7.2 seconds left, he calmly tossed in a deep three-point from the top of the key to tie the game. Before that clutch shot, Austin had never attempted a three-pointer in college.

Austin was the hero in overtime, too, as he made five of six free throws to seal a 74-69 State victory. Austin finished with 32 points and picked up a legion of new admirers around the SEC and the country.

That victory propelled the Bulldogs into the major polls for the first time since the 1996 season, but their appearance there was short-lived after consecutive losses to Arkansas and Ole Miss.

Mississippi State eventually slipped to 4-5 in SEC games before beginning a rally that saw the Bulldogs win five straight and six of seven to close league play. One of those victories was a resounding win over Alabama, which would go on to win the SEC's regular-season championship. And the lone loss was a meltdown at LSU during which the Bulldogs led by 15 points in the second half.

Mississippi St.
All-SEC Expansion Era Team

F-Dontae' Jones

F-Mario Austin

C-Erick Dampier

G-Darryl Wilson

G-Chuck Evans

Top Reserves-Tyrone Washington, Tang Hamilton

When the regular season ended, Mississippi State had done what it set out to do. The Bulldogs won 23 games, passing the 20-victory mark for the second time in Stansbury's tenure. They finished second in the SEC West after being picked to finish last in most polls, earning a first-round bye in the SEC Tournament. But the league tournament didn't matter—a coveted at-large bid to the NCAA Tournament, State's first since the magical 1996 season, had already been secured.

Just as important to Stansbury, his job security was no longer an issue. With a young team coming back for the 2002–2003 season and a strong class of high school recruits in Mississippi, the future of the program seemed bright.

"It's all about players, and we're starting to consistently recruit kids who can play in this league, and we're protecting our turf," Stansbury said. "Those days where people come into our state and think they're gonna get a kid are over. We're not going to get them all, but it's going to come down between us and somebody else for the best kids in Mississippi. Other schools know that now.

"I like where we're at with this program."

A week after that comment, after the SEC Tournament was over, Stansbury would be even happier about the state of his program.

Chapter Nine

Ole Miss

R ob Evans will never forget the day he was formally introduced to the great state of Mississippi.

The year was 1968. Evans and Ed Murphy, young assistant coaches on Lou Henson's staff at New Mexico State, were finishing a long recruiting journey that had taken them from Las Cruces, New Mexico, to Jackson, Mississippi. The coaches were the best of friends and made for a contrasting twosome: Murphy the big, gregarious Irish Catholic from Syracuse, New York; Evans a shorter, considerably more reserved African-American from Hobbs, New Mexico.

Evans had never set foot in Mississippi, but he knew the state's reputation, was aware of its role in the civil rights movement. As a teenager, Evans begged his mother to allow him travel to Mississippi so he too could become part of the movement. Fearing for her son's life, Gladys Evans refused to let him go.

As the two coaches drove across the state line that day in March 1968, Evans could feel his skin crawl.

"I was nervous," Evans recalled. "I'd read the newspapers and seen the reports on the news. I was aware of James Meredith and Medgar Evers. Once we crossed over into Mississippi, as a black man I could feel the difference."

In those days, NCAA rules governing recruiting weren't nearly so restrictive as they are now. Evans and Murphy had plans to set up headquarters in Jackson and stay for several days recruiting the entire state. No sooner did the two men arrive in Jackson they witnessed something that shook them to the core.

"We were stopped at a traffic light," recalled Murphy. "And right in front of us, two policemen pulled this black guy out of his car and started beating the hell out of him. They were working him over pretty good."

Suffice to say Evans's worst fears had been realized.

"I was scared and nervous anyway," Evans said. "Seeing that didn't help me any at all."

When it came time to find lodging, Murphy and Evans, whose families were close and shared a duplex in New Mexico, knew they would have to go their separate ways. Murphy got a room in the Holiday Inn. Evans had to settle for the Edward Lee Hotel, where Ray Charles and other black entertainers making their way through Mississippi always stayed.

During their time in Mississippi, Evans and Murphy took precautions. They rented another car so they could recruit separately, but were careful to let Evans drive the car with Mississippi license plates and let Murphy take the one with New Mexico plates. "You didn't want to be a black man driving a car with out-of-state plates around Mississippi," Evans said. "People could have thought I was a civil rights worker. And that would have been dangerous."

Evans made sure he did his business in daylight hours. And when he had to meet with Murphy, it was always in a park or a bus station, anywhere where blacks and whites were commonly seen together. Years later, Murphy described those meetings to the *Jackson Clarion-Ledger*. "It almost felt like we were in some kind of cheap spy movie," Murphy said.

Though Evans was justifiably scared out of his wits half the time, he and Murphy made their trip to Mississippi a successful one. Their hard work helped open a talent pipeline from Mississippi to New Mexico State.

"We signed a lot of those kids," Evans recalled. "And we were very successful with them."

Over the years, Evans returned often to Mississippi. "A lot of times, I'd stay with black families, sometimes a couple of weeks at a time," Evans recalled. "It was funny. Sometimes coaches from other schools would come through recruiting. I'd sit in the living room, listen to them making their pitches. They never knew I wasn't a part of the family."

Nearly a quarter century after his first visit to Mississippi, Evans considered returning there, only this time under different circumstances. The year was 1992, and the way Evans—then forty-five years old—saw it, he had long since served out a reasonable apprenticeship as an assistant coach. After seven years at New Mexico State, Evans went to Texas Tech, where he worked on head coach Gerald Myers's staff for fifteen seasons. Evans went to work for Oklahoma State coach Eddie Sutton in 1990, and after two years in Stillwater, he felt more than prepared to run his own program.

As fate would have it, Evans would be offered a head-coaching job in the spring of 1992. But there was one catch. The job was at the University of Mississippi.

As Evans tried to envision himself as the head coach at Ole Miss, its dark history in the struggle for equal rights wasn't his primary concern. What concerned him was the state of the program. As badly as he wanted to be a head coach, Evans didn't want to take over an impossible situation where he couldn't win. A quick check of some history gave Evans's pause. Ole Miss was last—by a good margin—in the all-time

SEC standings and didn't have a winning record against any of the eleven other league schools.

Some of Evans' most trusted advisers were convinced he was out of his mind to even consider the job. Sutton, who had coached at Kentucky, was well familiar with the SEC. During his days in the conference, Ole Miss was usually an easy mark.

"Coach Sutton told me not to take the job," Evans recalled. "He said you could take Hank Iba and John Wooden and Phog Allen—all those great coaches—and you can't get that thing done at Ole Miss."

Sutton's input weighed heavily on Evans's mind. And while he was considering Ole Miss, Evans also received offers from Rice and Baylor. The decision-making process was getting harder by the day.

"My wife said, 'Let's go to one of the Texas schools,'" Evans recalled. "She'd never been to Mississippi. But I just said it was time. I had a good feeling about Ole Miss."

Evans's degree of comfort came from two good sources. Gerald Turner, the chancellor at Ole Miss, was a former teammate of Evans's at Lubbock (Texas) Christian. And old friend Ed Murphy, who had just resigned as Ole Miss coach, had been urging Evans to consider the job even before he left.

The Rebels were in the midst of an 11-17 season when Murphy first called Evans. Murphy wasn't sure he would last much longer; his team was on its way to a third straight losing season. In 1990–91, Ole Miss finished 9-19 and 3-15 in the SEC. The year before, the Rebels were 13-17 and 8-10 in the league.

Murphy's problem was the same one that had plagued Ole Miss coaches for years. Though Bob Weltlich, Lee Hunt, and Murphy had all enjoyed periods of success, it was hard to sustain. Weltlich guided the program to its most consistent stretch—at that point in its history—from 1979 to 1982 and its first NCAA Tournament bid in 1981. Hunt led the Rebels to a 19-12 record and NIT berth in 1982–83, his first season. But Ole Miss was 8-20 the next year and finished below .500 in two other seasons under Hunt.

Murphy, popular with the fans and press because he was funny and quotable, squeezed a pair of NIT appearances out of the Rebels in his six seasons in Oxford. But even Murphy's media-savvy charm couldn't help reverse Ole Miss' dismal fortunes, at least not on a consistent basis. The problem as Murphy saw it was recruiting. For years, Mississippi had been an underrated producer of great high school basketball players. Unfortunately for a succession of Ole Miss coaches, those players had little desire to go to Oxford.

"It wasn't so much the kids as it was their parents," Murphy told the *Jackson Clarion-Ledger*. "They just weren't going to let their kids go to Ole Miss. Obviously,

Rob could address those fears [about racial unrest] in ways I just could not."

If Murphy was pulling for his old friend to take the Ole Miss job, so was Turner, whose stated goal when he arrived in Oxford was to create racial diversity at the university. Drawing from personal history, Turner knew Evans could help him achieve that goal.

At Lubbock Christian, Turner's career was ended when he blew out his knee. Evans made it a point to visit his teammate in the hospital.

"We'd come from two different backgrounds and I knew just in conversation that Gerald hadn't been exposed to a lot of blacks," Evans told the *Memphis Commercial-Appeal*. "I guess I went to the hospital to influence him somewhat, to show him things he hadn't been exposed to.

"After we left college, I lost track of Gerald, but he eventually wrote me a letter saying that I had taught him a lot about racial diversity."

After Murphy resigned, Turner and Ole Miss athletic director Warner Alford agreed that they would make it their quest to find a black head coach.

"It was time," Alford recalled. "We thought we needed to step out and make a statement in hiring a black coach for a major sport at our school, given the baggage the university had carried from past experiences. We needed to make a commitment."

Alford was given the task of finding the right man for the job, though Turner had a strong feeling he already knew who that was. Alford flew around the country, interviewing more than a dozen candidates. His list of potential coaches was eventually pared to Evans, Georgia assistant Tevester Anderson, and Georgia Tech assistant Sherman Dillard.

Anderson, a Mississippi native, had played at Rogers High School in Canton, Mississippi, and later coached his alma mater to two state championships. He'd served fourteen seasons as an SEC assistant at Auburn and Georgia. Dillard had spent fourteen seasons working for three successful head coaches at Maryland (Lefty Driesell), California (Lou Campanelli), and Georgia Tech (Bobby Cremins) and was ready to run his own program.

As qualified and experienced as they might have seemed to an outsider, Anderson and Dillard probably didn't have a chance for the Ole Miss job, given Turner's history with Evans.

"I always appreciated Rob, and the fact we had learned so much from each other about cross-racial relationships," Turner told the *Commercial-Appeal*. "He was part of my plan at Ole Miss. I did want very much to have African-Americans in significant leadership positions. I knew he had some missionary zeal."

After Alford interviewed Evans, he too was sold on Evans's personal magnetism.

"I just felt like, as we talked back and forth, that I had a comfortable feeling with him," Alford recalled. "I remember thinking that if this guy could coach basketball as well as he presented himself, he could really be something."

On March 30, 1992, Ole Miss hired Rob Evans. Like his new bosses, Evans knew he had a mission in Oxford that transcended the basketball court.

"I just happened to believe in what Gerald Turner was trying to get done," Evans said. "I felt in going to Mississippi that myself and my family could do some things outside of basketball for both the black and white communities."

———

Evans knew his new job was going to be tough. He didn't realize how tough until he had settled in.

"It was a tough from a lot of standpoints," Evans said. "But the toughest thing was the fans. People just didn't care. There was so much apathy."

The state of the program could well have been determined by the facilities Evans would have to work with. To say his new office was dingy wouldn't begin to describe the place.

"The offices were the worst in the world," Evans said. "When we first got there, my office was so bad my wife went in and did everything out of our own pockets. She put in new wallpaper and had to get it recarpeted. My assistant coaches' offices were just cubicles—three coaches side by side with the secretary. If one of them needed to have a private conversation they had to come to my office.

"And the gym [Tad Smith Coliseum] . . . I remember telling an assistant athletic director we needed the floor resanded. He said, 'Well, we resanded it ten years ago.' In the winter, you'd go into the coliseum at times and the heat was off. The players had on sweats and gloves and stocking caps."

Bad as they were, the facilities weren't the worst problem Evans had to deal with. The Rebels' lack of a winning tradition was a tough obstacle in recruiting, which Evans knew was the lifeblood of any program. And the university's role in the turbulent civil rights movement in the early 1960s, even after so many years, hadn't been forgotten.

Very few African-American student-athletes—and more importantly their parents—haven't heard, read about, or seen film clips of the story of James Meredith, who in 1962 was denied entry into the university because he was black. Forced by the Supreme Court to admit Meredith, Ole Miss steadfastly refused. Mississippi governor Ross Barnett personally blocked Meredith from enrolling, prompting President Kennedy to dispatch federal marshals to force the issue and protect Meredith. In a riot that ensued between the marshals and an angry mob of more than two thousand, two people were killed and hundreds wounded. The violence ended only after Kennedy sent in sixteen thousand federal troops.

"In recruiting, if I went into a home, especially a black home, I knew that was on their mind," Evans recalled. "Most of the time they wouldn't bring it up. I brought it up. I said, 'Let me just talk about some of these things.' I didn't want to leave that home with any questions not being answered.

"I basically told them the positive things going on at Ole Miss at the time. The dean of the law school and the dean of students and some of the academic advisers were black. There were black engineering professors. There was a lot of positive movement going on from the standpoint of blacks being given leadership opportunities at the school. Just the fact that I was the head coach at Mississippi told you positive changes were going on."

Evans knew that in order for him to make a difference at Ole Miss, he would have to start keeping Mississippi's better high school players at home. But unfortunately for Evans, familiarity had bred contempt. Why would players who grew up thinking Ole Miss was a loser or hostile toward African-Americans want to play basketball or go to school there? Any time a fan waved a confederate flag or the Ole Miss band played Dixie—common occurrences at the school's athletic events—it was a reminder to African-Americans that, no matter how far they had advanced since the days of James Meredith, their fight for respect and equality wasn't over.

Evans worked tirelessly to spread a message that Ole Miss had undergone a transformation from those frightening times in the 1960s. In his first few weeks on the job, he traveled to Jackson, Memphis, Atlanta, Birmingham, and numerous smaller towns in Mississippi, speaking to alumni groups. He personally visited high school and junior college coaches in the state, leaving them pleasantly surprised. For most, it was their first visit from an Ole Miss coach.

"When you don't show an interest in the in-state kids, it's magnified," former Ole Miss athletic director Warner Alford told the *Jackson Clarion-Ledger*. "They start to think, 'Ole Miss doesn't want us.' You get tagged with that."

It took Evans a few years to crack through some long-standing barriers and make significant progress recruiting Mississippi. In 1992, he tried hard to sign Antonio McDyess, a six-foot-nine *Parade* All-American from Quitman, Mississippi. But other SEC schools had the advantage of recruiting McDyess well before Evans came to Ole Miss. McDyess's choices came down to Mississippi State and Alabama, and he eventually settled on the Crimson Tide.

In 1993 Evans tried and failed to sign two quality big men, but he was encouraged by the fact he had at least gotten their attention. Jerod Ward, a six-foot-nine forward from Clinton, Mississippi, was generally considered the top high school player in the country. Ward's final choices came down to Ole Miss and Michigan, but the lure of the Wolverines, just coming off consecutive Final Four appearances, was too much for Evans to overcome.

Memphis, an hour's drive from Oxford, had long been known as a hotbed for talent, and Evans wanted to tap into it. In 1993, the top prospect in Memphis was McDonald's All-American Lorenzen Wright, a six-foot-eleven center. But Wright made the easy choice and stayed home to play for Memphis.

Evans could only wonder how quickly he would have reversed the Rebels' fortunes with a frontcourt that included Ward and Wright.

While Evans was having a difficult time convincing state or regional stars to come to Ole Miss, he still had to have players. His urgent need forced him to take some risks and become a little less conventional. Neighboring states and junior colleges would supply Evans with players for the next three years.

Hired too late in 1992 to work any high school recruits, Evans brought in two junior college players in the spring signing period, seven-foot-one center David Dean and forward Jarrell Evans. Were it not for those two, the Rebels might have really struggled in Evans's first season. As it was, they finished 10-18 overall and 4-12 in the SEC. But Ole Miss sent a message by sweeping rival Mississippi State and upsetting Florida, which would play in the Final Four a year later, in the SEC Tournament.

The Rebels were more competitive in 1993–94, finishing 14-13 overall and 7-9 in the SEC. That was good for fourth place in the Western Division and it represented real progress. Ole Miss had been picked to finish last.

Evans's recruiting efforts in his second season laid the groundwork for what would become a perennial postseason tournament team. Disappointed but undaunted by his failed attempts to land Jerod Ward and Lorenzen Wright, Evans ventured beyond the borders of Mississippi to sign two key recruits. Anthony Boone, a six-foot-seven forward from Arkansas, opened a pipeline of talent in that state, much to the future chagrin of the mighty University of Arkansas. And Ansu Sesay, a six-foot-nine forward from Texas, appealed to Evans because of his rare combination of inside-outside scoring skills.

Evans had to work overtime to convince Sesay that Ole Miss was the right place for him. Rather, Evans had to work overtime to convince Sesay's mother, Marie. Evans's wife Carolyn was credited with an assist on the play.

"Ansu's parents are from Africa," Evans said. "Everybody had been telling his mother about the past at Ole Miss. They only knew what people were telling them. It was tough to get involved."

Evans also had to work his way around some rules set up by the NCAA and the University Interscholastic League, the governing body of Texas high school sports. "I knew the rules because I'd worked fifteen years in Texas," Evans recalled. "They had a rule in Texas high schools that once [fall] practice started, you couldn't visit any schools until the season started. And the NCAA said you couldn't visit a school until you had passed the ACT or SAT. So we had a small window by the time Ansu got his test score and could visit. I wanted to be the first one to get him.

"He had two weeks and visited our place and Cal Santa Barbara. We got him in and he wanted to sign with us but his mother wouldn't let him. Because of what she'd heard about Mississippi."

Evans and his top assistant, Russ Pennell, wouldn't give up. They gathered a group of black professors and administrators from Ole Miss to talk with Sesay's mother.

"There were fifteen of us in the room," Evans said. "Every one of us got on the phone and talked to her. When it was over I told her she'd just talked to fifteen people in high places on this campus. If it was so bad, would they have been given their opportunities to advance?"

Still Marie Sesay didn't crack. Her resolve was surpassed only by Evans's resolve.

"A week later I was talking to her again," Evans recalled. "My wife was in the room, and she said, 'Let me talk to her.' I could hear a little bit of what was being said. After a few minutes I heard my wife say, 'I'm glad to know that.' She got off the phone and said, 'Ansu's [scholarship] papers will be in the mail tomorrow.'"

"This was mother to mother," Carolyn Evans told the *Jackson Clarion-Ledger*. "She was pretty hard-nosed. I told her to ask me any hard-hitting questions she wanted. I answered them as only a mother could. In the end, it came down to this: I told her, 'Do you think if Ole Miss and Mississippi were as bad as what you've heard, that Rob and I would be here and that we would have both our children at Ole Miss?'"

Evans's diligence in landing Sesay turned out to be of major importance in turning the program around. It took two seasons for Evans to break Sesay of relying too much on his perimeter game, but once Sesay was convinced he could do some damage inside, he became an All-SEC player. As Sesay got better, so did the program.

Ole Miss struggled through an injury-plagued 1994–95 season and finished 8-19, 3-13 in the SEC. There was slight improvement the next season as the Rebels doubled their conference victory total of the year before.

By the 1995–96 season, four more key players had been added. Ole Miss once again robbed Arkansas for talent, signing forward Jason Smith and guard Keith Carter. Carter became a four-year starter and an All-SEC player. Smith willingly assumed blue-collar roles, becoming the Rebels' top defender and a solid rebounder.

Ole Miss

He was also a leader.

"Jason Smith was a warrior," Evans recalled. "I remember we'd started out the season 0-5 [in the SEC] his freshman year. We played our first game at Georgia, the second game at Kentucky—which was going to win the national championship that year—our third game against Arkansas—which had been to the Sweet 16—our fourth game at Mississippi State—which was getting ready to go to the Final Four—and our fifth game at Florida, which had already been to the Final Four. It was a tough, tough schedule.

"I'll never forget after the Florida game Jason was chewing out his teammates. I just stepped back and let him go at it for a while. That's when I knew we were turning it around. Somebody cared as much about it as I did."

Evans found the second component of his starting backcourt in New Orleans. Michael White locked down the point guard position for four seasons. Ironically, the arrival of White would play a role in the eventual departure of Evans.

Though Carter, Smith, and White all became starters, another player in that class who rarely started in his career might have been the most critical recruit. Joezon Darby played high school basketball at Mississippi power Jackson Murrah. Overshadowed there by teammates Othella Harrington, who would later start at Georgetown, Ronnie Henderson, who played at LSU, and Jesse Pate, who played briefly for Arkansas, Darby was nevertheless talented.

"His teammates were more widely known on the national level," said Ole Miss sports information director Lamar Chance. "But it was well known in Mississippi that Joezon Darby was one of the top players in the state."

Darby started his career at Cowley County Community College in Kansas. Just as he did with Ansu Sesay's, Evans had to convince Darby's mother that Ole Miss was the right fit.

"Joezon was another key guy, a kid I felt like we had to have," Evans recalled. "I promised his mother that I would make sure he graduated from college, and that when he did, I would be there in the stands to watch him."

Evans eventually kept that promise, though he had to take a red-eye flight from the West Coast to do it. And Darby proved to have a twofold value. On the court, he willingly consented to a sixth-man role and excelled at it, coming off the bench to provide instant offense and clutch shooting. Twice during the 1996–97 season he knocked down game-winning shots. Off the court, Darby's presence in Oxford served as an example to Mississippi high school players. Years later, Ole Miss was still thriving off a steady stream of Jackson high school stars.

All the hard work put in by Evans, his staff, and his players was finally beginning to reap dividends. An 8-2 nonconference record gave the Ole Miss coaches reason to believe a breakthrough season was in their grasp. And the beginning of SEC play proved they were right. On January 2, 1997, the Rebels shocked the rest of the conference by going to Arkansas and hammering the Razorbacks, 91-74. Arkansas had won seven of the previous eight games between the schools. Making the victory sweeter was the fact that five Arkansas natives were on the Ole Miss roster.

"We'd really had some success going into Arkansas and getting players," Evans said. "[Then-Arkansas coach] Nolan Richardson and I grew up together. I knew his philosophy. He'd only take players from Arkansas if they were great players. He didn't want the aggravation from a kid's family, high school coaches, and fans if the kid wasn't playing. So we went into Arkansas and got some kids. Once we started winning, [Richardson] couldn't beat us on the best players in the state."

The Rebels followed their win over Arkansas by beating third-ranked Kentucky at home. Evans, his confidence in his scrappy band of players growing, told them before the game to expect to win. "And when you do win," Evans recalls saying, "tell the media it wasn't a fluke."

When the final horn sounded, Rebel fans that had been coming to games in steadily increasing numbers swarmed the floor. Ole Miss basketball had arrived. The next week, the Rebels found themselves ranked for the first time in school history. The win over Kentucky had vaulted them all the way to No. 20 in the Associated Press poll.

A tone had been set for the rest of the season. The Rebels finished 11-5 in the conference, winning the Western Division after being picked in some pre-season publications to finish last. It was the first time in school history Ole Miss had won a regular-season championship of any kind.

Ole Miss advanced to the NCAA Tournament for only the second time ever. And though Temple would handily knock the Rebels from the Big Dance in the first round, a trend had been established. Post-season play was about to become the norm, not the rare exception, at Ole Miss.

After the season, Evans had suddenly become a commodity, his name mentioned prominently in connection with several job openings. None of the rumors were taken too seriously until LSU athletic director Joe Dean called and asked for permission to speak with Evans. Dean was looking for a successor to Dale Brown, who announced his retirement before the 1998–97 season began. Even Brown, who had been pushing his assistant Johnny Jones to be his replacement, wouldn't have minded seeing Evans come to Baton Rouge. In a ceremony honoring him before LSU played at Ole Miss, Brown told the Rebel fans, "If they are looking for a first-class coach and a great man, I wish it would be Rob Evans."

Dean tried as hard as he could to convince Evans to make the switch. Dean had a significantly larger salary and better facilities to offer. Evans thought seriously about LSU as Rebel fans anxiously awaited his decision. Evans finally came to the conclusion he cared too much for his players to leave.

"After I went to visit LSU, I talked with my wife, weighed everything in my mind and the ultimate factor was that it was just very difficult to walk away from the kids," Evans recalled. "I knew how we recruited, how I promised them that if they came and gave themselves to the coaches and worked hard, that we had a chance to do something special everybody said couldn't be done at Ole Miss. For me to walk away for financial gain was something I just couldn't do."

Ole Miss had hung on to its coach for one more season. But Rebel fans were still nervous. Another good season and Evans would surely be gone.

In the meantime, Evans and his staff were beginning to put their recent success to work. Following Joezon Darby's lead, talented Mississippi high school players began showing interest in Ole Miss. Evans was able to sign two of the state's best in 1997: Rahim Lockhart, a burly center from Piney Woods and a national Top 100 player, and David Sanders, a versatile guard who led Jackson Murrah to the Mississippi 5A championship and was chosen the state's player of the year.

In 1997–98, the Rebels put together the best season in school history, finishing 22-7 and 12-4 in the SEC. Ole Miss won the Western Division for a second straight year with a strong finish that included a seven-game winning streak to close out the regular season. During the streak the Rebels won at Kentucky, LSU, and Mississippi State in successive games.

Ole Miss again played in the NCAA Tournament, losing to Valparaiso at the buzzer when the Crusaders' Bryce Drew tossed in a three-pointer. After the season, Evans was again tempted by job offers. This time, he found one to his liking.

Kevin White, the athletic director at Arizona State, had an association with Evans that few outside Oxford knew about. White's son Michael was the Rebels' starting point guard. When White came to Barnes with an offer to return to his western roots, Evans was tempted.

"I came in and interviewed, and Kevin White offered me the job," Evans said. "He wanted to have a press conference the next day. I said I couldn't do it, that I owed Ole Miss more than that. I owed it to the chancellor [Robert Khayat had replaced Turner in 1995] to sit down and tell him. I flew back and my wife and I wrestled with it. I talked with my staff, the chancellor and my players. I just decided it was the right move to make."

Evans's six-year record at Ole Miss was just 76-98, but the legacy he left behind won't be forgotten.

"Kevin White said I didn't rebuild the program at Ole Miss, I built it," Evans said. "It was one of the toughest jobs, maybe ever, because we were fighting so many things. There was so much baggage and no tradition. To turn that program around was truly satisfying."

Ole Miss moved quickly to replace Evans, whose two top assistants, Russ Pennell and Rod Barnes, were thought to be the leading candidates. Evans didn't have the heart to recommend one of his valued assistants over the other, so he remained silent. When, on April 9, 1998, Khayat announced that the job would be given to the thirty-two-year-old Barnes, who had never been a head coach at any level, fans were surprised and concerned about his lack of experience. The media was doubtful and critical. One SEC coach called Barnes's hiring "an experiment." But Evans wasn't surprised.

"I think the university wanted to stick with the same game plan," Evans said. "They wanted another African-American coach, and that was Rod."

Barnes—who had played for the Rebels and loved the school—wasn't about to let his lack of experience deter him from pursuing the Ole Miss job. For a man who had made a career of overachieving and proving his detractors wrong, this would be the perfect challenge.

———

When Rod Barnes showed up at Ole Miss in the fall of 1984, he was a skinny, awkward-looking, six-foot-one freshman with an unorthodox jump shot. And no one gave him a chance in hell to ever play a lick for the Rebels.

That this was the prevailing opinion about Barnes was a bit ironic. At Mississippi's Bentonia High School, Barnes had achieved all the requisite accomplishments to be considered a college prospect. As a sophomore and junior, Barnes led his team to state championships. As a senior, he averaged 23 points, 10 rebounds, and nine assists and played in the Mississippi High School All-Star game.

Perhaps recruiters couldn't get past the scrawny body or the funky jumper. Whatever the reason, Barnes was largely unnoticed by Division I schools. When Ole Miss coach Lee Hunt offered a scholarship, Barnes jumped at the chance. It wasn't as though he had choices.

In his freshman season, Barnes did nothing to make any rival coaches think they had missed on him. He played in just sixteen games, averaging all of 1.1 points. Undaunted by his lack of playing time and production in his freshman year, Barnes went to work on his game.

Barnes had learned the virtues of hard work honestly. His father, Charles, was a

Rob Evans. *Ole Miss Sports Information*

sharecropper.

"My dad got up every day and went out to work in the blistering sun," said Barnes, who was often asked to help out with the family business. "He never complained—not once did I hear him complain. He just went to work to provide for his family. His attitude was instilled in me: Take what you have and make the best of it."

The lesson applied to basketball as well as it did everyday life. So after his freshman year at Ole Miss, Barnes took his particular body type and skills and made the best of them. For the next three years, a span covering eighty-six games, Barnes didn't come out of the starting lineup. And by the time he was a senior in the 1986–87 season, Barnes, a player no other SEC team wanted, was an all-conference player.

Ed Murphy remembers Barnes in his senior season. One of Murphy's regrets in his time at Ole Miss was that he got to coach Barnes just one season. In that time, Murphy learned to appreciate Barnes like no other player he had before or since.

"I never coached a better person," said Murphy, now the coach at West Georgia. "You just always knew what you were going to get from Rod Barnes. And what a worker. He was the first guy in the gym, and the last to leave."

In the short time Murphy spent with Barnes, he learned to trust him completely. Murphy recalls a day when Barnes missed practice, a shocking occurrence. Murphy knew Barnes had to have a good reason. Barnes told his coach his car broke down.

"One of my assistants said, 'What are you gonna do about it?'" Murphy recalled. "I said, 'Nothing. I'm not going to even mention it.' Rod had built up so much trust with me. There were guys I would have hammered for missing practice. But not Rod Barnes."

Barnes got the most out of his talent as a senior, averaging 19 and shooting 50 percent from the field and 85 percent from the free throw line. He became the first player in school history to accumulate more than five hundred points, one hundred rebounds, and one hundred assists in a season. Barnes earned his All-SEC selection. For a player who had been so lightly regarded in high school, the honor was proof that he had made it.

"All my life, I have always been the underdog," Barnes said in an interview his senior season. "When I went to high school, people said, 'He was [good in] junior high. Those kids can't play. When he gets to high school, it'll be a different story.' After I left high school, people said, 'When you get to college you won't get a chance to play because you're too little, you're not quick enough, you can't shoot well enough.'

"I just try to prove them wrong. It's like a journey."

Barnes's journey has never taken him too far from his beloved Mississippi. When his playing career was finished at Ole Miss, he hung around for a year, finishing his degree in business administration and working as a student assistant for Murphy.

In 1990, Barnes left his home state, albeit briefly. With Murphy's help, Barnes hooked on at West Alabama, where he worked as an assistant coach for three years. Then in 1993, Barnes got the biggest break of his career. Again, Murphy paved the way.

"I can't claim I've been any great influence on Rod's career," Murphy said. "But I'll take credit for helping his coaching career get started. I coached at West Alabama and knew the athletic director. And when Rob Evans got the job at Ole Miss, I talked to him about Rod on several occasions."

Evans really didn't need to be convinced to hire Barnes, who returned to his alma mater in 1993 and has been there ever since. After a five-year apprenticeship working for Evans, Barnes was hired to replace his former boss.

After hearing all his life from skeptics who said he couldn't succeed at a higher level of competition, Evans was ready for anyone who doubted whether he could do the job. When a reporter for the *Jackson Clarion-Ledger* asked him about his lack of experience as a head coach, he had the perfect answer.

"Well, let me ask you this," Barnes said. "How much experience did the previous head coach have before he got the job?"

In talks with various alumni groups in the first month or so after he was hired, Barnes urged Ole Miss fans to buy season tickets while they still could. The way Barnes saw it, tickets wouldn't last long. He turned out to be right.

Some might have called that arrogance. Barnes called it confidence. In his mind, his career had mirrored the history of Ole Miss basketball.

"We talk a lot about Ole Miss being the underdog and overcoming the odds," Barnes said. "It's the same with me. People said I couldn't do certain things in my career, just like they said it couldn't happen for us at Ole Miss. I think that fit my personality.

"As far as my being ready to be a head coach, my philosophy is somewhat the same as Rob's was. The belief in taking the program to the next level. That was the thing. Coach Evans had laid the foundation for the success we had. But with my hunger and drive, I had the belief we could be even better."

After taking over for Evans, Barnes quickly surrounded himself with a staff that could help him implement his goals. First and foremost, he wanted to recruit hard-working, mature, and coachable athletes. And he wanted to find them within a two-hundred-mile radius of Oxford.

"You're talking about Mississippi, Tennessee, Arkansas, and Alabama," Barnes said. "That's the home base we wanted to cover. We feel like there's enough talented kids in that area to win with."

Barnes's philosophy was reflected in his choice of assistant coaches. From Arkansas, Barnes reached out to Eric Bozeman, then the head coach at Division II

Henderson State. And Bozeman brought a little bonus along with him—a five-foot-five walk-on guard named Jason Harrison.

When he was working at West Alabama, Barnes used to cross paths with Marc Dukes, then the coach at Mississippi's Jones County Junior College. "He came down and recruited my players," Dukes recalled. "I'd been an Ole Miss fan all my life. We used to talk about how we thought you could win at Ole Miss if you could get the best Mississippi kids year in and year out."

Barnes remembered those conversations and also knew Dukes had spent his entire career coaching high school and junior college basketball in Mississippi. Few people had more connections in the state. Like Bozeman, Dukes helped attract a key player to Oxford. Forward Marcus Hicks, a junior college All-American, had played for Dukes at Northwest Mississippi and wanted to be a part of an emerging program at Ole Miss.

Barnes made an astute call on his final hire, reaching to Jackson's Provine High School to take its coach, Wayne Brent. Provine won the Mississippi 5A championship in 1998, Brent's last season.

"Rod is probably among just one or two coaches I would have left my job at Provine to work for," Brent said. "He'd never ask you to pay for a player or do anything wrong. All he'd ask you to do is come to work early and stay late. That's who I wanted to work for."

———

In his first season, Barnes worked wonders with the strong nucleus Evans left behind. Riding seniors Keith Carter, Michael White, and Jason Smith for all they were worth, Barnes led the Rebels to a 20-13 record and a third-place finish in the SEC's Western Division. More importantly, the Rebels advanced to the NCAA Tournament for the third straight season. This time, they beat Villanova in the first round. It was the first NCAA Tournament victory in school history.

Ole Miss lost its second round game to Michigan State, which eventually advanced to the Final Four, but Barnes's message had been clearly stated. He would be no mere caretaker of the program Evans had built. He wanted to take Ole Miss basketball to an even higher level.

Two sidelights of the season involved players who couldn't have been more different. Jason Harrison, the smallest man in the SEC, quickly earned a scholarship by averaging 6.3 points and handing out 84 assists in a reserve role. And burly Rahim Lockhart learned a lesson about accepting responsibility and becoming a man. The

228

lesson was taught by Barnes.

Barnes prides himself on being a good Christian and a forgiving man. But Lockhart, a hell-raiser of the highest order, had done all he could to test Barnes's patience. If Barnes wanted to take control of his program and clearly demonstrate to his players who was in charge, he would have to get control of Lockhart, or run him off.

"I'm a forgiving person," Barnes said. "And I like to give kids chances. But it comes to a point where it hurts other players. We were at the point with Rahim Lockhart where I had done all the forgiving I could do. When it started affecting teammates, that's when I had to do something about it. That's basically what happened with him.

"As a sophomore he had been driving me up the wall with all kinds of crazy stuff. He'd be somewhere in a fight, around a fight, starting a fight. It just kept mounting up. In the incident that brought it all to a head, he was accused of shoplifting a CD or something. He still says to this day that he actually didn't.

"If he had been convicted, he was gone. But because they dropped the charges and because they said they didn't have evidence, I felt I couldn't end his career because of that particular situation. But I told him, now we're at the point where, if you're in here again, it's over. I talked to him about it a couple of years later and he said that was where he realized I wasn't playing anymore."

A few days after his confrontation with Barnes, Lockhart found out his girlfriend was pregnant. The double-barreled dose of reality he'd received in less than a week made a man out of him. From that point on, he was a model citizen. Lockhart found religion and became a devout family man. And just as important to the Ole Miss cause, he became a player.

As a junior, Lockhart averaged 12.2 points and 8.4 rebounds. He turned in career highs in points (29) and rebounds (16) and came up with thirteen double-doubles, second in the conference. Teaming with the backcourt duo of Harrison and Jason Flanigan, yet another Arkansas import, Lockhart helped lead the Rebels to a 19-14 record. Ole Miss didn't have the regular-season success it enjoyed the previous three seasons, finishing with a 5-11 SEC record, but the Rebels did advance to the NIT, where they won twice.

In two years as a head coach, Barnes's team won three postseason games, the first in school history.

––––––

While Ole Miss began to win consistently, Barnes and his staff also did a great job off the court, sustaining the program through strong recruiting. The class signed in the fall of 1999 and the spring of 2000 rivaled any in the history of the program. Barnes would begin his third season with a deep and talented roster, thanks in large part to the arrival of the Provine Posse, a trio of former Provine High School stars who had played for Ole Miss assistant Wayne Brent and won a state championship in 1997.

The first of the posse to make his way to Oxford was David Sanders, who had originally signed with Ole Miss when Evans was coaching in 1997. Sanders couldn't get eligible his freshman season, so he played a year at Tallahassee (Florida) Junior College, averaging 15 points, five rebounds, and nearly six assists.

In the 1999–2000 season, Sanders didn't play basketball, but attended Northwest Mississippi Community College, got his academic affairs in order, and re-signed with the Rebels.

Soon to follow was six-foot-seven Aaron Harper. Like Sanders, Harper had signed with Ole Miss before, in 1998. He, too, couldn't get eligible, but to preserve four years of eligibility, he sat out a year. The combination of Sanders, a great athlete, and Harper, a game-breaking shooter, might have been enough to get the Rebels into a post-season tournament for the fifth straight season. But an added bonus from Provine arrived along with them in the fall of 2000.

The recruitment of six-foot-eight Justin Reed was typically intense, the kind of war that is waged between SEC schools battling for players in close proximity. "The closer the schools are around you, the more times you have to be confrontational," an SEC assistant said. "It gets tough sometimes. But that's life in the SEC."

Reed, the player of the year in Mississippi and a *Parade* All-American in 1999–2000, is typical of the kind of athlete turned out in his home state. Long, lean, strong, and athletic, he has the ability to take over a game inside, outside, or through the sheer force of his will. Barnes and his staff knew Reed could be a breakthrough recruit for Ole Miss.

Given the presence of Sanders and Harper, Reed's former high school teammates, and Brent, his old coach, the Rebels would have seemed the likely leaders for his services. But all through the recruiting process, Reed seemed bound for Auburn, and he eventually committed to the Tigers. The Auburn staff was confident Reed would sign right up until the first day of the NCAA's spring signing period. When Reed instead signed with Ole Miss, it sent shock waves throughout the league.

Some long-time observers of SEC basketball cried foul, but Reed insisted his association with Brent and Barnes was the primary factor in choosing Ole Miss. Reed's relationship with Barnes began when Barnes was still an Ole Miss assistant.

"I knew the whole coaching staff," Reed said. "Wayne Brent was my high school coach. When I was at Provine and coach Barnes was an assistant at Ole Miss, I got to know him. I knew he wasn't just a coach, but a great person and a father figure. Over the years, we sort of had a father-son relationship. I call him 'pops.' We've got a strong relationship."

Brent, as Barnes hoped he would, laid the groundwork for the Provine Posse to take its act to Ole Miss as early as 1998.

"When I first asked about the job here with coach Barnes, I got the guys on my team together," Brent recalled. "I kind of expressed interest in going to Ole Miss. I asked them if they would mind. That was a major decision for me. They told me they supported me. Then after I talked to coach Barnes, I went and got those three guys [Sanders, Harper, and Reed] one day after school and we discussed the Ole Miss situation. They all told me they'd like to go to Ole Miss, which was one of the major factors that made me take the job."

Brent expected that Reed, who would be more heavily recruited, might change his mind. Reed still had to play two more years of high school basketball, during which a lot could happen. Brent insists he exerted no pressure on Reed to choose Ole Miss.

"I think Justin's mother wanted him to make his decision," Brent said. "Everybody had told him he had to go to Ole Miss because coach Brent and Aaron Harper and David Sanders were there. His momma told him to make up his mind where he wanted to go. She wanted him to make up his mind for Justin Reed instead of coach Brent.

"A week after he committed to Auburn he told his momma he actually wanted to go to Ole Miss. Once he said that, she agreed to let him come. She was comfortable with him going to Auburn. It was a hard sell going to Ole Miss. If we hadn't already set the tone by winning there, he'd have been another guy who would have gone out of state."

Parade All-Americans may come and go at Kentucky and Florida, but the successful recruitment of Justin Reed was a major deal at Ole Miss. Reed was the most highly decorated recruit to ever sign with the Rebels, and his signing made a statement. Gone were the days when top Mississippi high school players wouldn't even consider Ole Miss. The work of Evans, and now Barnes, had caught their attention.

Ole Miss would continue to attract attention in the 2000–2001 season. Rahim Lockhart, the previously angry young man whom Barnes came within an eyelash of kicking off the team two years before, became a star and a first-team All-SEC pick, leading the Rebels in scoring and rebounding. Guards Jason Flanigan and Jason Harrison again teamed to run the team efficiently from the point-guard position. Harrison was even chosen third-team All-SEC despite starting just two games, clear evidence of his value to the team.

While the veterans were performing as expected, the Provine Posse also lived up to its billing.

Barnes put Reed into the lineup from the beginning and Reed didn't disappoint, averaging 11 points and six rebounds. He became the first Ole Miss player to be chosen the SEC's Freshman of the Year, and he was also a third-team All-SEC pick.

David Sanders and Aaron Harper also made an impact. Sanders—the best athlete of the trio—became a defensive stopper. And with his ability to slash to the basket, he was also hard to handle in the open floor. Harper was a game-breaking shooter who scored in double figures sixteen times and tossed in 63 three-pointers, the third most in school history.

With so much talent at his disposal, all Barnes had to do for the Rebels to be successful was push the right buttons. And push them he did. Ole Miss won the SEC's Western Division title for the third time in four seasons and entered the SEC Tournament with a 23-6 record and ranked fourteenth in the country.

The Rebels advanced all the way to the tournament championship game, and despite being beaten handily by Kentucky, their enthusiasm for the NCAA Tournament wasn't dampened in the slightest. Their season-long efforts had earned them an at-large bid, their fourth trip to the Big Dance in five seasons. Counting the previous year's NIT appearance, this would be the Rebels' fifth straight post-season tournament. And it would be memorable.

Seeded third in the tournament's Midwest Region, Ole Miss drew a pesky first-round opponent, twelfth-seeded Iona. Barnes expected a tough game, and he got one. With 31.8 seconds to play and the Rebels ahead, 71-70, the Gaels had plenty of time to set up a game-winning shot. Iona point guard Earl Johnson drove into the lane, but, double-teamed, he tried to get the ball to teammate Courtney Fields. Rahim Lockhart reached in to intercept the pass, deflecting it to teammate Jason Holmes, who was fouled with 1.8 seconds to play. The Rebels escaped 72-70.

If the rare NCAA victory showed how far Ole Miss basketball had come, a gesture made by chancellor Robert Khayat before the game showed how far the university had come. Forty-four years before, Ole Miss refused to play Iona because it had a black player, Stanley Hill, on its roster. Hill and his wife were guests of Khayat at the NCAA Tournament.

"I'm so proud of the changes that have taken place in Mississipppi," Hill told the *Jackson Clarion-Ledger*.

The Rebels' second-round game against Notre Dame was no easier than their opener had been. With less than a minute to play, they trailed the Fighting Irish, 55-54. During a timeout, Harrison told Barnes what was going to happen.

232

Rod Barnes. *Ole Miss Sports Information*

"He told me he was gonna take the shot," Barnes recalled. "The thing about it was he had missed his two previous shots. But he came over to the sideline and said, 'Hey, do you want to win the game?' I said, 'Yeah.' He said, 'Alright, I've got it.'"

True to his word, Harrison took matters into his own hands. With two seconds left on the shot clock, Harrison lofted a twenty-three-foot jumper that swished through the net, giving Ole Miss a 57-55 lead.

"I really didn't hesitate about taking that three," Harrison recalled. "It felt good leaving my hand. I had been in a bad slump. But this was my one shining moment. There was my chance right there to redeem myself. If I made this shot we're going to the Sweet 16."

After Harrison's historic shot, what he did next surprised even Barnes.

"After he makes the three-pointer, he calls timeout," Barnes said. "He comes over to the bench and says, 'Coach, put Buck [Jason Flanigan] in. He's a better defender.' Took his own self out of the game. That shows the kind of kid he is."

Harrison made the right call again. After David Sanders blocked a three-point try by Notre Dame's Matt Carroll, Flanigan was there to scoop up the loose ball. He was fouled, hit one of two free throws, and Ole Miss won, 59-56. The first Sweet 16 appearance in school history and a matchup with Arizona was next.

The Rebels, with the expectations of an entire state on their shoulders, gave everything they had against the Wildcats in taking a 12-point first-half lead. But Arizona, on a mission of its own after the death earlier that season of coach Lute Olson's wife, Bobbi, rallied and won, 66-56. The Wildcats would eventually reach the championship game.

The greatest season in Ole Miss history had come to an end, but much had been proven during a year in which the Rebels won twenty-seven games and Barnes was voted the Naismith Coach of the Year.

"You've got ten or twelve teams that are national contenders," Barnes said in assessing the Rebels' ever-improving status. "Year in and year out they're gonna have a chance to win the championship. Florida's one of them now. Kentucky. Duke. UCLA. Then you've got another group of teams in the top twenty-five that could maybe slip in there and make it happen. That's where we want to be. We're not there yet, but it's where we want to be."

In three seasons under Rod Barnes, Ole Miss had won sixty-six games. The Rebels played in two NCAA Tournaments and an NIT and won five post-season games. No less an expert than Rob Evans thought Barnes's work with the program had been extraordinary, especially considering the fact Barnes was just thirty-two when he took over.

"He's done a fabulous job," Evans said. "Rod's really grown in that job. To be very honest, he was very fortunate we had a championship team coming back, which gave him time to make mistakes going in. I don't think [the fans] were going to be real patient. He's done a magnificent job of maturing in that position, which doesn't surprise me. Rod understands discipline. He understands there are no shortcuts. He won't compromise his principals."

————

Despite all he had accomplished in his first three seasons, Barnes had no lofty expectations for his team as the 2001–2002 season began. The Rebels had lost Rahim Lockhart and Jason Flanigan to graduation. John Gunn, a promising big man, had become ill with a kidney disorder and wouldn't play a minute all season. An untested junior college transfer, Derrick Allen, was going to have to approximate Lockhart's contributions in the post.

"This was a team that had a lot of questions in the beginning of the year," Barnes said. "I thought if we could just have a winning season that would be really good. I didn't really imagine, as I looked across the league, that our team could do much more than that."

There was evidence to suggest Barnes's preseason assessment of the Rebels was accurate.

Ole Miss
All-SEC Expansion Era Team
F-Ansu Sesay
F-Justin Reed
C-Rahim Lockhart
G-Keith Carter
G-Jason Harrison
Top Reserves-Joe Harvell, Jason Flanigan

In the Top of the World Classic in Alaska, they lost their season opener to Bowling Green when they couldn't hold a lead in the final minute and were forced into overtime. In its second home game of the season, Ole Miss lost to George Mason, 71-70. That loss hurt, because it broke the Rebels' forty-four-game home-court winning streak over nonconference competition.

At that point of the season, Barnes was concerned about his team's ability to win close games. But less than a week after the loss to George Mason, the Rebels regrouped with a win over No. 22 Memphis. The game wasn't decided until the final seconds, when Derrick Allen blocked a shot by the Tigers' Dajuan Wagner and Ole Miss guard Emmanuel Wade made a pair of free throws.

The Rebels won the rest of their nonconference games and took an 11-2 record into their SEC opener at Tennessee. The Rebels lost to the Vols but proceeded to win six of their next seven league games. Halfway through the SEC season, Ole Miss stood at 6-2. Barnes thought if the Rebels could squeeze out three more wins, they had a realistic chance to make the NCAA Tournament field yet again.

As it turned out, Ole Miss would win just three more SEC games. The Rebels proved to be a poor road team in league play, winning only at Arkansas. But down the stretch, they came up with three convincing victories at home, running their SEC home-court winning streak to fifteen, tops in the league. First the Rebels beat Arkansas. It was their tenth win in their last twelve games against Arkansas, a statistic that by itself underscored how far Ole Miss, and SEC basketball in general, had progressed.

Next, the Rebels rocked sixth-ranked Florida, 68-51, then manhandled eventual regular-season champion Alabama in the regular-season finale, 84-56. The Crimson Tide was also ranked sixth at the time.

The win was Ole Miss' twentieth, the fourth time in the last five seasons the Rebels had reached that magic number. All things considered it was a solid season, one that exceeded even Barnes's expectations. Ole Miss would go on to have a disappointing performance in post-season play, but at the end of the regular season, Barnes was pleased with the progress of his program.

"This season tells me more than anything that we do have a good program," Barnes said. "We haven't gotten to the level of greatness. But now people look at our program with respect. We're no longer looked at as the doormat of our league. This year we put some things in place and kept some continuity. We had so many question marks and we answered them. That tells me we may be a little farther at this stage than even I could have imagined."

Chapter Ten

South Carolina

I t was early December 2001, and Dave Odom had just finished a press conference to discuss a game his South Carolina team would play the next night against Georgetown. As the media slowly filed out of the room, a writer approached Odom, who was bedecked in garnet and black—colors familiar to Gamecock fans, but not to Dave Odom fans. "What are you doing here?" the writer asked Odom.

Odom knew exactly what the question meant. After a dozen years coaching at Wake Forest—which, given its academic standards and the fact it competes in the rugged Atlantic Coast Conference, is one of the toughest jobs in the country—Odom, at fifty-eight years old, found it necessary to bail out in the spring of 2001. Though he had compiled a 240-132 record and taken the Demon Deacons to eleven straight post-season tournaments, Odom's contract hadn't been renewed beyond the 2001–2002 season. There was talk that Odom's relationship with Wake Forest athletic director Ron Wellman was strained. And there was grumbling among fans, who had been thrilled with how the Demon Deacons started the 2000–2001 season—twelve straight wins, including a 31-point whipping of Kansas—and devastated over how it ended—eleven losses in the last nineteen games, including a 79-63 upset by Ball State in the first round of the NCAA Tournament.

That his boss and some fans weren't all that happy with the state of Wake Forest basketball wasn't surprising to Odom. Basketball coaches know if they stay anywhere for twelve years, they'll develop their share of detractors and second-guessers. In the four seasons after star center Tim Duncan left Wake Forest in 1996, the Deacons had played in three National Invitation Tournaments and that lone NCAA, from which they were booted rudely by Ball State. That was enough for some Wake Forest fans—and, apparently, Wellman—to deduce that the program had begun a downturn from which Odom couldn't direct a recovery. Thus Wellman's decision to not renew Odom's contract. That forced Odom to take some serious stock of his present, and his future.

"By all reasonable estimates," wrote columnist Lenox Rawlings in the *Winston-Salem Journal*, "Odom faced expectations he detested and lacked solid support from athletics director Ron Wellman. If the Deacons couldn't improve on their 19-11 finish and No. 23 national ranking, Odom couldn't count on staying any longer. Teams rarely get better when everyone knows that the coach dangles by a thread, his centers gone, his contract expiring, and his recruits inching away from the signature line. Odom faced purgatory, quite likely followed by hell. All of a sudden, the garnet parachute looked more heavenly. Not many fifty-eight-year-old men get to keep their wife, their beach house, their investments, and their loyal assistants while embarking on a second coaching honeymoon. He took it."

Such is life as a coach at a major Division I school. Odom's record at Wake Forest, impressive as it was, wasn't good enough to ensure job security. The NCAA Tournament has become the standard by which coaches are measured. And it isn't enough just to get there, or even, as the Deacons did under Odom, reach the Sweet 16 or the Elite Eight. Never mind how hard the coach at Wake Forest has to work to keep pace with the dynasty Mike Krzyzewski has built at Duke, or the perennial power at North Carolina (just throw out the 2001–2002 season) or Maryland, Virginia, North Carolina State, et cetera, et cetera.

College basketball coaches are judged by the familiar what-have-you-done-for-me-lately standard, and most can live with that. But for some coaches, that measuring stick seems unfair. Thus the writer's question to Odom, who had traded in his gold-and-black coaching togs for the garnet-and-black of South Carolina and looked strangely out of place: "What are you doing here?"

Odom smiled at the question and nodded his head. But at that late date, he wasn't about to debate anyone over whether he got the shaft at Wake Forest, or whether coaches are judged by too harsh a standard.

"This is something I've always said," Odom said. "I always had as my goal for the Wake Forest program that when I left there, when my time was over, that the only thing I wanted was for the program to be in better shape than it was when I came. And I'll let history decide that. I feel good about it, but that's not for me to say. I'll let others say that."

There are plenty of others willing to assess the job Odom did at Wake Forest. But even his closest friends acknowledge that by accepting South Carolina athletic director Mike McGee's offer to replace Eddie Fogler on April 10, 2001, Odom made the smartest decision he could.

"I think everybody who knows Dave was surprised he ended up at South Carolina," said former University of Virginia coach and athletic director Terry Holland, who first got to know Odom well when he hired him as an assistant. "But to be honest, if he'd asked me—which he didn't, because it happened so quickly—I would have said that, as much as I wanted him to stay in the [ACC], and I know how much that league meant to him because he grew up in that area, South Carolina was a special opportunity. You've got a new arena being built, great players in the state. I think it's a good move for him.

"He had built the program at Wake up to the first level. I don't know that anyone can keep it at the level he had it at. But you always have a state where you start to plateau. And rather than Dave staying there and hitting that plateau, maybe ending up with no place to go but down, he goes out on top. Wake's in great shape, had everybody back from a NCAA team, essentially. Dave's move worked out well for everybody."

Ernie Nestor, Odom's long-time friend and assistant at Wake Forest, supported Odom's move to South Carolina and eventually decided to follow him there. But Nestor couldn't help but note the irony of situation. Like Odom, former South Carolina coach Eddie Fogler had built a program under difficult circumstances, and despite his status as one of the game's most respected tacticians, couldn't avoid a downturn, the scrutiny of his athletic director, and the criticism of fans and the media. After the 2000–2001 season, Fogler chose to be bought out of his contract, which, like Odom's, had not been extended. He spent the 2001–2002 season working as a commentator for CNN and CBS and scouting for the Utah Jazz and Philadelphia 76ers, blissfully removed from coaching but still close to the game.

"There's one thing about coaching," Nestor said. "You come to periods in your life where you're either going to change what you're doing or change where you're doing it. In Eddie's case, he changed what he was doing. In Dave's case, he changed where he was doing it. In both cases, it might have been time for a change."

Gamecock fans and Odom's many friends and supporters are going to get an opportunity to see what the man can do in the next several seasons. Though he was pushing sixty when he took over at South Carolina, Odom has always maintained that as long as he's enjoying himself, he wants to coach. As Holland said, the move to South Carolina extended Odom's career and gave him a new challenge.

"I wouldn't say I was looking for a new challenge," Odom said. "But if I was going to leave, it was going to be for something I thought was truly unique. The University of South Carolina is truly unique. I've always thought that if you can say the name of the state and have it be the same as your university, you're a leg up."

One advantage Odom will have at a state-supported school is the opportunity to recruit a wider range of student-athletes. Freed from the high academic entry standards of Wake Forest, Odom looks forward to recruiting, a task he still enjoys even after all the years he's done it. And Odom has plenty of help. He made a good decision early to hire former Winston-Salem State head coach Rick Duckett, who had spent a year as an assistant coach at South Carolina in 1986 and knew the territory.

Odom wanted to make sure his staff concentrated on recruiting local talent.

"That was a big deal when we first got here, and always will be," Duckett said. "We went to the high school coaches' association convention and met as many coaches as we could. We went around to the various schools during the contact period. We called coaches and wrote them, just to make them feel a part of USC and the basketball program. And the coaches have been extremely warm and gracious to us. I've gotten a lot of good information and more effort to help us than you can ever hope."

———

South Carolina has a tradition in basketball, dating back to its days in the Atlantic Coast Conference, a league in which the Gamecocks competed for eighteen seasons, from 1953–54 to 1970–71. The program's glory days came under the direction of legendary Frank McGuire, who had come from the University of North Carolina in 1964 and coached for sixteen seasons, retiring in 1980. McGuire, by far the winningest coach in school history, produced some great teams—the 1969–70 Gamecocks, who went 25-3 and 14-0 in the ACC, are still discussed with reverence around Columbia. And he recruited some star players—John Roche, Alex English, Kevin Joyce, Bobby Cremins, Brian Winters, and Mike Dunleavy to name just a few.

Yet despite its success in basketball in the ACC, South Carolina administrators saw no future in that league. In a move that was directly related to the success of its football program, South Carolina left the ACC in 1971.

"At the time, the NCAA had no academic restrictions," said Tom Price, a South Carolina sports historian and former sports information director at the school. "It was all up to the individual conferences to determine admissions standards. The ACC was the first conference to institute admissions standards above and beyond what the individual schools had. The conference required a minimum of 800 on the SAT, which made it hard to recruit.

"As a result, ACC football had become vastly inferior to SEC football, which we were well aware of because of our proximity to the SEC. I can recall playing Georgia one year, and seven of their twenty-two starters were from South Carolina; they were kids we couldn't get in school."

The presence of McGuire was another reason South Carolina administrators began to feel uncomfortable in the ACC. His move from North Carolina had not gone over well with fans and administrators there. And McGuire kept running feuds with various people around the conference.

"Frank was a naturally controversial person," Price said. "He reveled in controversy.

He was roundly disliked by certain people in the ACC. There was a lot of animosity."

The decision was made for South Carolina to become an independent, a path Penn State, Pittsburgh, and Notre Dame, among others, had already traveled with great success.

"Paul Dietzel led the fight to leave the ACC," Price said. "He was our athletic director and football coach, and he had delusions of grandeur that South Carolina could become the Notre Dame of the Southeast."

Things didn't quite work out that way. South Carolina football became just as stifled by its independent status as it had been recruiting under the ACC's academic standards. And the basketball program found it increasingly difficult to play a quality schedule. Clemson was the only ACC school still willing to play the Gamecocks.

"The first few years, the Catholic schools bailed us out," Price recalled. "We filled out our schedule with Notre Dame, Marquette, Temple, St. Joseph's, St. Bonaventure. All those schools had outstanding basketball programs, but there were no natural rivals."

After twelve seasons as an independent, South Carolina joined the Metro Conference in 1983. That affiliation was good for basketball, considering fellow Metro schools included such established powers as Louisville and Memphis, but it was of no benefit to football. The Metro didn't sponsor the sport.

Searching for a solution that would benefit all South Carolina's athletic programs, the school's administration was in a good position to negotiate with the Southeastern Conference when the league made its decision to expand in 1990. The SEC courted several schools, including Miami and Florida State, but ultimately, Arkansas and South Carolina proved to be the most comfortable fit for all concerned.

"I can't speak from a coaching standpoint," said Dr. John Moore, South Carolina's senior athletic administrator. "But from an administrative standpoint, we knew that we had to move our program to a different level. That's not a knock on the Metro. But we needed an all-sports conference. Obviously, we had great concerns for our football program continuing to operate as an independent at a time when the noose was closing in on independents."

Though South Carolina came into the SEC well aware of that league's success in athletics, there was an adjustment period for all sports.

"It took some time for us to be competitive," Moore said. "It wasn't a shock to us to see the level of competition in this league. We were well aware of what the SEC was all about and the tremendous resources available to every school in the league. But adjustments had to be made."

That was particularly true in basketball.

241

After McGuire retired in 1980, he was replaced by Bill Foster, who led the Gamecocks to a 22-9 record and an NIT appearance in 1982–83 but couldn't make the program competitive in the Metro Conference. After a 12-16 1985–86 season that included a 2-10 record in the Metro, Foster stepped down and was replaced by George Felton, who had played for McGuire, albeit sparingly, in the early 1970s. With the help of a hard-working assistant named Tubby Smith, Felton directed a brief resurgence; in 1988–89, Felton's third season, the Gamecocks earned their first trip to the NCAA Tournament in fifteen years.

Off-the-court problems proved to be Felton's undoing, however. Just two years after directing the Gamecocks to the NCAAs, Felton was gone, fired after a 20-13 season in 1990–91. Felton later said he didn't learn of his demise until reading about it in the paper.

If South Carolina's then-athletic director King Dixon had botched Felton's firing, his performance in hiring a replacement was even worse. It took Dixon and a search committee two months to hire Steve Newton away from Murray State. Murray State has a proud history competing in the Ohio Valley Conference and had enjoyed success under Newton. But when Dixon announced Newton's hiring, he proclaimed that Newton had been his first choice all along. South Carolina fans didn't buy that company line for a second. And they were underwhelmed by the straight-laced Newton, a deadly dull speaker who on his best day was never going to excite the masses with any great oratorical style or magnetism.

Neither did Newton overwhelm anyone on the court. Under his direction, the Gamecocks were 20-35 overall and a woeful 8-24 in SEC games. His tenure was mercifully short, though, ending in 1993 after just two seasons. A brief dalliance with well-traveled junior-college transfer Cortez Barnes proved to be Newton's undoing; he was fired after five secondary NCAA recruiting violations were uncovered.

After Newton's ouster, athletic director Mike McGee pulled what seemed like a coup by hiring Bobby Cremins away from Georgia Tech. Not only was Cremins in his most successful period at Georgia Tech—having directed the Yellow Jackets to the 1990 Final Four—he was practically a native son. Cremins was a link to South Carolina's proud past, having played for McGuire from 1968–70.

Cremins's hiring excited Gamecock fans that had been eager for the program to assert itself in the SEC. But two days after accepting the job, Cremins had a change of heart and decided to stay at Georgia Tech.

Suffice it to say McGee wasn't pleased with Cremins's decision. But he regrouped by entering into a whirlwind courtship with Eddie Fogler, who had just directed Vanderbilt to a 28-6 record, the regular-season SEC championship and an appearance in the NCAA

Tournament's Sweet 16, earning consensus national coach-of-the-year honors.

Those accomplishments made Fogler a hot commodity, but he had resisted the overtures of other schools offering jobs before, and was prepared to again. By all accounts, he loved Nashville and wanted to finish his career there. All Fogler wanted from Vanderbilt athletic director Paul Hoolahan was a show of support and a reasonable increase in pay. Fogler made his wishes known to Hoolahan, who agreed to discuss the matter with Vanderbilt chancellor Joe B. Wyatt. But when a few days passed and Fogler hadn't heard back from his boss, he asked to speak to Wyatt.

In the meantime, McGee had called Vanderbilt for permission to speak to Fogler. Fogler was expecting some sort of sign from Wyatt, but got frustrated when he didn't hear from the chancellor. By that point Fogler was ready for the recruiting pitch of McGee, who didn't realize how uncanny the timing of his job offer had been. Fogler, angered by the apparent reluctance of his administration to reward him with a new contract, stunned Vanderbilt fans by bolting for South Carolina.

Years later, Fogler was reluctant to revisit his final days at Vanderbilt.

"Coaches move for a number of reasons," Fogler said. "I had reasons to move. That's water over the dam."

Fogler might be unwilling to discuss his departure from Vanderbilt. But it hasn't been forgotten in Nashville.

"Eddie's leaving caused an uproar in the Vanderbilt community that I'm convinced exists to this day," said Joe Biddle, a columnist for *The Tennessean*. "It cost the program thousands of fans and who knows how much financial support."

It took Fogler a couple of years to sort through the mess he inherited at South Carolina. In Fogler's first season, the Gamecocks were 9-19 and 4-12 in the SEC. A year later, South Carolina was 10-17, 5-11. The breakthrough came in 1995–96, when Fogler coaxed a 19-12 record, 8-8 SEC finish, and three NIT games out of the Gamecocks. South Carolina beat Davidson and, fittingly, Vanderbilt in the NIT before losing to Alabama.

"What Eddie did in a short period of time was one of the most phenomenal things I've ever seen in this game," said Tennessee-Chattnooga coach Jeff Lebo, who worked on Fogler's staff at Vanderbilt and South Carolina. "When we took over at South Carolina, I can't imagine a program in any worse shape at that level.

"There were no players in the program. We had to sign seven guys in the late signing period, and we'd gotten there late in the game, obviously. That's like going to Wal-Mart on the third day of a sale. You get the best of what's left, and a lot of times, that isn't good enough."

By the 1996–97 season, Fogler's fourth in Columbia, the Gamecocks were ready to roll. The team was extremely strong in the backcourt, and Fogler started three guards to take advantage.

North Carolina transfer Larry Davis had been a star in 1995–96 after regaining his eligibility. A native of Denmark, South Carolina, the six-foot-four Davis averaged 44 points a game his senior year at Denmark-Olar High School. But despite his obvious skills and reputation as a scorer, Davis was inserted at the point-guard position at North Carolina. That move didn't work out for Davis or North Carolina, and after transferring to South Carolina for his junior season, Davis led the Gamecocks in scoring, averaging 18 points.

Joining Davis in the Gamecocks' quick and explosive backcourt were Melvin Watson, a clever point guard from Charleston, South Carolina, and B. J. McKie, a strong, athletic scoring machine who had been a breakthrough recruit for Fogler's staff. McKie was a *Parade* and McDonald's All-American at Irmo High School in Columbia. McKie averaged 15 points as a freshman and would eventually become South Carolina's all-time leading scorer, passing the great Alex English.

In all, eight native South Carolinians were on the roster in 1996–97, and Fogler had supplemented the homegrown talent with Ryan Stack, a versatile six-foot-eleven forward from Tennessee, and Nate Wilbourne, a strong, six-foot-eleven center who had transferred from Ohio State.

That team steamrolled through the SEC schedule with a 15 1 record, but the Gamecocks gave no indication of that kind of dominance in their nonconference games. They lost five games before December was over, the latter two shocking homecourt defeats to UNC Asheville and Charleston Southern. Disappointing as they were, those two upsets had a positive benefit, awakening the Gamecocks from their early season slumber.

South Carolina proceeded to win its first eleven SEC games—three of them on the road with clutch baskets in the closing seconds. B. J. McKie's runner in the lane with five seconds to play gave the Gamecocks an 80-79 win at Florida in a game where they rallied from 16 points down with 5:16 to play. That victory, Fogler said after the season, gave his team a boost of confidence it would draw from the rest of the season.

A week after the Florida game, Melvin Watson was the hero, as his lay-up with 3.9 seconds left gave South Carolina a 62-60 win at Alabama. A week after that, the Gamecocks stole a 65-64 win at Fogler's old school, Vanderbilt, when Watson knocked down a jumper with twenty-seven seconds left. The Gamecocks were beginning to look invincible.

South Carolina won four more games after the close call at Vanderbilt and finally entered the Associated Press poll at No. 25 in late January. The Gamecocks proved they were worthy of being ranked in a February 4 game against Kentucky, the defending national champions. It took an overtime period, but South Carolina, then ranked No. 19, beat the No. 3–ranked Wildcats, 84-79. The win gave the Gamecocks a two-game lead in the SEC's Eastern Division standings.

The lead became a little more precarious on February 12. South Carolina finally lost at Georgia when a William Gallman lay-up attempt spun out of the basket late in the game. Holding a one-game lead over Kentucky, the Gamecocks knew they were headed for a showdown with the Wildcats. To make sure that showdown took place, Carolina won six straight games, including two out of conference against Cincinnati and The Citadel, before the March 2 game at Kentucky. By this time, Gamecock fans had become infatuated, supporting the team with a fervor and in numbers unseen since the glory days of Frank McGuire.

"That year taught us a lot about the good and bad of college basketball," Lebo recalled. "People were so down on us in December. But then we beat Auburn on the road and beat Tennessee. We got to 7-0 in the league. We'd get back from road games and there would be five people at the airport. The next game, there was 150. The next game it was 550 people waiting on us. It was amazing. We went from nobody wanting to talk to you to heroes."

The Gamecocks were particularly heroic at Kentucky with the outright SEC championship on the line. The game has since carved out its own exalted place in South Carolina basketball history.

The chances of South Carolina winning seemed remote at best. Kentucky hadn't lost its last home game of the season, the always-emotional Senior Day, in thirty-three years. The Wildcats had won twenty-seven straight games in their intimidating Rupp Arena. And South Carolina had lost ten straight at Kentucky.

The game was a classic. The lead changed hands several times, but when Kentucky went ahead 49-45 with 10:14 to play, the game seemed to be slipping from the Gamecocks' grasp. Somehow amid the deafening noise and hostile atmosphere of Rupp, South Carolina regrouped, went on a 10-2 run and claimed the lead for good, winning 72-66. After the game, Kentucky coach Rick Pitino gave the Gamecocks their due.

"It was not a fluke," Pitino told reporters. "They are better than us right now."

South Carolina was the only SEC team to pull off a two-game season sweep of Kentucky in Pitino's eight years as coach.

Fans and the media hailed the Gamecocks' win at Kentucky and SEC championship as an accomplishment to match any in South Carolina's long history. Having won the league title at Vanderbilt, Fogler knew how difficult it was.

"It was the first SEC championship in the history of the school," Fogler said. "So it was a benchmark of sorts. SEC championships in any sport are hard to come by because this conference is so competitive. We showed it could be done at the University of South Carolina. And we did it basically with South Carolina kids. That was fun."

The post-season wouldn't be so much fun. The Gamecocks drew a first-round bye in the SEC Tournament, but were beaten by Georgia in the quarterfinals. That didn't end up hurting South Carolina too terribly—the Gamecocks were seeded No. 2 in the NCAA Tournament's East Regional—but it might have served notice that something was amiss. In the first round of the NCAAs, South Carolina was knocked out by Coppin State, the fifteenth-seeded team in the East. That game was the stunner of the tournament—only two other No. 15 seeds had won since the sixty-four-team format began in 1985.

"The No. 2 seed in the NCAA Tournament should beat the No. 15 seed," Fogler told *Blue Ribbon College Basketball Yearbook* a few months later. "But on a neutral court in the NCAAs, anything can happen. That's no excuse. Coppin State was the better team that day."

Those words proved to be as prophetic as they were reflective. In 1997–98, South Carolina, without Davis and Wilbourne, put together a 23-8 record that included an 11-5 mark and second-place finish in the SEC's Eastern Division. The Gamecocks even ended their string of three straight post-season losses by beating Florida and Ole Miss in the SEC Tournament and reaching the tournament finals against Kentucky. But any momentum South Carolina might have gathered from those wins was squashed under the heels of the mighty Wildcats, who won by 30 points and would go on to win the national championship.

South Carolina's own foray into the NCAA Tournament was brief. Entering the tournament as the No. 3–seeded team in the East Regional, the Gamecocks were again left for dead in the first round, losing 62-61 to fourteenth-seeded Richmond. To South Carolina fans, a disturbing trend had been established, and their worst fears came to fruition in the 1998–99 season, when a total meltdown occurred in the program, and for two years after that. The Gamecocks' travails underscored how difficult it is to maintain a high level of success in the SEC.

With Watson, who finished as South Carolina's all-time assist leader, and Stack having graduated, McKie was left to carry on. As talented as he was, McKie couldn't carry the load by himself. South Carolina had trouble putting the ball in the basket—the Gamecocks finished the season last in the SEC in average points per game and shooting percentage. Fogler also had some discipline problems with senior forward LeRon Williams, a Florida transfer who was booted off the team six games into the SEC schedule.

The result was a shocking 8-21 record. South Carolina finished last in the SEC East, winning just three of sixteen league games.

The next two years were slightly better. The Gamecocks were 15-17 in 1999–2000 and won five SEC games. In 2000–2001 they wound up 15-15, won six league games and played in the NIT. Fogler might have gotten his team back into the NCAAs if the Gamecocks could have held onto big leads in home-court losses to Ole Miss, Arkansas, and Tennessee.

South Carolina's cause wasn't helped by some personnel problems. An injury to sophomore Chuck Eidson, a versatile swingman who blew out his knee in the early portion of the SEC season, was crippling because Eidson had become the Gamecocks' most valuable player. *Parade* All-American forward Rolando Howell, a freshman, had some off-the-court troubles that merited a suspension and hampered his early development.

Despite the injuries and personnel problems that were beyond anyone's control, South Carolina athletic director Mike McGee didn't have enough confidence in the future of the program to offer Fogler a contract extension.

That concerned Fogler, but the truth was that he had already begun to feel restricted by some of the requirements of his job that had nothing to do with coaching.

"I got to the point where, after thirty years as a coach, fifteen as a head coach, I had basically had enough of recruiting to some degree," Fogler recalled. "The coaching, I enjoyed. The kids, I enjoyed . . . watching tape, doing the Xs and Os. It was just the other stuff. . . . April was a tough month. You'd have recruiting, alumni talks. Finding your seniors jobs. There was a coaches' convention to go to. I was never home. It just got to be that there were so many demands, it just wasn't very fun in the off-season."

Fogler might have had more fun if he and his assistants had been able to coax South Carolina natives Kevin Garnett and Jermaine O'Neal into Gamecock uniforms. Both were six-foot-eleven, mobile and highly skilled. But both opted to head to the NBA after high school—Garnett in 1995, O'Neal in 1996—helping pioneer a trend that continues to this day. An ever-increasing amount of young big men are bypassing college for the lure of NBA dollars.

"If we'd just gotten one of those guys," said Lebo, who left to become head coach at Tennessee Tech in 1998 and then switched to Tennessee-Chattanooga in 2002. "They were both just so good. You take the guards we had with one of those guys in the mix, and I think we could have had a team capable of winning the national championship."

Ironically, South Carolina never won an NCAA Tournament game under the leadership of Fogler, who had been able to do so at his two previous coaching stops at Wichita State and Vanderbilt. Despite those celebrated NCAA Tournament flameouts, Fogler didn't think he was underappreciated at South Carolina. But his experience in Columbia left him thinking the Big Dance had become too much of a barometer by which a coach's performance is evaluated.

"I said this before I started my last two years [at South Carolina]," Fogler recalled. "Only Kentucky and Arkansas [from the SEC] had been to more than five NCAA Tournaments in the previous ten years. That's the problem as I see it. You're damned if you do, damned if you don't. If you get there—you go to the tournament two or three years in a row—and then you have two years where you don't, you have created your monster. You can now find a coach who is going to have problems with his contractual situation. If you don't get [to the NCAAs], well, you're gone anyway."

As a coach, Fogler was never afraid to say what was on his mind. After leaving the sidelines, he was just as candid in assessing the state of the game.

"It's very difficult to get to the NCAA Tournament," Fogler said. "There are a very select group of ten or fifteen schools that can realistically say they can do that every year. My last year at South Carolina, we played the 1999 national champions [Connecticut] in the NIT. The point is it's tough. What is realistic? What else is the coach doing?

"Unfortunately, it's based on wins and losses. It's not based on graduation rates. It's not based on the caliber of kid you bring in. The director of athletics can say all that stuff at a lot of schools, but the fact of the matter is it's all about winning. I believe that's a sad state of affairs."

If all that sounds as though Fogler is bitter, he isn't. His closest confidants knew he wouldn't coach far into his fifties. Fogler had other things to do with his life, including spending time with his two young children. He left the game with no regrets, and no intention of returning to the sidelines. After fifteen years as a head coach, the last eight at South Carolina, he was ready to let somebody else handle the job.

———

Terry Holland will never forget the impact Dave Odom had on his life. The year was 1982, and Holland, then coaching at Virginia, had hired Odom as an assistant. After one early-season game against an opponent Holland can't remember, he got to really know Odom after having admired him from afar for years.

"We'd beaten somebody by like fifteen," Holland said. "Jimmy [Larranaga, another Virginia assistant] and I were just killing the kids in the locker room. After we were through, Dave looked at us and said, 'Look, I know you guys have been here a while. But if you can't enjoy a fifteen-point win, it's time to do something else.' Because of what we were going through, particularly with [Ralph] Sampson, there was so much pressure. It was an impossible situation. But Dave was a little calmer than Jimmy or me. He impacted us."

After three years as a Virginia assistant and another dozen coaching in the crucible of the Atlantic Coast Conference at Wake Forest, Odom is still the same guy who quietly told Holland to chill out back in 1982. He wants to win as badly as anyone, but it doesn't devastate him if he doesn't. It's precisely that attitude that has allowed him to stay in coaching at an age when many others have long since found other things to do. It's that attitude, Odom's friends believe, that made him the right man for the job at South Carolina.

South Carolina athletic director Mike McGee didn't offer the job to every top Division I coach in the country after negotiating Eddie Fogler's buyout in the spring of 2001. It just seemed that way. But after entering into serious negotiations with the likes of Tubby Smith and Jim Calhoun and getting turned down cold, McGee had an alternate plan.

The basketball coach at South Carolina has to have the right attitude about the game and its inevitable highs and lows. Competing in the SEC at a school that has had only a smattering of success in the last two decades is tough, and it takes a special coach to handle it. Odom, McGee reasoned, could handle it.

"To be successful in this business, you have to be a people person," said Ernie Nestor, Odom's long-time assistant. When I say people, that means players, coaches, people in your school's administration, media, and the fans. Dave does a great job balancing all those areas. Anyone who writes him a letter, he writes them back. He returns phone calls. He's just a guy that sees beyond basketball to the personalities he deals with."

"The best way to describe Dave Odom is that he's like the guy next door," said South Carolina assistant Rick Duckett. "He's the kind of guy where you go home and he's the one working in the yard next door and you stop and start chatting. He's very approachable. If you didn't know he's a coach, you'd think he was an everyday businessman."

None of this is to suggest that Odom doesn't have a tough side to him. Odom's pleasant demeanor belies an inner fire that has stoked his competitive drive throughout his career in athletics. He was a two-sport star at North Carolina's Guilford College in the mid 1960s, also playing quarterback for the football team. Odom, far from the biggest, strongest player on the football field, had to be tough to survive.

249

After he evolved into safer pursuits as basketball coach at hometown Goldsboro (North Carolina) High School in 1965, Odom found out that stressing toughness to his players was a key to success.

"Dave's philosophy is a sound one," Nestor said. "He wants his kids to be tough. He wants them to be competitive. And he doesn't want them to do crazy things on the court. If you can be tough, compete hard, and take care of the basketball, you're going to have a chance."

In Odom's view, part of being tough is a willingness to expend energy on the defensive end of the floor.

"I think I've always believed in the defensive end of it because it goes back to my playing days," Odom said. "I was never a great offensive player. I was a better-than-average playmaker, but I was not geared toward scoring a lot of points. The way that I played college basketball was with my head, and defense was a part of that."

Odom's philosophy served him well on the high school level. After four years at Goldsboro and another seven at Durham High School, he was ready for the next step. Odom had made it a point to be visible to and develop a rapport with college coaches, hoping some day that might lead to a job.

"I first got to know Dave as a high school coach," Holland recalled. "I never recruited any of his kids, but Dave was just always around. He was one of those guys who had to be where something was happening."

In 1976, Odom landed his first college job at Wake Forest as an assistant to Carl Tacy. After three years in Winston-Salem, he was ready for his first head-coaching job. The opportunity came at East Carolina, where Odom worked as hard as he could to lead the Pirates to a 38-42 record in three seasons. Then Holland came calling.

"I had sort of kept an eye on him when he went to East Carolina," Holland recalled. "I remember thinking that maybe after a couple of years, he'd get tired of it and be ready to come back to the ACC. And I sort of just took a wild shot. Sure enough, when I had an opening, I talked to people who knew Dave. I came to the conclusion to try and go after him. I guess I just hit him at a good time."

If Odom was a calming influence on Holland, Holland gave Odom a few things to think about, too. As competitive as Odom was, he learned a lot about toughness from Holland.

"Any time you coach at a Davidson or Virginia, where the players tend to come from certain types of backgrounds, they're just not as tough as you need them to be," Holland said. "So we had to get them tough. I called it just making sure we kept a firm hand in the small of their back."

Odom loved the concept.

"Virginia is where I completely bought into defense," Odom said. "That's where I really said, 'This can make a difference with my team.' Terry was very good defensively. The one thing that was missing from my experience as a defensive coach prior to Virginia was the element of toughness. Terry taught the element of toughness in his defense. Of not backing off. Taking the fight to your opponents. Taking away the play of the offense as opposed to reacting to what the offense does. I learned all those things at Virginia. My time there was invaluable."

And Odom was invaluable to Holland. The two grew close in Odom's seven years at Virginia, so close that Holland wanted to make sure Odom would have the first chance at his job when he stepped down. After Wake Forest parted company with coach Bob Staak in 1989, Holland sought to gain assurances that Odom could replace him at Virginia.

"I told our athletic director at the time that at some point I wanted to turn the program over to Dave," Holland recalled. "He said, 'Well, Dave would be a candidate, but I can't guarantee him the job.' And I said, 'Well, Dave should leave then.'

"That sort of set the clock ticking for me, too. I'd felt that I'd done all I could do."

Odom beat Holland to the door. When Wake Forest offered the chance to replace Staak, Odom was ready. Though he inherited a team that had gone 13-15 and 3-11 in the Atlantic Coast Conference in 1988–89, Odom was excited to be a head coach in what he considered the strongest league in the country.

Considering where the program was when Odom took over, and given the competition in the ACC, his rebuilding job was impressive. After a 12-16 season in 1989–90, Odom led the Deacons to a 19-11 record and NCAA Tournament trip the next season. Wake would play in seven straight NCAAs, reaching the Elite Eight in 1995–96. As the program coped with the loss of All-American center Tim Duncan, the Deacons had to settle for the NIT for three straight years, from 1998 to 2000. In 2000, Wake won the NIT title.

That was a springboard to the next season, when the Deacons started 12-0 with lopsided victories over Kansas and Virginia. Those wins helped propel the Deacons to as high as No. 4 in the national polls. But they eventually lost that early season momentum and struggled to a 19-11 finish. Weary of working under unrealistic expectations and wary of his relationship with Wake Forest athletic director Ron Wellman, Odom saw a chance to leave on his own terms when the South Carolina job came open. He couldn't have found a better bail out opportunity if he'd tried.

Odom and his staff had to get busy once they got to South Carolina. A recruiting class had to be salvaged in a hurry. Odom had four scholarships to use and, though he didn't want to waste one, he knew the Gamecocks needed depth.

The biggest find in Odom's first recruiting class turned out to be the first player he signed, six-foot-seven forward Carlos Powell of Florence, South Carolina. Powell played with his back to the basket at Wilson High School, but would become a perimeter threat with the Gamecocks and a key player as the season progressed.

After adding three more players, Odom turned his attention to existing personnel. He was concerned about rumors that Chuck Eidson was contemplating a transfer.

Eidson, who played most of his time as a point guard for Eddie Fogler, was seriously injured in a game against Vanderbilt on January 17, 2001. While boxing out for a rebound, Eidson tore the anterior cruciate ligament in his right knee.

"I didn't exactly jump that high," Eidson recalled. "I just kind of floated up. When I came down, I felt my [right] leg give out, like I had been hit by a baseball bat. I knew the pain I felt was not something I could just walk off."

Without Eidson, the Gamecocks lost their next two games and eight of their last twelve. Seven of those losses were decided by six points or less.

Eidson left school in the spring semester to return home to Charleston, South Carolina, and continue rehabilitating his knee. After Fogler left and was replaced by Odom, the inevitable rumor began circulating that Eidson, who had been loyal to Fogler, wouldn't be back.

Odom didn't let the story of Eidson's departure get too far along. He acted quickly, meeting with Eidson and his family.

"I have told him and his parents I want him here," Odom told *The State* newspaper. "I know his teammates want him here. In his heart of hearts, he wants to be here. I know that."

Odom was right. Eidson returned to Columbia to complete his rehab work and was declared physically fit to start the 2001–2002 season, just nine months removed from his injury.

———

With Eidson's recovery, Odom was able to cross one item off his list of concerns as he entered the 2001–2002 season, his first at South Carolina. The next item wouldn't be resolved so quickly, for it was out of Odom's hands.

In the summer of 2001, the NCAA instituted a serious crackdown on the eligibility of international players. The NCAA sought to identify athletes who could have been paid for playing in their respective countries, or who could have affected their amateur status by knowingly playing with professionals. The NCAA was prepared to suspend players on a game-for-game basis. If an athlete played fifteen games for a pro team overseas, he would have been suspended for fifteen games in college.

That drew the ire of several college coaches who had come to rely on a talent flow from overseas. Dozens of schools had international players on their rosters, including South Carolina.

Marius Petravicius, a six-foot-ten, 250-pound center from Lithuania, had played for South Carolina for two years, even though, ironically, it was Odom who discovered him.

"I actually brought him over," said Odom, who had great success finding and developing international players at Wake Forest. "He came in right behind Darius [Songaila]. I recommended he go to the same school [New Hampton Prep] and I actually wanted to recruit him. But Marius wisely decided it was not in his best interest to come to Wake because we already had five post players in front of him. The South Carolina people at that time did a great job of recruiting him."

As it turned out, Petravicius did make a good decision. He started sixty-one of sixty-two games in his first two seasons at South Carolina, averaging 8.5 points and 4.5 rebounds. But when the NCAA learned that he played seventeen games with a pro team in Lithuania in 1997, Petravicius's junior season was in jeopardy.

Odom argued that Petravicius, who had just started playing basketball in 1997, didn't know he was violating rules.

"I knew nothing," Petravicius recalled. "I had just started playing basketball. I lived in a small town, and it was about forty-five minutes away to play basketball. I wasn't that familiar when I started to play, and I didn't know much about leagues, anything.

"If someone had asked me the difference between Duke and USC-Aiken at that time, I couldn't tell them. I didn't know NCAA rules either. That's the thing. If I would have known, maybe I'd have tried to do something else. But at that time, I knew nothing."

Petravicius's fate was uncertain through the summer and early fall. Practice had already begun when the NCAA made an announcement. Based on a recommendation by its Division I Management Council, the NCAA decided to reduce the number of games an international player could be suspended if he was found in violation of the amateur status rule. Instead of a game-for-game suspension, the number was reduced to 20 percent of games played in a pro league, with a maximum of eight games.

Suffice to say Odom was elated. The new rule meant Petravicius would sit out just three games.

"Not knowing was tough," Odom said. "But to find out we were going to have Marius for most of our season was important for our team."

―――――

Petravicius missed South Carolina's season-opening trip to Hawaii, where the Gamecocks were to take part in the Maui Classic in late November. But it's doubtful he could have done much to stave off the two whippings South Carolina received there.

The Gamecocks started the tournament with a 74-61 win over Chaminade, but all that did was set up a second-round game with Duke, the defending national champion and preseason No. 1 team in the major polls. Showing no regard for his father's alma mater, Duke forward Mike Dunleavy shot the Gamecocks out of the game late in the first half. With the score tied at 25, Dunleavy, whose father, Mike, is the No. 5 all-time scorer at South Carolina, tossed in two three-pointers under heavy defensive pressure and made another jump shot as the Blue Devils pulled away and eventually won, 81-56.

After that beating, the Gamecocks didn't have enough energy to return to the court in less than twenty-four hours and take on UCLA. The Bruins had been beaten in the tournament's second round by upstart Ball State, which had upset Kansas a day earlier. It would take four months, but the Gamecocks would eventually extract a little revenge on the Cardinals for forcing that matchup with UCLA.

The Bruins showed no mercy on South Carolina, shooting 78.6 percent from the field in the first half and taking leads of as large as 20 points. UCLA won 89-77. The Gamecocks couldn't get back to the continental United States fast enough.

After a five-day layoff, the schedule became a lot less brutal and South Carolina won four straight games. The highlight of that ministreak was the return of Petravicius, who started and played twenty-three minutes in a win over East Tennessee State. He scored eight points and grabbed five rebounds, but showed his rustiness by making five turnovers. Still, another big body in the lineup was going to help the Gamecocks.

Only a heartbreaking, last-second loss to Georgetown, then ranked No. 15, put a damper on the rest of South Carolina's nonconference season. Playing on their home court, the Gamecocks had desperately hoped to beat the Hoyas, and almost did, leading 68-67 with 1:07 to play. But Kevin Braswell calmly knocked down a seventeen-foot jumper with 2.2 seconds left to pull out a 70-68 Georgetown victory.

South Carolina closed out nonconference play with five straight wins, including a big one at in-state rival Clemson. The Gamecocks roughed up the Tigers, 81-59, which was South Carolina's largest margin of victory over Clemson since 1971 and the largest ever at the Tigers' Littlejohn Coliseum.

The Gamecocks finished nonconference play with a 10-3 record, and Odom could live with it. Never had a South Carolina team won ten games before January. And at Odom's urging, the Gamecocks had begun to take pride in their defense.

"The defense that we continue to play is beginning to look more like we draw it up on the board and more like we hope that it will game in and game out," Odom told *The State* newspaper. "What's happening so far is our kids are beginning to catch fire with the defense and beginning to enjoy it."

That defensive intensity would continue into Southeastern Conference play.

South Carolina's SEC season began in similar fashion to its nonconference season. No league team had a more brutal start, with games at Florida, at home against Kentucky, and at Arkansas. The Gamecocks lost at Florida, but that wasn't as unsettling as their loss a week later to Kentucky.

Ahead 50-47 with a minute to play, South Carolina couldn't contain Kentucky guard Cliff Hawkins, who had been struggling much of the season while taking—and missing—clutch shots against Duke, Mississippi State, and Georgia. Hawkins wouldn't be denied a fourth time. His ten-foot jumper brought Kentucky to within 50-49.

With twenty-eight seconds to play, Marius Petravicius went to the free throw line for a one and bonus, but he missed his first shot, giving the Wildcats life. South Carolina appeared to have a chance to defend Kentucky's last shot when Hawkins picked up his dribble beyond the three-point line. But when South Carolina guard Jamel Bradley slapped the ball from Hawkins's grasp, picked it up, drove into the lane, and sank a fourteen-footer for a 51-50 win.

"My heart right now is broken in a thousand pieces for our team, who I think gave so much, and for our fans, who I know wanted to win that basketball game more than life," Odom told the press after the game.

South Carolina regrouped quickly with a 62-60 win at Arkansas that seemed to start the Razorbacks' season on a downward spiral. If the Gamecocks derived any momentum from that win, they didn't show it. Much of the rest of their SEC season was inconsistent. South Carolina could never put together a winning streak, but there were some big victories along the way, including a 94-60 road win at Tennessee, an 80-67 victory over nationally ranked Georgia at home, and another bashing of the Vols. If the Gamecocks could have played Tennessee every game, they might have gone undefeated in the SEC.

Despite another heartbreaking home-court loss, this time 52-51 to Alabama in mid

B. J. McKie. *USC Sports Information*

February, the Gamecocks believed they still had a chance for an NCAA Tournament bid. Their record at the time stood at 14-10 overall and 4-7 in the SEC, but consecutive wins at Vanderbilt and at home over LSU provided some hope.

At that point, the Gamecocks collapsed. Sophomore forward Rolando Howell, whose improving game would be so important in the weeks to come, was suspended for a game at Auburn. South Carolina lost to the team with the worst record in the league.

Four days later, the Gamecocks had Georgia beaten in Athens, but couldn't seal the deal. Ahead 70-67 with 11.5 seconds left, South Carolina could have put the game out of reach with Aaron Lucas at the free throw line for two shots. Even one free throw would have won the game, but Lucas missed both, allowing Georgia guard Rashad Wright to tie the score at 70 with a three-pointer with 5.8 seconds left. The Bulldogs won 82-75 in overtime.

Four days later, South Carolina ran into a surging Mississippi State team and was beaten 64-57 at home. With an overall record of 16-13 and an SEC mark of 6-10, the Gamecocks would have to win the league's tournament to earn their way into the NCAA Tournament field.

"I'm disappointed we didn't win more games," Odom said as his team prepared for its first round SEC Tournament game in Atlanta in early March. "If I'd looked at it from the very beginning and somebody told me we'd win sixteen games, I'd say that's not too bad. That's more than they won last year. That would give us a winning season. No player on our team has ever had a winning season. In some ways, it's been a very good year.

South Carolina
All-SEC Expansion Era Team
F-Chuck Eidson
F-Larry Davis
C-Ryan Stack
G-B. J. McKie
G-Melvin Watson
Top Reserves-Tony Kitchings, Rolando Howell

"But once you play into your season and you find out you have a chance to do more, it leaves you with an empty feeling. We lost three games at the end of our season, and we felt like we had a chance to win all three. And that doesn't count Georgetown, or Kentucky, or Alabama. You tack those games onto what we have and you're looking at the NCAA Tournament. We played ourselves right to the edge, but we couldn't get over."

Odom didn't know it at the time, but the Gamecocks were about to put aside the disappointment of their regular season and perhaps build a foundation for the remainder of his career in Columbia. Some personnel changes and reassignment of duties were about to give South Carolina a much-needed boost.

Chapter Eleven

Tennessee

I t wasn't as though the University of Tennessee's administration wanted its men's basketball program to be mired in mediocrity throughout most of the 1990s. With the cavernous, twenty-five-thousand-seat Thompson-Boling Arena exposing the program's ineptitude on a nightly basis with disinterested, half-capacity crowds, athletic director Doug Dickey and his various bosses in the chancellor's chair would have liked nothing better than to make that embarrassment go away by putting a winner on the floor.

It didn't help matters that while the Volunteers were stumbling their way through much of the 1990s, the Lady Vols of hall-of-fame coach Pat Summitt were winning four national championships—including three straight from 1996 to 1998—and playing to substantially larger crowds. As each championship banner was hung in Thompson-Boling Arena, it underscored the fact that people will support a winning basketball team, even at a football-mad school like Tennessee.

Adding to the frustration of Vol fans who favored the men's game was the fact that, albeit in a different era, Tennessee had clearly proven it could put a competitive team on the floor. In fifteen seasons from 1962 to 1977, former coach Ray Mears, the consummate showman, won 71 percent of his games and proved the Vols could stand up to mighty Kentucky, the SEC's perennial power. Mears coached the Vols in thirty games against the Wildcats. Tennessee won fifteen of those games.

More recently, Don DeVoe coached the program to a reasonable degree of success in the early 1980s and at one time wielded enough power to become the catalyst for the construction of Thompson-Boling Arena. DeVoe led the Vols to seven straight postseason tournaments from 1978–79 to 1984–85.

The decline of DeVoe's regime—the Vols suffered two straight losing seasons from in 1985–86 and 1986–87—signaled the end of an era for Tennessee basketball. By 1987, DeVoe's critics had become legion, and interest in the program was waning. When Dickey called a late-season press conference in 1987, most assumed it was to announce DeVoe's firing. Instead, Dickey gave his beleaguered coach a vote of confidence.

The next year, though the Vols fashioned a winning record and went to the NIT, speculation ran rampant at the SEC Tournament in Baton Rouge, Louisiana, that

DeVoe was about to be fired. Again, he lived to fight another season.

Dickey's reasoning for keeping DeVoe then was fair enough—five seniors, including future NBA player Dyron Nix, were returning, and the Vols figured to be one of the favorites to win the SEC championship.

Tennessee managed a 19-11 record in 1988–89 and even returned to the NCAA Tournament after a six-year absence. But when the Vols got pounded, 84-68, by West Virginia in the tournament's first round, DeVoe was finally ousted.

Even DeVoe's staunchest supporters might have agreed that it was time for him and Tennessee to part ways. But his departure began a streak of futility that endured for nearly a decade.

———

It was apparent in the spring of 1989 that Tennessee wanted to replace Devoe with an African-American coach, a pioneering move in the SEC. Tennessee's administration reasoned that such a hire would give the program an advantage over the rest of the league. The new coach would be able to penetrate the fertile recruiting hotbeds of Memphis and Atlanta, which Tennessee had failed to mine consistently under DeVoe's watch.

Tennessee quickly identified two candidates for the job—Oklahoma State head coach Leonard Hamilton and Louisville assistant Wade Houston. The school was hot on Hamilton's trail for a time and also interviewed Houston. But somewhere in the process, the search veered off-course and focused on Florida State's coach at the time, Pat Kennedy, who eagerly negotiated with Tennessee, only to bail out when FSU came through with a salary increase.

Dickey apparently felt confident on a Sunday night that Kennedy was taking the job. A press conference was tentatively set for the next morning. But after finding out early Monday that Kennedy was staying put, Dickey quickly redirected his search. A call was placed to Houston, who was in the process of interviewing for the Central Florida job. The next day, Houston was announced as Tennessee's new coach, even though, some program insiders insist, he was not impressive in his initial interview.

Part of the attraction of Houston could have been that his son Allan was a *Parade* All-American. But the elder Houston's hiring wasn't necessarily a package deal. Allan Houston had already signed with Louisville, and its coach, Denny Crum, desperately wanted to keep him. Crum eventually changed his mind and released Houston from his scholarship, but it was another two months before a special NCAA committee ruled he could switch to Tennessee without having to sit out a redshirt season.

Few could have forecast it at the time, but Allan Houston was the only legitimate blue-chip recruit to play for the Vols when his father ran the program. Wade Houston never turned out to be the master recruiter Tennessee's administration had hoped for when he was hired. Houston had his share of recruiting successes during his five seasons in Knoxville, but there were just as many misses. Worse, the concept of running an entire program as opposed to just focusing on recruiting was foreign to him. Discipline was lacking, as players seemed to come and go as they pleased. Relations with the media were strained. There was no genuine effort to cultivate a fan base. Assistant coaches drifted in and out of the program.

Tennessee's record fluctuated wildly under Houston. The Vols were 16-14 and played in the NIT in 1989–90, his first season. The next year, Tennessee finished 12-22 and 3-15 in the SEC. The Vols nearly pulled a shocker in the SEC Tournament after abandoning the man-to-man defense they had played all season and turning to a zone. Tennessee beat Ole Miss, Mississippi State, and Georgia to advance to the tournament finals, where Alabama finally squashed the uprising, presumably after having had plenty of time to figure out the Vols' zone.

In 1991–92, the year the SEC expanded by adding Arkansas and South Carolina, Tennessee reversed its fortunes yet again, finishing 19-15 and a respectable 8-8, good for third place, in the new Eastern Division. The Vols advanced to the NIT for the second time in Houston's tenure, but their trip was short. After a home-court win over UAB in the first round, they were beaten, 77-52, at Virginia.

Tennessee fans by this time were wary of the Houston regime, but they had some reason for optimism in 1992–93. Finally displaying the recruiting prowess that got him the job, Houston pulled a coup by signing three players from west Tennessee, an area of the state that usually produces the most talent, yet a place where the Vols had been the least productive. After bringing in Steve Hamer, a seven-foot center from Grand Junction, LaMarcus Golden, a point guard from Memphis, and Stanley Caldwell, a rugged forward from Union City, Houston thought the program was on an upswing. With Allan Houston returning for his senior season and solid starters Corey Allen and Lang Wiseman also back, the Vols seemed to have enough talent to contend for a post-season tournament bid for a second straight season.

Any post-season hopes Tennessee might have harbored were quickly dashed. The Vols lost five of their first six SEC games, finishing a disastrous 4-12 in the league and 13-17 overall. Fans were calling for Houston's scalp, even though, ironically, the Vols beat the two best teams in the league, Arkansas and Kentucky, in the span of a week in late February. Those wins served to frustrate long-suffering Tennessee fans even more.

The end for Houston came in 1993–94. After a season-opening win over Tennessee-Martin, the Vols proceeded to lose five straight games, including an embarrassing, 78-71 home-court loss to lightly regarded Western Carolina of the Southern Conference. After the game, Western coach Benny Dees couldn't believe what he'd just seen. "We're just a little ole team from the Kmart league," Dees told the press. "We aren't supposed to go into an SEC team's building and come away with a win."

Tennessee finished 5-22 overall and 2-14 in the SEC, forcing the school to finally admit Houston wasn't going to be the savior of the program. He was fired shortly after the season ended.

One again Dickey, the old football coach, was forced to go out and find another basketball coach. The pressure was on to find a coach who could quickly undo the residual damage from the Houston regime. Would Dickey make the right decision?

———

In replacing Wade Houston, who had never run his own program on the college level, Dickey was determined to hire someone with previous head-coaching experience. Marquette's Kevin O'Neill quickly became a front-runner for the job, his candidacy receiving a huge boost after his team ousted Tennessee's bitter rival Kentucky from the 1994 NCAA Tournament. Marquette's victory over the Wildcats earned it a bid to the Sweet 16, which was played, coincidentally enough, at Thompson-Boling. Vol fans had a unique chance to see O'Neill up close and personal, and he had a great opportunity to check out Tennessee.

Given the circumstances, it seemed as though fate had intervened on Tennessee's behalf, and O'Neill became the logical choice of many to replace Houston. His hiring was all but expected.

Still, some Tennessee fans and program insiders were concerned. There was no denying O'Neill's success at Marquette, but anyone who knew the maverick coach's reputation wondered how soon his penchant for bucking authority would alienate his new athletic director, or how long it would take O'Neill to revolt under the leadership of the demanding Dickey. It seemed anyone even remotely connected to the program had heard the tales of O'Neill throwing Marquette's president out of his locker room. "Just wait until he tries that crap with Dickey," said one athletic department employee.

In O'Neill's first few months in Knoxville, he did a thorough job of ridding the program of some bad characters recruited during the Houston regime. Several players O'Neill inherited didn't bother to meet him the day he was hired. They already knew they were gone.

Other players parted ways with their new coach in dramatic fashion. Cortez Barnes, a forward who had been one of Houston's prized recruits, was kicked off the team in the summer of 1994 after he refused to cooperate with the team's strength coach. Barnes later went to O'Neill's office to protest the decision and ended up trashing the place in full view of DePaul's then coach Joey Meyer. "It's a little crazy around here right now," O'Neill told Meyer.

Still another player got canned after directing some obscene gestures at O'Neill behind the coach's back, or so he thought. While O'Neill was having a conversation with Stanley Caldwell in the Tennessee basketball office, the player, who thought he was out of O'Neill's sight, was giving his coach the business with both hands. O'Neill caught his reflection in a glass-enclosed picture on the wall. "Get the hell out, and don't ever come back," were O'Neill's last words to the stunned player.

One particularly amusing departure involved guard Chris Brand, who had quit the team when Houston was coaching but asked O'Neill if he could return. Desperately in need of bodies, O'Neill agreed, but Brand didn't last long. One day, after O'Neill lashed out at him over some practice transgression, Brand stalked off the court. O'Neill called after him, but Brand didn't look back. After practice the press asked why Brand bolted. "I don't know, guys," O'Neill said in his best deadpan delivery. "Maybe he had a meat loaf in the oven."

Even Caldwell, who had started out in O'Neill's good graces, quickly fell into disfavor with the coach over some off the court issues. O'Neill cut him loose just a few games into the 1994–95 season.

It took a strong-willed sort to survive O'Neill, who ran his practices like a boot camp, constantly screaming at his players with creative sequences of profanity, making them run steps in Thompson-Boling Arena, and even banishing them to the locker room. In O'Neill's first season, there weren't many strong-willed players in the program. For that matter, there weren't many *players* in the program. Eventually, O'Neill had just seven scholarship players at his disposal, but he didn't seem to mind. With the problem cases having been dealt with, O'Neill was glad to have only solid citizens remaining.

Staunch Tennessee fans will never forget the names of Shane Williams and Damon Johnson. The pair of junior college transfers had played together in the early 1990s at Science Hill High School in Johnson City, Tennessee, a traditional power in the state. After two years at junior college, Williams and Johnson became O'Neill's first recruits as he frantically tried to restock his roster in the spring of 1994.

Neither player was a star, but O'Neill credits Johnson and Williams with being the first component parts in the process of rebuilding Tennessee's program. Johnson, an undersized power forward at six-foot-four, could be a dynamic scorer at times but was mistake-prone and often incurred O'Neill's wrath. Williams was a steady if unspectacular point guard who might be the only player who was never screamed at by O'Neill. "He just doesn't make mistakes," O'Neill said often during Williams's two seasons.

Another player who helped turn Tennessee's program around was Steve Hamer, who, not long after O'Neill's arrival, almost quit school. Hamer was not used to being pushed in practice and wasn't sure he wanted any part of O'Neill's hellish workouts. At one point, Hamer actually had his bags packed and was headed for his car. "Steve said he just wants to be the tallest guy in the mall," O'Neill said while Hamer took a day to ponder his decision. The press wasn't quite sure what that meant.

Somehow, O'Neill convinced Hamer to stay. And in the two years O'Neill coached him, Hamer became the best center in the SEC. He was one of the few legitimate seven-footers to have an impact on the league in the ten-year period that is the focal point of this book. With huge hands and long arms, Hamer could catch even the worst of entry passes into the post and could score with a short-range jumper or a power move to the rim. O'Neill eventually made Hamer more of a threat by teaching him to pass out of the double- and triple-teams he often faced.

Hamer led the Vols in scoring, rebounding, and blocked shots as a junior and senior. Somewhere deep down, O'Neill must have appreciated Hamer, but he never let on that he did. Yet opposing SEC coaches raved about the big man. "He's the hardest player in the league to prepare for," said Jeff Lebo, then an assistant coach at South Carolina. "He's really disruptive."

Hamer was disruptive on both ends of the floor, which O'Neill loved. O'Neill prided himself on being able to coach defense and the Vols quickly became a defensive-oriented team (as if they had a choice). Under O'Neill, Tennessee played a tight man-to-man, but placed an emphasis on shutting down high-percentage shots in the post. Players were expected to leave their man to help defend players in key scoring positions. O'Neill thought a player could be as selfish defensively (by guarding only his own man) as he could offensively by taking too many shots.

Low-scoring games were the order of the day and Tennessee wasn't very exciting in O'Neill's first season. The Vols did everything they could to survive, and sometimes the results were comical. During a lopsided Tennessee loss at Arkansas, foul trouble left O'Neill with but five scholarship players. Late in the game, O'Neill had to guard the Razorbacks' hulking star Corliss Williamson with baby-faced walk-on guard Clint Newman, who was six-foot-two and 170 pounds at best. Williamson, who would go on to have a productive NBA career, took pity. "Don't worry Huck Finn," Williamson told Newman. "I'll take it easy on you."

Somehow, Tennessee scratched out eleven wins in O'Neill's debut season. The Vols still finished last in the SEC East, but their fans had hope. At long last, effort was being demonstrated on the court.

As a recruiter, O'Neill had few peers in the business. Arizona coach Lute Olson, for whom O'Neill worked, likes to tell a story about the first recruiting trip he took with his new assistant.

"He was full of energy, always on the go," Olson recalled. "We were on the road recruiting, and I remember lying there in the next bed in our hotel room, trying to get to sleep. Kevin was going over his recruiting files. It had to be after two in the morning before he finally turned the light off. About six o'clock, the phone rings. Kevin had asked for a wake-up call so he could get up and go running. He had more energy than I did."

That energy served O'Neill well at Marquette—O'Neill's first Division I head coaching job—and was even more important to his rebuilding efforts at Tennessee. Because O'Neill was a tireless recruiter, he worked overtime thinking of ways to bombard players with pro-Tennessee propaganda. Given the limitations of the NCAA's rules of contact, O'Neill's work to convince recruits to come to the downtrodden program he had inherited was remarkable.

O'Neill's first full recruiting class, signed in the fall of 1994 and the spring of 1995, included four freshmen who would go on to play key roles. The catch was Nashville guard Brandon Wharton, who turned down a football offer from Notre Dame before deciding on the Vols.

The next year, O'Neill's key recruit was Charles Hathaway, a six-foot-ten center from Nashville who was a *Parade* and McDonald's All-American and, in the opinion of several recruiting analysts, a Top 10 player nationally. Though Kentucky and Rick Pitino had shown an interest in Hathaway, O'Neill and his staff convinced him to commit in the summer of 1995.

Hathaway's decision influenced other good players to follow him to Knoxville. C. J. Black, a six-foot-eight, 260-pound hulk from Chattanooga, had become friends with Hathaway on the AAU circuit, and though Kansas, Virginia, and North Carolina were also on his list of schools, he spurned those established powers to help rebuild his home-state school. Black and Hathaway signed in the fall of 1995.

In the spring of 1996, though he already had Black and Hathaway in the fold, O'Neill somehow managed to sign six-foot-nine forward Isiah Victor away from home state Kentucky, which apparently wasn't all that interested until O'Neill started camping on the player's doorstep. Victor would later become a point of contention that led to O'Neill's shocking departure.

In 1995–96, O'Neill's second season, the five-man freshman class led by Wharton gave the Vols some much-needed depth. Tennessee finished the regular season 14-14 and 6-10 in the SEC East. That was good for fifth place, the first time in four seasons the Vols didn't finish last in their division. Tennessee even got a chance to host a first round NIT game, but lost to the College of Charleston to fall under .500 for the year.

O'Neill's third and final season in Knoxville began with controversy when Doug Dickey advised him to redshirt Victor, whose high school academic work had come under question, presumably when another SEC school reported the situation to the league office. The SEC eventually found no problem with Victor's academic record, but the damage had been done. And O'Neill wasn't happy.

Still, O'Neill continued to recruit in an effort to add what he believed were the final pieces of a championship team. He landed a much-needed point guard by winning an intense recruiting battle with Memphis for Tony Harris, then signed another player who came with a bonus. Del Baker, a forward from Cleveland, Tennessee, had a half brother who would become a *Parade* and McDonald's All-American the next year, Vincent Yarbrough. Though O'Neill wouldn't hang around to see his ploy succeed, the signing of Baker proved to be a strong lure for Yarbrough, who spurned Kentucky and committed to Tennessee in August 1997.

The program seemed in great shape for the future. But the present brought a return to the bad old days. In 1996–97, Tennessee finished 11-16 and 4-12 in the SEC. That bought the Vols a return trip to last place in their division. O'Neill ranted all season how much the Vols could have used Victor, whom he predicted would one day become an NBA lottery pick.

After the Vols' season ended with a first-round ouster in the SEC Tournament, O'Neill fended off rumors that he was bound for Northwestern. But that's eventually where he went, abruptly leaving Tennessee despite the promise of a pay raise and other perks, and the fact that a potential NCAA Tournament team had been put in place, given his improbable recruitment of Tony Harris.

For the third time in eight years, Dickey had to find a basketball coach.

The list of coaches who expressed interest in the Tennessee job was impressive. So too was the list of coaches reportedly contacted by Dickey. But if Tim Floyd (then at Iowa State), Dave Odom (then at Wake Forest), and Rick Barnes (then at Clemson) weren't interested, three younger, promising coaches were.

Oral Roberts coach Bill Self would have taken the job in a second. Steve Alford, in his first Division I head-coaching job at Southwest Missouri State, was reportedly very interested.

In fairness to Tennessee, it might have taken a leap of faith and more basketball knowledge than the school's hiring committee could have mustered to hire Self and Alford, then young coaches who had yet to prove their skills at a higher level. Both eventually did prove themselves, Self at Tulsa and Illinois and Alford at Southwest Missouri State and Iowa. Some Vol fans still wonder how the program might have turned out had Self or Alford been hired.

Dickey—after trying unsuccessfully to convince an older, established coach to come to Knoxville—did manage to bring a hot young coach to the negotiating table in Illinois State's Kevin Stallings. The courtship seemed serious, prompting two Tennessee newspapers to report that Stallings had accepted the job. Though it seemed like a natural progression in Stallings' career, he didn't feel comfortable about Tennessee. His decision to remain at Illinois State stunned Vol fans and left them questioning Dickey's ability to identify and hire a capable coach.

Left with few choices and feeling pressure to make a respectable hire, Dickey turned to another experienced head coach, albeit one who was on the downside of his career.

When a representative from Tennessee called Oregon's Jerry Green and asked him if he would be interested in speaking with Dickey, Green couldn't believe his good fortune. A former assistant to Roy Williams at Kansas and a head coach at UNC Asheville, Green turned around a struggling program at Oregon but in the minds of many Duck fans had worn out his welcome. Green, a native of South Carolina, was eager to leave for a job closer to his roots.

Green knew a good deal when he saw it. After trying without success to get involved at LSU, Green had resigned himself to staying another year at Oregon, a job he deemed as purgatory, a million miles from anywhere he had ever known. The Tennessee job appealed for a lot of reasons. Green had earned a degree at East Tennessee State and coached at UNC Asheville, neither very far from Knoxville. This was a chance to return to familiar territory. And the money wasn't too bad, either; Tennessee's offer nearly doubled what Green had been making at Oregon.

Better still, O'Neill had left behind a loaded team at Tennessee. That baffled many

266

Tennessee fans still questioning O'Neill's departure. Why would he have worked so hard for three years to recruit a team full of good players, only to leave for the worst job in the Big Ten, and one of the most difficult in college basketball?

Once Tennessee's search centered on him, Green didn't have to agonize over a decision. Green met with Dickey on a Friday and by Sunday had taken the job. He was introduced as the Vols' new coach on April 1, 1997.

Some Tennessee fans weren't thrilled about Green's arrival after having been teased with names like Tim Floyd, Rick Barnes, and Kevin Stallings. But Dickey was convinced he had made a solid choice.

Green came with the full endorsement of his friend Roy Williams. Though Green was twice removed from the North Carolina lineage from which Williams hailed, even the slightest connection to the great Dean Smith seemed like a plus.

Williams, and other coaches contacted by Tennessee, agreed that Green was a good tactician. He seemed personable enough, which would help in reconnecting with fans that felt jilted by O'Neill's abrupt departure. And there was no question Green was intensely loyal to those in his inner circle, which Dickey took as a sign that Green wouldn't dump Tennessee for another job, as O'Neill had.

Williams has often told the story about a life-altering decision he had to make early in his career. A successful high school coach at the time, Williams had been offered a low-paying position on Smith's staff at North Carolina. If Williams had accepted the job, he would have had to take a pay cut.

Green knew about Williams's dilemma and made an offer that stunned his friend. Green had just received some insurance money after the death of his mother. Without hesitation, he offered the check, which totaled about twenty thousand dollars, to Williams. Williams took the job at North Carolina, but not the check.

———

Just hours after the press conference that introduced him as Tennessee's new coach, Green had to get busy. His most pressing order of business was to fly to Memphis to re-recruit Harris, who by that time had earned the reputation of being the best player to come out of his talent-rich hometown since Penny Hardaway. After O'Neill left, Harris wasn't sure he still wanted to come to Tennessee, which left some Vol fans puzzled. Why was Harris, a cat-quick point guard who loved the transition game, so disappointed over not getting to play for O'Neill, who favored a grind-it-out halfcourt offense?

The process took a week, but after meeting twice with Harris and his family, Green was able to bring Harris back into the fold. For the first time in nearly ten years, Tennessee had the makings of an NCAA Tournament team in place.

Another component part—albeit for the following season—would be acquired a few months later. Green and assistant coaches Chris Ferguson and Byron Samuels did a great job of shadowing Yarbrough throughout the open recruiting period in the summer of 1997. Wherever Yarbrough traveled with his AAU team, the Tennessee Travelers, he couldn't turn around without seeing Green or one of his assistants, all of them hard to miss in their orange shirts. That made a positive impression on him. After Kentucky coach Rick Pitino left for the Boston Celtics, Yarbrough—who had been enamored with Pitino and rumored to be bound for Lexington—had an easy decision to make.

——————

Green turned in his best coaching job in 1997–98, his first season, after season-ending injuries to Hathaway and guard DaShay Jones shook the team. Hathaway nearly died after a blood clot was discovered in his right shoulder; he had to have emergency surgery. Jones, a junior college transfer who might have passed on some veteran stability to Tony Harris, blew out his knee.

Despite the loss of two starters and minor injuries to other key reserves, Green guided the Vols to twenty victories for the first time since the 1984–85 season and to an NCAA Tournament berth for the first time since 1988–89.

The addition of Harris was a plus for Tennessee. But there was a strange dynamic going on between Harris and Brandon Wharton, who had started at point guard the previous two seasons. Outwardly the two seemed a good match as Wharton slid over to shooting guard, but it wasn't the smoothest of transitions. Harris, best described as an offensive-minded point guard, often tried to do too much by himself rather than get his teammates into the flow of the offense.

Harris got a lesson in point guard play from Wharton, who had to take over in early January when Harris, recovering from a minor injury, missed a game against Ole Miss. The Vols had started out 0-3 in the SEC, but with Wharton running the show to perfection, they upset the Rebels and began to resurrect their season. Tennessee eventually finished 9-7 in SEC games, its best finish since the league expanded.

A four-game winning streak in February and a win over LSU in the SEC Tournament sealed the Vols' NCAA Tournament bid. Though they were seeded eighth in the West Region and would have to travel to Sacramento, they were happy to be in the Big Dance.

In a matchup that seemed too compelling to be coincidental, Tennessee's first-round opponent was ninth-seeded Illinois State, coached by Kevin Stallings. Tennessee fans thought they'd seen the last of Stallings after he rejected an offer to coach the Vols a year earlier. And there was another piece of history involved in the game: Green and Stallings had worked together on Roy Williams's first staff at Kansas.

Not even Stallings gave his team much of a chance to win after his starting point guard was declared unfit to play because of a back injury. But in a game that was a harbinger of things to come, Harris played poorly—making just one of thirteen shots—and the Vols lost at the buzzer in overtime.

Tennessee fans were disappointed, but it was far too early in the careers of Green and Harris to think that a trend of NCAA Tournament futility had been established. And there was ample evidence to suggest the program had been turned around. The signing of Yarbrough, who was picked by one recruiting service as the No. 1 high school player in the country in 1998, gave the fans confidence in the ability of Green and his staff to recruit blue-chip players.

The faith Tennessee fans had in the resurgent program was justified in 1998–99. The Vols won twenty games for the second straight year and won the SEC's Eastern Division with a 12-4 record. The addition of Yarbrough had given Tennessee the most athletic lineup in the conference, though his contributions as a freshman weren't as great as some had anticipated. With so many veteran players wanting the ball, Yarbrough would have to wait his turn.

Some experts considered the Vols the most talented team in the SEC. Tennessee, it seemed, was capable of doing some damage in March. Instead, it was March that did damage to Tennessee.

After earning a first-round bye into the SEC Tournament, the Vols collapsed in their quarterfinal game against Missisippi State, losing 62-56. The lethargy that plagued Tennessee in that game carried over to its first round NCAA Tournament game against Delaware. The Vols were seeded fourth in the East Region, Delaware thirteenth.

Tennessee was lucky to avoid an upset, but survived despite the fact guards Harris and Wharton shot a combined eight-for-26 from the field. Disaster was just two days away.

In its second-round game, Tennessee would play twelfth-seeded Southwest Missouri State. Kevin Stallings, who had seen plenty of Steve Alford's Bears in the Missouri Valley Conference, tried to warn the Tennessee staff about Danny Moore, a six-foot-ten center with great shooting touch. Before the game, Stallings called Vol assistant Eric Pauley, whom he had coached at Kansas, to suggest Tennessee double-team Moore. The suggestion was carried to Green, who chose not to put an extra defender on Moore. Tennessee hadn't double-teamed a post player in the SEC. Why should it worry about a center from the Missouri Valley?

Stallings's concerns about Moore were justified. He scored 25 points on eight-of-14 shooting, his inside work eventually opening the perimeter for the Bears, who shot 41 percent from three-point range. By contrast, Tennessee's guards struggled. Harris was two for 11 from the field and Wharton five for 16.

Those numbers added up to an 81-51 Southwest Missouri State win. After the game a grim, ashen-faced Green stood in stunned silence in a corner of the Vols' locker room. Harris refused to come out of the shower to speak to reporters.

That loss unleashed the critics on Green, who made matters worse by skipping his weekly radio show two days after the debacle, sending instead assistant Chris Ferguson to take the heat. Vol fans thought Green had ducked criticism, and some never forgave him for it.

There were even whispers around the program and among fans that Green, who had a hands-off approach to his player's off-the-court lives, needed to instill more discipline in the program. In a story that appeared in the *Chattanooga Times*, Vincent Yarbrough's mother questioned Green's lack of discipline and predicted a grim future if the problem wasn't corrected.

Green won back some lost followers after Tennessee went 26-7 and tied for the SEC East and overall league championship in 1999–2000. A solid recruiting class had fortified the Vols' bench with five freshmen who all made contributions. John Higgins, a tough-minded guard, replaced Brandon Wharton, and forwards Ron Slay and Marcus Haislip combined with Isiah Victor and Yarbrough to give Tennessee its most athletic frontcourt in years.

Tennessee started 11-0, got bashed by Tulsa and then won seven of its next eight games. In the stretch run of the SEC season, the Vols beat Florida twice and handled Kentucky and Arkansas.

Were it not for Tennessee's inability to beat an old nemesis, the Vols could have claimed the outright SEC championship. Vanderbilt, led by new coach Kevin Stallings, swept Tennessee, winning in Knoxville after trailing until the final minute.

March would hold a little more promise for Tennessee than it had the two previous years, but the result was all too familiar.

For the second straight season, the Vols earned a first-round bye in the SEC Tournament. And for the second straight year, they were upset in the quarterfinals. This time the deed was done by South Carolina, a team Tennessee had beaten twice in the regular season.

The Vols still managed a No. 4 seed in the NCAA Tournament's South Region. Just as it did the year before, Tennessee struggled to beat a No. 13 seed. The Vols needed some late free throws from Tony Harris to slip by Louisiana-Lafayette, 63-58.

The game ended in controversy, or at least the Lafayette side thought so. With less than a minute to play, Tennessee might have gotten a break when Harris drove to the basket and seemingly turned the ball over. But officials called a reach-in foul on the Ragin' Cajuns' Brett Smith with fifteen seconds left, sending Harris to the free throw line. He finished with his best game in the NCAA Tournament, scoring a team-high 15 points.

There was no doubt the Vols caught a break in their next game against fifth-seeded Connecticut. All-American point guard Khalid El-Amin had suffered a high ankle sprain in the Huskies' first-round game and wasn't expected to play against Tennessee. El-Amin actually took the court, but was so ineffective UConn, the defending national champions, were no match for Tennessee, which won, 65-51. Harris turned in his second straight solid game, leading the Vols with 18 points. The win marked the first time in school history Tennessee won two games in the NCAA Tournament. Up next in the Sweet 16 was North Carolina.

For nearly thirty-six minutes against the Tar Heels, the Vols looked as though they were going to bury the memory of their postseason disappointments of the previous two seasons. They led 64-57 with 4:48 to play, and seemed all but assured of victory after Brendan Haywood, North Carolina's high-scoring center, fouled out.

Instead of folding after Haywood departed, the Heels went on the offensive, outscoring the Vols 17-5 and stealing a 74-69 win. North Carolina's comeback was greatly assisted by a series of bad shots and poor decisions by the Vols that Green seemed powerless to stop. Afterward, Green described his team's breakdown as "dementia of the game." Few could argue with that assessment. Tennessee fans were sickened when North Carolina went on to beat Tulsa in the Elite Eight and advanced to the Final Four.

———

In 2000–2001, Green's last season, the Vols gave their fans the biggest tease of all, jumping out to a 16-1 record and No. 4 ranking in both major polls before beginning a shocking decline that saw them finish 6-10 the rest of the way. After being mentioned for a time as a possible No. 1 seed, the Vols had to scramble for an NCAA Tournament bid. By early March, most of them played as though they just wanted to get the season over with.

Tony Harris in particular seemed to have lost all hope, his confidence all but gone after enduring a prolonged bout of erratic shooting and criticism by the fans and media. During a home game against Kentucky, Harris, who was on the bench in street clothes after suffering an ankle injury, ran to the Wildcats' bench to jump in the middle of a skirmish involving teammate Isiah Victor. The next day, the press ripped Harris, one columnist going so far as to call him a punk. Tennessee assistant coaches thought Harris's competitive drive was essentially gone after that.

The same might have been said for Harris's teammates, which they clearly demonstrated once again in the postseason. Tennessee had to struggle to get past Auburn in a first round SEC Tournament game, and then got manhandled in a second-round loss to Ole Miss.

The Vols were lucky to earn an NCAA Tournament bid, but they received no favors from the selection committee. Seeded eighth, Tennessee got a killer draw in ninth-seeded Charlotte, just the type of solid, well-coached team that gave the Vols fits. The game's outcome never seemed in question. Charlotte won 70-63.

Harris played just twenty minutes and took only four shots. His last shot of a Tennessee career that many expected would include a trip to the Final Four was a miserable brick that crashed against the backboard. Somehow it seemed fitting.

Not long after that loss, Dickey and Green met to discuss the state of the program. At least that's what Dickey told the press. Most people thought Tennessee's then-president J. Wade Gilley had ordered Dickey to negotiate Green's departure and that Dickey didn't want to do it. With one year left in his own tenure at Tennessee (or so he thought at the time), the last thing Dickey wanted to do was conduct a coaching search. He'd gone through three protracted searches in his career and had been criticized by the fans and media for his three previous hires.

Green didn't make things any easier on Dickey. During the course of losing control of his team, Green told the media several times that if the administration didn't like the job he was doing, it should show him the door. Gilley took that advice to heart.

Green's contract had been rolled over after his first three years, so it was going to take a lot of money to get him to walk away quietly. After a few days of negotiating, Dickey and Green's attorney reached an agreement: For a buyout of $1.1 million, Green bid a fond farewell to the program he had coached to the brink of college basketball's elite. Under Green's watch, the Vols drove around the neighborhood occupied by the Dukes, Arizonas, and Michigan States of the game, but never found a place to park.

Even before the announcement of his departure was made, Green had put his house in Knoxville up for sale. After the deed was done, he beat a hasty retreat to his beach home in North Carolina and safely removed himself from the pressure cooker of Southeastern Conference basketball. He was later mentioned as a candidate for vacancies at UNLV and St. Bonaventure, but his coaching days seemed finished.

————

Buzz Peterson was in a hotel room in Minneapolis when he heard the news. Jerry Green was out at Tennessee.

"I'm getting ready to take a shower and someone—I can't even remember who now—called and said coach Green had stepped down," recalled Peterson, who had just gone through his own disappointing season at Tulsa, his first after coming from a four-year stint at Appalachian State. After winning thirty-two games and advancing to the NCAA Tournament's Elite Eight the year before under Bill Self, the Golden Hurricane lost in the finals of the Western Athletic Conference Tournament, played on its home floor, and missed out on a Big Dance bid. Thus Peterson's trip to the frozen north. Tulsa was in Minneapolis to play the University of Minnesota in a second-round NIT game. Hungry to atone for the disappointment in the WAC Tournament, Peterson was focused on the NIT, until that phone call to his hotel room.

"I've got a game to play that night," Peterson said. "But my mind's racing. The Tennessee job was a dream opportunity. I tried to tell myself if it was meant to be, it would happen. But I couldn't help but think. Man, if we just beat Minnesota, we'll probably get a home game, then maybe we'll win that and maybe that'll get [Tennessee's search committee] interested a little bit more."

As fate would have it, Tulsa wasn't awarded an NIT home game, despite beating Minnesota. The Golden Hurricane's next opponent would be Mississippi State, one of Tennessee's SEC rivals that had given the Vols a tough time in the latter stages of Green's career. When Tulsa went to Starkville and pulled out a win, it was on to the NIT Final Four in New York, where the opponents would be Memphis and Alabama, like Mississippi State, two schools Tennessee plays every season.

Tulsa and Peterson followed the script perfectly, beating Memphis and then Alabama in the championship game. But Peterson probably didn't need to win the NIT. His list of references had been impeccable. By the time Gilley and Dickey had

273

to decide on a coach, they had heard from all corners of college basketball about Peterson's virtues. Foremost among those who called Dickey in Peterson's behalf were Dean Smith and Roy Williams, but there were numerous other recommendations. After about the tenth phone call, Dickey got the idea Peterson was a popular guy.

Peterson's only real competition came from an old friend, Tennessee Tech's then-coach Jeff Lebo, who had replaced him in North Carolina's backcourt years before. Lebo impressed Tennessee's committee and would have been next in line had Peterson turned the job down. But there was no way that was going to happen.

Peterson will never forget the day his life changed forever. He was in his sophomore year at the University of North Carolina and the Tar Heels were playing Virginia. In an instant, his lifelong dream of playing in the NBA was shattered.

"It was 1983," Peterson recalled. "The year after we won the national championship. We were playing Virginia. The play was a two-on-two situation. I was the back guy, and Steve Hale was up front. [Virginia guard] Othel Wilson tried to take Steve one-on-one, and I went over to help. Othel got by Steve a little bit, and Ralph Sampson was on my right side.

"All of a sudden, we kind of all came together. Sampson's pushing my upper body and Othel stepped on my foot. They collapsed and both of them fell on top of me. Something had to give."

Something did give. It was the medial collateral ligament in Peterson's right knee.

"Our medical people kept telling me it didn't look good," Peterson said. "The team doctor took my knee and moved it to show me [the extent of the damage]. When he did that, I just got sick to my stomach and laid down."

Peterson was quickly taken to the hospital, where he begged to watch the rest of the game on television. What he saw eased his pain: Michael Jordan helped rally the Tar Heels from 16 points down. After the win, Jordan, Peterson's roommate, friend, and confidant, was interviewed on TV. Jordan knew Peterson was watching. "I miss you buddy," Jordan said. "I wish you were here."

The next game, Jordan wore a tribute to his fallen friend, taking a sweatband and placing it halfway up his left forearm. The sweatband became a trademark, almost as identifiable as Jordan's baggy shorts. He wore it the rest of his career.

Peterson was finished for the season and, though he returned the next year, he was never the same player. Neither was he the same person.

274

"The injury changed my life dramatically," Peterson recalled. "It gave me a better perspective on life. I was always so focused on basketball. That's when I began to say, 'Hey, you're not a pro player.' My grades went up. And then I started thinking about my future. In the back of my mind, I'd always wanted to coach. After the injury, I started thinking about that a lot more seriously."

Peterson and Jordan had always been competitive, nearly from the first day they met at a summer camp at North Carolina. They didn't play against one another at the camp, but shared a room.

"We got to really know each other at night," Peterson recalled. "We had a lot of stuff in common. We stayed in touch. And after a while, we started talking about going to school together."

Jordan, little known outside his home state, committed to North Carolina in the fall of 1981. Peterson, too, eventually decided on the Tar Heels, and he was convinced Jordan wouldn't stand in his way for an eventual starting job.

After Peterson and Jordan arrived in Chapel Hill, Peterson quickly learned Jordan was his equal as a competitor.

"He hated to lose, at anything," Peterson said. "Cards, pool, whatever. And you could tell he was going to be a great player."

That much was obvious after Jordan earned a starting job as a freshman and hit that famous game-winning shot against Georgetown in the 1982 NCAA championship game. By Jordan's junior season, Peterson knew his friend was something special. His knee injury had long ago taken Peterson out of the personal competition he enjoyed with Jordan—"Michael said it took the heart right out of me," Peterson recalled—and allowed him to judge his friend's talent with an unbiased eye. A pre-season trip to Europe was the clincher.

"We were playing an Italian team that had [former Indiana star] Scott May on it," Peterson said. "Scott guarded Michael, and Michael got 34 [points] on him. Then we go into the locker room, eat a candy bar, coach does another pre-game talk, and we play a Yugoslavian team. Michael goes for 34 again. That was back when we scored in the low 60s a game.

"I'll never forget telling coach [Roy] Williams, 'I think Michael's gonna be another Doctor J or something.'"

Jordan left North Carolina after his junior year to fulfil Peterson's prophecy. Peterson stayed behind and finished a playing career that had once held so much promise.

Peterson left North Carolina in 1986 and briefly played in Belgium, then came back home to work for recruiting analyst Bob Gibbons. In 1987, that job led to a position on Tom Apke's staff at Appalachian State. Peterson was on his way.

A year later, Peterson was hired by East Tennessee State coach Les Robinson, who was about to parlay his success into the top job at his alma mater, North Carolina State. Peterson followed Robinson and worked three years in Raleigh. But ultimately, his North Carolina ties ran too deep. Peterson felt pressure to leave.

In 1993, Peterson left N. C. State for Vanderbilt, where he worked for three years. During his time in Nashville, Peterson was a serious candidate for three head-coaching jobs. After missing on Murray State and East Tennessee State, he finally achieved the goal he'd set for himself during the time he spent rehabilitating his knee injury thirteen years before. At thirty-three, Peterson became the head coach at Appalachian State.

Throughout his career, Peterson has always turned to North Carolina coach Dean Smith for guidance. Smith had his doubts about Appalachian State.

"He wasn't real gung-ho about that job," Peterson said. "But he said, 'If you want to be a head coach, go ahead and take it. Just get discipline in there and work hard in recruiting.'"

Peterson did as he was told. And though Boone, North Carolina, where Appalachian State is located, is one of the more remote outposts in college basketball, he was able to recruit enough talented players to help him win. The Mountaineers were 14-14 his first season and won no fewer than 21 games his final three seasons there.

After Peterson's third year, he had chances to move on. Southwest Missouri State beckoned and actually called a press conference to announce Peterson's hiring, but he didn't feel comfortable about the job. Peterson probably would have been hired at Georgia had Jim Harrick not taken it. Peterson wound up staying put, won twenty-three games, and led Appalachian State to the NCAA Tournament in 1999–2000. That was his last season in Boone.

After the season, when Bill Self left Tulsa for Illinois, Peterson got involved at Tulsa, for which he has a debt of gratitude to Duke coach Mike Krzyzewski.

"[Tulsa athletic director] Judy McLeod called Mike after Bill Self left," Peterson recalled. "She was really into what Mike had done at Duke. She asked if he had any assistants who were ready. Mike said not yet. But he offered to go over Judy's list of candidates. She read them off. And he said, 'Well, I thought you had another guy on there, Buzz Peterson.' It turned out Judy didn't want to ask coach about a North Carolina guy. Basically, how I got the Tulsa job was Mike saying, 'Hey, if you can get him, you'd better hire him.'"

Once Peterson became a serious candidate at Tulsa, he put in a call to Smith.

"He really wasn't excited about the Tulsa job," Peterson said. "He said, 'You're taking over the hardest job in the country right now. They just won thirty-two games. They'll expect that again. That's hard to do if you're not at a high major school.'"

Once again, Peterson didn't heed his old coach's warning. And once again, his gut decision proved to be the right one to make. Peterson did an admirable job following Self, but when he heard the Tennessee job had come open he couldn't stop thinking about it.

For Peterson, Tennessee was a dream job. Though he probably didn't need any career advice, Peterson dutifully called Smith again.

"He said, 'You'd didn't listen to me the first two times,'" Peterson said. " 'But if you want my advice, this is the job you should take.'"

———

When Peterson took over at Tennessee, he was careful not to be too critical of former coach Jerry Green. But several times, when asked about the seemingly unlikely series of events that landed him in Knoxville, Peterson alluded to problems in the program. "There must have been problems," Peterson would say. "Or I wouldn't be here."

Peterson was right. He quickly learned of one major problem. Forward Marcus Haislip, thought by many to be the most gifted player on the team, was in trouble academically.

"I found out as soon as I got the job," Peterson recalled. "He didn't have the GPA or the right amount of classes. We thought we could make up for it in the summer. But he was just too far behind."

Haislip would miss the first semester, a total of six games, but at least he would return. That wasn't the case for guards Harris Walker and Terrence Woods, who ran afoul of team rules and were kicked off the team. At the time, the departure of Walker and Woods seemed to be a case of addition by subtraction. Both players had been critical of Green and complained about a lack of playing time. Peterson didn't want any attitude problems.

Tennessee would lose more bodies after practice started in October. Little-used sophomore Andy Ikeakor went down with a stress fracture in his foot. Peterson might have been able to live with that one, but when junior forward Ron Slay, an All-SEC pick in 2000–2001, also pulled up lame with a stress fracture, Peterson started to get a little nervous.

"I compared it to getting to play a round of golf at Augusta National," Peterson said. "You get there, and somebody stole some of your golf clubs out of the back of your car. You don't have all your weapons. Here I get this opportunity to coach a great

C. J. Black. *Tennessee Sports Information*

program like Tennessee, and two weeks into practice I've got seven players."

The Vols' lack of depth and frontcourt talent would hamper their early season progress. After barely getting past Tennessee Tech, then coached by Peterson's old friend Jeff Lebo, Tennessee traveled to the Great Alaska Shootout and got hammered twice, by Marquette and St. John's. About the only good thing to come from the long journey was that Ron Slay, though not quite at full strength, played in two of the three games.

Wins over Peterson's old school, Appalachian State, and on the road at SMU seemed to get the Vols back on track. And having served time in purgatory, Marcus Haislip would return in time for a game at Memphis.

Though Haislip didn't start against the Tigers, he had an impact, scoring 14 points and grabbing five rebounds before fouling out. But Haislip's presence couldn't prevent the first of what would become an uncanny string of last-minute losses. Memphis won, 71-69, in a game where one more defensive rebound might have made a difference.

If Peterson thought the Memphis game was a heartbreaker, he couldn't have imagined what was coming. Five days later, the Vols lost at Louisville despite leading 70-64 with thirty-six seconds left. Those frantic final seconds left Peterson in a state of disbelief.

After Tennessee guard Thaydeus Holden made two free throws to give the Vols that six-point lead, the Cardinals' Reece Gaines came downcourt and tossed up a deep three that bounced hard off the backboard and into the net. Just like that, the lead was cut to three.

"When I saw [Gaines] taking that three and Thaydeus contesting him, I actually turned around toward the basket happy," Tennessee guard Jon Higgins said. "That's what you want—them jacking up thirty-footers. Then you see it go in off the glass and you think, 'Maybe it just wasn't meant for us to win.'"

Higgins was right. Vincent Yarbrough's in-bounds pass was intercepted by Louisville's Erik Brown, who tossed the ball to teammate Bryant Northern at the top of the key. Northern quickly hoisted a three-pointer that went in and tied the score at 70 with twenty-six seconds left.

Tennessee was stunned, but was able to get the ball in play, get downcourt, and slip a pass inside to Haislip. His basket gave the Vols a 72-70 led with seven seconds to play, but the lead didn't hold up. Gaines streaked downcourt and let fly with another deep three that, like the Cards' other two desperation shots before it, went in to put Louisville ahead 73-72. Tennessee had 1.8 seconds left and actually got a decent final shot from Haislip, but it bounced off the rim.

"I was shocked," Peterson said. "It happened so fast. Maybe there was something else we could have done, but except for the bad in-bounds pass, we didn't make mistakes. Louisville just made shots."

In the days and weeks that followed, several other teams made critical last-second shots against the Vols. Less than forty-eight hours after the Louisville nightmare, the Vols lost at home to West Virginia when guard Jonathan Hargett pulled up with 4.3 seconds left and drained a three-pointer with Tennessee's Jenis Grindstaff hanging all over him.

In SEC play, three-pointers continued to haunt the Vols. Ahead 94-91 with ten seconds left against Florida, all Tennessee had to do was prevent a three. But after the Gators in-bounded the ball from under Tennessee's basket, Brett Nelson drove to the arc, jumped over Jon Higgins's outstretched arm and knocked down a game-tying basket. Florida won in overtime.

In a game at Georgia, Ron Slay's three-pointer with 15.8 seconds left tied the score at 70, and it looked as though the game would go into overtime when Georgia lost control of the basketball on its end of the floor. As (bad) luck would have it, the Bulldogs' Ezra Williams picked up the ball outside the three-point line, and with the seconds ticking down, calmly tossed in a shot that won the game at the buzzer.

Four days later, the Vols led at Mississippi State, 91-88 in overtime, but a missed defensive assignment allowed the Bulldogs' Michal Ignerski to slip free for a three-pointer that tied the score. State won 92-91.

Tennessee's misfortune wasn't limited to losses. In an upset of then–No. 8 Syracuse, Ron Slay came down on his right knee awkwardly and tore the anterior cruciate ligament. He was lost for the season.

"By that time, I was wondering if I'd done something somewhere to make somebody mad," Peterson recalled. "What more could happen to us?"

The string of close losses ended when the Vols were waxed at home by South Carolina, 94-60. Ironically, Tennessee responded with its best stretch of basketball. The Vols beat Auburn convincingly at home, pulled out two key road wins at LSU and Vanderbilt—the latter when a last-second three-pointer by the opposition finally missed—and came home to upset then–No. 7 Kentucky.

An unsung hero in the winning streak was Jenis Grindstaff, a hard-luck senior guard who had lost both parents to cancer and blown out his knee during his time in Knoxville. Desperate for a playmaker, Peterson moved Grindstaff to the point, Higgins to shooting guard, and Thaydeus Holden to the bench. Grindstaff was a catalyst in a second-half comeback against Kentucky.

Tennessee's winning streak came to an abrupt end at South Carolina, which crushed the Vols again. After a win against Arkansas, Tennessee lost four straight, including yet another heartbreaker at Kentucky. The Vols led the Wildcats for thirty-eight minutes before breaking down. Another crippling defeat in the streak came at home to Vanderbilt. That loss effectively ended Tennessee's chances of salvaging an NIT bid.

The Vols ended the regular season by upsetting No. 16 Georgia, once again giving their fans a tantalizing glimpse of what might have been. The ebbs and flows of Peterson's first season at Tennessee took their toll on the young coach, but the damage wasn't permanent. Peterson even learned a few things about his craft during the difficult season.

Tennessee
All-SEC Expansion Era Team

F-Vincent Yarbrough

F-Marcus Haislip

C-C. J. Black

G-Allan Houston

G-Tony Harris

Top Reserves-Brandon Wharton, Ron Slay

"I used to think I had to become one of the best X and O guys," he said. "But this season, I've learned it isn't just that that makes you a good head coach. It's also the art of communication. Trying to find the right chemistry. What motivates kids. Getting them ready to play. Every team has a different personality. I've learned that now. A lot of coaches, friends of mine who've been in this a lot longer than I have, have told me this year will make me a better coach. I've always thought whatever doesn't kill you makes you tougher. Man, was that ever true this season."

Tennessee's postseason foray would end after two games in the SEC Tournament, but Vol fans seemed pleased with the job Peterson had done. Their comments on radio talk shows, Internet bulletin boards, and letters-to-the-editor columns in newspapers suggested a general belief that finally, Tennessee had found a coach who could bring consistency to the program.

"It was a rough year on all of us," Peterson said. "But it gets me fired up to think that in tough times, we didn't quit. And the fans didn't give up on us. That's a good sign for the future of this program."

281

Chapter Twelve

Vanderbilt

There's no task too big for a loyal, hard-working assistant coach. That's why Vanderbilt's Tim Jankovich found himself on an eighteen-hour flight to Poland in mid April 2001. Many times during the trek, Jankovich thought back to how suddenly the trip had become necessary. All it took was one phone call—from a high school player named David Harrison. Harrison, a six-foot-ten *Parade* and McDonald's All-American, had called the Vanderbilt office a few days before and informed head coach Kevin Stallings that he wouldn't be attending the university, that he intended to sign with Colorado.

Stallings was disappointed by the news, but not nearly as disappointed as Vanderbilt fans, who had eagerly anticipated Harrison's arrival for two years. It seemed such a no-brainer: Harrison played high school basketball in Nashville, at Brentwood Academy. His father Dennis was an assistant on the Vanderbilt football staff. And Stallings, the energetic, emotional rising young coaching star, had the program headed in a positive direction.

In the end, Harrison reluctantly turned his back on all those reasons he should attend Vanderbilt and focused on the one reason he shouldn't—his brother D. J. played for Colorado.

"I kind of wanted to go away and be on my own," Harrison told the media after his decision. "D. J. is like a step-stool for a year before I'm really on my own."

That comment gave Vanderbilt fans another reason to curse the good name of former Commodore coach Jan van Breda Kolff, who had parted ways with the university two years before. A big reason van Breda Kolff was no longer in Nashville, said some of those disgruntled Commodore loyalists, was that he didn't do a good enough job recruiting Nashville area players. One of those players was D. J. Harrison, who played at Martin Luther King High School, then honed his skills for two years at Nashville's Aquinas College.

Most people assumed that the key to landing David Harrison, who had become one of the nation's premier big men, was signing his brother. It wasn't a reach—Harrison later became a starter at Colorado, so he was talented enough to play in the SEC. But Vanderbilt seldom pursues junior college players, and under van Breda Kolff's watch didn't recruit D. J. Harrison.

When Stallings took over the program in 1999, it was too late to do anything about D. J. Harrison, but he worked David Harrison as hard as anyone could have. Though the younger Harrison had flirted with North Carolina, Duke, and in-state rival Tennessee, Stallings always thought he had a chance to sign him. Vanderbilt fans assumed that family ties would keep Harrison in Nashville.

In the end, family ties influenced Harrison's decision, but they weren't the ties Commodores fans had hoped would influence him. April 10, 2001, was a dark day in Vanderbilt basketball history—at least as far as the fans were concerned. Stallings, though understandably deflated by Harrison's decision, knew business had to proceed as usual.

"Everybody had the impression when David Harrison didn't come to school here that that was it for our program," Stallings said. "I've lost recruits before. And I'm gonna lose them again. Guys that we really want. Guys that we spend a lot of time with. But no one player is going to be the reason we're successful. And no one player is going to be the reason we're not successful."

Vanderbilt supporters might have criticized van Breda Kolff for being a passive recruiter. But they'll never say that about Kevin Stallings. "Kevin is a competitor," said Gene Keady, who coached Stallings at Purdue and later hired him as an assistant. "He lives for the competition that the game provides. He loves challenges, and he's gonna work hard to overcome them."

So it was when David Harrison signed with Colorado. Stallings had put a lot of effort into signing Harrison, but even during the recruiting process, he was making contingency plans. A good friend of Stallings—"I could tell you his name, but then I'd have to kill you," he said—tracks European basketball and gave Stallings a list with six post players on it. Three were from Poland, a couple more from Italy, and another from Yugoslavia.

After evaluating the list, Stallings made a decision. A few days later, Jankovich was headed for Slupsk, Poland, where he was to watch seven-foot center David Przybyszewski play. Jankovich was a little wary of what he might encounter when he landed—he didn't know a word of Polish.

"I know two words now, but none when I got there," Jankovich said. "I just tried to learn please and thank you. It's a big leap of faith when you go somewhere so far away, where you've never been before. It can get scary when you're driving around. You think you're on the right road, but they're marked differently from ours. You just hope you see a town name that looks familiar."

Jankovich drove around until he got to his destination, a huge, dark gym where he was to find Przybyszewski playing a pickup game. As he got out of his car, Jankovich had a sobering thought: "What if I've come all this way and the kid can't play?"

Luckily for Jankovich and Vanderbilt, Przybyszewski could play. Jankovich was pleased with the big man's mobility and shooting touch. And considering Przybyszewski had played for just four years, he had adapted to the game quickly.

"He wasn't a polished player, but amazingly good for somebody who had only played that long," Jankovich recalled. "To say the least, I was relieved. There probably aren't too many worse feelings in recruiting than traveling eighteen hours and within the first five minutes you're there you think, 'What am I doing here?' That's every coach's nightmare."

After meeting with Przybyszewski, Jankovich returned to Nashville the next day. Not long after his plane landed, Jankovich gave his report to Stallings.

"Tim said, 'I think he can be pretty good,'" Stallings recalled. "He wasn't totally sure, but he said, 'I know one thing. He's big. He's long. He looks like he's got real good touch, and he runs pretty well.' Well, that was enough for me to go on. I went totally on Tim's evaluation."

When Przybyszewski arrived in Nashville and Stallings could see him in preseason individual workouts, the coach was elated.

"He's got a chance to be better than good," Stallings said while watching the big man drain three-pointers during a November 2001 practice. "We're thrilled for two reasons. One, because he's got a chance to be a heck of a player. And two, because he's a great kid. David will be an instrumental part of our success the next four years."

Clearly, Stallings and Jankovich—who's logged a lot of frequent flyer miles since he's worked in Nashville—are prepared to do whatever it takes. At Vanderbilt, a school known and respected for its academics, entry standards are high. Student-athletes who can meet those standards aren't exactly standing around on every street corner.

"You have to use your resources," Stallings said. "Over the course of my career, I have always thought what I would describe as outside the box. Unconventional. At Kentucky and Kansas, you can do it in a conventional way, recruit highly recruited kids, and win your share of the battles. If you're any place else, you'd better have some resourcefulness to you."

In Stallings's first three seasons at Vanderbilt, Commodore fans learned that not only was he resourceful, but as Gene Keady said, very competitive, almost combative. That was the way he had been trained, ever since his high school playing days. Those traits would serve him well at Vanderbilt, judged by many to be the toughest job in the Southeastern Conference.

———

When Kevin Stallings, at just thirty-two years old, became the head coach at Illinois State in 1993, he was considered young for the job. What people didn't know was that through sheer good fortune, his formal education in the game had made him wise beyond his years. Few coaches in college basketball, in their formative stages, had a better group of mentors.

He didn't realize it at the time, but Stallings began preparing to be a head coach in the late 1970s during his career at Collinsville (Illinois) High School. Stallings's coach there was Virgil Fletcher, who in a career that lasted thirty-two years compiled a 792-234 record. In Collinsville, Fletcher was a pillar of the community, known and revered by all. Rare is the coach—at any level of the game—who is successful enough and stays at one job long enough to have the gym in which his team plays named after him. At Collinsville, the building was re-christened Virgil Fletcher Gymnasium while Fletcher was still coaching.

"It's hard for me to put into words what coach Fletcher meant to me," Stallings said. "Other than my father, he had almost all the influence on me. And his influence has carried over to this day. Because in every practice that I run, every team that I coach, just about every way I think, he in some way has affected me.

"But it wasn't just me. He had such a profound impact on so many guys who played for him. We were all scared to death of him. I'm still scared to death of him. He had God-like stature to me. He was the reason I wanted to coach."

Stallings had good reason to be afraid of Fletcher, for the old coach was apparently all-knowing and all-seeing. Stallings remembers the time he skipped class after his junior season, a year in which he had become one of the top players in Illinois and a big-time college prospect.

"One day I decided to cut class," Stallings recalled. "It was me and another player, a senior. He and I were the stars on our team. It was the only time I ever skipped school. That night, I went home, and I was sort of smug that I was going to get by with it. Then the phone rings and it was coach. He asked to talk to my dad. I could hear my dad's side of the conversation: 'Hi coach. Uh huh. Oh is that right? I see. Sure coach, that would be fine. I'll have him see you first thing in the morning.'

"The way I was raised, my dad would have happily been willing to administer any disciplinary action that needed to take place. But coach said he'd handle it. Which was worse. The next day, he calls me in his office and told me something I'll never forget, something I tell my teams to this day. He said that all year long, for several months of the season, players are used to getting attention. And that when the season was over, inevitably, somebody will do something to get attention, even if it's negative attention. I've never forgotten that, because it seems like every spring, somebody does something, albeit for negative attention."

That episode convinced Stallings that Fletcher held absolute power over him. Even Stallings's father wouldn't stand in the way.

Stallings recalls another quick lesson when he was a senior. He can't remember the specific transgression that occurred during practice, but won't ever forget the shock he felt when Fletcher hurled a basketball at him.

"He was standing about eight feet from me and threw that ball at my head as hard as he could throw it," Stallings said. "I ducked and it sailed over my head. Trust me when I tell you that parents today would say they would never ever allow somebody to do that to their child.

"At that time, I was a highly recruited player being sought after nationally and was very full of myself. Coach Fletcher had a tremendous way of knowing when you needed to be brought down. I went home that night and I proceeded to tell my father that coach Fletcher had lost his mind. My dad looked me square in the eye and said, 'You better figure out what you're doing wrong and get it fixed.' That was the way parents felt about coach Fletcher because he had so much credibility. A guy wouldn't get by with that now—he'd be in front of the school board and fired.

"Looking back, I not only deserved to have the ball thrown at me. I deserved to be hit with the ball. I'm sure coach missed on purpose. I can only imagine he felt that I thought I knew more than he did. And I probably did think that."

The doses of humility imparted on him by Fletcher did much to prepare Stallings for his future with another strong-willed and forceful coach. After a season at junior college, Stallings signed with Purdue, where he played on a Final Four team as a sophomore in 1980. His first coach at Purdue was Lee Rose, but after Stallings's sophomore season, Rose left for South Florida and was replaced by Gene Keady. In Keady, who had coached under Eddie Sutton at Arkansas and had been successful running his own program at Western Kentucky, Stallings found another mentor who would help shape his career.

"Coach Keady was another strong influence," Stallings recalled. "Another strong personality. Another person who has a terrific way of impacting lives if you're smart enough to learn the lessons. I was greatly influenced by Gene Keady, because he gave me an opportunity to coach and to advance in this business when I was very young."

In time, Keady became almost a father figure to Stallings, whose father died of a heart attack while Stallings was still in college. It was Keady who provided emotional support during Stallings's time of need.

"I was devastated," Stallings said. "My father and I had a special relationship and were very close. But coach Keady was real big. It happened just before the season started. But coach told me to go home, to take as much time as I needed. I never forgot what he did for me."

After his playing career ended, Stallings joined Keady's staff as a graduate assistant in 1983. And every time Keady had an opportunity to elevate Stallings on his staff, he did so without hesitation. In eight years at Keady's side, two as a player and the last six as an assistant, Stallings absorbed all he could. Keady's teachings mean more to Stallings now than when he was around Keady every day.

"Coaching is both art and science," Stallings said. "But I've come to learn that it is more art than science. It is the ability to motivate people. To get people to understand what role to play and to accept it and be happy with it. That's the art of coaching. And coach Keady does that better than anyone. When it comes to the art of coaching, he gets an A-plus."

Stallings had one more apprenticeship to serve before he would become a head coach. When Roy Williams was putting together a staff at Kansas in 1989, he remembered Stallings from the recruiting trail. As a North Carolina assistant, Williams had run into Stallings a few times over the years, most notably when the Tar Heels were able to pluck Rick Fox out of Indiana and away from the Boilermakers.

"Roy was about to get the Kansas job, and Rick Callahan, one of Eddie Fogler's assistants at Wichita State, called me and told me I should think about going with Roy as an assistant," Stallings said. "I remember exactly what my response was. I told him there was nothing about being an assistant at Kansas that excited me. We had just gone 29-4 at Purdue and won three Big Ten championships in six years.

"But I got off the phone and my wife asked me who it was and I told her. And she said I should talk to Roy. That night I couldn't sleep thinking about it. And the next day I called Rick back and told him if Roy was interested, I'd like to visit with him."

Stallings did meet with Williams. And as much as it hurt him to finally leave Keady, Stallings decided his career would benefit from learning a different way of doing things. Though Williams had never been a head coach, he had absorbed Dean Smith's system in ten seasons as a North Carolina assistant. If Kansas had enough faith in Williams to hire him despite the fact he had never led his own program, that was good enough for Stallings.

The five years Stallings spent on Williams's staff were invaluable to his career.

"I learned a much different way of doing things," Stallings said. "But the most important thing was how Roy paid such unbelievably close attention to detail. That was a different thing for me. But Roy was always in control. Things always ran efficiently, in the office, on the floor, in recruiting. And it did because that was the way it was set up.

"For me, who was more a by-the-seat-of-the-pants guy, that was a real eye-opening experience. It was one of the best things to happen to me professionally. And I was also tremendously impacted by Roy's success."

In Stallings's five years at Kansas, the Jayhawks were 132-37 and played in two Final Fours. College athletic directors across the country who were looking for head coaches couldn't wait to plunder Williams's staff.

In 1993, Stallings's fifth season at Kansas, he had begun to command serious attention. Stallings actually had two jobs to choose from—Miami of Ohio and Illinois State. He eventually decided on Illinois State because he was impressed with athletic director Rick Greenspan. Stallings's decision turned out to be a good one.

Learning how to be a head coach without the glare of a major program blinding him, Stallings quickly became successful. His first team at Illinois State was 16-11, and for the next four years, the Redbirds won no fewer than twenty games and played in four consecutive post-season tournaments.

Given those accomplishments, Stallings quickly became a commodity, his name linked with seemingly every major job opening. Each year Greenspan and Redbird fans crossed their fingers and waited, worried that Stallings might finally find a job that interested him. For six seasons, he happily stayed put.

Stallings had several legitimate opportunities to leave. In 1997, he seemed all but out the door when Tennessee offered him the chance to take over a talented team left behind by former coach Kevin O'Neill. Two Tennessee newspapers actually reported Stallings had accepted the job, but though the move to Knoxville seemed like a logical progression in his career, something didn't seem quite right about the fit. On the day he was supposed to conduct a press conference, Stallings called Tennessee athletic director Doug Dickey and told him he was staying at Illinois State.

"I was as serious about the Tennessee job as a person could be," Stallings recalled. "Turning it down was in some ways difficult to explain then and it's difficult to explain now. You make decisions that you feel are in the best interests of your family and your future. I did not feel that [taking the Tennessee job] was the right decision to make."

Many Tennessee fans were upset when Stallings turned down the job. And Stallings wouldn't let them get over it. He kept coming back to haunt them. In 1998, the Vols, under first-year head coach Jerry Green, reached the NCAA Tournament for the first time in nine seasons. Green had served with Stallings on Roy Williams's first staff at Kansas. Coincidentally—or was it?—Tennessee's first-round opponent in the tournament was Illinois State.

The Redbirds, despite playing without their starting guards, who had been injured, managed to pull out a one-point victory at the buzzer in overtime.

After that bitterly disappointing loss, Tennessee fans might have thought they had finally seen the last of Stallings. But little did they know they hadn't.

———

When stacked up against that of mighty Southeastern Conference stalwart Kentucky, Vanderbilt's tradition and history in basketball doesn't seem like much to get excited about. But the periods of success that the Commodores have enjoyed over the years are still remembered fondly in Nashville.

Mention the name of coach Roy Skinner, and the typical Vanderbilt fan can reel off the names of the legendary "F Troop" of Jeff Fosnes, Joe Ford, and Butch Feher. Together with Jan van Breda Kolff, that trio led the Commodores to the 1974 SEC championship, a No. 13 national ranking, and an NCAA Tournament appearance, just the second in school history.

C. M. Newton's name will likewise never be forgotten in Nashville. Newton had earned his SEC reputation at Alabama, where he led the Crimson Tide to six post-season tournament appearances before quitting to take a job in the SEC office in 1980. In 1982, Newton was compelled to return to coaching at Vanderbilt, where he promptly rescued the program from a down period that began after Skinner's departure in 1976. Behind stars Will Perdue, Barry Booker, and Barry Goheen, Newton led the Commodores to the NCAAs in 1988 and 1989. In 1988, Vanderbilt advanced to the Sweet 16.

Vanderbilt's loss to Notre Dame in the first round of the NCAA Tournament turned out to be Newton's last game. He left to become athletic director at Kentucky, where his mission was to resurrect a scandal-ridden program. He quickly did so by hiring Rick Pitino as coach, and eight years later put the finishing touches on a basketball hall-of-fame career—he was elected in 2000—by hiring Tubby Smith to replace Pitino.

Newton's replacement at Vanderbilt was Eddie Fogler, a bright protégé of North Carolina coach Dean Smith who had forged his own success at Wichita State. After leading the Shockers to NCAA Tournament trips in 1987 and 1988, Fogler became a hot commodity. Surely, thought those who knew him best, Fogler's next stop would be at an upper-echelon program in a power conference as he continued his preparation to eventually replace his mentor at North Carolina.

When Fogler left Wichita State for Vanderbilt in 1989, some people were puzzled. "When I went to Vanderbilt, a number of people questioned whether you could [consistently] win there," Fogler recalled. "It was a very tough league and had very high academic requirements, nationally, not just for the Southeastern Conference. Some people didn't consider Vanderbilt a great job. But I think that's proven not to be true. You can have a successful program at Vanderbilt."

It was Fogler who led Vanderbilt basketball into the 1990s, which became a decade of unprecedented success for the SEC. For one glorious season, the Commodores took their place alongside the SEC's best teams of the ten-year period from 1992 to 2002.

Fogler was immediately successful at Vanderbilt, leading the Commodores to the NIT championship in 1989–90 and the NCAA Tournament the next season. A 15-15 1991–92 season didn't derail Vanderbilt's progress—Fogler had been patiently stock-piling the component parts of what would become an SEC championship team and knew better days were ahead.

Three key players from the 1992–93 teams were transfers. Two of those, Chris Lawson, a burly, redheaded center who came from Indiana, and Billy McCaffrey, who left a national championship team at Duke so he could play point guard for the Commodores, had just become eligible after sitting out the 1991–92 season. Bruce Elder, an undersized power forward who started at Davidson but wanted to test his skills against a higher level of competition, had been on the team for two seasons. The other starters were a pair of rangy guards, Ronnie McMahan and Kevin Anglin, who joined the program as freshmen.

"Ronnie McMahon was the only one of that five who could go up, flat-footed, and dunk a basketball," Fogler said, smiling at the recollection. "It wasn't the most athletic group, but they were tough as hell, smart and unselfish. They were also very good defensively and they could shoot the basketball."

Jeff Lebo, one of Fogler's assistants and now the head coach at Tennessee-Chattanooga, recalls that the Commodores weren't a team that could intimidate the opposition. "Elder was our four man at six-four, six-five," Lebo said. "Anglin was our three man at six-three. Ronnie McMahon was a long, skinny kid. This was not the most imposing group of guys in the world, especially playing in the SEC."

Vanderbilt lost to Illinois in its second game of the season, but then won ten straight to get to 11-1. Commodore fever began to grip Nashville.

"That gym was jam-packed every night," Lebo recalled. "People were falling out of the rafters. That was all before [Tennessee] Titan football. Vanderbilt basketball was on the front page of the sports section. Basketball, at that time, was it in

Nashville."

The Commodores ran through their SEC schedule with a 14-2 record, losing only to Florida and Kentucky. Vanderbilt won the SEC's Eastern Division by a game over the Wildcats, and also won the league's overall regular-season championship.

Vanderbilt stumbled in the SEC Tournament, losing to LSU in the quarterfinals, but advanced to the NCAA Tournament and beat Boise State in the first round. Paired against Illinois in the second round, the Commodores gained a measure of revenge with an 85-68 victory. Next it was on to the Sweet 16, but the ride ended there when Vanderbilt lost to Temple.

The loss didn't diminish the Commodores' accomplishments. They had won a school-record twenty-eight games. Their fourteen conference victories were also a record. They had been more than competitive with the two acknowledged best teams in the league, splitting with Kentucky and beating Arkansas in the only game between the two. Their trip to the Sweet 16 was only the second in school history.

When the season was over, Fogler had to build a new trophy case after making a clean sweep of national coach-of-the-year honors from the Associated Press, United Press International, CBS, the United States Basketball Writers Association, Scripps-Howard, *Sports Illustrated*, *The Sporting News*, and *Basketball Weekly*.

No one could possibly have imagined it at the time, but Fogler wouldn't coach another game at Vanderbilt.

For at least the previous two years, it wasn't a secret that there was no love lost between Fogler and Vanderbilt athletic director Paul Hoolahan. After the great season Vanderbilt had, Fogler approached his boss about a salary increase. The request was hardly unreasonable, especially considering that Fogler had been one of the lowest-paid coaches in the SEC.

Hoolahan promised to take Fogler's request to Vanderbilt chancellor Joe B. Wyatt and get back with him. But when Fogler hadn't heard from Hoolahan in a few days, he became concerned. Fogler had also requested to speak with Wyatt, but again, he heard nothing.

In the meantime, South Carolina was looking for a coach, and its athletic director, Mike McGee, called for permission to speak with Fogler. Years later, Fogler didn't want to recount the details of his departure from Vanderbilt. But his final days in Nashville are well documented.

McGee was under a great deal of pressure to hire a big-name coach after Georgia Tech coach Bobby Cremins, a South Carolina graduate, accepted the job and then shocked Gamecock fans by returning to Georgia Tech two days later.

That made the conditions ripe for something dramatic to happen. McGee needed a big-name, successful coach. Fogler wanted to be fairly compensated and wanted to work at a school where the administration would fully support him. Fogler couldn't have been blamed for thinking that his bosses at Vanderbilt didn't appreciate him. Their silence seemed to support that contention. Or perhaps Wyatt and Hoolahan didn't think Fogler would leave for another SEC school. Imagine Hoolahan's surprise when Fogler announced he was leaving for South Carolina. After flying to Columbia to accept the job, Fogler returned to Nashville, where he gave a final press conference. One reporter asked Fogler why he'd been so hasty, considering Wyatt had been out of town and unable to speak with the coach. Fogler's response was classic.

"The last I checked," Fogler said, "they had telephones in all fifty states."

With that, the most successful era in Vanderbilt basketball came to an abrupt end. And Commodore fans weren't happy about it. The masses were stirred up even more when the media duly reported how easily Wyatt and Hoolahan could have sewed up Fogler to a long-term deal.

"He loved Nashville," said Joe Biddle, a columnist for *The Tennesean*. "His wife loved Nashville. He wanted to retire there. I remember asking him if Vanderbilt could have come up with a million-dollar, ten-year annuity, would that have been enough to get him to stay. And he said it would have been. That might have cost the university three hundred thousand dollars."

Some Vanderbilt fans are still sickened at the thought of how Fogler's great work was dashed. The program was on solid foundation and figured to contend for more SEC championships. Former Vanderbilt assistant Jeff Lebo could only shake his head when he thought back to the players the Commodore staff might have signed.

"We were all over Ron Mercer [one of the nation's top recruits and a Nashville native who signed with Kentucky in 1995]," Lebo said. "Who knows what might have happened there? We could have signed Kirk Haston [a six-foot-eleven center and middle Tennessee native who went to Indiana, where he became a first-round NBA draft pick]. I know we would have signed Ryan Stack [another six-foot-eleven middle Tennessee native who followed Fogler to South Carolina and was also taken in the NBA draft]. We would have kept that program going at a high level."

———

Hoolahan wasn't prepared for the firestorm that had been unleashed after Fogler's departure. Scrambling around to find a replacement, Vanderbilt realized the best chance it had of saving face after the Fogler debacle was to hire a coach who was well known to Commodore fans.

That turned out to be Jan van Breda Kolff. VBK, as he was known in Nashville, was one of the more popular players in Vanderbilt history. He was a first-team All-SEC pick in 1974 and was so versatile he was used at all five positions. That 1974 team played in the NCAA Tournament, a rare occurrence in school history and another reason van Breda Kolff had been so revered.

VBK came with a first-rate basketball pedigree and the requisite experience after his collegiate playing days had ended. His father, Butch, had coached five NBA teams, including the Los Angeles Lakers, and four college teams, including Princeton. After Vanderbilt, van Breda Kolff played in the ABA and the NBA. He began his coaching career in the Italian pro league in 1983, then returned to the United States in 1987 to take a spot on Princeton coach Pete Carril's staff.

The apprenticeship with the crafty Carril was a learning experience for van Breda Kolff. The Tigers won Ivy League championships and played in the NCAA Tournament in 1989, 1990, and 1991, van Breda Kolff's last three years there.

In 1991, VBK was hired at Cornell. After a 7-19 debut season, van Breda Kolff coached the Big Red to a 16-10 record in his second year. Then his alma mater called.

Van Breda Kolff's six-year tenure in Nashville isn't remembered fondly, though the record shows he didn't fare all that badly. Some of VBK's harshest critics forgot that when he came to Vanderbilt, where he would take over a program in one of the nation's toughest conferences, he had been a college head coach for all of two years.

Learning on the job was only part of VBK's problem. He also suffered by comparison to the highly successful Fogler regime. Still, in his six seasons, van Breda Kolff led the Commodores to a 104-81 record, three trips to the NIT, and one to the NCAA Tournament. He won twenty games twice, nineteen another season, and eighteen another—not bad numbers, just not great ones.

Because he was a private person who disliked mingling with fans and was uncomfortable courting the media, VBK never could develop enough of a following to help him through tough times. After Vanderbilt finished 14-15, with a 5-11 SEC record, in 1998–99, van Breda Kolff was gone.

"Jan was an exceptional basketball mind," said Todd Turner, Vanderbilt's athletic director since 1996. "But the key thing at this level, particularly in a program that is trying to find itself, trying to develop a name, trying to emerge, is leadership. And effective leadership encompasses more than Xs and Os. It's about people. It's about the big picture. Jan's strengths were not in that area.

"When he was forced to do PR work, he was pretty good at it. But it didn't come naturally. When we made the decision to go in a different direction, we told Jan that at that point in our history, we were unfair to him, asking him to do some things that were not easy for him to do. It just wasn't the right time."

VBK's tenure was marked by some recruiting problems, perhaps attributable to the fact his staff was constantly changing. He wasn't he easiest guy in the world to work for.

"During the VBK era, the amount of Division I prospects in middle Tennessee and Nashville was unprecedented," said Greg Pogue, who covered high school athletics and later Vanderbilt for the *Nashville Banner*. "A lot of good ones in the area got away to other schools, guys like Brian Watkins, who went to Maryland, Ryan Stack, who went to South Carolina, Kirk Haston, who signed with Indiana, and Niki Arinze, who went to Wake Forest. All of those kids were from Nashville or a neighboring county."

But the best area player to get away from Vanderbilt in VBK's tenure was Ron Mercer. The *Parade* and McDonald's All-American had played three seasons for Nashville's Goodpasture High School before leaving town in the fall of 1994 for Virginia's Oak Hill Academy. Mercer's final choices came down to three schools—Tennessee, Kentucky, and Vanderbilt. That the Commodores were in the running was a tribute to the hard work put in by van Breda Kolff's staff, much of it by assistant coach Buzz Peterson.

At one point, Mercer had reportedly agreed to commit to Vanderbilt, and the plan was for him to do so by giving Pogue the story at the McDonald's All-American game in St. Louis in April 1995. But before Mercer could announce a decision, Vanderbilt cut him off short. Though Mercer was fully qualified under NCAA guidelines, his academic background fell short of Vanderbilt's exacting standards, and no exception was going to be made, regardless of how talented he was.

Pogue had been tipped off to Vanderbilt's decision and approached van Breda Kolff, who asked him to hold the story until he could appeal the decision on Mercer. When a few days went by, the *Banner* ran the story for fear it would leak in another media outlet. When the story broke, Vanderbilt fans went crazy.

"It was unbelievable," recalls Joe Biddle. "For days on our talk show, it was nothing but calls about Mercer. Hundreds of people called in and cancelled their membership in the National Commodore Club. It was as volatile an issue as I can remember in my twenty-two years in Nashville."

Commodore fans were incensed because, as both Nashville newspapers later reported, exceptions had been made to other athletes trying to gain admission into Vanderbilt. Wyatt might have intervened on van Breda Kolff's behalf, but chose not to.

What might have happened had Mercer been admitted to school? He eventually went to Kentucky, where he stayed just two years, but helped the Wildcats win a national championship in 1996. Years later, Mercer said he had never intended to commit to Vanderbilt.

But what if he had? Could that have stimulated interest in the program and helped van Breda Kolff save his job? Could the Commodores have regained the conference-winning form they showed in 1993 in Fogler's last season?

Long-time Vanderbilt fans are still debating those questions.

VBK's coaching career took a turn for the better after he left Vanderbilt. Just days after his departure from Nashville in 1999, VBK was hired by Pepperdine. The Waves were 25-9 overall and won the West Coast Conference with a 12-2 record in 1999–2000. And VBK was the last coach to beat Bobby Knight at Indiana when the Waves ousted the Hoosiers from the 2000 NCAA Tournament in the first round. In VBK's second season, Pepperdine was 22-9 and played in the NIT.

In March 2001, van Breda Kolff, who wanted to return to his East Coast roots, accepted the job at St. Bonaventure, where he led the Bonnies to wins over Connecticut, Temple, and Xavier and a trip to the NIT in 2002. Those who knew VBK at Vanderbilt and have kept up with his career say he's a better coach now than when he was thrown into the maelstrom at his alma mater in 1993.

———

When Todd Turner, who had taken over from Paul Hoolahan as Vanderbilt athletic director in 1996, began his search for a replacement for van Breda Kolff in the spring of 1999, he knew what he wanted. Turner had previously served as athletic director at North Carolina State, where he couldn't help but observe how successful Mike Krzyzewski's Duke program had been in the previous decade. Turner wanted to tap in to what Krzyzewski had going on—arguably, the Blue Devils were the team of the 1990s, having won two national titles and appeared in five Final Fours in the decade. Krzyzewski assistant coaches were hot commodities.

"I was trying to find a coach that had experiences that paralleled the experiences our coach would have to deal with at Vanderbilt," Turner said. "That list is pretty short, and it's really short when you start talking about those that have had basketball success. Duke was at the top of that list. I called Mike and spent most of a day with him. I went to practice, and later we talked about what it would take to be successful at Vanderbilt. And we spoke at length about the fraternity of coaches he had developed on his staff."

The first coach Turner contacted was Delaware's Mike Brey, who had worked for Krzyzewski. Brey wasn't interested. Neither was former Duke player and assistant coach Tommy Amaker, who at the time was only two years into his career at Seton

Hall. Even though Amaker's wife had attended graduate school at Vanderbilt and he had an appreciation for the university, he felt compelled to stay put.

Turner had talks with Bob Bender, then coach at Washington and another former Duke assistant. Bender visited Nashville, but decided to stay in the Pac-10.

Getting close to the end of the short list he kept, Turner called two coaches with whom he worked at Virginia, Terry Holland and Dave Odom, even though he was sure what their answer would be. Holland was Virginia's athletic director at the time, and Odom was coaching at Wake Forest. Neither was interested.

Turner went back to Brey a second time, but his answer was the same. Quin Snyder, yet another Duke assistant, fascinated Turner. But before Turner could get too far along with Snyder—who later became the head coach at Missouri—he received a phone call that would drastically alter the course of the search.

"We have a mutual friend who called me and said, 'Why aren't you talking to Kevin?'" Turner recalled. "And I said, 'I know he's not available.' And he said, 'Don't be so sure.'"

Most people who had followed Kevin Stallings's career at Illinois State assumed his next coaching job would be at a Big Ten school. As Stallings continued to produce winning teams at Illinois State, his name had been mentioned prominently with openings at Michigan and Iowa. In 1997 the Ohio State job had apparently come down to Stallings and Jim O'Brien before the school settled on O'Brien. And there was always the possibility that Stallings could take over at Purdue when his mentor Gene Keady decided to retire.

Turner knew Stallings's background, knew that Purdue or another Big Ten school could be in his immediate future, but decided to pursue him anyway. To Turner's surprise and delight, Stallings was interested. After meeting with Stallings, Turner convinced him to visit Nashville.

"We went to Disney World complex in Orlando and stole him out of there," Turner recalled. "His family was on vacation. We later sent a plane down for them. His children have held that against me ever since because I ruined their vacation."

Turner was armed when he met Stallings a second time. He brought with him Jim Foster, then the school's women's coach. Foster had achieved a high degree of success at Vanderbilt. Turner also brought a notebook he had put together that graphically illustrated his vision for basketball. In the notebook was an artist's rendition of planned renovations to Vanderbilt's aging Memorial Gym. The results of a 1996 report of Vanderbilt's Board of Trust were also included. In that report, the board reaffirmed its commitment to competing in the SEC, and stated its intention of making basketball the flagship sport at the school, much like Duke and Wake Forest had done.

Turner's hard work paid off when Stallings accepted the job. Now Turner had to sell Vanderbilt chancellor Joe Wyatt.

"I had to convince Mr. Wyatt that Kevin was worth an investment that Vanderbilt had never made before," Turner recalled. "It was a significant sum beyond what we'd ever paid. The board supported it. And Mr. Wyatt understood it as long as we could justify it and it was market-competitive."

In looking back at his decision to leave Illinois State for Vanderbilt, Stallings recalls that Turner's offer came at the right time. The challenge of building a consistent winner at Vanderbilt intrigued him. And he didn't want to grow old waiting to take over a Big Ten program.

"As a person goes along in their life, they make decisions based on the timing of events that occur," Stallings said. "Some people might have wondered why I turned down Tennessee but came to Vanderbilt. When I was involved at Tennessee, at that time, I did not feel that was the right decision to make. Vanderbilt, for me, was a situation that very much appealed to me."

———

Hired too late to impact his new team through recruiting, Stallings took essentially the same team that finished 14-15 the season before and turned it into a winner. Leaning heavily on seniors Dan Langhi, a skinny, six-foot-eleven forward who would be chosen the SEC's player of the year, point guard Attiba Prater, and shooting guard James Strong, Stallings reversed the Commodores' fortunes in a hurry. Fourteen games into the 1999–2000 season, Vanderbilt was 12-2, its best start since the 1978–79 team went 14-2. The record caught the attention of the pollsters; Vanderbilt turned up at No. 20 in the Associated Press poll in mid January. Stallings wasn't all that impressed.

"I would like to get our program to the point where it is not a novelty-type situation to be ranked," he told *The Tennessean*.

The Commodores improved their record to 16-4 overall and 6-3 in the SEC before their season unraveled. They lost five of their last seven games, including a 72-71 home-court heartbreaker to South Carolina and former Vanderbilt coach Eddie Fogler. The Commodores won their opening-round game in the SEC Tournament, but lost to LSU the next day. That left them at 19-10 overall and 8-8 in the league. Stallings hoped that resume would be enough to attract the attention of the NCAA Tournament selection committee.

Unfortunately for Vanderbilt, Arkansas picked the right time to get hot. The Razorbacks came into the SEC Tournament needing to win the championship to earn an NCAA bid. But doing so seemed improbable—Arkansas would have to win four games in four days. When the Razorbacks did just that, it forced the tournament selection committee to take Vanderbilt off its board and replace it with Arkansas. The Commodores had to settle for the NIT.

"That was a very bitter disappointment," Stallings recalls. "I still can't rationalize it, and I've had fairly detailed explanations given to me. It's not been something I've been able to wrap my arms around. They said it was our record in our last ten games [4-6]. But those last five or six teams on the selection committee's board are all going to have blemishes. The ones that don't make it, they're going to point to your blemishes."

Unable to shake off the disappointment of the NCAA snub, the Commodores—and their coach—seemed as though they were going through the motions in a first round NIT loss to Wake Forest.

Stallings had no postseason aspirations for his second team.

"I told Todd Turner it should be the worst year we have here," Stallings said. "Because there were going to be a lot of freshman and sophomores playing. In the Southeastern Conference, that is not a recipe for success."

Defying even Stallings's expectations, the Commodores found themselves 15-7 heading into the second half of their SEC season in 2001. One or two more wins would have secured at least an NIT berth, which would have been much more welcome the second time around. To Stallings's dismay, Vanderbilt fell apart, going 1-7 in February, losing its final regular-season SEC game in March and falling to Alabama in the first round of the SEC Tournament. The Commodores finished 15-15 and couldn't even get a call from the NIT.

The collapse was particularly painful to Stallings.

"I had told Todd the second year would be our toughest," Stallings said. "Then we get our record to 15-7. I'm thinking, 'Gosh, we've got a shot to defy all odds and even my wildest expectations. And then of course we lose eight straight. That was easily the biggest disappointment, or most disappointing season, I've endured as a coach. We were on the verge of a great year."

―――

Eight years after Eddie Fogler couldn't get a phone call from his athletic director or chancellor after he'd been chosen national coach of the year, things had dramatically changed at Vanderbilt. Under the leadership of chancellor Gordon Gee and athletic director Todd Turner, sports would be emphasized as a vital part of the university. And coaches would be paid accordingly.

An unprecedented influx of private giving under Turner's watch had given Vanderbilt more operating cash. And Gee, a sports-friendly administrator who recognizes the positive publicity winning sports programs can generate, isn't afraid to spend it. Gee had a history of encouraging strong athletic programs in other stops in his career, at West Virginia, Colorado, and Ohio State.

"The best thing I can say to describe Gordon Gee's interest in athletics is to tell you about his first meeting with our alumni and friends," Turner said. "He stood up there and said winning and losing starts in the chancellor's office. And then we had to pick up about fifteen people in the back of the room who'd passed out. They'd been fans for thirty years, and they'd never heard anything like that before."

After the 2000–2001 season, Stallings's second at Vanderbilt, Gee and Turner approached the coach with an offer to tear up his old contract and significantly increase his compensation package. Stallings had been hired at about five hundred thousand dollars per year. He was stunned to hear that, even after a year in which the Commodores couldn't advance to a postseason tournament, he was offered a raise of more than two hundred thousand dollars per year and an extension through the 2005–2006 season.

"I told the chancellor, 'You know, I've not done anything to deserve what you're doing,'" Stallings recalled. "And he said, 'Just consider this an investment in the future.' That kind of forward thinking makes me excited to be here and makes me be excited to be a part of this program. [Gee and Turner] have been people of action. Their actions have backed up their words. They've said winning is important, and we're going to try to help you win. That's what means something to me."

Turner recalls trying to be proactive when dealing with Stallings.

"I went to the chancellor and said, 'We've got a great basketball coach here. We need to do something to keep him at Vanderbilt, or else people will think they can steal him,'" Turner said. "Gordon said, 'Let's do what we need to do.' So we tore up Kevin's contract."

In addition to Stallings's salary and those of his assistant coaches—Tim Jankovich is one of the SEC's highest-paid—Vanderbilt has devoted considerable funding to other aspects of the program, including a twenty-five million dollar renovation of venerable Memorial Gym. The coaching staff previously had to walk the equivalent of two city blocks to get to the gym. Now, their state-of-the-art offices are in Memorial with a perfect view of the floor. A practice facility has been added, meaning the Commodores no longer have to worry about a conflict for court time.

Matt Freije. *Neil Blake/Vanderbilt Athletic Media Relations*

When Stallings discusses the support he's received, he thinks back to a conversation he had with another SEC coach.

"Without naming names, I've had another league coach tell me you can't win a national championship at Vanderbilt," Stallings said. "But I don't believe under any circumstances it can't be done here. Don't get me wrong—winning the national championship is hard at any school. But I'll go back to when Eddie Fogler won the SEC championship here in 1993. If you win this league, you're good enough to win the national championship, because the SEC is as good as any league in the country."

Stallings knows Vanderbilt's chances to win the national title won't come along often. And though he holds up Duke and Stanford—strong academic institutions that have won national championships and appeared in Final Fours—as examples of what can be accomplished, his goals are reasonable.

"A lot of things have to go right," Stallings said. "You have to be the recipient of some breaks along the way. But I think this program is capable of winning this league. Now, do I think we're going to do it every year? Heck no. Do I think we should do it every year? Heck no. But I do think we should be able to elevate this program to the point where we're an NCAA Tournament team on a regular basis. Yeah, I really think that."

That belief has made Stallings content, happy to be where he is, and not necessarily looking to move. Some Vanderbilt fans live in fear that Stallings will eventually return to his Big Ten roots. But Stallings seems in no hurry to leave.

"I'm happy to be past that stage where I was sort of the flavor of the month, where jobs would come open and my name would always be mentioned," Stallings said. "That was not a comfortable time for me. I'm not your average guy. My thoughts aren't the same. I'm not saying most people are opportunists, but I certainly am not. I'm very happy here. I'm expected to say I'm thrilled to be at Vanderbilt, but I am thrilled to be at Vanderbilt and thrilled with my perception of how the program is moving."

Stallings has moved the program along by turning what many perceive to be a negative aspect of coaching at Vanderbilt into a positive aspect. Some believe recruiting to an institution with the academic standards of Vanderbilt is next to impossible. In truth, the talent base Stallings and his staff can draw from is considerably smaller than that of the eleven other SEC schools. But Stallings has learned to live with working a smaller number of recruits than his opponents each year. And he's embraced the benefits of recruiting to Vanderbilt.

"I enjoy recruiting here because we don't have to deal with the bad elements of recruiting," Stallings said. "And there are some bad elements in the recruiting process. We have to deal with next to none of that. Because we're not going to attract a kid with his hand out. We're not going to get a kid who's looking to be bought or his coach is on the take. If he's surrounded by bad influences or whatever I consider to be negative, the kid won't even consider us. Hallelujah, because that's not the guy we're trying to recruit. That's not the kind of guy we have to recruit.

"We have got good kids who are good players. Eventually we'll have enough of them to where we're impacting some of the things that are going on in this league."

————

Stallings knew his prediction that Vanderbilt could become a perennial NCAA Tournament wouldn't begin to come true in the 2001–2002 season. After having spent two years in Nashville and seen the state of his program and the difficulty of competing in the SEC, he knew there was still work a lot of work to do.

"I think the one thing I underestimated was the length of time it takes to change the course of a program at a school like Vanderbilt," Stallings said. "You go to a school like Illinois State, and one class can turn it around because you can recruit a couple of junior college players. It's a different thing here. You can't do it that way. Kentucky loses Tayshaun Prince and goes out and signs an Antwain Barbour [one of the nation's top junior college recruits in 2001–2002]. We've got a glaring hole, we've got to get a high school kid to come here and fill in."

Stallings's third season began on an ominous note. On October 19, 2001, Stallings announced that sophomore Billy Richmond had been dismissed from the team. The stock explanation was a "violation of team rules." Stallings didn't elaborate, but team insiders said Richmond had an annoying habit of defying authority. Suffice to say that didn't sit well with Stallings.

The loss of Richmond was a blow to the Commodores. Or rather, the loss of a Richmond who was willing to buy into Stallings's program was a blow. Richmond had been a breakthrough recruit for Vanderbilt, the first player from talent-rich Memphis to sign with the school in seventeen years.

When Richmond signed, Stallings hoped other talented Memphis players might follow, and it wasn't unreasonable to suggest there were more high school players in the Memphis area that could fit Vanderbilt's criteria. In the fall of 2001, Derrick Byars, a six-foot-seven top-fifty player from Memphis Ridgeway High School, signed with Virginia. The Vanderbilt staff tried hard to recruit him and had a home visit set, but after his visit to Charlottesville, Byars was sold on leaving the state.

Properly motivated, Richmond had a chance to be a special player. He labored

302

through an inconsistent freshman season, but was capable of playing three positions and had been Vanderbilt's best athlete. From a physical standpoint at least, he would be hard to replace. Richmond eventually resurfaced at Memphis.

Another potential problem was the health of sophomore point guard Russell Lakey, who broke a bone in his right foot in late summer. Though he took part in preseason practice, Lakey's status was questionable.

Just days after cutting loose Richmond, Stallings was realistic when assessing the Commodores' chances.

"The rational truth is we're still a year away," Stallings said. "We have eight freshmen and sophomores out of eleven players. And we have no juniors."

Stallings knew his young team would be inconsistent, so he didn't put the Commodores through an overly demanding nonconference schedule. The results were fairly predictable. Vanderbilt lost at Connecticut and Tulane, but won all its home games, including an early December game against nationally ranked Western Kentucky played in Nashville's new downtown arena. The Commodores got lucky in that game and didn't have to face seven-foot-one, 290-pound All-American Chris Marcus, who had just gone down with a stress fracture in his foot.

Vanderbilt finished its nonconference season at 10-3, the lone puzzling loss coming against Monmouth in the Hawaii Pacific Honolulu Classic.

The momentum of three straight nonconference wins didn't carry over to 2002 and SEC play. The Commodores lost three straight league games to Georgia, Alabama, and Florida, running their frustrating SEC losing streak to twelve games, dating back to 2001.

Vanderbilt finally ended the streak with a home-court win over Auburn, then pulled two consecutive mild surprises by winning at South Carolina and beating nationally ranked Georgia at home. Two straight losses ended that brief run of success, and after a win over LSU, the Commodores' season nearly bottomed out with four straight losses.

Once again, February had not been kind to Vanderbilt. The four-game losing streak, coupled with February collapses the two previous seasons, left some Vanderbilt fans doubting whether Stallings was capable of getting his teams to peak at the right time. But the Commodores answered the critics, stealing a critical win at Tennessee and then upsetting No. 11 Kentucky, 86-73. The win broke a nine-year, eighteen-game losing streak against the Wildcats.

After the regular season ended with a loss at Arkansas, Stallings gave a candid assessment. The Commodores had finished 16-13 overall and 6-10 in the SEC.

"Our season was predictable in the fact it was very unpredictable," Stallings said.

"Consistently inconsistent. I mean that seriously. With a team as young as ours, they're going to play at high levels and low levels. And that's what we did. I wish I was a better coach than that and could have coached them away from that. But I couldn't get that done."

Stallings might have been a little harsh. One reason the Commodores were inconsistent was the fact they had to live and die by the jump shot. Without an experienced low-post scoring threat or the presence of Lakey, who re-injured his foot three times and was healthy only the last five games of the season, Vanderbilt had no choice but to fire away from the perimeter.

"If your big guys can command a double team and you have one or two perimeter guys who can consistently break down people off the dribble, then you're a good offensive team," Jankovich said. "But we're not there yet. We have to execute offense, find good shots, and knock down jump shots all night to win games. When we do that, we've beaten the best. But it doesn't happen every night."

Vanderbilt did begin to develop the kind of players who could eventually give the Commodores a balanced offense. Freshman Brian Thornton showed signs of becoming a solid contributor at power forward, and freshman Corey Smith proved capable of finding his own shot. Like Lakey, David

Vanderbilt
All-SEC Expansion Era Team

F-Dan Langhi

F-Matt Freije

C-Chris Lawson

G Ronnie McMahan

G-Billy McCaffrey

Top Reserves-Bruce Elder, Frank Seckar

Przybyszewski, the player Jankovich had traveled so far to see, also battled foot problems but gave indications he could become a consistent scorer. Sophomore Matt Freije, who had been chosen to the SEC's All-Freshman team the year before, continued to fine-tune his emerging game, leading the Commodores in scoring and rebounding.

Stallings couldn't help but wonder how much difference a healthy Lakey might have made.

"Russell's injury was damaging, sure, because he's a guy who controls our tempo," Stallings said. "He controls our pace. He's our best on-the-ball defender. Everything you want in a good point guard, Russ is, and we played without him most of the year."

Lakey reentered the starting lineup with three games to play, just in time to help the Commodores salvage their season. Unlike the year before, Vanderbilt did what it had to do in the stretch run to secure a postseason tournament bid.

Some Vanderbilt fans were happy with the NIT and others weren't, pointing to three straight years without NCAA Tournament bids. Turner, the man Stallings has to please first and foremost, saw progress.

"Our strategic plan has been to invest first and foremost in the sport of basketball," Turner said. "We thought it was do-able. Duke and Wake Forest have done it, and our tradition in basketball shows it's possible here. I think Kevin is right on task. It's a process. It's not going to happen overnight. Kevin has to build this program around his personality. We're excited about the way he's going about it."

Chapter Thirteen

SEC Tournament

N olan Richardson was gone but not forgotten.
The ouster of the long-time Arkansas coach the week before was still the hot topic of conversation as the eight SEC teams that had to play first-round tournament games gathered at the Georgia Dome on March 6, 2002, for practice and press conferences. To a man, the eight coaches expressed shock and sadness that Richardson, whose program was a central figure in the SEC's rise to prominence, was now out of the league. Some wondered whether Richardson, at sixty, would have the inclination or the energy to take another job.

The media was a little less surprised at Richardson's sudden demise. It was during a press conference, after all, that Richardson's scathing diatribe against sports writers, discrimination, Arkansas fans, and the school's administration was unleashed for the world to see. And if the world was stunned to hear Richardson talk about how he was treated differently than other Arkansas coaches because he's black, the media wasn't. Long-time SEC beat writers had witnessed Richardson's rants before.

"Nolan didn't say anything he hadn't always said," said Ray Melick, a columnist for the *Birmingham Post-Herald*. "I think the university didn't like to hear it, and if they were looking for a way to get rid of him, Nolan provided it for them."

"Nolan was a good coach," said *Memphis Commercial-Appeal* reporter Ron Higgins. "A hall-of-fame coach. But he never got over the fact that he didn't think other people believed that. Any time he got criticized, and he got criticized very rarely, he'd play the race card, and he usually used national tournaments and national forums to bring it out. This time, it did him in."

Tim Brando, who does play-by-play of SEC games for CBS and Jefferson-Pilot, thought Richardson had no ulterior motive when he began his fateful press conference, and that Richardson's emotions and frustrations got the better of him.

"I'm of the belief that when he started that press conference, he had one comment to make about an article regarding recruiting that he thought was negative. But once he got started, he couldn't stop himself," Brando said. "I know him well enough to think that he had no idea where he was going with those comments."

When Jerry Tipton of the *Lexington Herald-Leader* heard about Richardson's blowup with the press, his first thought was a comment Rick Pitino had made when he was coaching at Kentucky. "A lot of coaches think if you stay in the same place too long, the worm turns," Tipton said. "I think that's one reason why Rick Pitino left Kentucky [for the Boston Celtics]. He had been there long enough and he sort of knew—I'd heard him say—that you can overstay your welcome. Everybody's heard your stories and they're tired of you. They need a new flavor."

———

Who would be the new flavor at Arkansas? When the media got wind of a rumor that it could be Ole Miss coach Rod Barnes, he was swarmed as he tried to get his team on the practice floor.

"I'll never say never," Barnes said when asked about the Arkansas job. "I don't expect Ole Miss to say never. If we're not making progress, if I'm not doing things to represent the university in a class manner, they should get rid of me. So I'll never say never."

The media probed further. Had Barnes been contacted?

"All I can say is that's speculation," he said.

Does that mean you'd like to get a phone call?

"It's speculation."

If Barnes was a candidate to replace Richardson, it wasn't difficult to see why. Carrying on a trend that began at Ole Miss under his boss, Rob Evans, Barnes had helped lead the Rebels to ten wins in their last twelve games against Arkansas.

As Ole Miss sports information director Lamar Chance pulled him away from the media pack, Barnes headed to practice with a final thought for the media.

"Mike Anderson is the coach at the University of Arkansas at this present time," Barnes said. "As long as he's the coach of Arkansas, there's no vacancy. And as long as there's no vacancy, I don't have a comment."

———

Mike Anderson came to Atlanta hoping to win a job. Earlier in the week, Arkansas athletic director Frank Broyles told reporters that if Anderson were to lead the Razorbacks to four wins in as many days and bring home the SEC Tournament title and the NCAA Tournament berth that went with it, the job was his.

Anderson had patiently waited for years for such an opportunity. His dream had been to eventually replace Richardson, and Richardson desperately wanted his protégé to succeed him. But Anderson never thought his big break would eventually come at the expense of Richardson.

"You don't get a whole lot of sleep," Anderson said when asked about the days immediately following Richardson's firing. "This is something I have been looking forward to, but under these circumstances, it's bittersweet."

Nevertheless, Anderson was prepared to show Broyles and Arkansas fans that he was the right man to replace his mentor. The prospect of winning four straight games was daunting, but Anderson was ready for the challenge.

"All eyes are really on me now," Anderson said during his pre-tournament press conference. "But that is no problem. I can handle eyes being on me."

What Anderson and the Razorbacks couldn't handle was Tennessee. The two teams would play the second game of the afternoon session on Thursday, March 7. LSU had beaten Vanderbilt in the first game in a battle of two teams trying to solidify their chances for an NIT bid. The Tigers won, but as it turned out, Vanderbilt got the better end of the deal. When NIT pairings were announced three days later, it was the Commodores, not LSU, who received a home game in the first round.

Tennessee, too, had come to the SEC Tournament with the NIT in mind. Considering the travails that had plagued the Vols in coach Buzz Peterson's first season, making the NIT field would have been a real accomplishment. But even though postseason play meant everything to his team, Peterson was wary of Arkansas. The Razorbacks were on a mission.

For almost thirty-six minutes, the Razorbacks played one of their best games of the season. Looking like the Hogs of old, they harassed Tennessee into turnovers and attacked the basket with abandon. Rather than settling for jump shots, as it had during the latter stages of the regular season, Arkansas worked for high-percentage shots. With 8:44 to play, the Razorbacks led, 50-42. Tennessee star Marcus Haislip was on the bench with four fouls, and it seemed as though Arkansas would bring home the first of the four wins Anderson needed to take the interim tag off his title.

That wasn't to be. When Haislip returned, the Vols switched to their high-low offense. In the low post, Haislip had been held in check with the Razorbacks' double-teaming. At the high post, he could catch the ball and make things happen. In a two-minute span, Haislip scored twice and passed to Brandon Crump for another basket. Haislip's second basket gave the Vols a 55-53 lead with 3:34 to play, and they hung on the rest of the way for the win.

After the game, Arkansas's locker room was a dreary place. But the Razorbacks were unanimous and vocal in their support of Mike Anderson.

"Mike Anderson's the man for the job," said T. J. Cleveland, though no one expected a different opinion from him. Anderson is his uncle.

"Mr. Broyles said if we won the SEC championship, the job was coach Anderson's," said freshman J. J. Sullinger. "But I believe the job already is. I'm not thinking any other way. But if hell freezes over and he doesn't get it, then I'll have to look seriously at my future."

In the day's final two games, Florida, seeded No. 3 from the Eastern Division, took out Auburn, the sixth-seeded team from the West. That was expected. What wasn't expected was South Carolina's 69-67 upset of Ole Miss.

Unbeknownst to all but the Gamecocks, first-year coach Dave Odom had challenged his talented but underachieving low-post tandem of sophomore Rolando Howell and junior Tony Kitchings. South Carolina had been guard-oriented much of the year, understandable considering the guards were senior Jamel Bradley, the school's all-time leader in three-point goals, and the dependable Aaron Lucas. But as the season progressed, Odom decided that the Gamecocks wouldn't get any better if their big men didn't come to the fore.

Kitchings looked like a changed man as he attacked the Ole Miss defense with jump hooks and strong post moves. He scored 16 points and grabbed nine rebounds as the defensive-minded Rebels had no answer for him. Howell chipped in with nine points.

"Dave just got in their faces and challenged them," said South Carolina assistant Ernie Nestor. "We asked Rolando if he wanted to play in the NBA some day. He said yes. We told him there aren't too many guys getting drafted who average 8.5 points a game."

"I should have had my butt kicked for waiting so long [to inspire Howell and Kitchings]," Odom said. "But that's my fault. It's not theirs. Tony Kitchings is the one guy on our team that can make a difference. If he plays, then we've got a chance to be a good basketball team. If he doesn't, we'll just be mediocre."

———

LSU came into the SEC Tournament with nothing to lose. After squeezing out sixteen regular-season wins, the Tigers had all but assured themselves of an NIT bid. With that in hand, they locked in on a bigger prize—the NCAA Tournament berth that came with winning the SEC Tournament. A remarkable win over Georgia on Friday brought LSU two steps closer to its goal.

Those two steps were attained only after LSU center Brad Bridgewater took one step—one extra step—on his way to a win-securing slam dunk with fourteen seconds to play. The basket put LSU ahead, 78-74, but luckily for the Tigers, no one wearing a striped shirt noticed Bridgewater's fancy footwork.

"He walked," LSU guard Antonio Hudson told the *Baton Rouge Advocate*. "I was right behind him. He stopped dribbling. It looked like the NBA. But I figured the ref wasn't going to call anything, because it was close and it happened so fast."

"It was a close call," Bridgewater told the *Advocate*. "Some of my teammates said I walked. But I wasn't even thinking about that. I just wanted to make sure I didn't miss the shot."

After Bridgewater's dunk, Georgia guard Rashad Wright, the hero in Georgia's win at LSU only thirteen days before, made a lay-up that cut the margin to 78-76. Then, after LSU reserve point guard Charlie Thompson threw away the ensuing in-bounds pass, the Bulldogs' Ezra Williams got fouled and went to the line for two shots.

Williams missed the first shot, then intentionally missed the second, hoping one of his teammates could rebound the ball and score. But it wasn't to be. LSU survived 78-76.

LSU coach John Brady was elated with the win, and he was also pleased with another trend that continued in the SEC Tournament. Antonio Hudson was becoming a scoring machine. He scored a career-high twenty-four against the Bulldogs after getting twenty-three the day before against Vanderbilt.

For the second straight year, Georgia had been knocked out of the first round of the tournament by LSU. It was the fourth straight year the Bulldogs lost their first game. As disappointed as he was, Georgia coach Jim Harrick wasn't going to dwell on the loss. The Bulldogs' NCAA Tournament berth was already secure.

———

For much of the SEC season, Alabama forward Rod Grizzard's jump shot had been AWOL. In one dizzying stretch against Tennessee, it resurfaced with a vengeance.

The six-foot-eight Grizzard has a tantalizing game, one that attracted the attention of NBA scouts as early as his sophomore season. But the knock on Grizzard is his shooting touch. Grizzard is the ultimate streak shooter. "He can shoot you in games," said one NBA scout. "But he can also shoot you out of them."

On this day, it was Tennessee that Grizzard shot out of the game. If anyone was due to have a shooting performance for the ages, it was Grizzard, who didn't make a three-pointer in seven of the Crimson Tide's last eight regular-season games and shot 14 percent from three-point range in sixteen SEC games. In February, Grizzard was one for 23 from three-point range.

310

Mario Austin. *teamcoyle*

Tennessee coach Buzz Peterson had seen all those numbers, and given that Alabama's Erwin Dudley, the SEC's Player of the Year, was a much more consistent low-post scorer, the Vols' defensive strategy was to make sure he didn't go off. That meant a defender sneaking away from Grizzard to double down on Dudley.

"I probably wouldn't have guarded myself after that month," Grizzard said.

Given Grizzard's slump and Tennessee's defensive strategy, it was perhaps an ominous sign that Grizzard hit his first three-pointer of the game, with 17:49 to play in the first half. After that Grizzard was quiet for a while, but with the Tide holding on to a 24-19 lead, he took control of the game.

With 7:24 left in the half, Grizzard struck from the right wing, knocking down a twenty-two-foot three-pointer. In the next 1:30, Grizzard drained three more from behind the arc, pushing Alabama's lead to 36-19. He wasn't through. With 4:53 left, Grizzard tossed into a fifth three-pointer with the Vols' Marcus Haislip hanging all over him. Grizzard was fouled and hit the free throw for a four-point play.

When the carnage was over, Grizzard had scored 16 points in two minutes and thirty-one seconds. Alabama led, 40-19, and the game was essentially over. Grizzard scored 27 points in the first half, and, his damage already done, came back to score six in the second for a career-high 33.

Afterward, Grizzard talked about what it felt like to be in the zone.

"It's kinda quiet," he said. "Basically, you just catch and shoot. If you look down, you'll be contested [defensively] and won't get to shoot it. So when you're feeling it, you just put it up."

"You saw the real Rod Grizzard tonight," Alabama point guard Mo Williams said. "I've got other teammates, but if I see him pop open even for a split second, I'm going to try to let him touch it at least. If he gives it back I'll go somewhere else, but he gets the first option."

Still smarting from the 92-71 loss that ended his team's season, Peterson said Grizzard's outburst had a familiar look. "I was thinking that was M. J. [Michael Jordan]," Peterson said. "Once a guy like that gets in a zone, there's not much you do with them."

———

In the days before the SEC Tournament, Mississippi State coach Rick Stansbury embarked on a quest. Despite a five-game winning streak to end the regular season, the Bulldogs, in Stansbury's opinion, hadn't been given the proper respect by the media. State was nowhere to be seen in the major polls, even though it had a 23-7 record and was No. 11 in the RPI rankings.

That snub by the pollsters became a rallying cry for a team that had been picked to finish last in the SEC's Western Division. If few people outside of Starkville, Mississippi, knew that the Bulldogs were for real, Stansbury reasoned, the SEC Tournament was the perfect forum to gain a few converts.

"We knew coming in here we had a good basketball team," Stansbury said. "We'd won five in a row, six of our last seven and seven out of ten. No one else in our league had done that. Our goal is to win this tournament."

To do that, the Bulldogs had to get past their quarterfinal game against Florida. Though they had finished second in the SEC's Western Division and earned a first-round bye, Florida, the third-seeded team from the East, was considered the favorite. Even Stansbury thought the Gators were the best team in the league. He had formed that opinion after doing the proper field research—a month earlier, Florida pounded State by 28 points in Gainesville.

Stansbury and his staff stressed to the Bulldogs that defense was the way to beat Florida, and their advice was well taken. Mississippi State held the normally high-scoring Gators to 31 percent shooting and 52 points, their second-lowest total in coach Billy Donovan's six seasons. Udonis Haslem and Matt Bonner, the Gators' two leading scorers, were held to just seven points each, and Haslem put up a mere five shots. Meanwhile, Florida guards Brett Nelson and Justin Hamilton were a combined nine for 26 from the field.

Though State shot just 37 percent, the 62 points it scored were more than enough for a win that spoke volumes.

"This was a statement," Stansbury said after the game.

South Carolina was ready to make a statement of its own in the final game of the tournament's second day. The Gamecocks had lost twelve straight games to Kentucky, including a one-point home-court heartbreaker in the regular season. That loss and two others in the closing seconds to Georgia and Alabama had probably cost the Gamecocks an at-large bid to the NCAA Tournament. That left them no choice. If they wanted to play in the Big Dance, they had to win the SEC Tournament. And to do that, they would have to get past the tournament's darling, Kentucky.

The Wildcats, seeded No. 2 from the Eastern Division, had fashioned an impressive 9-1 record in the SEC Tournament in coach Tubby Smith's five seasons. Three times under Smith's watch, Kentucky had won the tournament. In the previous ten years, the Wildcats had won the tournament eight times.

But the team that Smith brought to Atlanta was hardly the confident group that had taken the floor in previous SEC Tournaments. Beset with internal problems, the

Wildcats were susceptible to being taken out. Though "Team Turmoil," as the media had been calling Kentucky, was ranked No. 12 in the country and had earned a share of the SEC East's regular-season championship with Georgia and Florida, it was a fragile group. The last thing the Wildcats needed was more distractions.

But that's exactly what the Wildcats had to deal with. Adam Chiles, the freshman point guard that Smith had railed on during an ESPN-televised game against Tennessee in February, was left in Lexington after being suspended for a second time in three games. And Gerald Fitch, who had endured a rough couple of weeks after getting suspended twice, was—unbeknownst to even Brooks Downing, Kentucky's sports information director—not going to play, suspended this time for missing curfew the night before.

Once again getting an assertive effort from big men Tony Kitchings and Rolando Howell, the Gamecocks took the fight to Kentucky early. South Carolina led 35-27 after a first half that saw the Wildcats shoot 28 percent from the field and miss all nine three-pointers they attempted.

Things got worse in the second half. Amid cries of "We want Fitch," from the five thousand or so Kentucky fans in attendance, the Wildcats fell behind by as many as 18 points. Kentucky wouldn't make its first three-pointer of the game until Tayshaun Prince connected with 3:56 to play. By that time, the outcome had long since been decided.

Behind six players in double figures, South Carolina pulled off a 70-57 win, becoming the first sixth-seeded team in the expanded SEC Tournament's eleven-year history to reach the semifinals.

As Smith and his team walked through a tunnel in the Georgia Dome to get to their locker room, fans rained down boos, curses, and insults on them. "It was so loud, you could barely make out what they were saying," said a radio reporter from Alabama. "It reminded me of [football coach] Mike Dubose's last game at Alabama."

Elsewhere in the building, a group of Kentucky fans chanted, "We want Nolan."

In the post-game press conference, an exasperated Smith told the media Fitch didn't play because of a coach's decision, but it was later learned the player had been caught in roommate Marquis Estill's room after curfew.

"We've played through a lot of things," Smith said. "There has been a lot of turmoil and distractions. Gerald is a big part of our team and a big part of our twenty wins. We've certainly had some things go on. It does tear a team apart. We have to be focused on the same thing."

Kentucky players and South Carolina coach Dave Odom were in agreement that Fitch's suspension had played a part in the loss.

314

"Gerald Fitch not playing was big factor," Odom said. "He hurt us as much as anybody in the last game. I'm not saying we couldn't have won with him playing, but he is a big key."

"We needed him out there," Prince said. "Especially when I had two fouls. We needed him in there in the first half to contribute."

"This is not the time in the season for this stuff to happen," said guard J. P. Blevins. "There has to be a bond and some cohesiveness."

———

If Kentucky wasn't the cohesive, finely tuned machine it usually is in March, there was a new team around to take its place. Mississippi State entered Saturday's semifinal game against LSU still on its appointed mission to show the SEC and the rest of the country it could play.

This one wouldn't be easy. The Tigers of fiery coach John Brady had been the last team to beat the Bulldogs, erasing a 15-point second-half deficit and claiming an overtime victory three weeks before. Stansbury knew the game would come down to the final minutes.

The game wasn't textbook by any means, but by this time the Bulldogs were priding themselves on the fact they could turn a game ugly with their defense. LSU, which all season had been prodded and cajoled by Brady to play beyond its personnel limitations, was equal to the task.

Neither team could build much of a lead, and with 3:27 to play the score was tied at 51. Mario Austin's two free throws with fifty-eight seconds left gave Mississippi State a 53-51 lead. That's when things got interesting.

On LSU's in-bounds play, the Tigers' Jermaine Williams passed the ball to point guard Torris Bright. The Bulldogs' Derek Zimmerman slapped it out of Bright's hands and out of bounds. The officials ruled it touched Bright last. Suffice to say Brady wasn't pleased.

"On that play, Torris Bright was going backwards," Brady told the *Baton Rouge Advocate*. "And the ball goes that way? And we knock it out of bounds? I've never seen something like that. Sounds like a defiance of gravity. My guy goes this way and the ball goes that way, but we knock it out of bounds? That's a phenomenon. But you can write that the play didn't work."

After the Bulldogs regained possession, they went ahead 55-51 on Marckell Patterson's lay-up. Five seconds later, Zimmerman sealed State's seventh straight win with a steal.

"When things are not going very well offensively, you're struggling a little bit, you've got to find a way to make basketball plays," Stansbury said. "Those steals in the last minute of the game really changed the outcome."

In the second game of the day, Rod Grizzard's shooting touch returned to its February form, but a new hero stepped up for Alabama. Kenny Walker scored 21 points as the Crimson Tide held off South Carolina, 65-57, but the game was marred by some poor officiating in the final minute.

With thirty seconds to play and the score tied at 57, South Carolina had the ball and a chance to score the winning basket. But when the Gamecocks' Chuck Eidson collided with Alabama guard Mo Williams and fell to the floor, no call was made, even though television replays showed Williams clung on to Eidson for a second or two, preventing him from bouncing up quickly.

Meanwhile, the ball popped loose and was picked up by Grizzard, who tossed it to Antoine Pettway, who went streaking downcourt for an apparent lay-up. But South Carolina's Aaron Lucas caught up with Pettway and slapped the ball loose. Referee Anthony Jordan blew his whistle to indicate he had called a foul on Lucas.

Inexplicably, the play was allowed to continue. Walker gathered Pettway's miss and jammed it home. Another official, Tom Lopes, blew his whistle and called a foul on South Carolina's Carlos Powell, who had been trailing the play.

That prompted a huddle among Jordan, Lopes, and the third official, Andre Patillo. Lopes's call was allowed to stand, and Alabama led 60-57. Powell missed a three-pointer that would have tied the game with eighteen seconds to play, and the Tide secured the win at the free throw line.

South Carolina coach Dave Odom was as diplomatic as he could be in the post-game press conference.

"[Patillo] communicated to me that a foul had occurred before the whistle," Odom said. Odom couldn't explain why Walker's dunk was allowed to count.

"I have a hard time with that one," he said. "I'm sure [the officials] are right. I hope they're right. I'd probably feel a lot better about it if they were."

Odom didn't feel very well after John Guthrie, the SEC's director of officials, reviewed the game tape. Steve Wiseman of *The State* reported the next day that Guthrie told Odom two incorrect calls had been made. A foul should have been called on Williams for holding back Eidson. And even if that one wasn't called, Walker's game-winning basket shouldn't have counted, because Lucas had fouled Pettway first.

"[Guthrie] was very concerned about the way things were handled," Odom told *The State*. "The one thing we agreed upon is the whole situation was regrettable, at best. We also agreed that we always want to see the game decided by the players and not the officials."

———

Alabama's win set up a compelling championship game between two teams that battle nearly as much off the court as they do on it.

"We're playing against what we consider our greatest rival," Stansbury said. "Our fans might think it's Ole Miss. But we go head-to-head in recruiting more with Alabama."

Because of that head-to-head recruiting, there's no love lost between Stansbury and Gottfried. "I think it's safe to say we won't be going out to dinner any time soon," Stansbury said. "But you can put all twelve [SEC] coaches in a room, and I don't guess anybody would say they love all of them. There may be respect, but there's no love."

Gottfried demonstrated what Stansbury was talking about before Alabama and Mississippi State tipped off in Sunday's championship game. Rather than offer a chilly, blow-by handshake, Gottfried stopped to tell Stansbury he thought the Bulldogs would make an impact in the NCAA Tournament.

"I really meant it," Gottfried said after the game. "I told him I really believe they have the potential to go deep into the tournament."

The championship game was the season's rubber match between the two teams. Each had taken no prisoners on their home courts, Alabama winning 85-73 in Tuscaloosa and State winning 76-62 in Starkville. Though Alabama won the Western Division, had been ranked all season, and had gotten considerably more attention from the media, the Tide and Bulldogs were similar in a lot of respects and fairly evenly matched. Both had a quality post player. Both had good, athletic guards. And both prided themselves on their aggressive, man-to-man defense.

Mississippi State led throughout the first half, stretching its lead to 30-20 on a pair of Mario Austin free throws with 4:28 to play. But Alabama cut the deficit to five by halftime and kept chipping away at the lead in the second half until finally going ahead, 45-44, with 9:30 to play. The Tide led until Timmy Bowers drained a three-pointer to give State a 54-52 advantage with 3:52 left.

Derek Zimmerman's three with 2:13 to play increased the Bulldogs advantage to 57-52, but Alabama wasn't finished. Rod Grizzard's two free throws with forty-nine seconds left brought the Tide to within one at 59-58.

Zimmerman gave the Tide a chance to win the game when he missed the front end of a one-and-one with twenty-four seconds to play. Mo Williams went for the kill with a three-point try from the left wing, but he missed and State's Michael Gholar grabbed the rebound.

Gholar was fouled by Erwin Dudley and made the two free throws for a 61-58 lead. The victory was sealed when Zimmerman stripped Williams of the ball at halfcourt.

As the final horn sounded, the Bulldogs mobbed one another in jubilation. For Mario Austin, the victory was particularly sweet. As he took the court on Sunday, Alabama fans greeted him with a chorus of "Sellout. Sellout." They hadn't forgotten Austin's decision to spurn the Tide and sign with Mississippi State.

"That makes it so sweet," said Austin, who finished with 15 points and eight rebounds and was chosen the tournament MVP. "I didn't let what they said bother me. But I put it in the back of my mind. And I just let it all out when we played the game. I figured I'd make their team pay. And show them what they missed out on."

Stansbury, who some thought had begun the season with his job in jeopardy, didn't conjure up the anger he felt when he was said to be on the "hot seat," in some pre-season publications. In his shining hour, he reached out to family. Stansbury's wife, Meo, who would give birth to the couple's second child a month later, brought Stansbury their two-year old son, Isaac. From the ribbon-cutting ceremony to the Bulldogs' post-game press conference, the youngster rested quietly in his father's arms, all the while sporting a hat emblazoned with the words "SEC Champions" and the State logo.

"I keep him with me, win or lose," Stansbury said. "Because when we lose, momma doesn't talk to me. This boy will talk to me."

As the Bulldogs cut down the nets on the Georgia Dome floor, Stansbury saved the last snip for his seventy-one-year-old father, Robert. The elder Stansbury was battling cancer, but had traveled with his son most of the season.

"I love my team to death," Stansbury said. "But I'll never forget family. My son and my wife. And my father. He's going through a lot right now. He's fighting for his life. So to see him [cut the net] was the most special thing for me."

Tears were welling in Stansbury's eyes as he tried to compose himself.

"Nothing means more to me than that," he said. "Nothing. I'm where I'm at because of my mother and father, the work ethic they gave me. I can remember a lot of hours in barns, hanging tobacco. At the time, I didn't like it. But I wish everybody could go through it. It makes you appreciate some other things about life."

Stansbury might have his detractors in the league, those who would question everything he does from recruiting to coaching. But few could argue his work ethic. For seventeen years, he'd paid his dues as an assistant. In his fourth year as a head coach, the prize he'd coveted—an SEC championship—was his.

"This is a tremendous win for assistant coaches," said Mississippi State assistant Phil Cunningham. "Sometimes assistants get labeled as recruiters and they never get considered for head-coaching jobs. To see Rick the way he's evolved, everything he's been through as an assistant, building this program. He's proven that he learned something when he was working for some great coaches. He took all he could, put his own style in, and molded it all together. And now he's won the SEC Tournament."

"As an assistant, you see all sides of it," Stansbury said. "I came up through the trenches and the ditches. I learned to work and do a lot of different things at a lot of different levels. This wasn't something I walked into my first year."

In the losing team's locker room, Gottfried and his players didn't try to mask their disappointment. But in a few hours, their mood would change dramatically. When the NCAA Tournament pairings were announced, their one-year mission to gain the respect of the selection committee would be fulfilled.

Epilogue

C oming as it did on the heels of the regular season and just before postseason play, the firing of Nolan Richardson very nearly overshadowed March Madness, at least as far as the Southeastern Conference was concerned.

As promised, Richardson didn't go away quietly after his March 1, 2002, dismissal. Richardson contested the decision by Arkansas chancellor John White and athletic director Frank Broyles in the hope it would be overturned by Alan Sugg, president of the University of Arkansas system.

The appeal process delayed Arkansas' search for a new coach as Sugg took his time, sifting through hundreds of pages of documents in Richardson's personnel file and interviewing more than a dozen people. Sugg's decision, outlined to Richardson in a detailed letter, was released to the media on March 21.

"Based on my review, I am firmly convinced that the termination of your Employment Agreement by John White in consultation with Frank Broyles was legal and fair," Sugg wrote. "I find no evidence of discriminatory conduct or motive in the making of this decision by John White and Frank Broyles."

With that, Broyles was free to begin looking for a basketball coach. He knew the search would be important, for in the final season of Richardson's seventeen-year tenure at Arkansas, the program had slipped significantly.

Despite the challenge facing Richardson's replacement to restore Arkansas basketball to its previous high level in a league as tough as the SEC, there was no shortage of candidates. Broyles quickly appointed a search committee and began interviewing. Former Richardson assistant coach Mike Anderson was granted the first interview, as promised. Arkansas-Little Rock coach Porter Moser was given a courtesy interview. Tim Floyd's name was mentioned prominently, but the former Chicago Bulls, Iowa State, and New Orleans coach declined to interview. So did Kansas assistant coach Neil Dougherty, who had already been offered the top job at TCU.

Broyles had plans to take key members of his committee to the Final Four in Atlanta, but those plans were changed in late March when Kent State coach Stan Heath was interviewed. On March 28, Broyles stood before the media and a room full of Arkansas fans to announce Heath's hiring.

"Coaching is dealing with people," Broyles said at the press conference. "Coaching is motivating and teaching. Coaching is persuading and convincing, and this coach has been a part of this sport at the very highest level. So we have a coach here who can continue the great traditions of Eddie Sutton and Nolan Richardson. We were going to interview about eight other people, but we saw Stan and that was it—no more interviews. People asked why didn't we go to Atlanta [Final Four]—we didn't need to, we didn't need to because we have the man we think is the perfect fit, the perfect fit for the Razorback program. I'm very proud and very pleased to announce Stan Heath as our new basketball coach."

Heath could barely believe his good fortune, for in the span of a year he had gone from working as an assistant at Michigan State to the head coach at Arkansas. He did his best to parlay his one season at Kent State, leading the Golden Flashes to school records in victories (thirty) and consecutive victories (twenty-one) and to a Mid-American Conference record of seventeen league victories. In a glorious NCAA Tournament run, Kent State reached the Elite Eight by beating Oklahoma State, Alabama, and Pittsburgh.

Did Arkansas take a leap of faith by hiring the thirty-seven-year-old Heath on the strength of one great season as a head coach? Clearly, Heath had paid attention during the five years he spent working for Michigan State coach Tom Izzo. In Heath's time with Izzo, the Spartans played in the Final Four in 1999, 2000, and 2001 and won the 2000 national championship. At Kent State, Heath installed virtually the same system that Izzo won with at Michigan State. He promised to do the same at Arkansas.

"I have four staples," Heath told the media. "We are going to rebound. And people say, 'That sounds good,' and 'You did that at Michigan State but you had athletes.' Well, our team at Kent State started 6-9, 6-4, 6-2, 6-1 and 5-10. We were sixteenth in the country in rebounding. We put an emphasis on it and we got it done.

"Secondly, we are going to defend. To win championships you have to play defense.

"You are going to like our up-tempo style because we are going to be one of the few teams in the country that runs on makes and misses.

"Lastly, we are going to be a team that executes. Execute not just on the halfcourt, but on the free throw line and in situations where the clock is running down. Because that's when you win is down the stretch."

That all sounded good to Arkansas fans, but not necessarily to all its players. Freshman guard J. J. Sullinger asked for his release so he could transfer. Two incoming recruits, including talented Andre Iguodala, asked for their releases. Sullinger eventually wound up at Ohio State and Iguodala resurfaced at Arizona.

Heath had to scramble to restock his roster, but the man who helped recruit a national championship team at Michigan State was ready for the task.

321

Though the attention of SEC fans might have been diverted by all the proceedings at Arkansas, there was still the little matter of the NCAA Tournament. Would the SEC, based on its regular-season accomplishments, be competitive, as had been the case so often in the previous decade?

All season long, the SEC had generally been considered the strongest league, from top to bottom, in the country. The league's ratings percentage index (RPI) led the nation. No conference had as many teams ranked in the RPI's top forty (seven) or top fifty (eight) than did the SEC. The league was also tops in nonconference winning percentage (.784, well ahead of the Big East, which was No. 2 at .738). And that record wasn't inflated with patsies. Nine SEC schools were ranked among the top twenty-five in schedule strength by CollegeRPI.com.

The SEC ended up with nine postseason tournament bids. Six league teams were chosen to the NCAA Tournament and another three earned NIT berths.

Some experts believe the true measure of a league's strength is how it fares in the NCAA Tournament. Under that barometer, talk of the SEC's strength in the regular season faded after a rash of upsets in the NCAAs.

Florida and Ole Miss were the first to go. The Gators, playing in their school-record fourth straight NCAA Tournament, had put together an impressive record in the previous three, advancing to the Elite Eight, the championship game, and the Sweet 16. Given that past performance, some experts thought Florida was the best hope among SEC teams to make a deep run into the tournament.

Unfortunately for the Gators, they ran up against the first of two Missouri Valley Conference teams that would rough up their SEC opponents. Seeded fifth in the Midwest Region, the Gators were paired against twelfth-seeded Creighton. Florida coach Billy Donovan expected a tough game, and he was right.

With 2:42 to play, the Gators seemed in control with an eight-point lead. They weren't. Creighton battled back and with thirty seconds left trimmed Florida's lead to 82-80. At that point, all the Gators had to do was in-bound the ball, force the Blue Jays to foul, and make free throws.

It seemed easy enough, but things got scary when Florida's Orien Greene couldn't get a pass away in time and was called for a five-second count. That turned the ball over to Creighton, which won the game on Terrell Taylor's three-pointer.

Donovan gave the impression after the game that the loss would haunt him for a while.

"I have no explanation as a coach what transpired on the sidelines," Donovan told the press. "Obviously, maybe I did not articulate that well enough to Orien, but to let that happen . . . That play will certainly baffle me throughout my coaching career."

There was nothing baffling about Ole Miss' loss to UCLA. A first-round loss to South Carolina in the SEC Tournament probably doomed the Rebels to the dreaded No. 9 seed in the West Region. That meant a matchup with No. 8 seed UCLA. Coaches always hate the eight-versus-nine games because, for starters, the two teams are usually evenly matched. And the winner always draws the winner of the one-versus-sixteen game in the second round.

Ole Miss didn't have to worry about playing No. 1 seed Cincinnati. The Bruins, hungry to atone for a disappointing regular-season performance, pounded the Rebels, 80-58.

"We said if they played their game it would be in their favor, and if we played our game, it would be in our favor," said Ole Miss coach Rod Barnes, who had led the Rebels to the Sweet 16 the season before. "Clearly, it was in their favor."

If the Rebels were off their game, so was Alabama, the SEC's regular-season champion. If it weren't for the efforts of freshman point guard Mo Williams, the Crimson Tide might have gone in the NCAA history books as that rare No. 2 seed that was upset by a No. 15 seed.

Alabama hadn't played in the NCAAs since 1995, the longest dry spell in the SEC. And it showed in a South Region first-round game against Florida Atlantic, which came into the game confident.

The Owls showed they weren't afraid of the Tide by overcoming a 30-19 first-half deficit with a 15-0 run that gave them a 34-30 lead. But despite making seventeen turnovers, Alabama wouldn't lose. Williams was too good.

Realizing he had to score, Williams aggressively sought his shot and finished with 33 points, nearly double his career high of 17. He also grabbed 10 rebounds and passed for six assists as Alabama escaped 86-78.

"We wanted to be here so bad," Alabama coach Mark Gottfried said by way of explaining the Tide's apparent jitters. "We're going to let it all hang out from here on out."

That didn't quite happen, thanks to a Kent State team that was about to lose its head coach. The Golden Flashes had won nineteen straight games under first-year coach Stan Heath after upsetting Oklahoma State in the first round of the tournament. Its confidence boosted by that win, Kent State proceeded to demolish Alabama, 71-58, in a game that was never close. At one point, the Tide trailed by 24 points.

"I thought Alabama was going to be a tougher team," said Kent State guard Trevor Huffman, who contributed 20 points and five assists against the Tide. "We knew how good Alabama was, but I don't know if they came out with the kind of energy they wanted to. If they had, it would have been a closer game."

With the SEC's regular-season champion gone, it would be up to its tournament champion to uphold the league's honor. Mississippi State, which had earned a No. 3 seed in the Midwest Regional, did its best, after a slight first-round scare from McNeese State.

The Cowboys took a 21-13 lead and looked to be in control until State's Mario Austin, MVP of the SEC Tournament, began to assert himself. Austin scored 14 straight points over the next seven minutes as the Bulldogs took the lead. He finished with 25 points and nine rebounds as State won its school-record twenty-seventh game.

"The No. 1 problem was that Mario Austin showed up for the game," McNeese State coach Tic Price said. "After I watched the film of them, I was hoping the bus driver would take him to another facility."

Mississippi State's season lasted one more game. Texas coach Rick Barnes knew what to do against the Bulldogs in the second round. He surrounded Austin with defenders and dared other State players to beat him. They couldn't.

Texas took a 23 point lead with less than seven minutes to play in the first half and, though the Bulldogs rallied, the big deficit was too much to overcome. They lost 68-64.

On the same day Mississippi State was getting booted from the tournament, so too was Georgia, which had the misfortune of tangling with another pesky Missouri Valley team in the second round of the East Regional.

The Bulldogs, seeded third in the East, had handily won their first-round game, 85-68 over Murray State as the Hayes twins introduced themselves to the nation. Jarvis Hayes scored a career-high 31 points and brother Jonas scored 14 and grabbed 14 rebounds.

"I'm his biggest fan," Jarvis Hayes told the *Athens Banner-Herald*. "He's one of the best players nobody's heard of, too. This was the first NCAA Tournament game for either of us and we both had career-nights. I was just real happy for him."

The Hayes boys couldn't save the Bulldogs from a second-round ouster, even after Georgia took a 30-11 lead on Southern Illinois. Hoping to steal a bit of rest for over-worked point guard Rashad Wright, Georgia coach Jim Harrick pulled him with 8:02 to play in the first half. That, Harrick later admitted, might have cost the Bulldogs some momentum.

The Salukis scored six straight points, prompting Harrick to send Wright back into the game with 6:41 left. But it was too late. Wright could do nothing to correct Georgia's cold shooting. The Bulldogs missed their last seven shots of the first half and their first four of the second. By that time, Southern Illinois had taken the lead, regained its confidence, and held off Georgia for the win.

Within four days, all but one of the SEC's entrants in the NCAA Tournament had been sent packing. As has been the case so many times over the years, it was up to Kentucky to carry the SEC's banner.

Before the tournament, Kentucky, seeded fourth in the East Region, had been a fashionable upset pick of the media and in office pool brackets across the country. The Wildcats, dubbed "Team Turmoil" after a tumultuous regular season that was marred by injuries, transfers, fights, and suspensions, seemed vulnerable. And their first-round opponent was No. 13 seed Valparaiso, a dangerous team with a history of springing NCAA Tournament upsets.

Little did anyone who picked against Kentucky know, but before the tournament, junior guard Keith Bogans vowed to atone for what had been a disappointing regular season. Bogans took out his year-long frustrations on Valpo, scoring a game-high 21 points while making five three-pointers. The Crusaders couldn't have been blamed if their scouting report advised them to back off Bogans. In his previous six games, he made just two of 24 shots from behind the three-point line.

Buoyed by Bogans's offensive output, Kentucky won 83-68.

"It's really been needed," Bogans told the *Lexington Herald-Leader*. "For the majority of the season, I haven't been there. But that's in the past."

In the second round, Kentucky had to face Tulsa, a dangerous team. Smith, who had taken Tulsa on a pair of Sweet 16 trips in the early 1990s, knew better than to overlook the Golden Hurricane.

Bogans continued his strong play, scoring 19 points, but the big story in Kentucky's 87-82 win was Tayshaun Prince, who destroyed Tulsa with 41 points. The performance bore an uncanny resemblance to the night when former Kentucky star Jack "Goose" Givens dropped 41 points on Duke in the 1978 NCAA championship game. Both games were played in St. Louis. Both players were left-handed and both wore the number twenty-one.

On this day, Prince was so dominant he scored 28 of Kentucky's last 46 points.

"We put every guy we had on Prince, and it just didn't work out," Tulsa coach John Phillips said.

"It got pretty frustrating," Tulsa guard Greg Harrington said. "It got to the point where I was just shaking my head. There wasn't a whole lot we could do."

The win sent the Wildcats to the Sweet 16 for the fourth time in Kentucky coach Tubby Smith's five seasons. Unfortunately for the Wildcats, their weaknesses were exposed against No. 1 seed Maryland, which would go on, as many predicted, to win the national championship.

After Jason Parker's injury and Marvin Stone's transfer to Louisville, Kentucky became vulnerable in the post. Maryland's game plan was to pound the ball inside to big men Lonny Baxter and Chris Wilcox. The Wildcats battled until the end, but unable to stop Baxter and Wilcox, they lost, 78-68.

Thus ended the SEC's NCAA Tournament participation in 2002. The performance was disappointing to SEC fans, but it shouldn't have come as too much of a shock. As deep and balanced as the league was all season, no team emerged as a legitimate national championship threat. With Parker and Stone, Kentucky might have qualified. Had center Kwame Brown spurned the NBA's millions and guard Teddy Dupay been around for his senior season, perhaps Florida could have contended.

To their credit, neither Tubby Smith nor Billy Donovan moaned about their particular misfortunes and loss of personnel. No sooner did the 2001–2002 season end than both men got started on 2002–2003.

———

The SEC fared slightly better in the NIT than it did in the NCAA Tournament. A berth in the NIT often means a team didn't quite live up to its preseason goals or expectations. But the three SEC teams that landed bids didn't see it that way.

In some preseason polls Vanderbilt and LSU were picked to finish last in their respective divisions. That each advanced to postseason play was ample evidence that they had progressed more than most thought they could. Neither Vanderbilt coach Kevin Stallings nor LSU coach John Brady complained about playing in the NIT.

And both teams started out with first-round victories. Vanderbilt had the easier match-up, with a home game against Houston. The Commodores won behind 14 points by senior Sam Howard, who told the press later that he had played perhaps his best game ever.

Unfortunately for the Commodores, their usually loyal fans weren't overly enthused by the NIT. A season-low crowd of 3,439 turned out for the game, which doomed Vanderbilt's chances of hosting the second round. Dispatched to Louisiana Tech, the Commodores lost, ending their season at 17-14.

LSU, which had beaten three NCAA Tournament teams—Georgia, Mississippi State, and Ole Miss—in the previous month, felt good about its first-round NIT game at Iowa. At one time ranked No. 7 in the country, with a 12-3 record, Iowa ended up 19-16, and though it advanced to the final of the Big Ten Tournament, wasn't extended an NCAA bid.

Epilogue

Before a hostile crowd of nearly 11,000, LSU played perhaps its best game of the year. Behind 19 points from team MVP Ronald Dupree and some clutch free-throw shooting, the Tigers stole a 63-61 victory.

That earned LSU a home game, and LSU fans, appreciative of the effort Brady's injury-plagued team had put forth in the last third of the season, showed their appreciation. But despite the presence of nearly 13,000 fans, the Tigers couldn't stop Ball State's three-point shooting and lost 75-65.

Brady was obviously disappointed at the outcome. But he was pleased to have led the Tigers to a pair of postseason tournaments in his first five years in Baton Rouge despite NCAA sanctions, more knee blowouts than most coaches see in a lifetime, and defections to the NBA.

Ball State, which had won two NIT road games, was about to play away from home again, and face another SEC team.

South Carolina's players had been convinced by coach Dave Odom and his staff that the NIT was a good thing.

"It is a good thing," South Carolina assistant Ernie Nestor said. "The way we presented it to our kids, you've got 105 teams that are playing basketball [in the NCAAs and NIT] the first week of the postseason. You win one game and the next week 32 are playing. You win two games and the next week eight are playing. And what an honor it is to be playing the last week of March."

And that's exactly what the Gamecocks did. Earlier in the year, Odom had gotten into a bit of trouble by suggesting to the media that the SEC was a stronger conference than the ACC, where he had coached for twelve seasons at Wake Forest. Odom had a chance to back up his words when South Carolina was sent to Virginia for a first-round NIT game.

Virginia had been ranked in the top ten through December and January, but like Iowa, had fallen on hard times, losing nine of its last twelve games. Still, the Cavaliers are always hard to beat at home.

Odom knew that, but somehow he coaxed the Gamecocks to a 74-67 victory as they rallied from nine points down in the second half. The win earned South Carolina the right to play a second-round game at home.

The Gamecocks easily dispatched UNLV in their next game, and in the third round would play host to Ball State. South Carolina had seen the Cardinals but didn't play them in the Maui Classic four months earlier. The Gamecocks knew Ball State had beaten Kansas and UCLA in Hawaii and had won two consecutive NIT road games.

Playing their last game in Carolina Coliseum, which gave way to a new, state-of-the-art arena in the 2002–2003 season, the Gamecocks hit nine of their first thirteen shots, jumped out to a 23-4 lead, and destroyed the road weary Cardinals 82-47. It was on to New York for the NIT semifinals.

At Madison Square Garden, South Carolina took out Syracuse as Odom won his three hundredth game as a head coach. That set up a showdown with Memphis for the NIT championship, but any hope of salvaging the SEC's postseason pride was dashed when Tiger reserve post player Earl Barron stunned the Gamecocks with nine-of-nine first-half shooting and a career-high 25 points. South Carolina's inability to handle the inside game of the Tigers, who shot 49 percent from the field, was the difference in the game as Memphis won, 72-62.

The Gamecocks, who finished 22-15, had taken a while to adjust to Odom and Odom took a while to adjust to them in his first season in Columbia. But once that adjustment period was over, South Carolina had become a competitive team.

"I don't know if I've ever asked more from a team and gotten it than I did with this group," Odom told the press after the game.

Any writer or broadcaster who covers college basketball on a regular basis knows that assistant coaches are the best source of information. In researching this book, the author relied heavily on SEC assistant coaches to provide background information. The coaches were selected because of their experience and their potential to one day run their own programs.

After the 2001–2002 season, four of the SEC assistants used as primary sources in this book landed head-coaching jobs. And two others were finalists for jobs.

The first to go was Florida assistant John Pelphrey, who had long been considered a hot commodity. A year before, Pelphrey turned down opportunities to coach at New Orleans and Rutgers because he wasn't comfortable with the fit. In the spring of 2002, he had three more options to consider.

After its long-time coach Gale Gatlett resigned, West Virginia approached Pelphrey. Coaching in the Big East appealed to him, but then Pelphrey realized how far behind the rest of the pack West Virginia had sunk. Six Big East schools made the NCAA Tournament in 2002, and traditional powers Georgetown and Syracuse weren't among them. That was scary enough, but the fact that the Mountaineers were 1-15 in Big East games in 2002 didn't make the job any more attractive.

Pelphrey later considered Tennessee-Chattanooga, and his most trusted advisers all agreed the Southern Conference school that had a winning tradition would be a great place for him to start a head-coaching career. But Chattanooga was searching for an athletic director at the same time it was trying to find a basketball coach, which scared Pelphrey away.

South Alabama athletic director Joe Gottfried seized that opportunity. Hours after it was announced that former South Alabama coach Bob Weltlich had been fired, Gottfried met with Pelphrey and made him an offer he couldn't refuse.

"I just felt comfortable," Pelphrey said. "I think it's a good fit for me. I can win here, and I'll have the support of the administration to do it."

The next SEC assistant to land a head-coaching job was Mike Anderson, who had been Nolan Richardson's top assistant at Arkansas before replacing his boss as interim coach in late February. Though Arkansas officials interviewed Anderson for the job, he was never considered a serious candidate.

Without a job after Arkansas hired Stan Heath to replace Richardson, Anderson got into the mix at UAB, which was looking for a coach after firing Murry Bartow. When Anderson, a Birmingham, Alabama, native, got the job, his career had come full circle.

Anderson played high school basketball at Jackson-Olin and stayed in Birmingham for two years of junior college basketball at Jefferson State. After two years there, he wanted to move on to UAB, but wasn't recruited. Anderson ended up playing for Richardson at Tulsa, and stayed with him for the next twenty-two years.

"My dream was to come here and play at UAB," Anderson said at a press conference after he was hired. "Now my dream is to coach at UAB. I'm fulfilling a dream."

LSU assistant Kermit Davis, Jr., was the next to go when he beat out several candidates for the top job at Middle Tennesee State. Davis had been a head coach before, sandwiching two tours of duty at Idaho around an abbreviated stop at Texas A&M, from which he resigned after one season when NCAA rules violations were uncovered.

That was in 1990, and Davis had spent his time since trying to distance himself from the violations and resurrect his reputation. He was hired for the second time at Idaho in 1996, but stayed there just one season before joining his friend John Brady at LSU.

Davis wanted to be a head coach again—he had a 71-49 record at Idaho and Texas A&M—and knew he could handle a top job. But he wanted to stay in the South. When Middle Tennessee athletic director Boots Donnelly was assured by Davis's legions of friends that his problems at Texas A&M were an aberration, the deal was done quickly.

"Middle Tennessee State is a gold mine," Davis said when he was hired. "We'll bring excitement back to basketball here because it's just waiting to happen."

Kentucky coach Mike Sutton might have thought he'd landed in a gold mine, too, when he was hired to replace Jeff Lebo at Tennessee Tech. Lebo, who departed for the Chattanooga job, left behind a great program. The Golden Eagles were 27-7 in 2001–2002 and reached the quarterfinals in the NIT, no small accomplishments for a mid-major Division I school.

Sutton had been a trusted aide to Tubby Smith at Tulsa, Georgia, and Kentucky, and was deemed ready by his former boss to take over his own team.

"He was as ready [to be a head coach] as any coach I've been around," Smith said. "He's brilliant, the most organized person you'll see. He's got things I don't have— the computer skills, video coordinating. He's got it all. He's run our office before. He's been everything. He's come up the right way. He'll do a great job."

Compared to the previous season, the SEC wasn't hurt too badly by underclassmen or recruits jumping to the NBA in the spring of 2002. Mississippi State coach Rick Stansbury got a scare when sophomore center Mario Austin, who had announced in March he was staying in school, changed his mind in April and said he would declare for the NBA draft. Days later, Austin changed his mind again and said he was staying.

The league might have escaped with just one early defection were it not for the surprising decision of Tennessee forward Marcus Haislip to sign with an agent shortly after the season ended.

Haislip's decision caught Tennessee coach Buzz Peterson by surprise. Peterson assumed Haislip would test his marketability by declaring for the draft but not hire an agent. Haislip would have then had until late June to change his mind and return to school. No one on the Tennessee staff knew Haislip had abandoned school for good until someone saw him tooling around campus in a new Cadillac Escalade.

"It took me by surprise he signed with an agent," Peterson said. "But I didn't recruit the kid. I didn't get a chance to know him in a personal way. It takes time to get to know them to where you could help them make life decisions. He had said originally that if he would be picked in the top ten in the draft, he'd go out. If he wasn't going to be picked that high, he'd consider staying. But then he called [Tennessee assistant] Chris Ferguson and said he'd leave if he was a Top 20 pick."

Agents had begun to pursue Haislip as early as January. Finally given a chance to showcase his skills after playing less than thirteen minutes per game as a sophomore, Haislip impressed NBA scouts with his combination of height, quickness, and jumping ability. The thought of being a first-round draft pick intrigued Haislip. And it was no secret he wasn't a big fan of school.

"I wish him well," Peterson said. "But you can't help thinking he would have

330

boosted his stock by staying another year and working on his perimeter skills. And there's no question we'd have had a great front line."

The departure of Alabama forward Rod Grizzard was much more predictable, though scouts were wary of his inconsistency. Grizzard did say after the Crimson Tide was ousted from the NCAA Tournament that he'd return, but to his credit he changed his mind without pressure from an agent. In a press conference announcing his decision, Grizzard told reporters that confidence in his ability made his final decision easy.

Unlike Peterson, who wasn't a part of Haislip's decision-making process, Alabama coach Mark Gottfried was involved with Grizzard's decision from the beginning.

"I tried to let him make up his own mind," Gottfried said. "But once he did that, I wanted to help him. I'm excited for him. I'm disappointed obviously. We sure would have loved to have him play his senior year, but at the same time he needs to pursue his dream. He knows what's in his heart, and we're all 100 percent behind him. He knows how I feel about him. I care a lot about him. We're all wishing him the absolute best."

Even as Gottfried spoke those words, he knew that Alabama wouldn't exactly be destitute without Grizzard. Erwin Dudley, the SEC's player of the year in 2001–2002, had already announced he was staying in school. And two weeks before Grizzard's announcement, Alabama made a fortuitous recruiting acquisition when Kennedy Winston, a six-foot-seven forward from Mobile, Alabama, asked for a release from the scholarship papers he had signed in the fall with California.

Winston, the Alabama player of the year who was ranked among the top thirty prospects in the country by most recruiting experts, had been the subject of an intense, even bitter recruiting battle between Cal and Alabama. But four months after he signed with Cal, Winston, citing the poor health of his mother, asked for a release so he could play closer to home.

Gottfried was only too happy to extend a scholarship offer to Winston, even though he didn't have one available at the time. Grizzard's decision paved the way for Winston, whose arrival at Alabama proved once again that in the SEC, the stream of talent never stops flowing.

All around the league, the cycle that began in 1991–92, when Kentucky was officially declared back from the dead and Arkansas joined the league, continued as teams reloaded with talent.

At Kentucky, which lost All-American Tayshaun Prince to graduation, high-scoring high school star Kelenna Azubuike was brought in to replace him. Azubuike averaged 39 points as a senior and scored 3,530 in his career at Tulsa's Victory Christian.

And in May 2002, Kentucky received a commitment from high school junior Bobby Perry, a forward with an inside-outside game that reminded Tubby Smith of none other than Tayshaun Prince.

Florida, too, restocked its roster with talent. Coach Billy Donovan signed two of the top thirty players in the country, including *Parade* All-American guard Anthony Roberson. At Tennessee, Peterson and his staff signed two *Parade* All-American guards in a five-player recruiting haul that should return the Vols to a post-season tournament in 2003. LSU signed the top junior college big man in the country and the best high school player in Louisiana. And at Vanderbilt, Kevin Stallings signed two consensus Top 100 high school players. That's big news in Nashville.

On and on it goes. Once known only for its football, the Southeastern Conference became a big-time basketball league in the 1990s, a distinction that doesn't figure to change in the foreseeable future.

"From top to bottom, the SEC has been the best league in the last few years," Gottfried said. "It should be, in the future, the best league. I think it's here to stay. Everybody's competitive now. The stat that jumps out at me is that all twelve teams have won or shared a division championship in the last ten years. That separates the SEC from everybody, because I can promise you in the Pac-10 Washington State and Oregon State haven't done it. Clemson and Florida State haven't done it in the ACC. Baylor and Kansas State haven't done it [in the Big 12]. This league is so balanced."

"I definitely see the SEC continuing to play at this high level in the future," said Ole Miss coach Rod Barnes. "This league has a lot of outstanding young coaches and tremendously talented players. But more than the coaches and players is the commitment the universities in the SEC have made to the sport of basketball. The schools' administrations have realized now there is a large market of fans who watch and love SEC basketball and are giving strong support to the sport.

"That support is what has helped this league get to where it is today, and it is what will help the SEC basketball continue to be great."

Index

Dampier, Erick, 191–92, 194–95, 197, 200, 212
Daniels, Al, xi
Daniels, Chris, 107, 113–14, 130–31
Daniels, Erik, 162
Daniels, Marquis, 74, 80
Darby, Joezon, 221, 223
Davender, Ed, 134
Davis, Kermit, Jr., xi, 163, 173–75, 176–80, 185, 328–29
Davis, Kermit, Sr., 172
Davis, Kyle, 81–82
Davis, Larry, 244, 257
Davis, Merlene, 152
Day, Todd, 14, 36, 42, 44, 53
Dean, Brandon, 181
Dean, David, 219
Dean, Joe Jr., viii–ix, 171
Dean, Joe Sr., ix–x, 166, 169–70, 222
Dean, Mike, 128
DeClercq, Andrew, 90
Dees, Benny, 116, 261
Delk, Tony, 145, 147–49, 162
Dent, Rodney, 146
DeVoe, Don: Florida coach, 88–89; Tennessee coach, 258–59
Diame, Abdou, 82
Dickey, Doug, 6, 9, 258–59, 261, 265–67, 272, 274, 288
Dickey, James, 171
Dietzel, Paul, 241
Dillard, Al, 47, 49
Dillard, Sherman, 216
Dixon, King, 242
Dollar, Cameron, 109
Donnelly, Boots, 329
Donovan, Billy, x, 9, 83–84, 87, 92–106; as Kentucky assistant coach, 138, 140, 143, 147, 313, 322, 325, 331
Dooley, Vince, 108,

124–27, 151
Dorsey, Marlon, 191
Dougherty, Neil, 320
Drew, Bryce, 223
Drew, Homer, 166
Driesell, Lefty, 127, 208, 210
Duckett, Rick, xi, 239, 249
Dudley, Erwin: Alabama's recruitment of, 21–22, 23, 28, 30–31, 33, 318, 330; dominance in NIT, 12
Dukes, Derrick, 124
Dukes, Marc, xi, 228
Duncan, Tim, 237
Dunleavy, Mike, 240
Dunleavy, Mike, Jr., 254
Dunn, T.R., x; hired as Alabama assistant, 28
Dupay, Teddy, 95, 98, 100, 102, 104–5, 325
Dupree, Ronald, 179, 181, 184–86, 326
Durham, Hugh, 13, 96; as Georgia coach, 122–23, 151, 167

Eagles, Tommy Joe, 65
Earl, Lester, 169, 173, 176
Earl, Louis, 176
Eaves, Joel, 63
Edwards, Allen, 150, 153
Eidson, Chuck, 8, 247, 252, 257, 316
El-Amin, Khalid, 271
Elder, Bruce, 290, 304
Ellis, Cliff, x, 29, 60–62; 65–66; as Clemson coach, 67; musical career, 68–71; 72–81
Ellis, LeRon, 134, 136
English, Alex, 240
Epps, Anthony, 148, 150
Estill, Marquis, 314
Evans, Anthony, 111, 127
Evans, Carolyn, 220
Evans, Chuck, 212
Evans, Heshimu, 154, 156
Evans, Jarrell, 219

Evans, Rob, 75, 76, 201; rebuilding Ole Miss program, 213–25, 227–28; 234–35, 307

Farmer, Larry, 110
Farmer, Richie, 136, 138, 140, 145
Faulkner, Jamall, 60
Feher, Butch, 289
Feldhaus, Deron, 136, 138, 140, 143–45
Felton, George, 138, 242
Ferguson, Chris, xi, 268, 270, 330
Finney, Shawn, 123
Fishback, Daymeon, 60, 62, 73, 75, 77–78
Fitch, Gerald, 162, 314–15
Flanigan, Jason, 229, 231, 234–35
Fletcher, Virgil, 285–86
Floyd, Tim, 170–71, 173, 266–67, 320
Fogler, Eddie, xi; departure from South Carolina, 8; 96–98, 238–39, 242–48; Vanderbilt coach, 289–93; 297–98
Foley, Jeremy, 84, 86–87, 91–92, 104
Ford, Deuce, 168
Ford, Joe, 289
Ford, Travis, 142, 146, 162
Fosnes, Jeff, 289
Foster, Jim, 296
Fox, Rick, 287
Freije, Matt, 304

Gaines, Reece, 279
Gallman, William, 245
Garfinkel, Howard, 61, 148
Garnett, Kevin, 247
Gee, Gordon, 298–99
Gholar, Michael, 318
Gillen, Pete, 21
Gilley, J. Wade, 272
Givens, Jack, 325

Index

Index

About the Author

Chris Dortch covered Southeastern Conference basketball for four different newspapers over the course of a fifteen-year career. He left newspapers to edit the *Blue Ribbon College Basketball Yearbook* and launched the *Blue Ribbon College Football Yearbook* in 2000. He currently edits the *Blue Ribbon College Basketball Forecast*™ and the *Blue Ribbon College Football Forecast*™. Dortch lives in Chattanooga, Tennessee, with his wife Patty, son Chris II, and daughter Jennifer. This is his second book.